Lecture Notes in Computer Science 10254

More information about this series at http://www.springer.com/series/7409

Carlos Delgado Kloos · Patrick Jermann
Mar Pérez-Sanagustín · Daniel T. Seaton
Su White (Eds.)

Digital Education

Out to the World and Back to the Campus

5th European MOOCs Stakeholders Summit, EMOOCs 2017
Madrid, Spain, May 22–26, 2017
Proceedings

Springer

Editors
Carlos Delgado Kloos
Universidad Carlos III de Madrid
Leganés (Madrid)
Spain

Patrick Jermann
École Polytechnique Fédérale de Lausanne
Lausanne
Switzerland

Mar Pérez-Sanagustín
Pontifical Catholic University of Chile
San Joaquín, Santiago de Chile
Chile

Daniel T. Seaton
Harvard University
Cambridge, MA
USA

Su White
University of Southampton
Southampton
UK

ISSN 0302-9743 ISSN 1611-3349 (electronic)
Lecture Notes in Computer Science
ISBN 978-3-319-59043-1 ISBN 978-3-319-59044-8 (eBook)
DOI 10.1007/978-3-319-59044-8

Library of Congress Control Number: 2017941499

LNCS Sublibrary: SL3 – Information Systems and Applications, incl. Internet/Web, and HCI

Printed on acid-free paper

This Springer imprint is published by Springer Nature
The registered company is Springer International Publishing AG
The registered company address is: Gewerbestrasse 11, 6330 Cham, Switzerland

Preface

Aristophanes once said that "education is kindling of a flame, not the filling of a vessel." That quote remains true today. The best education is the one that engages the students in emotional ways. When this is achieved, learning becomes a joy for all involved and the educational outcomes are best achieved.

We would like to move that statement one level up, to the meta-level, about learning on how to educate best. There are many questions open about how to teach best. Very little is known about how the brain learns, so it is of no surprise that we are still struggling with the teaching practices. In this context, massive open online courses (MOOCs) appeared just a few years ago, and in relation to the quote of Aristophanes, we can say that MOOCs have ignited the learning conversation about education. Professors started to reflect more on how to teach best, universities have reinforced and reformed their teaching and learning units, and the world is discussing how to best use technology for teaching and learning.

About five years have passed since platforms like edX, Coursera, MiríadaX, and FutureLearn were founded, and after the initial hype, MOOCs have secured a milestone in the history of education. MOOCs are now well established and have evolved into multiple forms. On the one hand, they have found their way back into campus in the form of SPOCs (small private online courses) where they enable the use of various blended pedagogies such as flipped classrooms. Additionally, they are increasingly used in companies for training purposes of employees and partners. Also, professional education is another big area where MOOCs are used. Professionals are using the MOOCs to develop their skills and adapt to the changing needs of the labor market. In these proceedings, you will find a long list of MOOC use cases. These use cases make you reflect on the potential of MOOCs, their impact, and the implications that their use entails in several contexts.

The EMOOCs 2017 conference, the 5th in the series of European MOOCs Stakeholders Symposia, was held in Leganés (Madrid, Spain) on the campus of Universidad Carlos III de Madrid (UC3M) during May 22–26, 2017. It followed on from the initial closed conference at EPFL in Lausanne (Switzerland) in 2013. A second open conference was also held in Lausanne in 2014. In 2015, the Université catholique de Louvain hosted the event in Mons (Belgium) and 2016 it was Universität Graz in Graz (Austria). This year, Open edX con 2017, the conference for developers around the open source Open edX platform, was co-located with EMOOCs 2017 on the UC3M campus, allowing for interesting synergies to occur.

Altogether 137 contributions were submitted after the different calls for paper of the conference. Of these, 53 papers were submitted to the Experience and Research Tracks, from which 23 were accepted for presentation at the conference and publication as full papers, 10 for the Experience Track, and 13 for the Research Track, making an acceptance rate of 43%. Additional papers were accepted at a subsequent deadline that are included here as short papers (three for the Experience Track and seven for the Research Track).

Apart from this, the program featured many other interesting events:

- Eight panel sessions from the Business Track and the Policy Track
- Work-in-progress contributions presented as posters
- Nine workshops
- A Spanish Track with contributions from Ibero-America

Brilliant keynote speakers rounded up the program:

- Anant Agarwal, CEO, edX
- Armando Fox, Professor and Advisor to MOOClab, UC Berkeley
- Javier Hernández-Ros, Director, Data, DG CONNECT, European Commission
- Carolina Jeux, CEO, Telefónica Educación Digital
- Rick Levin, CEO, Coursera
- Simon Nelson, CEO, FutureLearn
- Sir Timothy O'Shea, Principal and Vice-Chancellor, University of Edinburgh

Many people participated in making this event a success. We would like to thank the authors for their contributions, the Program Committee members for their reviewing activity, the chairs of the different tracks, the Organizing Committee with members from the UTEID (Unidad de Tecnología Educativa e Innovación Docente) and the Department of Telematics Engineering, both of UC3M. Furthermore, UC3M supported the event through many of its services. Additional collaborators include PAU Education, the eMadrid network, the UNESCO Chair for "Scalable Digital Education for All" at UC3M, the European University Association, Springer, and EasyChair. We are grateful to the generous sponsors who supported EMOOCs 2017: McGraw-Hill Education, edX, Coursera, and FutureLearn as gold sponsors; Telefónica Educación Digital and SmowlTech as silver sponsors.

March 2017

Carlos Delgado Kloos
Patrick Jermann
Mar Pérez-Sanagustín
Daniel Seaton
Su White

Organization

Program Committee

John Aiken	Michigan State University Physics Education Research Lab, USA
Gudrun Bachmann	University of Basel, Educational Technologies, Switzerland
Aneesha Bakharia	University of Queensland, Australia
Chris Brooks	University of Michigan, USA
Gavin Clinch	Connatch-Ulster Alliance, Ireland
Ruth Cobos	Universidad Autónoma de Madrid, Spain
Dan Davis	TU Delft, The Netherlands
Max De Mendizábal	Universidad Nacional Autónoma de México, Mexico
Inge de Waard	The Open University, UK
Carlos Delgado Kloos	Universidad Carlos III de Madrid, Spain
Pierre Dillenbourg	EPFL, Switzerland
Gulustan Dogan	City University of New York, USA
E.A. Draffan	University of Southampton, UK
Martin Ebner	Graz University of Technology, Austria
Rebecca Ferguson	The Open University, UK
Silvia Elena Gallagher	Trinity College Dublin, The University of Dublin, Ireland
Davinia Hernández-Leo	Universitat Pompeu Fabra, Barcelona, Spain
Tanja Jadin	University of Applied Sciences Upper Austria, Austria
Patrick Jermann	Ecole Polytechnique Fédérale de Lausanne, Switzerland
Lukasz Kidzinski	Stanford University, USA
Irwin King	CUHK, Hong Kong
Rene Kizilcec	Stanford University, USA
Michael Kopp	University of Graz, Austria
Anja Lorenz	Lübeck University of Applied Sciences, Germany
Guy Lories	Université catholique de Louvain, Belgium
Katherine Maillet	Institut Mines-Télécom, Télécom Ecole de Management, France
Jorge Maldonado	Pontificia Universidad Católica de Chile, Chile
Kim Manturuk	Duke University, USA
Colin Milligan	Glasgow Caledonian University, UK
Andreina Parisi-Amon	Coursera, USA
Mar Pérez-Sanagustín	Pontificia Universidad Católica de Chile, Chile
Juliana Raffaghelli	University of Florence, Italy

Jeanine Reutemann	University of Applied Sciences Basel FHNW, Switzerland
Ulla Ringtved	eLearningLab, University of Aalborg, Denmark
Martín Rodriguez	IE Business School, Spain
Ido Roll	University of British Columbia, Canada
Yigal Rosen	Harvard University, USA
Ilia Rushkin	Harvard University, USA
Andy Saltarelli	Stanford University, USA
Daniel Seaton	Harvard University, USA
Nicolas Sennequier	IMT, France
Kshitij Sharma	CRAFT-EPFL, Switzerland
Gideon Shimshon	Leiden University, The Netherlands
Marinke Sussenbach	TU Delft, The Netherlands
Selen Turkay	Harvard Initiative for Learning and Teaching, USA
Guadalupe Vadillo	UNAM, Mexico
Su White	University of Southampton, UK
Ahmed Yousef	Fayoum University, Al Fayyūm, Egypt
John Zornig	The University of Queensland, Australia
Judith Zubieta	IIS, UNAM, Mexico

Additional Reviewers

Chan, Hou Pong
Dopper, Sofia
Estévez-Ayres, Iria
Marquis, Danika
Zhang, Jiani

Contents

Experience Track

From a Small Liberal Arts College to the World: Our Blended Courses, SPOC, and MOOCs in Italian Studies 3
Daniela Bartalesi-Graf

Giving Flexible Learners a Head Start on Higher Education: Designing and Implementing a Pre-induction Socialisation MOOC 10
James Brunton, Mark Brown, Eamon Costello, Orna Farrell, and Conor Mahon

The EMMA Experience. Emerging Patterns and Factors for Success 20
Rosanna De Rosa, Chiara Ferrari, and Ruth Kerr

Mentoring Learners in MOOCs: A New Way to Improve Completion Rates? 29
Lucie Dhorne, Jean-Pierre Deflandre, Olivier Bernaert, Sébastien Bianchi, and Maria Thirouard

Towards E-presence at Distance as a Way to Reach and Share E-quality: The Case of the ECO sMOOCs 38
Divina Frau-Meigs and Adeline Bossu

Additional Functionalities to Convert an xMOOC into an xLMOOC 48
Ana Gimeno-Sanz, Cristina Navarro-Laboulais, and Ignacio Despujol-Zabala

A Principled Approach to the Design of Collaborative MOOC Curricula 58
Stian Håklev and James D. Slotta

Towards Full Engagement for Open Online Education. A Practical Experience for a MicroMaster 68
Rocael Hernández and Hector R. Amado-Salvatierra

From Low-Scale to Collaborative, Gamified and Massive-Scale Courses: Redesigning a MOOC 77
Alejandro Ortega-Arranz, Luisa Sanz-Martínez, Susana Álvarez-Álvarez, Juan A. Muñoz-Cristóbal, Miguel L. Bote-Lorenzo, Alejandra Martínez-Monés, and Yannis Dimitriadis

Innovation in EU Communication: MOOCs from the European Committee of the Regions 88
Martin Gosset and Wolfgang Petzold

Does Gamification in MOOC Discussion Forums Work? 95
Matthias Reischer, Mohammad Khalil, and Martin Ebner

A MOOC-Based Flipped Class: Lessons Learned from the Orchestration Perspective 102
María Fernanda Rodríguez, Josefina Hernández Correa, Mar Pérez-Sanagustín, Julio A. Pertuze, and Carlos Alario-Hoyos

An International Collaboration in the Design Experience of a MOOC Series 113
Susanna Sancassani, Paola Corti, and Valeria Baudo

Research Track

Measuring the Degree of Innovation in Education Through the Implementation of an Indicator Based on Analyzing MOOC-Related Activities 123
Jose María Alvarez-Rodríguez, Antonio de Amescua, Javier García-Guzman, and Maribel Sánchez-Segura

Toward a Typology of MOOC Activity Patterns: Learners Who Never Rest? 134
Rémi Bachelet and Rawad Chaker

Improving MOOC Student Learning Through Enhanced Peer-to-Peer Tasks . . . 140
Borja Bordel, Ramón Alcarria, Diego Martín, and Diego Sánchez-de-Rivera

Who Wants to Chat on a MOOC? Lessons from a Peer Recommender System 150
François Bouchet, Hugues Labarthe, Rémi Bachelet, and Kalina Yacef

Weekly Predicting the At-Risk MOOC Learners Using Dominance-Based Rough Set Approach 160
Sarra Bouzayane and Inès Saad

#MOOC Friends and Followers: An Analysis of Twitter Hashtag Networks . . . 170
Eamon Costello, Mark Brown, Binesh Nair, Mairéad Nic Giolla Mhichíl, Jingjing Zhang, and Theo Lynn

Understanding Learning and Teaching in MOOCs from the Perspectives of Students and Instructors: A Review of Literature from 2014 to 2016 176
Ruiqi Deng, Pierre Benckendorff, and Deanne Gannaway

Effect of Free Certificate Discontinuation in Completion Rates of MOOC . . . 182
Ignacio M. Despujol, Carlos Turró, Linda Castañeda, and Jaime Busquets

Challenges of Identifying Second Language English Speakers in MOOCs . . . 188
Ismail Duru, Ayse Saliha Sunar, Gulustan Dogan, and Su White

MOOC Quality Evaluation System: Tomsk State University Experience. 197
Victor Dyomin, Galina Mozhaeva, Olesya Babanskaya, and Ulyana Zakharova

The Drivers of Employer Support for Professional Skill Development in MOOCs 203
Monika Hamori

To Change or Not to Change? That's the Question… On MOOC-Success, Barriers and Their Implications 210
Maartje Henderikx, Karel Kreijns, and Marco Kalz

Follow-Up of Learning Activities in Open edX: A Case Study at the University of Cauca 217
Daniel Jaramillo-Morillo, Mario Solarte Sarasty, Gustavo Ramírez González, and Mar Pérez-Sanagustín

Increasing Educational Value: The Transformation of MOOCs into Open Educational Resources 223
Michael Kopp, Ortrun Gröblinger, and Claudia Zimmermann

Implementation Intentions and How They Influence Goal Achievement in MOOCs 233
Karel Kreijns, Marco Kalz, Jonatan Castaño-Muñoz, and Yves Punie

A Social Learning Space Grid for MOOCs: Exploring a FutureLearn Case. . . 243
Kalpani Manathunga, Davinia Hernández-Leo, and Mike Sharples

The Double Classroom: Design Patterns Using MOOCs in Teacher Education 254
Anne-Mette Nortvig and Karsten Gynther

Early Prediction and Variable Importance of Certificate Accomplishment in a MOOC 263
José A. Ruipérez-Valiente, Ruth Cobos, Pedro J. Muñoz-Merino, Álvaro Andujar, and Carlos Delgado Kloos

Types of Dropout in Adaptive Open Online Courses 273
Maxim Skryabin

Exploring the Role of Assessment in Developing Learners' Critical Thinking in Massive Open Online Courses 280
Catherine Zhao, Sonal Bhalla, Lesley Halliday, Joanne Travaglia, and Julia Kennedy

Author Index 291

Experience Track

From a Small Liberal Arts College to the World: Our Blended Courses, SPOC, and MOOCs in Italian Studies

Daniela Bartalesi-Graf(✉)

Wellesley College, Wellesley, MA, USA
dbartale@wellesley.edu

Abstract. In this contribution I focus on the structure and contents of an online course in the Italian language and culture offered through different venues and formats, i.e. as a summer SPOC (Small Private Online Course); as a blended course on our campus and at MIT, and as a MOOC on the edX platform. I present and analyze some data on students' perception of the effectiveness of different online learning tools from a survey sent to all learners (MOOC and campus). Finally, I propose some concrete steps to advance our Italian language academic programs: these include the creation of a platform to share our best practices, evaluate our programs and assess learning outcomes.

Keywords: MOOC · Italian · Language teaching · SPOC · Blended learning

1 Our Contribution to Open and Free Access: ItalianOnline

In Fall 2013 Wellesley College was the first liberal arts college to join the edX consortium. With this decision, and the commitment to create and open four MOOCs, the College positioned itself with those institutions of higher learning that decided to welcome the new movement towards affordability and accessibility in the education system. Our Department has contributed to this endeavor by creating ItalianOnline, an online course that has been offered in many formats (online summer course, blended course on campus, and MOOC) and has reached a variety of learners.

In undertaking this effort, we had the following objectives: improve our enrollment in on campus courses by attracting students over the summer with a free Italian online course; test online modules over the summer in view of creating a new blended intensive language course to be offered on campus in the Fall; create a model for teaching a language online that other language programs might follow.

1.1 Contents and Design

ItalianOnline was first opened in summer 2014 and offered only to Wellesley College students and alumnae. For this reason, the course initially met the definition of a SPOC (Small Private Online Course), and not of a MOOC (Massive Open Online Course). The course corresponds roughly to the first year of College level Italian though its

C. Delgado Kloos et al. (Eds.): EMOOCs 2017, LNCS 10254, pp. 3–9, 2017.
DOI: 10.1007/978-3-319-59044-8_1

cultural material (video interviews with native speakers and readings) allows for its use in the second year as well. Since the platform allows for the upload of many different teaching media, such as videos, PowerPoints, audio files, images, etc., we decided to present the same content (language function and/or a cultural theme) in parallel but different ways. We also adopted a variety of teaching methods: formal and explicit presentations (for examples, grammar charts and video lessons) are accompanied by other components that focus on the functional use of the language (for examples, Podcasts and videos called Ciak! – these are slice-of-life videos illustrating natural conversations and idioms). The contents of this course (divided in three levels, i.e. Beginner, Intermediate and Advanced) are now available to all on the edX platform in the archived form since the course formally ran from January 25, 2016 to January 25, 2017: https://www.edx.org/school/wellesleyx.

2 From SPOC to Blended and Learning Outcomes in Blended Versus F2F Courses

The online course was first beta tested during three consecutive summers as a SPOC (Small Private Online Course) and offered to our campus students. Interest in this initiative was very strong, and particularly remarkable was the number of first year students in summers 2014 and 2015, equivalent to about 18% of the whole class. Unfortnately many of these students (39%) couldn't continue in the fall semester because they could not fit an Italian cours in their schedule. The intensive "blended" language course that we started offering in fall 2014 was designed to answer this documented student need for more flexibility.

The course has the following characteristics: three meetings F2F per week instead of five; 24/7 learning environment that provides more "time-on-task" and opportunities for "retrieval practice and learning" (see Glance et al. [4]); flipped methodology using exclusively ItalianOnline: students watch video lessons, video skits and complete other online activities before coming to class; in-class time is mainly used for practice and conversational activities; no cost to students as the use of any textbook is obsolete;

The blended format brought the following benefits:

- Improved pedagogy (see here the results of a "discourse analysis" conducted by Veronica Darer in Fall 2014). Students also completed a specific survey of the blended learning component of the course, and 70% stated that, compared to traditional language courses they had taken before, they learned "more or much more" in this blended language course.[1]
- Higher enrollment of first year students; this group is vital to our program as it is the most likely to continue at the advanced level. In the intensive non-blended courses of falls 2012 and 2013, first year students were only 31% of all students, compared to 67% of all students enrolled in the blended intensive courses offered in fall 2014, 2015 and 2016.

[1] This data was collected from a relatively small sample of students (33).

- A model for other languages to follow (French is now adopting a similar blended course version for their intensive beginner course.)

In the field of foreign language acquisition very few studies have compared learning outcome in courses where different media was used. To my knowledge, only Rubio [7] in Spanish has done comparative studies of students' proficiency in blended versus traditional courses. Their studies have both yielded similar results in favor of a blended learning format: despite a reduction in contact hours, students in the two groups had similar learning gains, and for some categories, like writing and vocabulary, the blended course students performed better. These results are consistent with Darer's discourse analysis of our Italian blended course at Wellesley College.

In conclusion, although more extensive qualitative and quantitative studies are needed, we can say with relative confidence that with blended learning we achieve greater flexibility without sacrificing achievement. Furthermore, we could infer that, if we were to keep the same F2F time and adopt a flipped classroom methodology, we could greatly improve learning outcomes, as suggested by some studies in other disciplines (Glance et al. [4] and Marcey and Brint [5]).

3 From Blended Courses to MOOCs

During the fall of 2015 ItalianOnline was further revised, updated, and divided into three levels (Beginner, Intermediate and Advanced). The three courses so created opened as MOOCs (Massive Open Online Courses) on the edX platform January 25, 2016 till January 25, 2017, and were offered as "self-paced", meaning that students enter and leave as they wish and may cover any part of the material in any sequence they choose, since all lessons were made available on the opening day. Although these MOOCs do not offer credit, learners can earn a Certificate of Completion for a small fee ($49), an option available to most other courses on edX.

By creating these MOOCs we wanted to offer free Italian courses to learners living in all parts of the world, many of them with limited or no access to traditional forms of instruction for geographical or financial reasons. We also wanted to test our pedagogical approach with large numbers of students: having thousands of online learners is an absolute first in Italian Studies and represents a unique chance to learn from large data about the effectiveness of our teaching tools and about the process of learning any foreign language.

4 Student Experience in MOOCs and Blended Courses

The interest for studying Italian worldwide is indeed very strong, as enrollment in the MOOCs attests. As of June 28, 2016, 42,865 learners enrolled from 188 different countries. While we had a relatively high number of learners from Brazil (6.4% of Italian Beginners versus 4% in all edX courses), a likely effect of the large community of Italian immigrants in that country, two countries were underrepresented in our courses: India, with 3.3% of Beginners versus 11% in all edX courses, and China with 1.1% of Beginners compared to 3% in all edX courses.

In June 2016, about six months after the course opened, we sent an online questionnaire to all MOOC learners; the objective of this survey was to collect data on student satisfaction with the program and specifically with the different learning tools offered online. Here are the numbers of respondents to the survey for the three levels:[2] Beginner: **1,225**; Intermediate: **195**; Advanced: **170**.

The survey's main objective was to compare campus and MOOC students' opinions on the effectiveness of the different learning tools. This information is particularly relevant because the two groups have different motivations, ages, geographical locations, levels of education, backgrounds, etc., and were taught using different media (online versus blended). Figure 1 shows students' ratings of the different online tools:[3]

p-values	
Ciak videos	**1.57619E-07**
Grammar charts	0.012169987
Video lessons	0.176732474
Exercises	0.421030452
Discussion forum	**1.00866E-05**

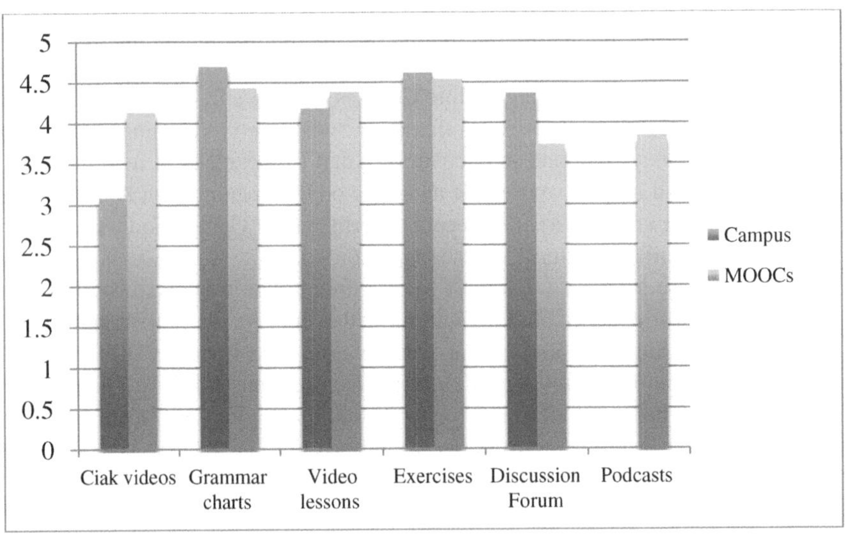

Fig. 1. Students' ratings of different online tools

[2] Although 25,000 students were officially enrolled in the Beginner course when we sent out the survey, only about 10% of these were active in any given week; for the intermediate and advanced students, about 4,500 were enrolled in each course, but weekly activity oscillated between 6–7% amounting at around 300–350 for both courses, with a slightly higher number for the Intermediate level.

[3] Figure 1 doesn't show the Podcast campus ratings because this tool was implemented relatively late, i.e. summer 2015, and was not available to campus students in Fall 2014.

We first notice that two learning tools (**Grammar charts** and **Exercises**) receive very similar ratings from all groups of students. These are the tools that receive the highest ratings, and they represent in many ways the most traditional offerings of the online course, if compared to the Ciak! videos, video lessons and Podcasts. Other comparative studies of students' and teachers' perception of the effectiveness of different learning tools have yielded similar results: students consistently value traditional language learning methods involving the formal study of grammar much more than teachers, as shown Brown [2]. It is likely that these tools are highly rated because they are familiar to most students, and they are connected to clearly defined expectations. We will see later that data collected on two versions of the Podcasts might point to a second explanation: the rating of online tools is also dependent on their close connection to assessment.

In contrast to the above ratings, the **Ciak! videos** receive relatively low marks particularly from campus students. In their narrative comments students mention the relative difficulty of these video's "natural language" (i.e. native speakers' speed of conversation and use of idioms), and the poor quality of sound. Also, Ciak! videos are not included in any tests (they are only followed by an exercise), so it might be that campus students, who are more concerned with their final grade, consider these tools "less useful". Conversely, Ciak! videos receive better marks from MOOC students, a group of learners that is less concerned with assessment results. Some of these students also mention the sense of connection with real people they derive from the Ciak! video, an understandable feeling for learners who study in relative isolation. We can draw a similar conclusion for the video lessons, i.e. they are more liked by MOOC students since they represent the only contact, though virtual, that these learners have with a teacher. Campus students, who go to class three times a week, value this tool as less useful.

The **Discussion Forum** ratings are also interesting as this is the only tool that campus students rate considerably higher than MOOC students. Discussion Forum entries are free writing activities with a certain level of guidance: we provide a subject for discussion followed by an example, and learners are invited to write one or two paragraphs in response to this prompt, and to respond to the entries of another learner. The discrepancy between the two ratings is probably due to the different ways this tool is used in the two courses: for MOOC students this is a voluntary activity that receives no feedback from the instructor whereas, for campus students, the Discussion Forum entries are a requirement and affect their final grade; campus students write two versions for each of these entries: the first is corrected by a teaching assistant, the second by the course instructor who also gives a grade.

Campus students' higher rating for the Discussion Forum confirms the result of several studies: students highly value teacher feedback on their writings (Ferreira et al. [3]). Conversely, some of our MOOC learners reacted negatively to this lack of teacher involvement as shown in some of their narrative responses. One possible solution would consist in establishing a peer-to-peer feedback system in which volunteers from the intermediate level provide feedback to learners in the beginner level and receive, in turn, feedback from learners in the advanced levels. Facilitators or teaching assistants could provide feedback for advanced learners only. Bárcena et al. [1] provide a creative solution to this impasse by proposing that MOOCs teachers identify, some time into the course, one or more e-leading student(s), i.e. learners who contribute consistently to the

Discussion Forum and who reach good academic results. These e-leading students could be empowered to act as mentors to the others online learners.

The **Podcast** rating is the final result that deserves a closer look. Although we don't have campus ratings for this tool (Podcasts were implemented on campus relatively late), we were able to compare two different offerings of the Podcasts: in the SPOC of summer 2015 when they were presented as an optional practice tool and were not connected to any assessment whereas in the current MOOCs they are placed right before a graded exercise. MOOC students reported a higher degree of use (82% in the MOOC versus 61% in the SPOC) and of usefulness to their learning (90% of MOOC leaners found this tool uselful or very useful versus 80% of SPOC learners). This result confirms one of our explanations for the high ratings of both Grammar charts and Exercises (and conversely, for the low ratings of the Ciak! videos): students appreciate, and therefore are more likely to use, the tools that are closely connected to assessment.

From this preliminary data we can learn some important lessons that can be applied to our teaching on campus, both in blended and F2F courses:

- We need to engage campus students in a conversation on learning strategies. Though many students understandably use only those studying tools that they perceive as closely connected to assessment and with which they are most familiar, we as educators need to communicate to these students that research shows that they will learn better and faster if they use a wide variety of learning strategies (Nyikos [6]).
- At the same time, we need to make sure that each online teaching tool is directly connected to a form of assessment that motivates students by marking the attainment of a certain skill.
- The video material that we use online must be only slightly above students' level; material that is perceived as too difficult, especially when is not clearly connected to assessment, is quickly abandoned.
- We need to be aware of most students' preference for structure, and include explicit tools, such as clear grammar explanations and charts. This need is equally felt among all learners (on campus and MOOCs).

5 Sharing Our Best Practices and Data: A Proposal

The creation of teaching material, especially online, takes an enormous amount of time and energy, and we would be wasting precious energies if we were to act individually, with the risk of replicating each other's work, and possibly mistakes. In what I am about to propose, I am inspired by the Open Educational Resource approach as described by Colpaert (in Bárcena et al., p. 169 [1]): "The OER approach should normally lead to 50% less work and 200% more result for language teachers". Two examples of such efforts are the following the Calper (Center for Advanced Language Proficiency and Research) at Penn State and Center for Open Educational Resources and Language Learning at the University of Texas Austin. Through their online resources these platforms share free teaching material and resources for all major languages.

I propose to take this approach one step further by introducing a circular process (adaptation/assessment/revision) that would result in improved teaching practices. More concretely, I propose to form a network of teachers of Italian interested in the creation and maintenance of a website for the uploading, sharing and free downloading of teaching material (digital and non digital) to use and test in our courses. The new feature of this website, if compared to the OERs mentioned above, would be the possibility to dowload, modify and customize any shared teaching material, the sharing of assessment results, the uploading of revised and improved material after assessment, further sharing, adapting and assessment phases, in a circular process that would ensure constant testing and revision.

References

1. Bárcena, E., Martin Monje, E., Read, T.: Potentiating the human dimension in language MOOCs. In: Proceedings of the European MOOC Stakeholders Summit 2015. http://www.emoocs2015.eu/sites/default/files/Papers.pdf. Accessed 1 Aug 2016
2. Brown, A.V.: Students' and teachers' perceptions of effective foreign language teaching: a comparison of ideals. Mod. Lang. J. **93**(1), 46–60 (2009)
3. Ferreira, A., Moore, J.D., Mellish, C.: A study of feedback strategies in foreign language classrooms and tutorials with implications for intelligent computer-assisted language learning systems. Int. J. Artif. Intell. Educ. **17**, 389–422 (2007)
4. Glance, D.G., Forsey, M., Riley, M.: The pedagogical foundations of massive open online course. FirstMonday (Peer-Reviewed J. Internet), vol. 18, Number 5–6 May 2013. http://firstmonday.org/ojs/index.php/fm/issue/view/384. Accessed 31 July 2016
5. Marcey, D., Brint, M.: Transforming an undergraduate introductory biology course through cinematic lectures and inverted classes: an assessment of the CLIC model of the flipped classroom. In: Proceedings of the 2012 NABT Biology Education Research Symposium. https://www.nabt.org/websites/institution/File/docs/Four%20Year%20Section/2012%20Proceedings/Marcey%20&%20Brint.pdf. Accessed 2 June 2016
6. Nyikos, M.: Variables affecting choice of language learning strategies by university students. Mod. Lang. J. **73**(3), 291–300 (1989)
7. Rubio, F.: The effects of blended learning on second language fluency and proficiency. In: Rubio, F., Thoms, J. (eds.) Hybrid Language Teaching and Learning: Exploring Theoretical, Pedagogical and Curricular Issues, pp. 137–159. Cengage, Boston (2012)

Giving Flexible Learners a Head Start on Higher Education: Designing and Implementing a Pre-induction Socialisation MOOC

James Brunton(✉), Mark Brown, Eamon Costello, Orna Farrell, and Conor Mahon

National Institute for Digital Learning, Dublin City University, Dublin, Ireland
James.brunton@dcu.ie

Abstract. This paper reports on a five week pre-induction socialisation MOOC that facilitates successful transition into Higher Education for flexible learners. In this context a broad definition is adopted of flexible learners, which includes adult learners in part-time and/or online/distance education. A number of national and international reports have emphasised the importance of bringing more adult learners into higher education, and adult learners have a preference for flexible programmes. The MOOC targets prospective learners during early parts of the study life-cycle, when they are considering entry into higher education and may benefit from advice about how to effectively prepare. The MOOC utilises a number of the OERs developed by the Student Success Toolbox project, and combines these readiness tools with supporting materials in order to deliver a comprehensive pre-induction socialisation course. A small pilot ran from the 15th Aug–19th Sept 2016. 150 people enrolled with 50 going on to receive a certificate of completion. Those selected to take part in this pilot were prospective flexible learners planning to start courses in Ireland in 2016/2017 and a cohort of approximately 70 learners from Kiron, an organisation supporting refugees in accessing higher education. The feedback received, albeit limited by the numbers of respondents, indicates that a course that uses the OERs developed by the Students Success Toolbox project, can have a positive impact on prospective flexible learners.

Keywords: Flexible learner · Pre-induction socialisation · Student success · Retention · Digital readiness tools

1 Introduction

The Head Start Online MOOC emerged from the Student Success Toolbox (SST) project, which was funded by the (Irish) National Forum for the Enhancement of Teaching and Learning in Higher Education Building Digital Capacity fund. A suite of digital readiness tools were created through this project for use in preparing adults for online/distance or part-time study at higher education level, and Head Start Online utilized several of these tools to develop a unified, assistive resource for prospective

C. Delgado Kloos et al. (Eds.): EMOOCs 2017, LNCS 10254, pp. 10–19, 2017.
DOI: 10.1007/978-3-319-59044-8_2

flexible learners. This MOOC aims to help flexible learners in the initial stages of the study lifecycle by addressing the salient issues of effective transitions and the bases for student success. Here flexible learners are represented by adults engaged in part-time or online/distance learning. Like many other MOOCs, Head Start Online is underpinned by an intention to widen access to education and be of assistance to higher education institutions [1].

Flexible learners are an extremely vulnerable proportion of the student population in that they have significantly lower completion rates than traditional on-campus students [2]. This highlights the need for Head Start Online to be readily available for higher education institutions worldwide in order to tackle this issue, as it poses problems on an international level. With many countries higher education student bodies consisting of up to 35% flexible learners [3], these disparities in completion rates represent a primary concern.

Head Start Online primarily aims to provide a useful, assistive resource for prospective/new flexible learners as they encounter key transition periods in the initial stages of the study lifecycle (i.e., thinking about study, making decisions, registration and the first few weeks of commencing study). Even though this period of time is vitally important for learners, it has been largely neglected in empirical research and relevant institution settings alike. Head Start Online directly tackles this pertinent issue through offering its target population expertly designed digital readiness tools alongside further resources as a support during these essential transitions.

2 Method

A design based methodological approach was harnessed in order to develop Head Start Online. This process is iterative in its nature; while evaluating an innovative intervention, it also systematically improves the innovation while providing design guidelines for succeeding relevant research and intervention formulation [4]. Further coinciding with the aims of this MOOC is design-based research driving to diminish the void between education research and practical real-world environments, be them online or traditional.

2.1 Literature Analysis

The first step was the conducting of a thorough analysis of the body of relevant empirical work; this was a necessity in order to discover what existing tools are working in relation to supporting flexible learners through the aforementioned important time period. Below are some of the key points from the full analysis of the literature [5].

Jones [6] notes that the literature indicates that students are most likely to leave in their year of entry. This is a long established fact [7–9]) but what has recently been added is the understanding that students who are actively supported over the course of this transition also develop the key academic skills needed to succeed in the longer run

[10, 11]. Given that students who exit will often not re-enroll [2], this highlights the importance of supporting students in the early stages of the study life cycle [12].

Personal circumstances are frequently and consistently listed in the literature as one of the top reasons flexible learners withdraw from study [13–15]. They may withdraw due to various reasons including employment demands, the needs of their dependents, workload, problems with finance, and organisation issues [15]. Poor course choice and poor support from friends and family are identified as triggers by McGivney [16], though older learners are less likely to pick the wrong course [17] and more likely to cite external circumstances and financial reasons for non-completion [16, 17]. Learners who drop out typically found study to be more work than expected [13, 15], and/or had believed that flexible study was going to be easier than attending an 'on-campus' programme [18]. To be successful, flexible learners need to be able to manage their time and self-regulate effectively, in order to both structure their study around their other responsibilities effectively, and make the most of the time available to them. If they cannot, they will fall behind in coursework. [19]. Ashby [19] found the top reason for withdrawal at the UK Open University was falling behind with coursework, followed by personal/family or employment responsibilities. It seems highly likely that the two are related, and the challenges around them could perhaps be better prepared for during the pre-entry period, for example by helping students to "calculate what is personally realistic during the path to enrolment" [13] (p. 12). The importance of time-management has also been emphasised by [20], who developed a simple time-management tool in the form of a 'progress bar' for students' online learning activities. Flexible learners also need to be helped to appreciate the benefits of having good support networks as part of their studies [13, 21].

This process saw the discovery of several relevant tools. The usefulness of support measures (e.g., compulsory support surveys, orientation course, general messages of support, personal contact/interaction with students) is established [15]. Another suite of effective tools identified were discussion forum platforms, active emails, and time-limited lecture postings [22]; these were demonstrated to increase student satisfaction and enhance their chances of successful progression. Murphy et al. [23] stressed the beneficial impact of offering the necessary information to help course choice, early access to timetables, and activity based learning to improve academic ability for mature learners in the initial stages of the study lifecycle. In addition they stated providing entrants with a suitable digital environment to interact with their peers and existing mature learners has a positive impact on their experience. While some interesting tools emerged from the analysis, the amount of relevant tools identified was limited.

2.2 Database of Existing Tools

The next stage of the approach was the development of a database of existing digital readiness tools. The database was compiled from analysing websites of international universities in order to detect the readiness tools they provide for their prospective learners. Following this the identified tools were thematically coded according to their main function; this resulted in the following themes: (1) Course match; (2) Preparation for higher education; (3) Orientation; (4) Addressing personal circumstances;

(5) Community and (6) Satisfactory student experience. Evidently, the themes coincide with Jones' [6] principle factors that prevent student progression and lead to drop out when lacking.

2.3 Creation of Digital Readiness Tools

The digital readiness tools to be included in Head Start Online were then developed by academic teams working, in many instances, with a Dublin-based digital design company Fluid Rock. Five overarching principles were adopted for the design of a suite of eight digital readiness and preparation tools for flexible learners: (i) self-regulation, (ii) personalization, (iii) customization, (iv) information at the point of need, and (iv) language and framing of the tools in the world of the prospective learner. In terms of this last principle it was noteworthy that we found most of the existing tools to help facilitate successful transitions for flexible learners were couched in institutional language.

3 Structure of Head Start Online

A number of factors contributed to the presentation of this MOOC, including existing knowledge of creating credit-bearing online courses, alternative MOOCS that team members had participated in as learners, guidance from a contact in Moodle HQ, a design workshop delivered by Yishay Mor, and trial and error development while constructing the MOOC. Head Start Online was developed on a new MOOC platform called Academy, created by Moodle HQ. The development process embodied a design based approach, however reflection on the best methodology for developing the MOOC was needed. The core of the course involved the students engaging with the digital readiness tools developed by the Student Success Toolbox. Other resources were also specifically created for the MOOC, i.e. text and video content, Moodle activities, and discussion forums. Two examples of this content were videos of flexible learning graduates telling their stories of higher education, used to reinforce messages contained within the readiness tools, and a 'complete the sentence' Moodle activity that facilitated participants reflecting on who they were and their motivations for study.

The course is designed to run over a total period of five weeks. A welcome area is made available to those enrolled on the course prior to the official launch of week one. The welcome area consists of a course overview and provides guidelines to setting up a course profile. The estimated time commitment for participants is two hours per week; this varies according to the learner as there are also optional, additional activities that can be accessed. Every Monday during the five week period a new section of the course is launched and becomes accessible to participants. While this method is maintained for the duration of the course, participants do not have to adhere to this timing. They can complete the course at their own pace, or commence the course at a later date than its original launch. The course content remains accessible for two weeks following the end of the course's fifth week.

The five sections of the course are as follows: 1. A good beginning - What is this course about? Who else is here? 2. What to expect - What should you expect of part-time/online learning? 3. Time is precious - How much time do you have for study? What supports do you have in your life? 4. Skills for success - What computer skills do you need? What is required to produce a successful assignment in your first semester of study? 5. Next steps - Where next? Is online learning for you? What will you decide to do?

3.1 SST Digital Readiness Tools

Am I Ready for Study? Participants encounter this tool during Week Two, enabling them to self-assess if they are ready to commence flexible study. A quiz is presented to students, entailing the following six sections tackling pertinent issues: (i) Previous Study, (ii) Work and Family, (iii) Study Intentions, (iv) Study Skills, (v) Computer Skills and (vi) Work Habits. Participants are provided with personalised feedback upon completion of each section and the quiz in its entirety (e.g., "you probably need to talk with your close family and friends. It's really important that they understand why you're thinking about undertaking further study…"). Two forms of feedback are given from differing perspectives (i.e., the higher education institution and a past/present flexible learner).

Do I Have Enough Time? Situated in Week Three of Head Start Online is a self-reflective 'life calculator', assisting the learners in assessing the time they spend on certain activities during a typical week. This assists the participants on gaining a realistic perspective of whether or not they will be able to manage their time effectively to include study amongst life, work and family commitments. The 'life calculator' consists of six sections: (i) Work, (ii) Family, (iii) Household, (iv) Hobbies, (v) Leisure and (vi) Sleep. Finally participants are provided with feedback on whether they have adequate time to include study or if they may have to make some necessary adjustments. (e.g., You can probably go ahead and register for your course but don't forget to talk with the staff and check the requirements for the particular programme of study you wish to undertake).

Who can I ask? Another tool placed in Week Three aims to get learners thinking about their available support network, and how they may receive the necessary support through their higher education degree. They are presented with advice on gaining support from Friends, Family, Employers, Universities and Other Students, and examples of student stories detailing individuals who are supported and other lacking in support are accessible. Furthermore, numerous typical student support boundaries matched with potential solutions and assistive support outlets are also demonstrated. (e.g., Problem: I am struggling with the technology on this course. Other Students Solution: Other students may be a good source of help with technology problems as they may have experienced similar problems themselves. However be careful not to share your user name and password with anyone.)

My Computer Skills: Am I Computer Ready to Learn? With this tool, placed in Week Four of the course, students hear from student voices in relation to the computer skills required for higher education. Upon commencing their interaction with this tool, the participant indicated their prior levels of computer skills, which influences their subsequent pathway. Information is provided regarding both the typical technology services offered by higher education institutions and the technology flexible learners tend to use. Student stories detailing first encounters with email services, online reading materials, Microsoft Word, and Microsoft PowerPoint are also provided. The main element of this tool is the quiz. The first section involves three fundamental questions yes/no questions, should a participant answer no to any of these they are directed to additional online resources designed to develop computer skills. The remaining students who answer yes to all three of the questions follow a different pathway and face questions regarding word processing, file management, and using the internet.

My First Assignment. The second tool contained within Week Four sees participants being guided once more by a student voice, however this time it relates to tackling that very first assignment in higher education. This tool also contains multiple navigation pathways based on participants' prior experience with higher level assignments. The development and planning of an assignment is covered and other students' views are provided in quotes throughout the tool. My First Assignment aims to allow prospective learners gain a sense of what it may be like to face an assignment early in their studies.

4 Learner Feedback/Results

In order to the gain knowledge of the efficacy of Head Start Online, participant feedback was sought from those enrolled during the soft pilot phase of MOOC development. As verified below, it is highly likely that learners will be positively impacted through their engagement with the course.

The pilot of Head Start Online was carried out over a five week period in 2016 from the 15th Aug to the 19th Sep. This was achieved through the utilisation of a new MOOC platform called Academy, created by Moodle HQ. This partnership resulted in Head Start Online being the first MOOC to be carried out on the new, developing platform.

4.1 Participants

In total 150 individuals enrolled on the course, with 45 of them failing to take further action in signing into the course. Of the remaining 105, 50 fully completed the Head Start Online pilot, receiving a certificate of completion. Participants in this soft pilot consisted of prospective flexible learners planning or thinking of commencing higher education course in Ireland in 2016 or the near future. Additionally, a cohort of roughly 70 prospective learners were recruited through collaboration with a German organisation Kiron, who are dedicated to supporting refugees in gaining access to higher education opportunities.

4.2 Procedure

Participant feedback was gathered through two separate methods.

Weekly Digital Readiness Tools Quiz. Firstly upon completion of the individual digital readiness tools within the five sections of the course (i.e., Am I Ready?, Do I have enough time?, Who can I ask?, My Computer Skills, My first assignment, and Study Tips for Me), participants were prompted to complete an optional feedback quiz assessing three aspects of the tool: (1) the usefulness of the resource, (2) the assistance it provided in preparing the learners, (3) how likely they are to follow the advice provided. A five-point Likert scale was used to gather responses (Strongly disagree-Strongly agree), where participants indicated their level of agreement to relevant positively worded statements (e.g., "I found this resource useful").

End of Course Quiz. Additionally, participant feedback was sought at the end of Head Start Online. Participants were prompted to complete the quiz within the MOOC platform upon completion of the last week's activities. The same five-point Likert scale method was harnessed here, with this concluding quiz assessing nine different aspects of the course: (1) decision to become a flexible learner, (2) readiness to become a flexible learner, (3) recommending the course to others, (4) time management ability, (5) awareness of sources of support, (6) appreciation of necessary higher education computer skills, (7) readiness to tackle a first assignment, (8) usefulness of graduate videos, (9) assistance in interacting with other prospective learners.

4.3 Results

Overall the feedback received was positive; indicating that Head Start Online, and its digital readiness tools, have a positive impact on prospective flexible learners.

Weekly Digital Readiness Tools. Response rates varied for each tool with a peak for "Tool 1- Am I ready?" in week one (n = 28), and the lowest for "Tool 7- Study Tips for Me" in the last week of the MOOC (n = 11). This is explained by the dropping out of some participants as the course progressed. Participants' favourable reactions were observed consistently toward every tool (see Table 1).

Table 1. Percentage of participants reacting favourably (Strongly Agree or Agree) to digital readiness tools

Tool	Usefulness	Preparation	Follow advice
Am i ready?	96	79	100
Do i have enough time?	100	78.95	84
Who can i ask?	92	83	92
My computer skills	72	61	89
My first assignment	94	83	100
Study tips for me	82	82	100

End of Course Quiz. Of the 50 participants who completed the course, half (n = 25) provided overall feedback data. Again, positive feedback was received indicating the course is achieved the desired learning outcomes (see Table 2). Similarly, positive feedback was received in relation to the items relating to whether the course helped participant's decide to become a flexible learner, and whether participants would recommend the course to others.

Table 2. Percentage of participants reacting favourably (Strongly Agree or Agree) to end of course quiz questions (n = 25)

Question	%	Question	%
I feel more ready to become a flexible learner after taking this course	96	The course helped me appreciate the computer skills I would need for higher education	92
I would recommend this course to others	84	I now understand better how I would do an assignment in my first year	92
I now feel better able to manage my time	92	The videos of graduates helped me understand the flexible learning experience	88
The course developed my awareness of different sources of support	92	Helped me interact with flexible learners	60

The majority of respondents to the end of course quiz also indicated that the course developed their awareness of the different sources of support they may access as flexible learners. Respondents also indicated that the course helped them appreciate the skills that they would need to succeed as a flexible learner in higher education, for example computer skills and the academic skills needed to produce assignments. With regard to the additional content created for the MOOC, beyond the digital readiness tools developed by the Student Success Toolbox project, participants who completed the quiz responded positively towards the video content of flexible learning graduates used in the MOOC. There was a mixed response on the question of whether or not the course helped participants to interact with flexible learners, with only 60% agreeing or strongly agreeing with the statement and 16% disagreeing or strongly disagreeing.

5 Discussion

There is an indication, from the evaluation of the Head Start Online MOOC pilot, and the digital readiness tools contained with it, that these tools can improve prospective flexible learners' preparation for higher education study through the provision of active developmental supports, early in the study life cycle [10–12]. While it is acknowledged that the pilot of the MOOC involved relatively low participant numbers the feedback received indicates that this type of pre-induction socialization course can help prospective flexible learners to form realistic expectations about higher education study [13, 15, 18]. The MOOC makes prospective learners more aware of: the need to reflect on their life in order to plan around their personal circumstances [13–15]; the importance of managing their time [19, 20]; the need to have good sources of support during their studies [13, 21]; and what skills they will need, e.g. study and computers skills, in order to stay on top of their studies in their first year [19]. The results from the Head Start Online pilot will inform future, full iterations of the MOOC, the data from which will help to fill an evident gap in the literature relating to the use of digital tools to facilitate flexible learner transition into Higher education.

References

1. Brown, M.: MOOCs as social practice: a kaleidoscope of perspectives. In: De Corte, E., Enwall, L., Teichler, U. (eds.) From Books to MOOCs? Emerging Models of Learning and Teaching in Higher Education. Wenner-Gren International Series, vol. 88, pp. 31–41. Portland Press, London (2016)
2. Woodley, A., Simpson, O.: Student dropout: the elephant in the room. In: Online Distance Education: Towards a Research Agenda, pp. 459–484 (2014)
3. Higher Education Authority: Part-time and flexible higher education in Ireland: policy, practice and recommendations for the future (2012). https://www.dkit.ie/system/files/HEA%20Report%20on%20Lifelong%20Learning%202013.pdf
4. Wang, F., Hannafin, M.: Design-based research and technology-enhanced learning environments. Educ. Tech. Res. Dev. **53**(4), 5–23 (2005)
5. Brunton, J., Brown, M., Cleary, A., Costello, E., Delaney, L., Fox, S., Galvin, C., Gilligan, J., O'Regan, L., Ward, J.: Lost in Transition: A Report on Enabling Success for Flexible Learners. Dublin City University, Dublin (2016)
6. Jones, R.: Widening participation - student retention and success. Research Synthesis for the Higher Education Academy (2008)
7. Yorke, M.: Leaving Early: Undergraduate Non-completion in Higher Education. Falmer, London (1999)
8. Quinn, J., Thomas, L., Slack, K., Casey, L., Thexton, W., Noble, J.: From Life Crisis to Lifelong Learning. Rethinking Working Class' Drop Out' From Higher Education. Joseph Rowntree Foundation, York (2005)
9. Yorke, M., Longden, B.: The First Year Experience of Higher Education in the UK: Report on Phase 1. Higher Education Academy, York (2007)
10. Armstrong, C.: An evaluation of initiatives implemented to support undergraduate students' transition into higher education at one post-1992 university. J. Hudders. Stud. Res. **1**(1), e10 (2015)
11. Thomas, L.: What works? Facilitating an effective transition into higher education. Widening Particip. Lifelong Learn. **14**, 4–24 (2012)
12. Brown, M.: Thinking about digital learning: opportunities for student support and development. Invited Presentation at Student Support and Development Services Retreat, Dublin City University, Dublin, 9 May 2014
13. Brown, M., Hughes, H., Keppell, M., Hard, N., Smith, L.: Stories from students in their first semester of distance learning. Int. Rev. Res. Open Distrib. Learn. **16**(4), 1–17 (2015)
14. McGivney, V.: Student retention in open and distance learning: understanding' 'persistence' in adult learning. Paper Prepared for the Retention Symposium, Madingley Hall, Cambridge, May 2003
15. Nichols, M.: Intervention for retention through distance education: a comparison study. Project output ed. National Centre for Tertiary Teaching Excellence, Aotearoa, New Zealand (2011)

16. McGivney, V.: Understanding persistence in adult learning. Open Learn. **19**(1), 33–46 (2004)
17. Yorke, M.: Retention, persistence and success in on-campus higher education, and their enhancement in open and distance learning. Open Learn. **19**(1), 19–32 (2004)
18. Nash, R.D.: Course completion rates among distance learners: identifying possible methods to improve retention. Online J. Dis. Learn. Adm. **3**(4), 1–27 (2005)
19. Ashby, A.: Monitoring student retention in the open university: detritions, measurement, interpretation and action. Open Learn. **19**(1), 65–78 (2004)
20. de Raadt, M., Dekeyser, S.: A simple time-management tool for students' online learning activities. In: Same places, different spaces. Proceedings of Ascilite Conference, Auckland (2009). http://www.ascilite.org.au/conferences/auckland09/procs/deraadt.pdf
21. Anagnostopolou, K., Parmer, D.: Practical Guide: Bringing Together E-Learning & Student Retention. STAR Resources, University of Ulster (2008)
22. Gallie, K.: Student attrition before and after modifications in distance course delivery. Stud. Learn. Eval. Innov. Dev. **2**(3), 69–76 (2005)
23. Murphy, E., Politis, Y., Slowey, M.: Contributing to an evidence base for the enhancement of the experiences and outcomes of mature students at an Irish University. In: New Voices in Higher Education Research and Scholarship, pp. 191–123 (2014)

The EMMA Experience. Emerging Patterns and Factors for Success

Rosanna De Rosa[1(✉)], Chiara Ferrari[2], and Ruth Kerr[3]

[1] University of Naples Federico II, Vico Monte di Pietà 1, Naples, Italy
rderosa@unina.it
[2] IPSOS, Via Tolmezzo 15, Milan, Italy
Chiara.Ferrari@Ipsos.com
[3] University of Naples Federico II, Softel, Via Partenope 36, Naples, Italy
ruthlizkerr@gmail.com

Abstract. Since 2008, when the first experiment with MOOCs took place, much has been said, written and explored. However, almost ten years later we are unable to say whether MOOCs are really a desirable learning experience and, moreover, what are the factors for success in the MOOC environment. Literature in the field seems to clearly endorse learner engagement and participation as activities that ensure a higher completion rate and a satisfying learning experience, yet a high degree of dropout can be attributed to a request for participation which learners find unsustainable. On many MOOC projects, the data opens opportunities for discussion but provides few answers, as so much depends on individual variables of the specific course. Far from being a limit of the research, this uncertainty is the only way to preserve learning from becoming a hostage of algorithms, thus leaving teachers and learners the freedom to plan, decide, and experience, and to evaluate their teaching and learning.

Keywords: Learning analytics · Learning data · MOOC

1 Introduction

In 2013 the MOOC phenomenon reached new heights. Many observers commented that it was like being «in the midst of a hype cycle» [1, 4, 5], while others feared that it was the overstatement surrounding the phenomenon that would prove their greatest obstacle to success [3]. Expectations were high in Europe too, but accompanied by a certain apprehension regarding the future of public universities and the way competition is increasing between old and new players for a position in this open and global education market. 2013 also marked the moment for new platforms to explore the European market. This was the case for the French FUN and the English FutureLearn, the first strongly supported by the government, the second by the Open University and other relevant stakeholders. One year later, after exploratory research based on a survey at a European Level [2], and thanks to EU funds, the EMMA project (European Multiple MOOC Aggregator: www.europeanmoocs.eu) came into being to create an innovative platform for MOOC delivery in a variety of European languages and pedagogical approaches.

C. Delgado Kloos et al. (Eds.): EMOOCs 2017, LNCS 10254, pp. 20–28, 2017.
DOI: 10.1007/978-3-319-59044-8_3

In this paper we focus on the data and look at some of the results emerging from cross-referencing of the learning analytics data, survey results, and qualitative observations, which enabled us to identify four main variables as key ingredients in a successful MOOC.

2 Methodology

The diverse and multi-faceted approach of EMMA provided a broad range of data from which to extrapolate information to make sense of the MOOC project. A solid and tested Evaluation Methodology of the processes of learning and of learners' behavior was obtained by cross-referencing two sources.

- The **Learning Analytics dashboards**, with real time data, which were made available to both teachers and learners during the course of the MOOCs.
- The **social survey-based analysis, which** includes 3 main steps:
  - A profiling of the students registering on the platform, via a combination of two tools: the **registration form**, collecting basic data (gender, age, profession, nationality, main language) and **the registration questionnaire (EXPECTATIONS),** collecting more detailed info (e.g. previous experience with e-learning, expectations vs. EMMA, etc.). The target of this survey includes all people registered.
  - A MOOC-Level questionnaire, adapted to each single MOOC, on course completion to evaluate the MOOC experience and to obtain feedback on the learning experience.
  - An Exit Questionnaire, which evaluates the experience on the platform. The target of this survey includes all people registering in at least one MOOC. Taking the survey was never mandatory, to avoid interference with course progress and/or learner fatigue.

2.1 Universe of Learners

The survey data were connected with Learning Analytics via the Unique Identification string. Learners were clustered as Enrolled, Observers or Contributors according to their level of commitment to the course as explained below. The universe of learners for this analysis was equal to 15.522.

Enrolled – participants who entered the MOOC up to five times: 5.708 or, 36.8%.
Observers – participants who entered the MOOC more than five times, but did not interact with the content or other participants: 3.939 or, 25.4%.
Contributors – participants who contributed with the assignment, comment or post to the MOOC at least once: 3.999 or, 25.7%.
Actives – participants who contributed with the assignment, comment or post to the MOOC more than once: 1.876 or, 12.1%.

3 Results of the User Surveys

The data reported and commented in this section refer to a sample of 1.483 individuals, i.e. 6% of the 23.800 profiles registered on the EMMA platform at the time of the last data dump (June 2016). This is a self-selected sample given the non-mandatory nature of all the surveys; the respondents have been selected as having submitted a complete set of data, i.e. both at registration and at expectation levels.

3.1 Distribution of Enrolments

The MOOCs which most appealed to the learners and therefore collected most of the enrolments are fairly diverse and presented by very diverse academic institutions. Besides the #OWU MOOC (which totaled over 2000 enrolments) and the course on *Adolescent Brain* (over 1.500 enrolments) both offered by EMMA Partners, two non-partner MOOCs around digital culture were definitely successful: *Coding in Your Classroom Now!* by A. Bogliolo (University of Urbino, Italy, 14.000 learners enrolled), and *Digital Libraries in Theory and Practice* by A. Tammaro (University of Parma, Italy – over 1200 enrolled students).

3.2 Opinion on the Experience with the MOOC Enrolled in

91% of EMMA learners found the learning experience an enjoyable one (+6% on previous round). 92% of the learners claimed that their course was well organized (+14%), which made the task of following it easy enough for 89% (+11%). This can be attributed to the care that the teachers and tutors took in designing their MOOC.

Opinions regarding quantity, quality and type of materials was positive (over 85% of users completely or fairly agreed that materials were "up-to-date", "appropriate", "engaging" and "innovative"), and registered little variation between different learner clusters, although the more opportunities the learners had to get familiar with the materials, the better their evaluation.

3.3 Opinion on the Quantity and Acceptance of Tasks and Assignments Proposed in the MOOCs

86% of respondents (+9% vs. 2015) found that the quantity of tasks and assignments requested of learners was just right considering the time they put in and what they got out of the task. Learners found the tasks and assignments useful (89%) and engaging (85%), and a good opportunity for self-assessment (88%). Moreover, 73% of the respondents enrolled in at least one EMMA MOOC claimed that they received the expected feedback from tutors and teachers (Fig. 1).

The difference in perception is more evident within the clusters, while the number of MOOCs followed doesn't seem to influence learner judgment significantly.

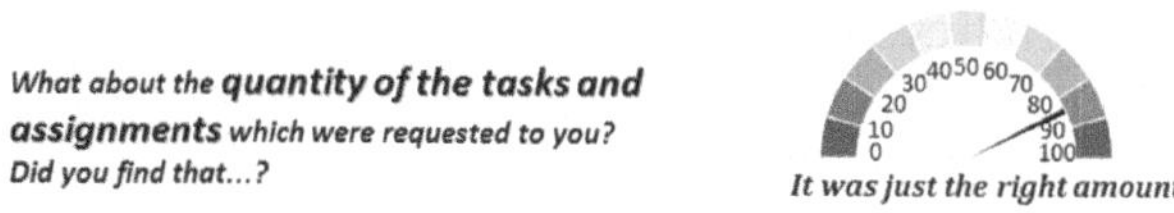

Fig. 1. Evaluation of assignments requested (data from the exit questionnaire)

3.4 Opinion on Interaction Tools

Over 2 out of 3 respondents claim that the conversation and chat functions are useful, productive, engaging and that they encouraged them to reflect. These functions are appreciated by the most active learners, with intensive MOOC users finding them a useful tool for creating connections.

3.5 Opinion on Video Materials

Over 90% of the respondents describe the videos as useful, of good quality and format, and enhancing the overall value of the MOOCs. Almost 2 out of 3 stated they are the right length and appreciated the subtitling. Again, these updates show a positive trend in increased appreciation. The length of videos apparently impacted learner willingness to remain on board. 41% of Enrolled learners found videos too long, so their participation might have been hindered by this. However, the main feature discriminating the high and low "users" of EMMA courses where video is concerned, is the availability of subtitles, which is seen as a further support in the learning process.

3.6 The Personal Blog

Respondents are generally satisfied with the availability of the personal blog: 61% stated it is useful, 57% engaging and 59% stated that it is a good opportunity for getting in touch with the other learners. 30% to 40% of learners could not express an opinion since they hadn't used the function (either because it wasn't expressly required, or it wasn't promoted by teachers/tutors). Once again, the most interactive learners fully appreciated the social potential of the function.

3.7 Personalisation Features

65% of the respondents found the personalisation features – Bookmarks, Notes and Comments, - useful and easy to use. 64% stated that they represent a good opportunity to track the relevant points of lessons. Values were 20% higher than on previous analysis.

3.8 Opinion on Topics for Future MOOCs

A wide variety of topics and subjects were mentioned as areas of interest by the respondents but digital skills for teachers, language learning and computer programming were amongst the most popular.

4 Learning Analytics Results[1]

4.1 Interactions Analysed

For analysing participants' interactions, data from Learning Locker and EMMA database were used. The following interactions were analyzed for learning analytics purposes:

- Learner visited page (lesson, unit, assignment, blogpost)
- Learner created post
- Learner commented/replied conversation
- Learner submitted assignment/peer-assessment
- Duration of different content

In order to make sense of the learning analytics data, the analysis results were compared with the intended MOOC design in the platform (Table 1).

One of the main results of the analysis indicates that it is almost impossible to say that shorter courses are more efficient than longer courses, as is sometimes suggested in MOOC research communities. One of the most successful MOOCs in the EMMA platform was *Coding in your classroom, NOW!* which lasted 13 weeks - the longest MOOC ever on Emma. It recorded the largest no. of participants (n = 6951 at the time of data collection) and it is interesting to note that the number of *enrolled* learners was only 27%.

Smart Toys for Smarter Kids is another good example. It lasted 12 weeks, yet more than 30% of the participants (n = 937) contributed to the MOOC and the number of *enrolled* learners was less than 40%. At the same time, several shorter courses were running where the number of learners who only enrolled on the course was pretty high (more than 70%) and, vice versa, the percentage of learners who actually contributed to the MOOC was rather low.

4.2 MOOC Designs

A further investigation into the different platform functionalities and activities used in individual MOOCs illustrates that EMMA was able to support different pedagogical approaches as shown in the table below.

At the same time it demonstrates that it is not possible to say if one kind of MOOC design is better than another. The MOOC "Designing online courses with 7Cs framework" design was mainly built on one functionality – conversation. Learners had a variety of options to use that tool for discussion, presenting tasks, asking questions, reviewing peers' and so on. Table 2 indicates that the number of only enrolled users is pretty high and only 15% of the learners actually contributed to the MOOC activities. A social network analysis of the same course showed that very few learners interacted with their classmates.

[1] For this paragraph, we thank Kairit Tammets (University of Tallin) for providing data and comments.

Table 1. Clusters distribution in the MOOCs analysed Oct 2015–July 2016

No. of participants	Duration	Enrolled	Observer	Contributor	Active
Drawing lights and shadows (n = 146)	4 weeks	57%	13%	15%	15%
Digital library in principle and practice (n = 726)	4 weeks	3%	25%	18%	14%
Circular economy (n = 74)	4 weeks	65%	9%	11%	15%
Lisbon and the sea: a story of arrivals and departures (n = 131)	5 weeks	58%	24%	15%	3%
Open Wine University (two runs together, n = 2512)	5 weeks	37%	12%	22%	29%
Copyright – DIY (n = 156)	6 weeks	67%	21%	11%	0.6%
Designing online courses with the 7Cs framework (n = 403)	6 weeks	71%	13%	8%	7%
21st century learning (n = 359)	6 weeks	64%	13%	12%	11%
The organisation of cultural enterprises (n = 292)	6 weeks	90%	2%	4%	4%
Climate changes: the context of life experience (n = 117)	9 weeks	78%	(9%)	(8%)	5%
Search in the internet (n = 186)	9 weeks	48%	12%	10%	30%
Computer-assisted Inquiry (n = 61)	9 weeks	57%	26%	13%	–
Assessment for learning in practice (n = 326)	8 weeks	39%	25%	36%	–
Adolescent brain (n = 1593)	8 weeks	34%	13%	35%	23%
FlotRisCo: seaside communities facing coastal risks (n = 77)	8 weeks	58%	42%	–	–
Guerrila literacy learners (n = 69)	7 weeks	65%	13%	19%	3%
Coding in your classroom (n = 6951)	13 weeks	27%	34%	32%	7%
Piattaforme digitali per la gestione del territorio (n = 405)	13 weeks	45%	50%	20 (5%)	–
Smart toys for smarter kids. Becoming a digital educator (n = 937)	12 weeks	38%	30%	29%	3%

The MOOC "Search in the internet" also used mainly one EMMA functionality – quizzes. Learners were expected to read or watch learning resources and then they submitted quizzes. The course was pretty capacious – 92 units and 61 quizzes is not an easy task. Further investigation of data demonstrated that:

- Only 3% (5 learners) visited all the 92 units;
- Only 10% (19 learners) visited at least 50% of the quizzes (31 quizzes);
- Only 9% (16 learners) submitted at least 50% of the quizzes;

Clustering of the participants demonstrated that ca. 50% of the learners became MOOC participants and 40% actually submitted quizzes.

The third example comes from the most popular MOOC – Coding in your classroom NOW. That MOOC used several EMMA functionalities: blogs, conversation, assignments, quizzes, peer-assessment, and external resources. Clustering demonstrates

Table 2. Comparison of MOOC design

	Search in the internet	Coding in the classroom now!	Designing online courses with 7Cs framework
N. of weeks	9	13	6
N. of lessons/units/ assignments	9/92/61	6/23/9	6/25/0 No assignments
Learning activities	Read materials Watch videos Submit quiz	Read materials Practical tasks outside platform Submit assignments (link tasks) Peer-assessment	Read materials Watch videos Practical tasks outside platform Reflect and comment in blog or conversation tool
Possible pedagogy	xMOOC	hybrid MOOC	cMOOC
Clusters of participants			
• Enrolled	48%	27%	71%
• Observers	12%	34%	13%
• Contributors	30%	32%	8%
• Active	10%	7%	7%

that nearly 40% of the participants contributed to the MOOC and less than 30% were just enrolled, which is really a good result for quite a massive MOOC. Further investigation demonstrates that 24% of the participants actually visited all the units and 33% of the participants visited at least 50% of the assignments.

4.3 Overview of Participants' Engagement in MOOCs

See Figs. 2 and 3.

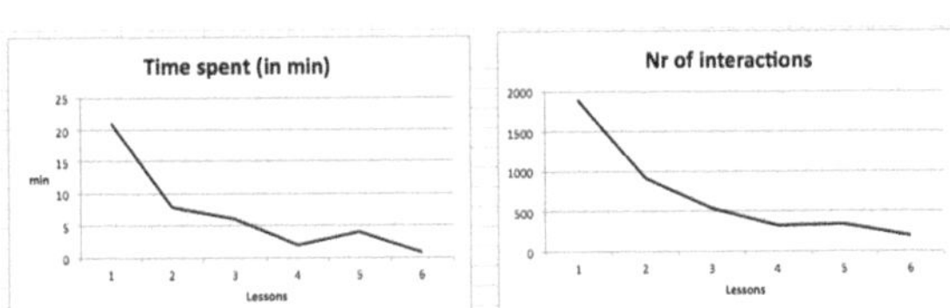

Fig. 2. 'Designing online courses with 7Cs framework': time spent and interactions in lessons

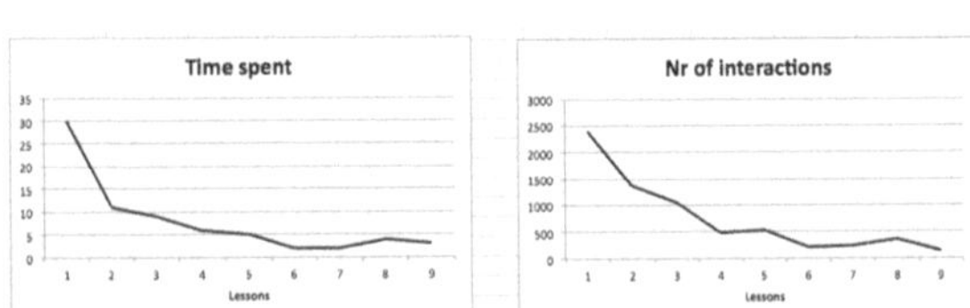

Fig. 3. 'Search in the internet': time spent and interactions in lessons

4.4 Clusters of Participants

Lesson engagement was also compared in relation to learner types. In the figure below, we can see an example of a course with 58% of the learners contributors or active learners, the "Adolescent brain "MOOC (Fig. 4).

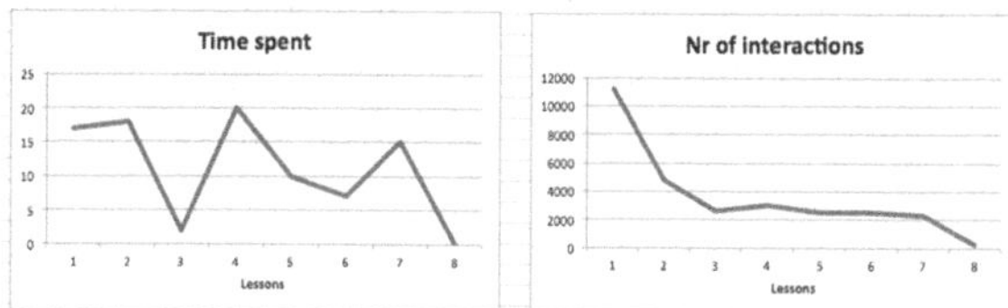

Fig. 4. Adolescent brain: time spent and interactions in lessons.

From these figures it is possible to assume that certain lessons were more time-consuming or interesting than others (lesson 2, 4, 7). It is also possible to see that interactions remained basically the same from lesson 3 onwards, though the same initial drop-off was recorded.

5 Conclusions

In this paper we briefly presented and discussed the cross analysis of survey data with LA clusters, which prove both that an intensive interaction with the platform is one of the keys to satisfaction and, possibly, to learner retention, and, on the contrary, that a successful relationship with the teacher and the MOOC design have an impact on the number of interactions with the platform. Expectations about the interactions within the platform were in fact rather high (75% stated they wanted to learn on EMMA by discussing with teachers/tutors, 67% by reading comments posted by other learners, and 61% by discussing with other learners), and the tools and functions made available by the platform responded well to their requirements, together with the opportunity of building a personal learning environment offered by the Coursebook functions.

Data from the Exit questionnaire were also crossed with LA data regarding learners enrolled in more than one MOOC, demonstrating that there is a connection between learner satisfaction and repeat enrollment (Fig. 5).

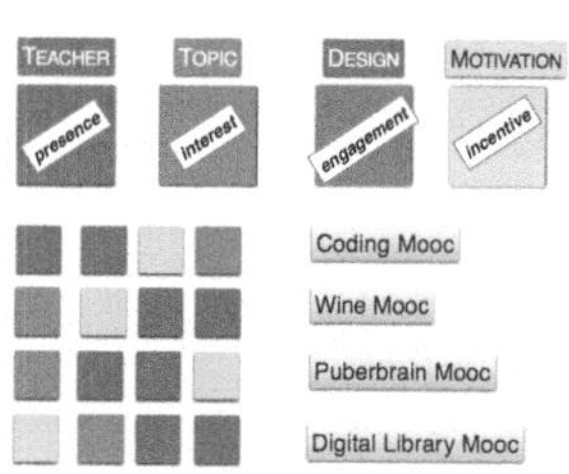

Fig. 5. The recipe for MOOC success

We can state that there is no unique recipe for success: MOOCs can be designed very differently using only the functionalities that are strongly necessary to support learning. We have identified four main variables as key ingredients of a successful MOOC. These components are the teacher presence (teaching, cognitive, social), the topic (socially or professionally interesting), the course design (how engaging the mix of materials and learning activities proves to be) and motivation (whether the course offers necessary credits or training in a necessary skill). Although these components are not to be considered as enabling factors - i.e. they cannot be put in place at the beginning of the learning to ensure success - they do all appear in a varying sequence in the most successful MOOCs.

References

1. Coates, K.: The re-invention of the academy: how technologically mediated learning will – and will not – transform advanced education. In: Cheung, S.K.S., Fong, J., Fong, W., Wang, F.L., Kwok, L.F. (eds.) ICHL 2013. LNCS, vol. 8038, pp. 1–9. Springer, Heidelberg (2013). doi:10.1007/978-3-642-39750-9_1
2. De Rosa, R., Reda, V.: La rivoluzione dei MOOCs: un'analisi di policy framework su scala europea. LEA - Lingue e letterature d'Oriente e d'Occidente **2**, 594–631 (2013)
3. Dillenbourg, P.: MOOCs in Europe, an overview, slides (2013)
4. Porter, S.: To MOOC or Not to MOOC: How Can Online Learning Help to Build the Future of Higher Education?. Chandos Publishing, Oxford (2015)
5. Yang, D.: Are We MOOC'd Out? (2013). huffingtonpost.com. Accessed 14 Mar 2013

Mentoring Learners in MOOCs: A New Way to Improve Completion Rates?

Lucie Dhorne(✉), Jean-Pierre Deflandre, Olivier Bernaert, Sébastien Bianchi, and Maria Thirouard

IFP School, IFP Energies nouvelles,
1 et 4 avenue de Bois-Préau, 92852 Rueil-Malmaison, France
Lucie.dhorne@ifpen.fr

Abstract. Since the launch of the MIT Open-Course Ware in 2001, MOOCs have developed exponentially. From a dozen in 2011, they have become ubiquitous in higher education nowadays. Far from bringing about a revolution in teaching practices, MOOCs are a new way of sharing knowledge. The so-called experimental phase facilitated exchanges between providers and users, and it now seems important to look at the first results of these courses in order to improve their effectiveness. Although MOOCs are mainly promoted by higher education establishments, they generally have very low completion rates (below 7%). After 3-years of experience with Massive Open Online Courses (MOOC) with good completion rates (28 to 33%) IFP School decided to improve these results by putting in place mentoring to motivate learners to not quitting before final achievement. This paper presents our MOOCs participation results and the approach we developed to enhance the coaching efficiency together with developing new pedagogical approaches.

Keywords: Massive Open Online Course (MOOC) · Mentoring · Adaptive learning · Completion rates

1 Introduction

In November 2014, IFP School launched its first MOOC devoted to Sustainable Mobility, up to 3,099 participants enrolled in the MOOC and 31% passed the certification. In May 2015, IFP School launched its second MOOC devoted to the whole Oil & Gas chain "From exploration to distribution" in partnership with Total S. A. and IFP Training. Up to 21,840 people from 140 countries participated in this edition and among them 28% passed the certification [1, 2]. During these three years, at least up to 50,000 people participated in MOOCs respectively on Sustainable Mobility (2014–2015) and The Oil & Gas Chain (2015–2016). These courses had already high completion rates (up to 28%) regarding other MOOCs [3] but nevertheless we aimed and are still aiming at improving them. Indeed for the re-edition of the two MOOCs and after an analysis of our results we introduced a mentoring approach by following students having difficulties more individually in order so they pass their assignments.

C. Delgado Kloos et al. (Eds.): EMOOCs 2017, LNCS 10254, pp. 29–37, 2017.
DOI: 10.1007/978-3-319-59044-8_4

2 Comments and Feedbacks on Our MOOC Experiences

The main objectives of our MOOCs were to improve IFP School worldwide visibility to attract excellent international students and to test on a large population of students new pedagogical approaches to be declined in our different educational programs. Both editions were very successful and allowed us to be confident in our approach. In addition to the video contents, the forums allowed students to communicate with others and the educational and pedagogical staff on the MOOC content. It creates a MOOC community and a very positive emulation that encourages learners to continue until the final certification.

From these first experiences we decided to introduce for the next sessions:

- a training week (called Week 0) to help participants to discover the platform environment and to advise them on how to participate and efficiently follow the MOOC program,
- a coaching support on the forums by peers (indeed students from IFP School) in addition to the educational and pedagogical staff support,
- a focused coaching program based on appropriate mailing actions to help groups of students who have difficulty in achieving their assignments in time.

2.1 MOOC's Re-editions

For the "Sustainable Mobility" (SM2) MOOC re-edition, main changes were associated with the coaching approach itself and associated pedagogy. We analyzed that part of the participation increase (5,205 participants in 2015 for 3,099 in 2014) is a result of, for part, the first Oil & Gas MOOC (run in May 2016) and we have been comforted by the fact that some Universities asked for integrating the MOOC in their courses. We also observed a 1% increase of the completion rate.

For the re-edition of "Oil & Gas" (OG2), with the support of Total S. A., we benefited from the experience of the initial session and the experience of re-editing a MOOC. As mentioned above we introduced new coaching actions and we also redefined the forums for them to better fit with engineering programs. We also replaced all the quizzes by mini-games. For this edition up to 21,009 people from 148 countries enrolled. But for this MOOC, we noticed a decrease of 3% of the completion rate - certainly the final certification mini-game rules were a little bit harder than for the previous final quiz but it is not the major cause. That's why we decided to analyze mentoring results in order to better understand these rates.

3 Mentoring Learners to Increase Motivation

One of the mechanisms that we have decided to put in place to discourage quitting is mentoring. With this approach in mind we worked with a consultant specialized in mentoring [4]. This study has allowed us to open up several paths for improvement of our MOOCs. After studying the data from the first two MOOCs and according to a study of Onah [5], we searched for identifying the possible pedagogical improvements to better follow-up of our MOOCers and reduce the dropout rates of our MOOCs. For Onah, the different reasons of dropout are: no real intention to complete, lack of time, course difficulty and lack of support, lack of digital skills, starting late (…). With the mentoring we decided to focus our attention on the three first reasons.

3.1 Training Week

The analysis of the demographic survey shows that 79% of the learners are very motivated to complete the MOOC. However, over the course duration, there is a strong disengagement of the participants with an increasing dropout rate over time. As a reminder in our first sessions 31% of participants obtained the Sustainable Mobility MOOC achievement certificate and 28% obtained the certificate of the Oil and Gas MOOC. Therefore our tutoring objective was to reduce the dropout rate by motivating the participants with a personalized supervision.

To do this we set up a tutorial system during week 0. The objectives were:

- To reduce the number of non-interactive visits of MOOCers by setting up activities and communication interactions;
- To provide MOOCers with methodological assistance with planning and management of training periods;
- To inform the participants about the tutors who will support them throughout the duration of the course.

This week was divided into seven actions that presented the MOOC and mentoring plan to participants. It aimed to be deliberately discussion intensive to show participants the active presence and benefit of tutors and therefore to encourage participants to attend the discussions.

3.2 Coaching Support on the Forums

Coaching support came in addition to the social network activity operated to motivate everyone to join the MOOC community. To accompany MOOCers during the course and to improve communication between those involved, we also set up a tutorial team (Fig. 1).

As explained below, mentoring aims to accompany MOOC knowledge acquisition. This mentoring was divided into three different types of forums. For the forum "General questions about the way to learn in a MOOC" only peer tutors and the program tutor were allowed to answer the MOOCers questions and in a set time period (24–48 h). We did the same for the thematic forums and the technical support forum. The whole community of tutors created a dynamic for the whole MOOC and also enhanced the motivation of students who felt monitored and supervised.

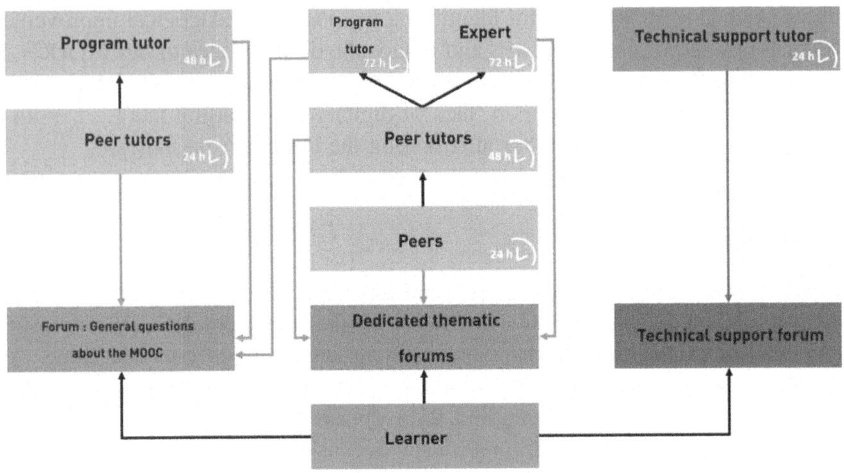

Fig. 1. Organization of the tutorial system

3.3 Focus Motivation and Support Coaching

The "group personalized" approach is based on a day-to-day information platform in combination with selective mailing actions to motivate the participants that are late in achieving their assignments. To be efficient a series of categories of participants is identified and updated over the MOOC program. We fixed a threshold of 200 participants per category to send a specific motivation mail. During week 0, the first pedagogical contact for students is the program tutor also called the learning community manager. Besides animating challenges on social network, this tutor is in charge of proactive activities for a specific audience identified from the demographic survey of week 0. In order to improve pedagogical effectiveness, we identify participants needing individualized tutorial follow up on the basis of the initial questionnaire following assumptions:

- Content difficulty would constitute a reason for quitting.
- Lack of time would constitute grounds for quitting.
- They want to devote less than two hours a week to the MOOC follow up.

4 Data Analysis

The aim of the analysis presented below was to identify the pedagogical actions considered as useful by learners in order to bring as many participants as possible to the final certification. To analyze the results of the four MOOC sessions, we focused on the data provided by the initial survey called "Demographic survey" and the final survey called "End of course survey" (Table 1).

For each MOOC session, the success rate was computed as a function of the number of activities (mini-games, quizzes or assignments) that participants completed.

Table 1. Participation rate in surveys

	OG1	OG2	SM1	SM2
Number of participants	21,840	21,009	3,099	5,205
Success rate	**31%**	**28%**	**32%**	**33%**
Demographic survey	53%	47,5%	54%	60%
End of course survey	31%	26%	30%	31%

We focused further data analysis on participants who completed the initial survey. Participants were assigned to two classes based on their final score: successful (final score > 60) and not successful (final score < 60). This analysis conveys the results of the respondents, i.e. approximately 50% of the participants in our MOOCs (60% for SM2).

4.1 General Analysis

Firstly, we conducted a more holistic analysis on the learner's profile who followed MOOC. When looking more closely at the results for each MOOC, we found that there was a clear threshold between the number of activities carried out and MOOC success rates. For the MOOC Sustainable Mobility, for example, the threshold was 4 out of 8 activities in total. We also noted that a learner who did all the activities had great chances to succeed (Table 2).

The time that participants decided to spend on each activity is also a determining factor for success (Fig. 2).

Table 2. Success rate according to the number of evaluation activities done

	OG1	OG2	SM1	SM2
All activities	43%	49%	46%	37%
Success rate	**99%**	**98,5%**	**100%**	**98%**
Some activities	43%	34%	41%	47%
Success rate	**33%**	**26%**	**24%**	**31%**
No evaluation activity	14%	17%	13%	16%

After analyzing the responses to the question "How much time do you think you will spend on the MOOC each week?" it appears that the participants who have decided to devote at least 2 h per week have a better success rate than those who decided to spend less than 2 h on all the four MOOCs. This supports the initial presumed time-to-spend that seems necessary to properly take each MOOC.

Finally, in this general analysis we were interested in the importance of the socio-demographic categories on the success rates. It must be firstly noted that the MOOC populations are very different. MOOC SM2 attracted more than 50% of students while the MOOC OG2 attracted only 35% of students but more young professionals. By analyzing the success rates according to status, professional or student,

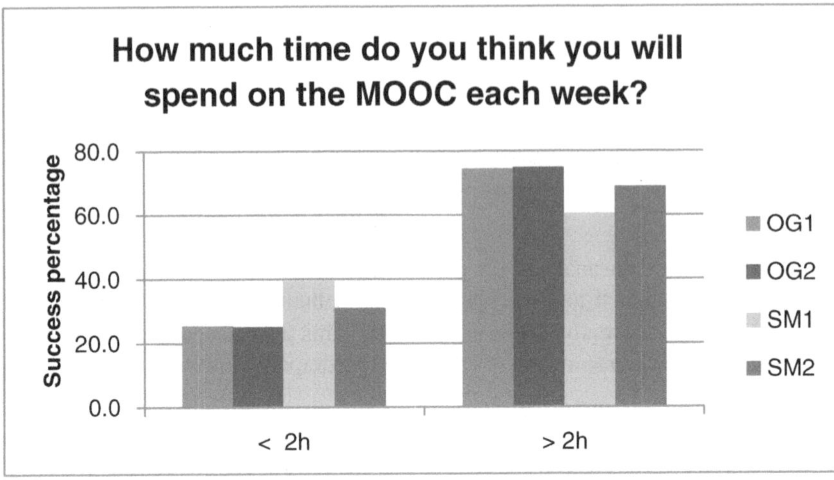

Fig. 2. Success percentage according to the response to the question

(Table 3) it appears that there are no significant differences in success rates according to socio-professional origins.

The success rate for MOOCs seems more related to the intrinsic motivation of the participants rather than their status. We therefore investigated whether or not the mentoring introduced during re-editions had increased the motivation of the participants.

Table 3. Success rate according to status (professional or student)

Success rate	OG1	OG2	SM1	SM2
Students	57%	57%	59.5%	49%
Professionals	57%	57%	52%	53%

4.2 Training Week Analysis

Week 0 was put in place during the re-editions of MOOCs Oil & Gas and Sustainable Mobility. Therefore the analysis below only relates to these two MOOCs. To the question "The information given during week 0 increases my motivation to follow the MOOC", it appears that 80 to 90% of the people who filled the demographic survey found that the week 0 allowed them to increase their motivation. However, when we look deep further to the results into the two groups "succeed" and "unsuccessful" (Fig. 3), it appears that there is a little difference between the results of the two groups. 76% of learners who succeeded to OG2 were motivated by the W0 (strongly agree + agree) against 69% of those who were unsuccessful. For SM2 the difference is 89% for those who succeeded against 84% for others. We can firstly notice a small difference between the two groups about the motivation produced by week 0.

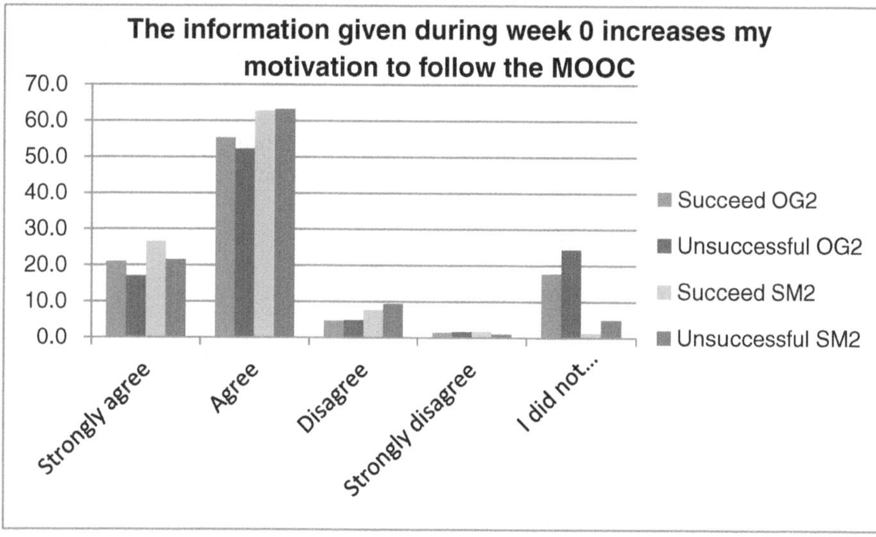

Fig. 3. Response rate in % to the assumption "the information given during week 0 increases my motivation to follow the MOOC"

4.3 Focused Goal and Support Coaching Program

During the End of Course survey of the MOOC OG2 we questioned the participants about the contribution of the personalized mails. These emails were sent each Monday morning to participants who had done their evaluations the previous week and were adapted according to the student profiles as described in Sect. 3.3.

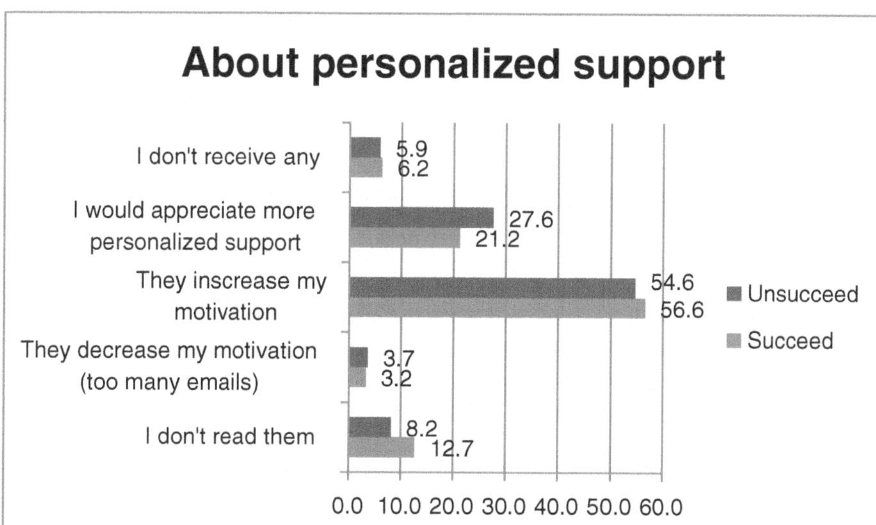

Fig. 4. Personalized support analysis depending on success

If we look at the responses we see that 56,5% of the participants find that the personalized messages contributed to enhance their motivation and that 21,2% of them would have enjoyed receiving more messages of personalized benefits. If we now examine in details the success rates of the respondents (Fig. 4), we see a small difference in the success rate for those who found that tutoring had increased their motivation. However, 27,6% of those who failed would have also liked more individualized tutoring.

5 Conclusions and Perspectives

When analyzing the results of the two re-editions of the MOOCs, we first note a difference in behavior in MOOC SM2 and MOOC OG2.

If we look at SM2 completion rates, we see a 1% increase in the rate, despite a strong increase in the total number of participants (+67%). This re-edition did not include major changes compared to the previous one (adding a serious-game and 3 videos). Concerning the results of OG2, the results differ. The number of subscribers for this re-edition is a little bit lower (−4%) and the completion rate has decreased too (−3%). In the same way, 31% of participants ran the certification mini-game, they were 33% that participated in the final quiz of the first edition. However, although the completion rate decreased, the satisfaction rate increased from 91% to 97.5%.

With regards to these figures and then to the analysis that we have led, it is evident that the motivation of participants plays on the MOOC completion rate. We have already spoke about our previous editions, and we think that the motivational aspect introduced by our serious games plays an important role in the high completion rates that we obtained. The engagement that the learners are ready to put in terms of hours of work is also a good indicator of motivation and this correlates with the success rate. The socio-professional origin does not have any effect on the results.

However, once we want to see if the tutorial system has an effect on success rates, the results are more mitigated. Week 0, which is the pillar of the tutorial activities is for example favored as it was motivating to more than 80% of responders. If we compare this 80% to those who succeeded and those who did not succeed, the difference between the two groups is 680 learners (7%). Concerning the coaching support on the forum, we haven't made reference to this in this paper because we haven't assessed the tutoring on the forums. Finally, concerning the "group personalized" approach, we find once again a slim difference in success between those who found individual support motivating and the others (+2% of success).

It is therefore difficult to deeper state on the effects of tutoring on motivation and rates of completion. Nevertheless we note an improvement in completion rates for SM2 which is very rare in view of the already high rates and the "reissue" aspect of the MOOC which often leads a public of "curious" not necessarily interested in taking the whole MOOC.

Concerning the decreasing completion rate of OG2 it was probably due to two main reasons:

- the first one is the more important participation of young professionals who seem to be less interested in being certified than students;
- also the conditions of certification were a little bit harder as it was not allowed to replay the final certification mini-game as it was for the quiz in 2015.

Thus, even if it is certain that the motivational impact of tutoring is less than the impact of the serious game, tutoring took part in the improvement of the completion and satisfaction rates of the two MOOC re-editions.

On the basis of what we learnt via these series of MOOC experiences we capitalized on some approaches to at least be able to improve the acquisition of knowledge by participant. This is fully profitable and applicable to our educational programs at IFP School but also for specific training to a limited group of students such as in the context of a SPOC (Small Private Online Course).

Acknowledgements. The authors thank Total S.A. for supporting the Oil & Gas MOOC second session and especially the Total education team for its contribution and fruitful support. They are also grateful to Myriam Bouchibi (IFP School), R. Crépon (aPi-learning), J. Rodet, C. Klein and L. Sidersky (Unow).

References

1. Thirouard, M., Bernaert, O., Dhorne, L., Bianchi, S., Pidol, L., Crepon, R., Petit, Y.: Learning by doing: integrating a serious game in a MOOC to promote new skills. In: eMOOC 2015 Conference, Mons (2015)
2. Thirouard, M., Bernaert, O., Dhorne, L.: How can motivation and completion rates be improved in a MOOC? Data analysis (2016)
3. Parr, C.: MOOC Completion Rates 'Below 7%' (2013). http://www.timeshighereducation.co.uk/news/mooc-completion-rates-below-7/2003710.article. Accessed 10 Jan 17
4. Rodet, J.: L'ingénierie tutorale. CreateSpace Independent Publishing Platform, p. 186 (2016)
5. Onah, D., Sinclair, J., Boyatt, R.: Dropout rates of massive open online courses: behavioural patterns (2014)

Towards E-presence at Distance as a Way to Reach and Share E-quality: The Case of the ECO sMOOCs

Divina Frau-Meigs[1] and Adeline Bossu[2(✉)]

[1] CREW, University Sorbonne Nouvelle, USPC, Paris, France
divina.meigs@orange.fr
[2] MICA, University Bordeaux Montaigne, Bordeaux, France
adbossu@hotmail.com

Abstract. This paper presents an original approach to e-presence in social participatory MOOCs (or sMOOCs), taking the case of EU-funded ECO project on sMOOCs. First it considers the model for e-presence based on the different layers proposed by Garrison and Anderson (2003): "cognitive presence" (emphasis on the reflexive) and "social presence" (emphasis on the collaborative) to which "designed presence" is added (emphasis on the platform constraints and opportunities) (Frau-Meigs 2013).

Using examples from a corpus of sMOOCs produced for ECO, the paper then proposes an ECO model for e-presence. It incorporates the various tools developed for the participants by the creative team of managers/trainers in this model, according to how they foster one of the types of e-presence (cognitive, social and designed). The results show that these tools tend to be more cognitive and designed than social, probably because social presence can be carried on with online commercial platforms for chatting and blogging.

The conclusions point to the use of e-presence to diminish distance and to bring awareness to pedagogical and technical design and functionalities. Such tools for e-presence produce a multiplier effect that can use the benefits of heavy prototype investment at the beginning by ensuring some sustainability over time and e-quality. Such e-presence is part of the ECO model that contributes to the specificity and originality of European MOOCs in the global MOOCosphere. This process indicates that e-quality itself is being redesigned by sMOOCs, in a qualitative manner.

Keywords: sMOOC · Quality · E-presence · Cognitive presence · Social presence · Designed presence · Model · Distance · ECO project · Sustainability · E-quality · Participants

1 Introduction

The EU-funded ECO project purports to design MOOCs that respond to the acquisition of digital competences for inclusion (www.ecolearning.eu). The project deployed in two main phases: the first phase developed 17 pilot MOOCs with diversified teams; the second phase enabled learners to become e-teachers themselves, on the basis of their

C. Delgado Kloos et al. (Eds.): EMOOCs 2017, LNCS 10254, pp. 38–47, 2017.
DOI: 10.1007/978-3-319-59044-8_5

participation in the pilot MOOCs, especially the sMOOC to learn how to make sMOOCs, the "Step by Step". Accordingly, ECO presents an original pedagogical design for social MOOCs (or sMOOCs), that recombines social-constructive approaches and connectivist approaches, with a strong reliance on tutors and mediators emanating from a strong community of inquiry (Siemens 2008; Siemens and Downes 2009; McAdam and McCreedy 2000). ECO sMOOCs are technically developed in accordance to a pedagogical design; they help participants to built their learning pathways; they provide learning analytics and all kinds of feedback (Frau-Meigs and Bossu 2016).

ECO sMOOCS also bring the online participants to a certain level of group dynamics as the de facto e-learning situation of isolation is compensated by felt presence in the e-community. They provide many affordances for establishing online presence or "e-presence". Far from discourses on digital identity, e-presence brings the learners' attention on issues of focus (interventional and accidental), reflexivity and self-knowledge rather than e-reputation and self-branding (Osuna et al. 2016). But the issue is not often looked into with MOOCs even though the discussion about the best strategy for e-learning becomes more and more centered on the learner experience. This implies the necessity to postulate that the presence of the learner has to be determined during the early design of the project (Conole 2013). ECO sMOOCs seem like a good test because of their iterative process and their agile methodology (three iterations of the pilots were deployed).

Another implication of this postulate is that e-presence needs to be related to e-quality as a multifaceted "process of co-production between the learner and the learning-environment" (Ehlers 2004: 2). E-presence needs to be taken more into account in the design of MOOCS and also in their quality assurance as it is an empowering process that enables the learner. Besides its potential contribution to (self) learning, e-presence embraces the learner's perspective while not ignoring the technological design embedded in the learning platform. If e-quality is posited at the end of the learning service, e-presence needs to be ensured all through, to ascertain that quality is not just an outcome of the e-learning platform.

2 Modelling E-presence

This kind of e-presence is a complex process in itself. Garrison and Anderson posit three different composite layers: cognitive presence defined as "the extent to which learners are able to construct and confirm meaning through sustained reflection and discourse in a critical community of inquiry"; social presence defined as "the ability of participants in a community of inquiry to project themselves socially and emotionally, as 'real' people (i.e. their full personality), through the medium of communication being used"; and "teaching" presence because they want to bring the focus on the role of the pedagogue in long-distance learning (Garrison and Anderson 2003: 28–30).

Cognitive presence is about all the mental processes that associate facts and events to ideas and concepts. It implies to make the transition from concepts to action explicit, and to communicate it via various outcomes, outputs and deliverables. It is thus associated to critical thinking, as a high-order reflection process that incorporates discourse, imagination, intuition and action. It is built on two knowledge bases: the public information that is available online and offline and the learner's private world of experience and needs. These knowledge bases allow for a cognitive scaffolding of the tasks that the teacher and learner have to conduct together, around learning strategies and pathways.

Social presence lays the emphasis on the collaborative whereas cognitive presence lays the emphasis on the reflexive. It is not at the same level as cognitive presence but it is necessary to turn online distance into proximity and engagement. Social presence is about affective socio-emotional feelings, open communication and cohesive communicative responses. It has to do with creating interactions in non-verbal environments as much as visual environments.

To Garrison and Anderson's third type of presence, "teaching" presence, Frau-Meigs prefers "designed" presence, because with e-learning in general and MOOCs in particular, the platform and its functionalities interact very much with the pedagogy. "Designed" presence is defined as "the extent to which learners are aware of the constraints and the affordances made available to them by the platform being used" (2013: 25–27). This implies full recognition that many of the tools that are available for learning are designed by others with their own finalities that in turn can affect their performance. The learners have to mobilize their own cognitive scripts and call on their experiences to adapt and control their own online performance and interaction with others. They have to call upon their representations of the authorities that control the performance of the digital tools and be able to tailor them to their own needs.

3 Methodology

E-presence in ECO sMOOCs can be described based on observational and empirical results. From the three layers of e-presence model, it ensues that one can observe e-presence (1) if there are pathways that foster reflexivity (2) if there are interactions and expressions of proximity; (3) if there is awareness of constraints and attendant solutions proposed. Two objectives guide the analysis: First, the research is concerned with the question (1) which layers of e-presence are most susceptible to appear in ECO sMOOCs; Secondly, which tools are more likely to emerge to palliate any technical or pedagogical constraints while ensuring e-quality?

The level of embedness of e-presence can be analysed both at the level of the available functionalities of ECO sMOOCs and the level of the Agile methodology used during service deployment (three iterations). The main focus is on the pedagogical teams (including tutors and engineers) and their ability to support the learner's autonomy and the process of co-production between them, the learners and the e-learning-environment.

The pedagogical designers worked in close discussion with the technical developers of the OPENMOOC platform. They have facilitated a number of options to ensure shareability and enhance participation and community-building. Such process has been made explicit especially in relation to platforms whose avowed economic model is data mining (via profiles, portfolios…): OPENMOOC whose model is open and participatory does not trace users and offers internal tools for communication (tchats, forums, micro-blogging) (Osuna et al. 2016).

Hence the choice of 3 main sMOOCs for the sample among a corpus of 17 pilot MOOCs and of more than 200 e-teacher sMOOCs: the DIY MIL, the PhDOOC and the Step by Step. The last one acted as a "meta-MOOC" for all the others as it was made by all the teams, cross-country (6 countries, 10 hubs). The first two ones embraced the specific innovative design approach of participatory sMOOCs and developed added features. The DIY MIL is a pilot sMOOC while the PhDOOC is an e-teacher sMOOC. They were carefully monitored by the authors, who were in charge of their service deployment and evolution.

The analysis used qualitative data on the basis of e-presence (reflexivity, proximity and design). They are mostly focused upon here as they provide in-depth insights on subjective quality choices. A quantitative questionnaire is available for each ECO sMOOC that elicits similar questions but was deemed less important here, as the focus is mostly on how the various teams applied and modified aspects of the pedagogical or technological interface design, to ensure e-presence.

4 E-presence in ECO sMOOCs

In ECO, the levels of embededness of the three layers of e-presence are all fully visible. Cognitive presence is facilitated in the different postures the learner can opt for. The sMOOC "DIY Media Information Literacy" proposes several pathways: "explorer", "analyst" and "creator", buttressed on a roadmap and a cognitive scaffolding (see Fig. 1).

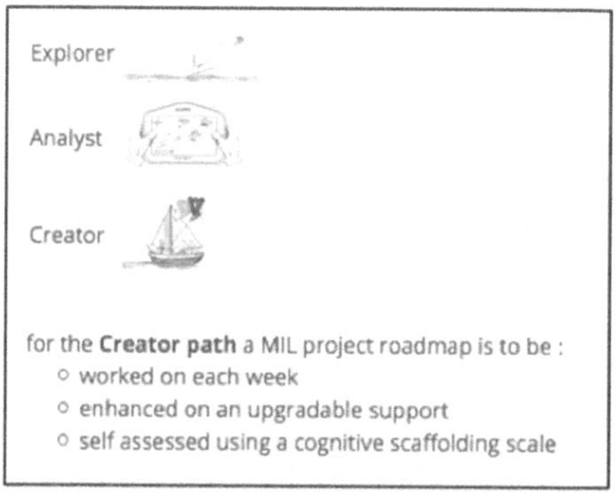

Fig. 1. The sMOOC DIY MIL critical pathways

In ECO, social presence is evinced by the extensive use of videos in sMOOCs and the links that point to other participants as a kind of social network of affinities that also present the benefit of fostering intercultural dialogue as visible in the sMOOC "Step by Step". The "groups" functionality also allows to work and solve cases by getting people to collaborate on projects (see Fig. 2). Live events help sustain a shared social presence as well as the possibility for the participants to "follow" each other and to geolocalize if they wish to meet face to face as seen with the "PhDOOC" (see Fig. 3).

Fig. 2. The group wall functionality with microblogging tool from the Step by Step sMOOC

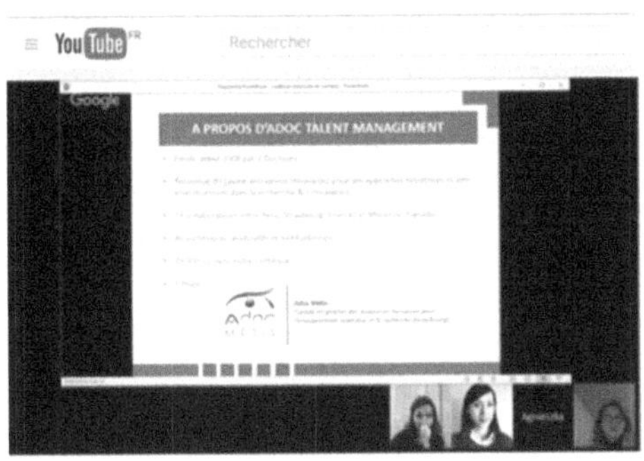

Fig. 3. A live-webconference from the sMOOC PhDOOC

Besides, the internal social networks and the external commercial networks allowed participants to express several levels of emotions according to their felt level of privacy and public openness (Haythornthwaite 2002; Frau-Meigs and Bossu 2016) (See Fig. 4).

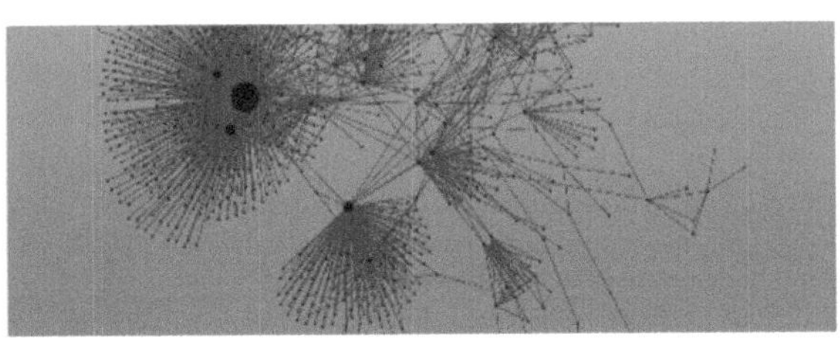

Fig. 4. Social network graph indicating connection between learners

Designed presence is very apparent in the sMOOC "PhDOOC", where the peer-to-peer evaluation was not about sanctioning and criticizing per se but about interaction and exchanges so that others were motivated to do it as well (see Fig. 5). In this video two participants show their work and how they have elaborated it with advices for other. In this live-event, there was an intense feedback experience from participants, some of whom evoked the fact that they needed to see other proposals and artefacts to be able to start their own work.

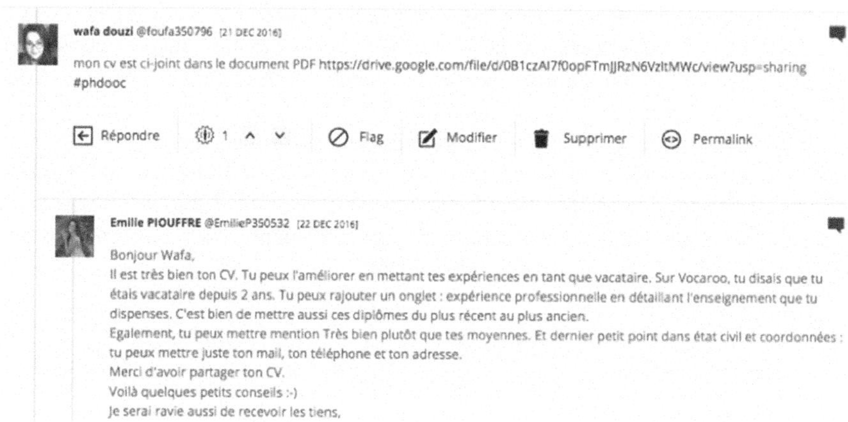

Fig. 5. The PhDOOC forum where one participant is giving feedback and advice about the work produced by another participant

This process of reflexivity on e-presence was first implemented and tested by the creators of the platform and its content according to the participatory sMOOC model. When applied to e-teachers, the early teams endeavoured to provide a similar experience, all the more so as the e-teachers were participants and had an early experience of learning via sMOOCs scheme. E-teachers as well as their trainers were exposed to similar questions and processes, the only difference being the scale and the level of reflexivity (Hodgson and Reynolds 2005; Wright 2005). The same person then gets to change status according to the phases of ECO in which she/he evolves. This increases reflexivity, proximity, awareness of representations of authority and knowledge, attention to others' diversity.

5 The Contribution of E-presence to E-quality

In ECO, the Agile iterative method produced a great variety of tools to facilitate e-presence over time, in a process that was not fully anticipated at departure. Nine were listed, some of which developed from their early stages (checklist, Learning Analytics, Satisfaction Questionnaire, Step by Step, self/peer-evaluation), while others emerged (guide, Learning Lab, FAQ, Back office application). They show a specific model of e-presence as developed by ECO (see Table 1):

Table 1. ECO model of e-presence

Presence	Tools								
	Guide	Check-list	sMOOC learning lab	Learning analytics	Satisfaction questionnaire	sMOOC step by step	Self/peer evaluation	FAQ	Backoffice application
Cognitive	X	X	X	X	X	X	X	X	X
Social			X			X	X		X
Designed	X	X	X	X		X	X	X	X

It is interesting to notice the emphasis on designed presence as the ECO project is about creating sMOOCs for e-teachers and bringing awareness to pedagogical and technical design and functionalities. This goes together with cognitive presence. Social presence is less emphasized in these tools because other functionalities already existed a part and parcel of the OPENMOOC platform (chats, forums, ….).

The tools most conducive to cognitive presence are the ECO guide, the Learning Analytics applications and the checklist forms (see Figs. 6, 7 and 8). They favour construction of knowledge, construction of course content. They confirm sustained reflexivity throughout the iteration of the sMOOC.

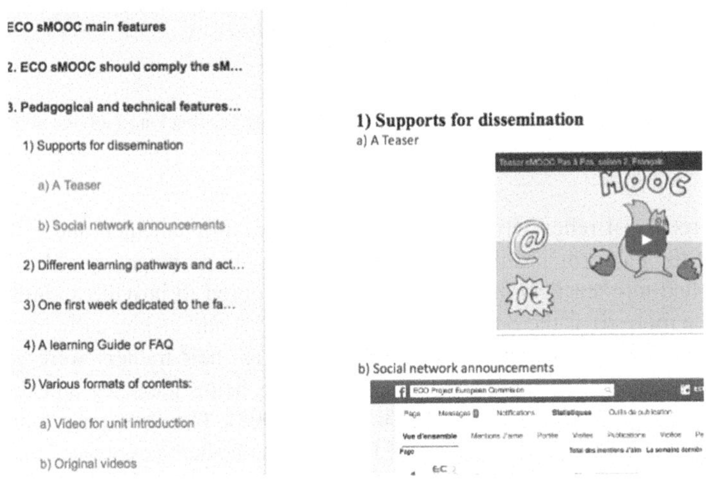

Fig. 6. Screenshot of the ECO guide

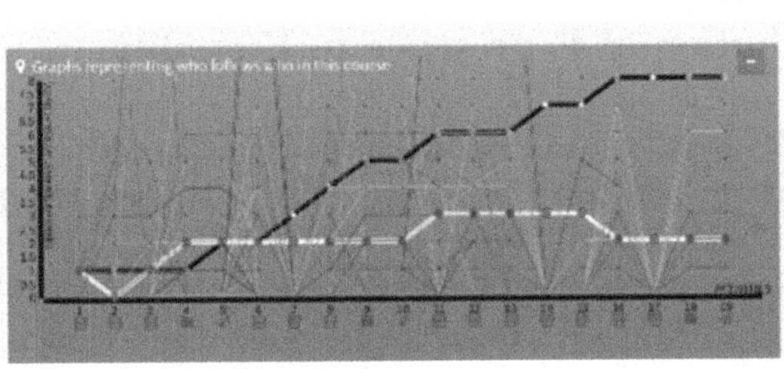

Fig. 7. Screenshot of the ECO learning analytics applications

The tools most conducive to social presence are the sMOOC Learning Lab and the sMOOC "Step by Step" itself, acting as a meta-MOOC (see Figs. 9 and 10).

They help the e-teachers and participants to project themselves socially and emotionally, with their full personality, not just their professional status. They used the "Step by Step" for instance as a means of communicating their experiences, their best practices, their doubts, their challenges.

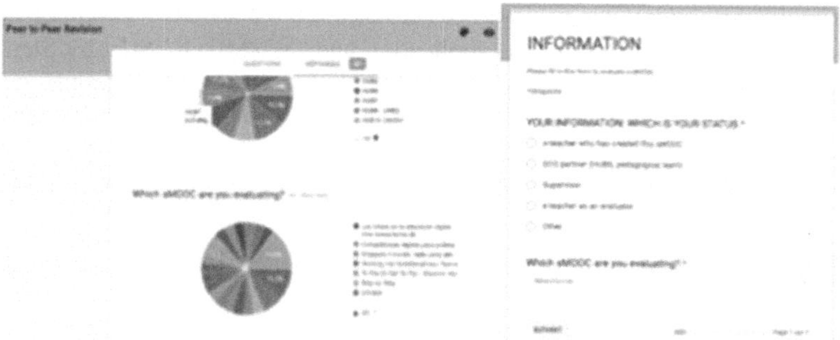

Fig. 8. Screenshots of the checklist form and one of the graph results

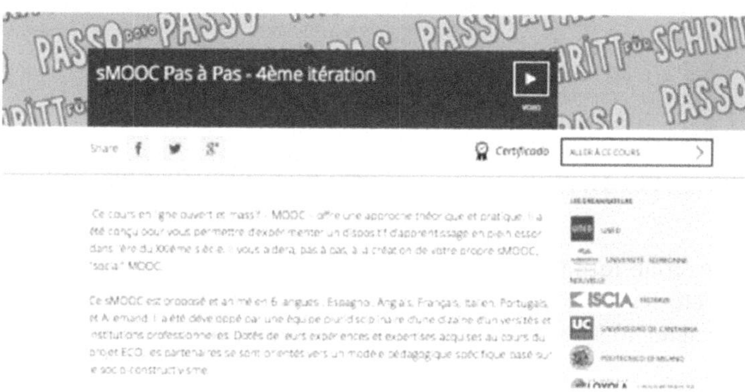

Fig. 9. Screenshot of the sMOOC "Step by Step"

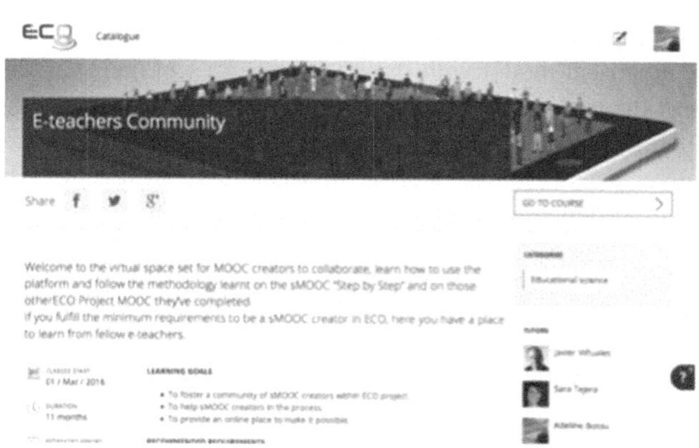

Fig. 10. Screenshot of the sMOOC Learning Lab

The tools most conducive to designed presence are the sMOOC Learning Lab, the checklist form, the ECO back-office application and the sMOOC Step by Step. They help the e-teachers and participants to mobilize their own cognitive scripts and their reflexivity of their needs and functionalities available (see Fig. 11).

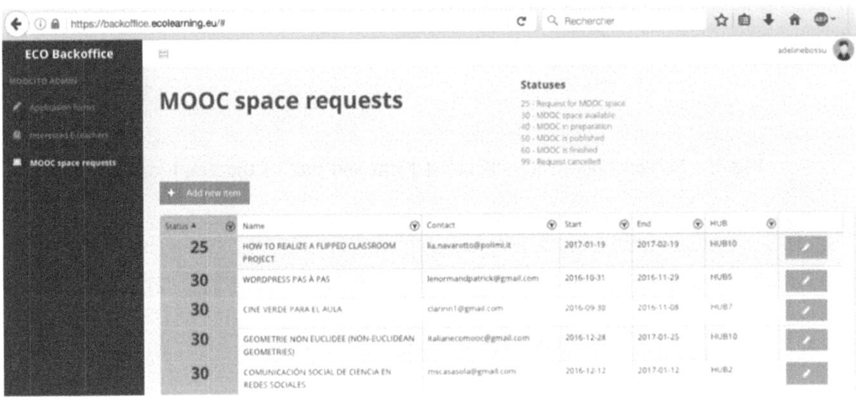

Fig. 11. Screenshots of the ECO Backoffice application

There is overlap for most of the tools. For instance the checklist favors cognitive presence but creates a lot of discussion and is also confronted to self and peer evaluation. They tend to strengthen the various dimensions of e-presence in an agile manner.

Since there is a need to create automatisms for robustness and scalability, there are constraints and limitations and as a result the social presence is less effective here than in the social networks. But it allows for scalability and all participants can benefit from it and gain autonomy and capacity.

In relation to e-quality, two results have contributed to a better understanding of e-presence: the empirical model with the three presences in their various dimensions; the description of the tools that were most conducive to it, due to the agile method and the constant attention to the learner's perspective. These tools show the participants' capacity to counter-balance the weight of the technology in favour of human preferences and thus re-introduce pedagogy in the heart of design.

6 Conclusion

All these tools help the e-teachers in the creation of their own e-presence. This process in turn benefits the other participants, which will be able to create sMOOCs and establish their e-presence as well. This snowball strategy produces a multiplier effect that can use the benefits of heavy prototype investment at the beginning by ensuring some sustainability over time.

Such a process is part of the ECO model whose reflexivity contributes to the specificity and originality of European MOOCs in the global MOOCosphere. After all these levels of presence, reflexivity and transferability, participatory pedagogy in sMOOCs helps presence at a distance, and makes it part of e-quality. As a result, e-quality is being redesigned by MOOCs. There is a qualitative shift: e-quality itself changes when the three types of presence (cognitive, social and designed) are brought together to ensure purpose, reflexivity and sustainability. This points to how the ECO model expands the institutional value of e-presence. This can also affect the future development of e-quality as guidelines are no longer general or applicable to all but can be personalized to serve individual learning paths.

References

Conole, G.: MOOCs as disruptive technologies: strategies for enhancing the learner experience and quality of MOOCs (2013). http://eprints.rclis.org/19388/4/

Ehlers, U.: Quality in e-Learning from a Learner's Perspective. Eur. J. Open Distance E-learn. (2004). http://www.eurodl.org/?p=archives&sp=full&article=101

Frau-Meigs, D.: Transliteracy: sense-making mechanisms for establishing e-presence. In: Carlsson, U. (ed.) Clearinghouse Issue on "Media and Information Literacy and Intercultural Dialogue". UNESCO, Goteborg (2013)

Frau-Meigs, D., Bossu, A.: The ECO Project for E-Teaching: Social MOOCs at the Crossroads of Actors Cognitive Logics and Strategies. Graz, Eden (2016)

Frau-Meigs, D., Bossu, A.: Le projet européen ECO: les MOOC participatifs au croisement des logiques d'acteurs publics/privés dans la formation ouverte des enseignants, TICEMED (2016). http://www.ticemed.eu/ticemed10-marseille-2016/

Garrison, D.R., Anderson, T.: E-Learning in the 21st Century. A Framework for Research and Practice. Routledge, London (2003)

Haythornthwaite, C.: Building social networks via computer networks. In: Renninger, K., Shumar, W. (eds.) Building Virtual Communities: Learning and Change in Cyberspace. Cambridge University Press, Cambridge (2002)

Hodgson, V., Reynolds, M.: Consensus, difference and multiple communities in networked learning. Stud. High. Educ. **30**(1), 11–24 (2005)

McAdam, R., McCreedy, S.: A critique of knowledge management: using a social constructionist model. New Technol. Work Employ. **15**(2), 155–168 (2000)

Osuna, S., Frau-Meigs, D., Bossu, A., Jansen, D.: Intercreativity and interculturality in ECO project's virtual learning environments. In: Jemni, M., Kinshuk, Khribi, M.K. (eds.) Open Education: from OERs to MOOCs. Lecture Notes in Educational Technology Series, pp. 161–187. Springer, Heidelberg (2016)

Siemens, G.: New structures and spaces of learning: the systemic impact of connective knowledge, connectivism, and networked learning. In: Communication Presented at Web 2.0 Conference, University of Minho, Braga (2008)

Siemens, G., Downes, S.: Connectivism and connective knowledge (2009). Accessed 28 Jan 2009

Wright, K.: Personal knowledge management: supporting individual knowledge worker performance. Knowl. Manag. Res. Pract. **3**(3), 156–165 (2005)

Additional Functionalities to Convert an xMOOC into an xLMOOC

Ana Gimeno-Sanz(✉), Cristina Navarro-Laboulais, and Ignacio Despujol-Zabala

Universitat Politècnica de València, 46022 Valencia, Spain
{agimeno, cnavarro}@upvnet.upv.es,
ndespujol@asic.upv.es

Abstract. This paper deals with the *Learn Spanish: Basic Spanish for English Speakers MOOC* designed at Universitat Politècnica de València, Spain, for the edX platform. It focuses on the tools that had to be implemented in order to convert a generic xMOOC platform into an LMOOC (or Language MOOC) to reinforce the learners' productive skills. Upon creating a foreign language learning course for a platform that has not been specifically designed for this aim, a number of shortcomings became apparent which had to be overcome, the main one being the need to encourage and facilitate oral interaction among enrolled students, a challenge which is still in an experimental stage. Firstly, to contextualize the difficulties encountered due to large registration numbers, basic information concerning course registration on this LMOOC will be presented. Secondly, the authors discuss the tools that were implemented in the MOOC specifically designed for foreign language learning.

Keywords: Language learning MOOC design · Speaking activities · MOOC add-ons

1 Introduction

McAuley et al. [13] define a MOOC as "an online course with the option of free and open registration, a publicly shared curriculum, and open-ended outcomes". Since the term was coined by David Cormier and Bryan Alexander in 2008 to designate a connectivist course offered by the University of Manitoba [15], an increasing number of universities around the globe have launched online courseware under this umbrella term.

In the fall of 2011, Stanford University experimentally launched the first MOOCs with huge enrolment numbers but they were different to the initial ones because they resembled a more traditional educational environment, later known as xMOOCs or content-based MOOCs [2]. They launched three courses, and to their surprise, over 100,000 students registered on each one.

Four years later, in 2015, there were over 4,200 MOOCs, produced by more than 500 universities worldwide with over 35 million students registered, doubling the figures of the year 2014 [14]. The vast majority of these MOOCs fit into one of the following categories: network-based, task-based or content-based [12].

C. Delgado Kloos et al. (Eds.): EMOOCs 2017, LNCS 10254, pp. 48–57, 2017.
DOI: 10.1007/978-3-319-59044-8_6

According to current data, average MOOC registration is between 35,000 and 43,000 students, although these numbers are constantly declining due to the increasing number of courses and platforms on offer. The average success rate is said to be between 6.5% and 7.5% and there is a proven negative relationship between course duration and dropout rates [6, 9]. Current literature highlights large registration numbers per course but very low percentages of course completion rates. However, given the practically non-existent registration barriers and the vast diversity of reasons for registering, it is commonly agreed that completion rates do not *per se* reflect the success of a MOOC and that there is therefore a need to establish more sophisticated gauging systems [5, 8].

In addition to registration numbers and success rates, literature also focuses on learner profile. For example, an edX MOOC student is typically a qualified professional 26 to 50-year-old graduate male, although there are, however, large differences in terms of the average demographics in each course [5]. For example, most students on Coursera have been awarded a university degree: 42.8% hold a graduate degree, 36.7% a master's degree and 5.4% a doctoral degree [7]. For example, the profile of the learners registered on the six Coursera courses offered by the University of Toronto was as follows: 80% held a higher education degree, there was a slightly higher percentage of male participants (52%) and most students ranged between 26 and 45 years of age [4].

2 UPV MOOCs

As from 2013, Universitat Politècnica de València (UPV) has used four different MOOC platforms, i.e. Google Course Builder, MiriadaX, a customised version of OpenedX called upvx.es and edX.org, of which it is still using the last two. Forty-two courses have been designed (with registration ranging from 80 to 128,000 participants), having run 220 individual editions with over 637,000 registrations and an average success rate of 9.6%.

2.1 Course Description

As its title suggests, the *Learn Spanish: Basic Spanish for English Speakers*[1] was designed for complete beginners of Spanish capable of learning the language through the medium of English. That is, all of the exercise instructions and theoretical explanations are presented in English. The course was launched as a self-paced MOOC in September 2015, with its content distributed into 16 weeks, and was closed to newcomers on 31st December 2016. Learners could therefore register at any point in time without the need of sticking to a strict academic calendar. In self-paced courses, instructor supervision is limited although there is constant teacher assistant support, mainly delivered by UPV students who have been hired specifically for that task.

[1] For further information, go to https://www.edx.org/course/learn-spanish-basic-spanish-english-upvalenciax-bsp101x.

The MOOC is comprised of 376 activities that are structured into one of four categories: video recordings (for explanations of theory and examples of use of language); written theoretical explanations; situational dialogues in audio-only format, and a variety of exercise typologies, which include gap-filling, reordering, true/false, association, and so forth. The course also integrates two tests, one delivered at mid-term and the other at the end of the course. Passing both of these entitles the student to a certificate of achievement awarded under a code of honour. All 16 learning units are preceded with learning objectives and outcomes.

2.2 Learner Profile

Throughout its duration, from September 2015 to December 2016, the course attracted 128,459 registered participants, 110,780 of which are still active, and 743 of these paid for a verified certificate. It is by far the course with the largest registration rate of all of those launched by UPV (the next largest attracted 29,543 registrations). There was a steep increase in student registration just before the MOOC was launched, when edX announced it in its weekly Bulletin. The course aroused a fair amount of interest and during its first week, nearly 30,000 students had completed an activity (i.e. 50% of the total registered population at that point, which comprises a higher percentage compared to the average rate for UPV courses, which stands at 30%). However, that initial boost soon declined and the course stabilised at approximately 2,000 students accessing the course on a weekly basis.

Demographic information regarding the Spanish language MOOC is very similar to that reported on other platforms, although there is a slightly higher proportion of female participants than is customary: just over 50%. Predominant ages range from 25 to 30. The percentage of students holding a higher education degree is higher than 67%, which is similar to the average reported on other major platforms.

Students have registered from 211 different countries worldwide, the United States of America providing the largest numbers with a total of 34%, followed by India with 9% and the United Kingdom with 5% in 2nd and 3rd place, respectively. Of the 128,459 students that have enrolled on the course at any one moment, 5,814 (4.5% of the enrolments) completed the mid-term exam, 2,599 (2%) passed the course and 743 (0.6%) paid for a verified certificate. This 2% rate of students who passed the course is lower than the average compared to other UPV MOOCs, which stands at 12.1% for courses that offered a free certificate. This is probably due to several factors such as course length and because learning a new language is an intellectually demanding task that requires a lot of effort and practice.

3 Discussion

As mentioned above, the *Learn Spanish: Basic Spanish for English Speakers* MOOC is a beginners' Spanish language course that uses English as its source language. The content is organised into 16 study weeks, distributed into 15 units plus 2 exams, one during mid-term and a final test. The first half of the course (up to the mid-term test) focuses on vocabulary and basic lexical and grammatical structures geared toward absolute beginners. The second half attempts to satisfy the communicative needs portrayed in common daily activities embedded in social life.

Compared to other UPV MOOCs, a 16-month course is far longer than the average (which is a little under 6 weeks for all UPV MOOCs). Its length, however, is a direct consequence of the wealth of content and large variety of resources offered aiming to support autonomous learning and learner engagement. Additionally, it was upon attempting to design a variety of exercises that it became apparent how (in)appropriate the edX platform was in order to satisfy the needs of a language MOOC or LMOOC.

When designing an LMOOC, materials writers have to ensure that the course satisfies the target group needs and complies with the set learning goals; that it caters for the needs of the different subgroups in terms of providing self-access and autonomous learning support, opportunities for collaboration (i.e. peer interaction), and expected rewards. Additionally, according to Colpaert [1], the system should adapt to personal differences based on an analysis of learner behaviour and performance. Furthermore, because each LMOOC is embedded in its platform (edX, Coursera, MiriadaX…), designers can make use of specific tools to share content, assess learner performance and establish channels of communication among users (via forums, wiki, chat, video management, etc.), all of which are very useful tools but scarcely flexible or adaptable.

Thus, in the first stages of the Spanish language MOOC design, the structure of the course was in line with the general features of our target audience: edX platform users, who are accustomed to a closed content-based course structure with quiz type exercises and explanatory video sequences, as well as being absolute beginners of Spanish. This led us to prepare, in addition to the activities, a wide range of didactic videos with captions in Spanish and English, which we shall refer to in the following section.

A second stage followed, after publishing and running the MOOC for a few weeks, where it became apparent that it was necessary to continue developments and provide functionalities to cater for different learning styles and personal preferences. The comments posted on the Forum by the users where of great help and aided us in developing further add-ons to comply with the specific requirements of an LMOOC, which the edX platform did not initially cater for. These tools include dictionary, glossary, compilation of external resources, voice recording, *Google Hangouts* with the course instructors and, lastly – for the time being – implementing the *Talkabout* tool.

3.1 Videos (with Captions and Translations into English)

Most xMOOCs typically rely on short video lectures for instruction [16]. Clearly, however, hardly anybody would be able to learn a foreign language by simply listening to another person's explanations but videos are certainly an extremely valuable asset in any LMOOC as they aid in keeping learners engaged [3]. Given the length of the Spanish language MOOC, several types of videos were recorded: those illustrating use of language in conversational contexts, grammar explanations, and basic comments describing the different varieties of Spanish spoken in the world.

To automatically generate the captions in Spanish and their translation into English, we used the *Translectures*[2] tool, which saved us from having to manually carry out these very time-consuming tasks. After the automatic generation, we used the same tool to correct the texts to obtain an error-free version of the captions. Because edX provides a video interface allowing users to read the captions whilst watching a video (text and audio are synchronised and the fragment being spoken is highlighted in bold typeface), students admitted that being able to do this and being able to select one of the two languages, depending on their mastery level, was of great help. Thus, this leads us to believe that this is one of the desirable features for a video to have in an LMOOC.

3.2 Reducing Playback Rate in Audio Files

Just as it was necessary to systematise textual support in the videos, it soon became obvious too – thanks to the comments on the Forum where there were a number of "complaints" regarding the speed of the audio recordings – that it was necessary to integrate a function to reduce the speed of the utterances. It was at this point that we developed the tool to reduce playback rate at intervals of 0.1 using Javascript.

3.3 Glossaries (Linked to *Multidict.net*)

Although the lexical items included in the course are introduced gradually and in context, learners are encouraged to become autonomous and are advised to look-up unknown words in an external dictionary. This has proven to be very useful for independent learners who have prior experience in learning a foreign language but not so much for those who are solely dependent on course resources and feel less confident about their personal learning capabilities. When these insecurities became apparent through posts on the Forum, we decided to offer lists of vocabulary organised into the same weekly structure as the units themselves under a menu item called *Glossary*. The tool used for this was *Multidict,*[3] created as one of the products of the *Tools for CLIL Teachers*[4] European-funded project, in which two of the course instructors participated. *Multidict* functions as a stand-alone online dictionary interface with over 100 languages catered for linked to multiple (monolingual and bilingual) free high quality online dictionaries. Due to the potential offered by this tool, which allows the user to look-up a word without leaving the text being read, we decided to make the most of it and integrate it into the MOOC.

---

[2] *Translectures* is a tool allowing us to generate, edit and download automatic video captions and translations, developed by the Machine Learning and Language Processing Research Group at UPV. For further information, go to https://www.translectures.eu and http://www.mllp.upv.es.

[3] The tool is available from http://multidict.net.

[4] For more information about the project, please visit http://www.languages.dk/tools.

3.4 External Resources

The huge number of participants generated a lot of enthusiasm on their behalf, which immediately materialised into setting up a *Facebook* group managed by the students themselves, without the intervention of the course administrators or instructors. This became the place, along with the MOOC Forum, where registered users shared resources, their learning experiences and gave fellow students their advice and recommendations. Some of the course weeks generated so much traffic that the same recommendations were given once and over again, some with outstanding pedagogic value and others lacking clear criteria because the learners themselves were overwhelmed with the amount of information at their disposal. It was then that we decided to intervene and scrutinise all of the resources mentioned by the participants themselves and, together with those in our own database, set about creating a comprehensive list called *External Resources,* which includes a very useful selection of additional resources organised by language skill, with a brief descriptive comment. The variety of resources included was kept to a reasonable limit on purpose so as not to overwhelm the learners who were less accustomed to working in self-access learning scenarios, but sufficient to satisfy the needs of those who were used to autonomous learning. Among them are webpages with cultural or didactic videos, fiction series, grammar pages, songs, collaborative sites, news sites in Spanish, applications and other methods to learn Spanish.

3.5 Voice Recording Tool (LanguageLab)

Judging by the comments posted on the Forum, approximately half of the registered learners had at some point studied Spanish before, meaning that Spanish phonetics were not entirely unknown to them but for the other half, this was their first encounter with the language and, on top of that, it took place in a self-paced autonomous context, with no direct constant guidance from an instructor. In this respect, there was clear evidence that a number of students admitted in the Forum that their self-confidence was obscured by this and by the fact that it was the very first time they had attempted to speak Spanish. In order for these students to start getting used to uttering new sounds, and short of authentic interaction, we developed and embedded a voice recording utility in all of the exercises containing audio, using javascript. Students may thus compare their utterances to the models provided by native speakers.

The Forum does not include comments regarding the presence of the voice recorder, presumably because it is only natural that such a tool should be present in a language course. However, considering the amount of technical "problems" reported, it seems that the tool is used abundantly and is a welcome add-on to practise pronunciation.

3.6 *Duolingo*

In order to integrate further practice into the MOOC, and given the gamification features of some of the most popular language learning apps, the *Duolingo*[5] free

[5] For more information, go to https://en.duolingo.com.

platform was also included as an add-on. *Duolingo* provides written lessons and dictation, with speaking practice for more advanced users. It has a gamified skill tree that users can progress through and a vocabulary section where learned words can be practiced. Users gain "experience points" when they complete a lesson.

The system also includes a timed practice feature, where users are given 30 s and twenty questions and awarded a skill point and seven or ten additional seconds (time depends on the length of the question) for each correct answer. Each skill (containing between 1 and 10 lessons) has a "strength bar" that corresponds to the computer's estimate of how strongly certain words or constructions still exist in the user's memory. After a certain duration of time, strength bars fade, indicating a need for a user to refresh that lesson, or to "strengthen weak skills". *Duolingo* uses a data-driven approach to lesson planning. At each step along the way, the system measures which questions the users struggle with and what sorts of mistakes they make.

In integrating this additional tool, our belief is that learners will benefit from combining different methods that no doubt supplement and reinforce the learning process.

3.7 *Google Hangouts* with Course Instructors

MOOCs relating to disciplines such as Law, Maths or Psychology, all commonly make use of social tools (forums, wikis, video-conferencing, etc.), through which participants may interact and exchange knowledge in the course's source language, be it English, Spanish or any other. In these cases, language is obviously instrumental and the fact that learners communicate in one or another language is not important. Conversely, however, in a beginners' level language MOOC, communication barriers can become a very serious obstacle that has to be tackled with a fair amount of imagination and skill if we want our students to interact in the target language in order to gain communication skills.

An LMOOC is an eclectic mix of practices and tools aiming to engage students in the use of the target language in meaningful and authentic ways [16]. The motivation underlying any learner's wish to learn a foreign language is precisely to be able to communicate in that language in interesting authentic contexts. Being aware, as we are, that the Spanish LMOOC lacks real communication possibilities for the learners where they can produce authentic language exchanges, we decided to organise programmed *Google Hangouts.*[6] The aim was two-fold, i.e. to get to know our students and for them to get to know us, as well as providing opportunities for them to put into practice some of the content included in the MOOC.

The first session took place with nine synchronous participants who had previously been given participation instructions: they should prepare a brief personal presentation and were aware that we would ask then a surprise question to challenge their interaction capabilities. In that first session, we had participants from Greece, Egypt, The United States of America, Kosovo, The United Kingdom, The Netherlands, Australia… from

[6] For more information, go to https://hangouts.google.com.

all latitudes, eager to speak with us, as well as a number of observers who only communicated with us and among each other through the integrated chat facility. The instructors acted as session moderators, inviting and seeing off participants, and managing turn-taking. The experience, although small in numbers, was very successful and allowed us to gain valuable insights into the learners' impressions.

This first video-conferencing session was very interesting because we were able to perceive the participants' satisfaction both during the session and afterwards in the Forum. *Google Hangouts* also allows you to record and store the live sessions so this enabled other course participants to watch the recording asynchronously at a later date. Favourable comments were also posted on the Forum. We witnessed how important it was for them to have been given the opportunity to participate in an authentic communication context and how this made an impact on their engagement and motivation. After that, video-conferencing sessions were programmed on a regular basis throughout the course.

The fact, however, that students were not able to interact autonomously among themselves and were obliged to address the moderators led us to experiment with another system, described in the following section.

3.8 *Talkabout* Discussion Planner

Talkabout[7] organises discussion sessions for MOOCs, which are later conducted through a *Google Hangouts* video conference. Its main aim is to allow course instructors to set-up synchronous online discussions. In our case, it served the purpose of organising speaking practice encounters so that students could interact live among themselves and practise the language together. Participants choose from a selection of possible schedules, and connect with each other on the set date and time to talk and complete the activities collaboratively in small groups of 3 or 4 [11]. The tool integrates an agenda of suggested topics and exercises to help guide the conversation and complement the work students are doing within the MOOC. It is a way of boosting the learning process through engaging activities and discussion prompts prepared by the course instructors.

On occasions, despite the materials writers' attempts to create attractive and engaging learner-centred activities, the truth remains that participation in synchronous activities is scarce and can even be frustrating due to this. High dropout rates and low student commitment is a proven fact affecting MOOC delivery [10] but this should become an incentive to continue researching into the reasons behind this lack of continuity. In our case, the first two *Talkabout* sessions were launched with 22 possible timeslots distributed in four different days. Each timeslot could take up to 5 participants; 19 students finally registered, of which only 3 turned up at the scheduled time. After rescheduling the *Talkabout* sessions, concentrating them and leaving only 4 weekly slots for each of the two activities, we were able to attract 130 people that participated in a session (out of 616 pre-registrations).

---

[7] *Talkabout* was designed by Carnegie Mellon University, University of California - San Diego and Stanford University. More information is available from https://talkabout.stanford.edu/welcome.

A number of studies [10, 11] echo the importance of including social media to keep learners engaged on any MOOC, as well as contributing in motivation toward the subject being studied. The low participation rates in our attempts to engage students in live speaking practice activities – one of the basic needs in language learning, leads us to believe that more effort should be placed on trying to encourage learners to practice their productive skills by participating in social networks.

4 Conclusions

The volume of registered participants in the *Learn Spanish: Basic Spanish for English Speakers,* its self-paced format (meaning that there is no specific start and closing date and that students therefore follow different calendars), as well as its lengthy 16-week duration comprised a number of obstacles that forced the course designers to imagine new learning strategies to support the specificities integral to foreign language learning. These, additionally, had to be appropriate for integration into a content-based MOOC and offer learners additional resources and methods to support foreign language learning, keep their expectations satisfied and try to decrease dropout rates. To this end, 8 add-ons were incorporated to the course, as described in Sect. 3 above, in order to convert an xMOOC into an xLMOOC, that is, a massive open online course capable of satisfying the specific needs of such a complex task as that of learning a new language, where not only is practice in passive skills like reading and listening comprehension necessary, but very specially in productive skills like speaking and writing.

In a second phase, the designers intend to conduct a qualitative study analysing student participation in the Forum in hope of being able to find hints that may lead to the integration new resources and functionalities in order to provide learners with maximum support and, thus, retain their motivation to continue learning the target language and not drop out before completing the course.

References

1. Colpaert, J.: Reflections on present and future: towards an ontological approach to LMOOCs. In: Martín-Monje, E., Bárcena, E. (eds.) Language MOOCs. Providing Learning, Transcending Boundaries, pp. 161–172. De Gruyter Open, Berlin (2015)
2. Daniel, J.: Making sense of MOOCs: musings in a maze of myth, paradox and possibility. J. Interact. Media Educ. **2012**(3), Part 18, 1–20 (2012). http://doi.org/10.5334/2012-18
3. Guo, P.J., Kim, J., Rubin, R.: How video production affects student engagement: an empirical study of MOOC videos. In: Proceedings of the First ACM Conference on Learning@Scale, pp. 41–50 (2014). http://dx.doi.org/10.1145/2556325.2566239
4. Harrison, L.: Open UToronto MOOC initiative: report on first year of activity (2013). http://www.ocw.utoronto.ca/wp-content/uploads/2013/08/Open-Utoronto-MOOC-Report-August-2013.pdf
5. Ho, A.D., Reich, J., Nesterko, S., Seaton, D., Mullaney, T., Waldo, J., Chuang, I.: HarvardX and MITx: the first year of open online courses, Fall 2012–Summer 2013 (HarvardX and MITx Working Paper #1), pp. 1–33 (2014). doi:http://dx.doi.org/10.2139/ssrn.2381263

6. Jordan, K.: Initial trends in enrolment and completion of massive open online courses. Int. Rev. Res. Open Distrib. Learn. **15**(1), 133–160 (2014)
7. Koller, D., Ng, A.: The online revolution: education for everyone. Seminar presentation at the Said Business School, Oxford University, 28 January 2013. http://www.youtube.com/watch?v=mQ-K-sOW4fU&feature=youtu.be
8. Koller, D., Ng, A., Do, C., Chen, Z.: Retention and intention in massive open online courses: in depth. Educ. Rev. **48**(3), 62–63 (2013)
9. Kolowich, S.: The professors who make the MOOCs. The Chronicle of Higher Education, 21 March 2013. http://chronicle.com/article/The-Professors-Behind-the-MOOC/137905/#id=overview
10. Kotturi, Y., Kulkarni, C.E., Bernstein, M.S., Klemmer, S.: Structure and messaging techniques for online peer learning systems that increase stickiness. In: Proceedings of the Second (2015) ACM Conference on Learning @ Scale - L@S 2015, pp. 31–38 (2015)
11. Kulkarni, C., Cambre, J., Kotturi, Y., Bernstein, M.S., Klemmer, S.R.: Talkabout: making distance matter with small groups in massive classes. In: Proceedings of the 18th ACM Conference on Computer Supported Cooperative Work and Social Computing - CSCW 2015, pp. 1116–1128 (2015)
12. Lane, L.: Three kinds of MOOCs, Lisa's (Online) Teaching Blog [Blogpost], 15 August 2012. http://lisahistory.net/wordpress/2012/08/three-kinds-of-moocs/
13. McAuley, A., Stewart, B., Siemens, G., Cormier, D.: The MOOC model for digital practice (2010). http://www.elearnspace.org/Articles/MOOC_Final.pdf
14. Shah, D.: MOOCs in 2015: breaking down the numbers. EdSurge News (2015). https://www.edsurge.com/news/2015-12-28-moocs-in-2015-breaking-down-the-numbers
15. Siemens, G.: What is the theory that underpins our moocs? Elearnspace [Blogpost], 3 June 2012. http://www.elearnspace.org/blog/2012/06/03/what-is-the-theory-that-underpins-our-moocs/
16. Sokolik, M.: What constitutes an effective language MOOC? In: Martín-Monje, E., Bárcena, E. (eds.) Language MOOCs. Providing Learning, Transcending Boundaries. De Gruyter Open, Berlin (2015)

A Principled Approach to the Design of Collaborative MOOC Curricula

Stian Håklev[1(✉)] and James D. Slotta[2]

[1] Ecole Polytechnique Fédérale de Lausanne, 1015 Lausanne, Switzerland
stian.haklev@epfl.ch
[2] Boston College, 140 Commonwealth Ave., Chestnut Hill, MA 02467, USA
slotta@bc.edu

Abstract. MOOCs have the potential to benefit from the large number of very diverse learners that participate in courses, but this requires a principled approach to MOOC curriculum development. Courses need to take into consideration the diversity of learner experience and intentions, and incorporate scripts that both benefit from the large numbers of learners (crowd-sourcing), as well as enabling small-scale intense collaboration. The real challenge is tying together a set of learning activities and the development of a community knowledge base, with the specific curriculum learning goals of the course. This paper offers a pragmatic approach to developing courses, based on the experience of a MOOC for teacher professional development.

Keywords: MOOCs · Scripting · Collaborative learning

1 Introduction

In a few short years, MOOCs have grown from a niche phenomenon, to a large scale movement involving universities, companies and organisations around the world. Thousands or tens of thousands of learners participate in courses, with very different backgrounds, levels of existing knowledge and motivation, and goals for their learning. This large number and distributed nature of participants in MOOCs suggests opportunities for innovative pedagogical designs, however the realities to date typically place the learner in an isolated context, with little direct peer interaction or sense of participation in a collective enterprise.

Researchers have already begun pushing at the boundaries of technology and pedagogy. Some have focused on the peer assessment, such as Dan Hickey, who launched a Big Open Online Course (BOOC), building on his research on peer assessment and WikiFolios for collaborative learning, where students engaged in small groups to promote and reflect upon the works of their peers [5].

Others have experimented with building better peer review systems embedded into traditional MOOC platforms, such as the PeerStudio platform [6]. There have also been attempts at designing stand-alone social platforms that are connected with the traditional MOOC platforms, such as the ProSolo system from the Data, Analytics and Learning MOOC (DALMOOC) [2].

C. Delgado Kloos et al. (Eds.): EMOOCs 2017, LNCS 10254, pp. 58–67, 2017.
DOI: 10.1007/978-3-319-59044-8_7

To strengthen the development of collaborative courses, there is a need for theoretically informed design principles and frameworks that integrate curriculum development, pedagogical scripting, and technological supports. This paper will present a pragmatic model for developing complex collaborative learning scripts that cater to, and benefits from a diverse student population, and responds to curriculum learning goals.

2 A Knowledge Community Approach to MOOC Design

One of the fundamental tenets of Computer Supported Collaborative Learning is the idea that interaction with other learners can improve learning outcomes. Students are forced to externalize their ideas, working with multiple shared representations of knowledge structures, and collaborating to converge on a shared understanding of meaning [3].

In addition, learning theories such as Connectivism [1] and social constructivism [7] emphasise the added value of diverse student viewpoints, experiences and identities to the learning experience. To increase the chance of real life transfer of learning, and applicability of theory to practice, it is necessary for learners to connect what they are learning with their own lives, and those of others. Especially in social science topics, the experiences and ideas from other students can be very valuable contributions to the learning process.

These learning theories become increasingly relevant given the emergence of user-created media, and the radical shift in how we access information and learn about the world. We learn by formulating and expressing our ideas and theories in language, posting on discussion forums and tweets. We gain access to deeply personal perspectives of others through personal blogs. We build on each other's knowledge by negotiating the successive editing of Wikipedia articles. And we harness input from thousands of peers through aggregation mechanisms like voting, folksonomic tagging, and even automated classification.

Knowledge Community and Inquiry (KCI), is a pragmatic framework for curriculum development to foster knowledge communities, which advocates scripting and coordinated grouping to assure comprehensive distribution across a targeted domain, but adds a layer of collective knowledge building, where students engage with Web 2.0 technologies to develop a shared knowledge base that serves as a resource for their subsequent inquiry [9].

Making ideas visible and accessible is at the heart of learning in a KCI design. This requires the use of existing Web 2.0 technologies, sometimes augmented by bespoke technology platforms or supports, as well as a pedagogical designs. Students work individually or in small groups collecting information, brainstorming ideas or solutions, supported by carefully designed prompts and scaffolds. Small group work alternates between cooperative work—divide and conquer—and collaborative—where group members build upon each other's knowledge.

Many KCI designs feature a group project in which students collaborate throughout the term, with new elements or dimensions added as the students gain access to a larger individual and community knowledge base, and become more conceptually sophisticated [10]. Such persistent, revisited projects can function as a means of guiding students' connection of principles throughout the course. Further, given that the projects are indexed to the learning objects of the course, these inquiry projects can support the summative evaluation of student learning.

3 Adapting the KCI Model to MOOCs

A number of design studies have tested the KCI model in primary and secondary classrooms, and university courses. In adapting the model for MOOCs, we faced a number of specific challenges, which will be addressed below. Students are much more diverse in terms of their location, experience, age, level of motivation, and what they want out of the course. The number of learners is much higher, making traditional social activities difficult (a discussion with 2,000 people becomes a cacaphony), and the largely asynchronous nature of MOOCs makes social coordination and a sense of social presence difficult to achieve.

The MOOC featured in this study was designed to support in-service teachers to integrate inquiry and technology into their lessons. It was explicitly marketed to in-service teachers, and was designed to build upon their professional experience and respond to their real challenges, providing tools, examples and approaches that could be directly applied within their professional settings. The course came out of a collaboration between the University of Toronto Schools (UTS), a university-affiliated private secondary school, and the Encore research group at University of Toronto led by Dr. Slotta, enabling us to provide an integration of academic and theoretical ideas, with applied practice.

The course ran on the EdX platform, however we designed several supplementary learning activities, which ran on a server hosted at the University of Toronto, and which were embedded within EdX pages using the Learning Tools Integration (LTI) protocol [8]. Below we will outline a number of the design features of the MOOC.

3.1 Special Interest Groups

Given that the course was catering to a wide variety of teachers, we decided to divide students into Special Interest Groups. Students went through a questionnaire on the external LTI site identifying their teaching level, subject area, and providing folksonomic tags for their specific interests. In order to have the course design be informed by its future learners, we opened a "pre-course lounge", where teachers could register, fill out the questionnaire, and begin submitting useful resources–all several weeks before the actual course began running.

Taking this initial data into consideration, we generated an initial list of Special Interest Groups, designed to group logically similar teaching levels and subject areas. The ability to gauge student demographics and interests before the course began, proved very important when it comes to the Higher Education and Online Learning SIG. Initially, we had targeted the course specifically towards

K-12 teachers, and not planned to include any groups for non-K-12 students, however upon seeing the initial interest, we were able to adjust our plans, and the Higher Ed SIG in fact turned out to be the most popular one.

The SIGs were generated on our external server, however we imported the CSV export into EdX several times per day to generate cohorts based on SIG memberships, for use in the EdX discussion forums. This meant that students maintained a consistent group membership both on the EdX platform, and within external activities (for example, students could only see and comment upon lesson designs within their own SIG, resources were mainly shared within SIG, etc.) This in practice creates a number of "parallel courses", each with a common starting point (the videos and prompts), but allowed to develop according to each community's interest.

3.2 Taking Advantage of the Crowds

Most of the students in the MOOC were in-service teachers, and collectively, they had used and explored hundreds of different digital resources and tools. Some of these resources are specific to their disciplines, such as a simulation of a particular physics phenomenon, whereas others could be used in a wide variety of disciplines in many different ways, such as Google Docs or Socrative. An example of harnessing the collective intelligence of the MOOC participants is the resource brainstorming script, where we asked teachers to share their favorites, with no limit on how many they could contribute.

First, we asked students to enter digital resources that they had personally found useful, or had heard positive things about. They added title, description,

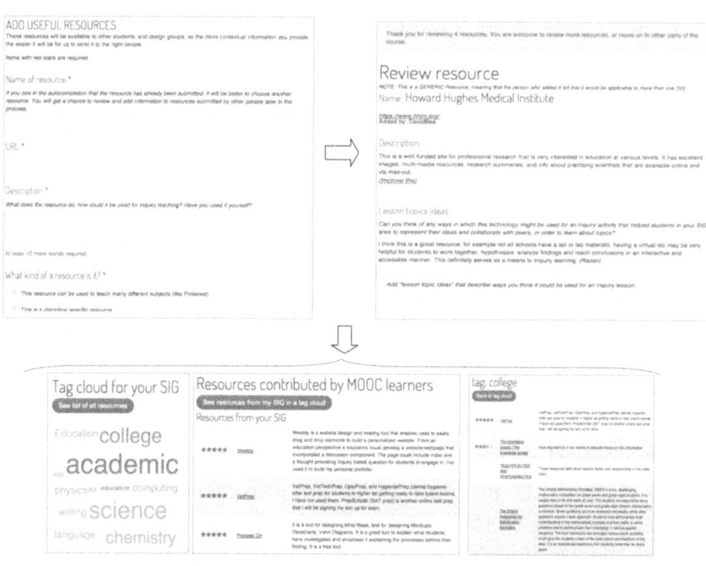

Fig. 1. Resource crowdsourcing script.

URL, and tags, and chose whether the resource was discipline-specific or "of general use". Once the resources had been submitted, the next step was for students to rate and review resources submitted by others. Upon entering this activity, students were presented with a random resource submitted either by a SIG member, or marked as "for general use" (i.e., applicable to all SIGs). They were allowed to modify the description, add more tags, and comment on how this resource could be used pedagogically, as well as to rate the resource.

Finally, students were able to further explore all the resources submitted, using the meta-data that were attached to the resources. We provided a list of all the resources that were submitted for that SIG (or marked as "applicable to all SIGs"), sorted by score, as well as a tag-cloud where students could choose only the resources belonging to a specific tag (see screenshots in Fig. 1).

3.3 Foundation Strand and Design Strand

MOOC students vary significantly in their approaches to learning and level of engagement. To address this variation, we needed to make the course appealing and useful to a wide audience, aiming for broad motivation, but also explicitly catering to different groups of learners. Ideally, we would not only offer different ways and levels of participation, but also design the script such that those different groups served as important resources for one another. This is one of the real promises of a knowledge community approach, that it captures and benefits from the diversity within the community, as opposed to conventional lecture-based or didactic pedagogies that typically address the lowest common denominator.

We chose a design path with two distinct modes of engagement, but where the different modes of engagement were inter-dependent, and benefited from one another. The levels of engagement can be described as a series of concentric circles.

None of the external (LTI based) activities were available before students had taken our LTI survey (since we could not access learner information from EdX through the LTI API, we had to ask students directly). Students that signed up for the course in EdX, but never completed the LTI survey were considered as auditors. They had access to all the content hosted on the EdX platform (videos, quizzes, discussion forums and further readings), but did not participate in any of the interactive exercises (whether Foundation Strand or Design Strand), and were thus not eligible to receive Course Certificates.

Any student that managed to make it through the LTI registration were considered as part of the Foundations Strand. Just like the auditors, they had access to the video material and other content, but in addition, they were asked each week to complete individual reflections, participate in forum discussions within their SIGs, self-assess their performance, and participate in various inquiry activities that were designed to promote reflection and learning while also providing inspiration and feedback to those in the Design Strand.

Students in the Design Strand completed the activities of the Foundation Strand, but in addition they had signed up to work as part of a small team on designing a technology-based inquiry lesson. They had access to the Collaborative Workbench as described below, and received weekly prompts to support their work. They built upon the resources and ideas collected by the Foundation Strand students, and received weekly feedback from the community on their design work.

To emphasize that participation in the Design Strand should be seen as an extra opportunity for rich engagement with other learners in creating a product that could be useful in one's future professional work, we explicitly chose to give no course credit for the Design Strand. Students could earn 100% marks simply by participating in the Foundation Strand activities (including submitting resources, providing feedback on lesson designs and contributing in other ways).

3.4 Collaborative Workbench

Once students had decided on a general topic, and joined together in a team, we needed ways of enabling and sustaining their collaborative effort, creating a sense of a collaborative team, among people who had never met before. A key part of orchestrating the Design strand was the collaborative workbench—a unified interface that provided a design team with all the necessary information and functionality required for doing its creative work and group coordination. Upon creating a new design team, or joining an existing design team, students entered the full-screen interface shown in Fig. 2.

The left sidebar of the Collaborative Workbench contained communication and social presence tools, including a list of the members of the group, with a green symbol showing who was currently online in the collaborative workbench. Students could send chat messages, which were persistent (i.e., students could scroll through the entire chat history of the collaborative workbench, including messages that were sent while they were not logged in)—a design that combined

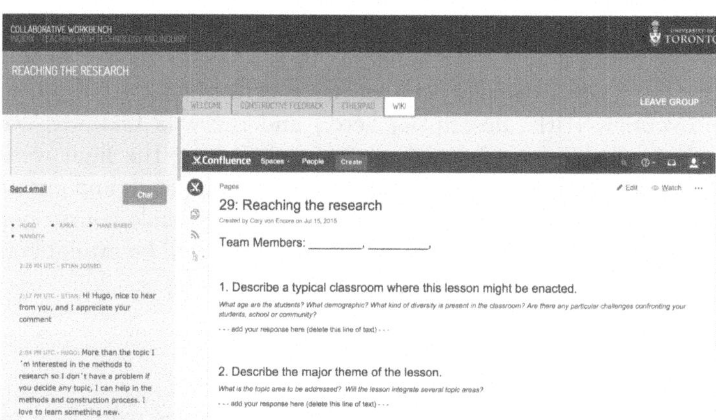

Fig. 2. Collaborative workbench.

the functionality of chat and notice boards. There was also a button to send e-mail, which opened a small window where students could send all group members an e-mail message. This worked by automatically creating an ad-hoc mailing list for the group, maintaining privacy of student e-mail addresses.

The right part of the Collaborative Workbench was for working on content creation and ideation, and had several main "tabs" that allowed various major functions to occur. The first tab contained a welcome message, including prompts and activity tasks for the current week. This message was updated each week. The other tabs varied with each week, often bringing content or ideas from the larger course. For example, the first time that students entered the Workbench, they got access to the resource explorer, to find resources that could inspire their lesson design. A third tab aggregated the feedback and suggestions from other students on their lesson design as it progressed. Because these different tools were presented as tabs instead of separate pages, students could switch between them without loosing context or data. This was important for students who were in the middle of editing the wiki, and wished to look something up in the Etherpad, or in the external review comments.

To begin sketching out ideas and approaches, we embedded Etherpad (live collaborative text editing) as a means of collaboratively developing their design ideas. A new pad was created each week with different prompts. During the first week, students were asked to use the pad to introduce themselves to their group members, and began brainstorming the topic of their lesson, how it was positioned in the wider curriculum, and its length.

A dedicated wiki page for the lesson was introduced in week 2, to serve as the platform for the final lesson design). This was a Confluence wiki page embedded directly into the workspace, where students were automatically logged in and sent to the right page. This page included a template, with pre-designed headers that would help ensure all major elements were present within their design. Initially, only a few headers were visible, in order to avoid distraction, and keep the design focus on the important early stages (i.e., coming up with a topic, some core technology resources, and a sketch of an activity plan). As weeks went by, new headers were added, corresponding to the weekly theme.

The chat and the Etherpad content were private to the group, and only the lesson overview (title, description, etc.) and the wiki text was ever made available to the wider Foundations community. During the final week of the course, we pooled all lesson designs that had been completed, and curated them into a "gallery walk" that was made available to the whole course population This gallery walk was later put on a public URL, and will be available to future course generation, as well as to the general public.

3.5 Scripting Across the Curriculum

Designing a complete course according to KCI principles requires a matrix of scripts that fulfill a number of objectives, while responding to course constraints. We had a number of learning objectives for students: we wanted them to learn

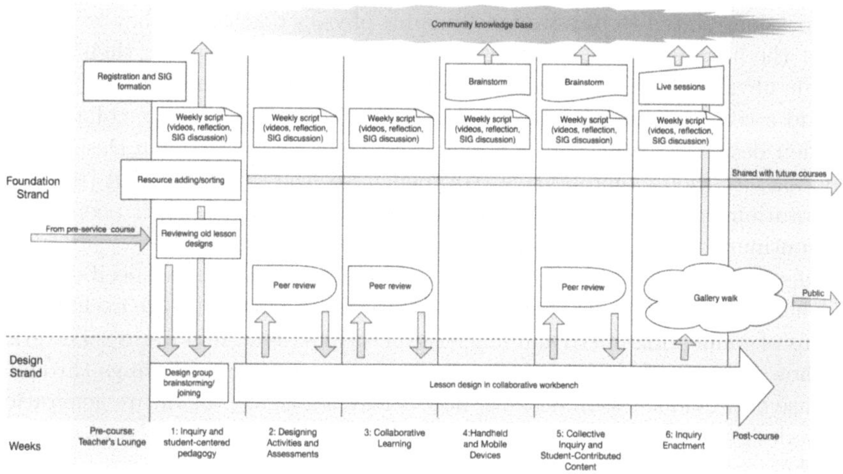

Fig. 3. Graphical depiction of interconnecting MOOC scripts.

about and experience a number of different technologies and resources for learning; to become familiar with a number of theoretical approaches and themes and have the opportunity to reflect on how these new ideas relate to their own teaching practices; and to use creativity and critical thinking in integrating the course topics with their existing knowledge to create a lesson design.

We were thus challenged to develop a script that addressed these various learning goals, without overly confusing students. Our design approach took the form of a matrix of scripts. Each week included a pedagogical script where participants worked through the videos, added personal reflections, participated in discussions, and completed short surveys. The Inquiry activities were divided into two categories, the Foundation Strand and the Design Strand. A smaller number of very motivated students could choose to form small persistent teams, which would work on a project to design a complete technology-infused lesson plan, scaffolded with prompts and guidance throughout the entire course. The larger course community would provide input to this process through initial brainstorming, and weekly constructive rounds of peer-review.

Thus, we were able to treat each of the course themes in a rich way, while simultaneously letting a number of course-scripts unfold from week to week. Each week, the students and groups increased in their knowledge and sophistication, having access to a growing personal and community knowledge space. For example, in week three, a student would begin by watching three videos about collaborative learning: an academic presentation by Professor Slotta, a school perspective by the UTS Principal, and an example of an application, through an interview with a teacher, and video from an actual classroom.

The student would continue by doing a personal reflection about collaboration (related to their own teaching practice), and respond to several prompts related to collaboration in their discipline-specific SIG (for example, how is collaboration related to physics teaching–for physics teachers). They would then look at the in-progress lesson design by a lesson design group (in their SIG, for example physics teachers trying to teach gravity using augment reality glasses), and add a comment about how this team could incorporate more collaboration into their design. Finally, a student who was a member of a Lesson Design group would log into their Collaborative Workbench, see the weekly prompt (related to collaboration), as well as the peer review comments from all their peers, before they continued work on improving their lesson design document.

Thus, scripts are indexed by the weekly themes, and also have specific interdependencies with each other, including pathways were artefacts are exchanged as a means of connecting micro and macro level scripts (as seen in Fig. 3). The graph also shows how the MOOC is connected to previous course offerings through a database of previous lesson designs, how it leaves a legacy for future generations (lesson designs and indexed resource collection), and even how it shares resources with the greater public.

4 Conclusion

In this paper, we have described an approach to designing a collaborative curriculum for a MOOC that explicitly addresses learning goals, harnesses the large number of students to crowd-source ideas, groups students based on their interests or characteristics to make the discussion more relevant, enables small intensive teamwork across multiple weeks, and ties together multiple long-lasting collaborative scripts with weekly course topics through a course matrix, and a set of inter-dependencies. We have shown that the KCI framework and a Knowledge Community approach can be applied to a MOOC context, taking advantage of the diverse backgrounds and experiences of MOOC participants, and making the learning more relevant to their professional lives.

In the end, more than 8,000 students registered for the MOOC, of which around 2,200 registered for LTI activities. Students submitted 1,320 resources, with 431 unique tags. 428 students joined one of 142 design groups (Design Strand), and visited the collaborative workbench on average 7 times each during the course, sending an average of 7 chat messages per group. 25 Design Groups were selected as being complete and high quality, and were displayed publicly as part of the gallery walk. While we hope to improve the participation, and especially the completion rate, in future iterations, there was already an impressive amount of knowledge exchange and community building happening in this course.

A key element in enabling the implementation of this script, was the large amount of external activities that we built. EdX offers no APIs for accessing student information, manipulating cohort membership, reading and responding to forum messages, or otherwise interacting with courses. The LTI protocol is also very minimalistic in the kinds of interactions it enables. However, because all of our LTI services lived on the same server, backed by the same database, we were able to build up a sophisticated student model available to all activities, taking into account group membership, student interests, past activity, etc. By embedding these LTI activities into the EdX activity progression, instead of offering a completely separate website, students never lost their place, and could easily understand what was expected each week. And hosting activities on our own server, enabled us to generate live dashboards with learning analytics, to be able to respond very rapidly to student behaviour while developing the course.

Unfortunately, the technology developed for this MOOC, while open source and available [4], cannot easily be adapted for other courses. More research and development is required to explore more flexible MOOC platforms or platforms for authoring and running rich collaborative scripts.

References

1. Downes, S.: Connectivism and connective knowledge: essays on meaning and learning networks (2012)
2. Ferschke, O., Yang, D., Tomar, G., Rosé, C.P.: Positive impact of collaborative chat participation in an edX MOOC. In: Conati, C., Heffernan, N., Mitrovic, A., Verdejo, M.F. (eds.) AIED 2015. LNCS, vol. 9112, pp. 115–124. Springer, Cham (2015). doi:10.1007/978-3-319-19773-9_12
3. Fischer, F., Mandl, H.: Knowledge convergence in computer-supported collaborative learning: the role of external representation tools. J. Learn. Sci. **14**(3), 405–441 (2005)
4. Håklev, S.: Software for INQ101x (2016). https://github.com/houshuang/survey
5. Hickey, D.T., Quick, J.D., Shen, X.: Formative and summative analyses of disciplinary engagement and learning in a big open online course. In: Proceedings of the Fifth International Conference on Learning Analytics And Knowledge, LAK 2015, pp. 310–314. ACM, New York (2015)
6. Kulkarni, C.E., Bernstein, M.S., Klemmer, S.R.: PeerStudio: rapid peer feedback emphasizes revision and improves performance. In: Proceedings of the Second ACM Conference on Learning @ Scale, L@S 2015, pp. 75–84. ACM, New York (2015)
7. McMahon, M.: Social constructivism and the world wide web-a paradigm for learning. In: ASCILITE Conference, Perth, Australia, vol. 327 (1997)
8. Severance, C., Hanss, T., Hardin, J.: IMS learning tools interoperability: enabling a mash-up approach to teaching and learning tools. Technol. Instr. Cogn. Learn. **7**(3–4), 245–262 (2010)
9. Slotta, J.: Knowledge community and inquiry. Paper Presented and Published for the Network of Associated Programs in the Learning Sciences (NAPLES). Technical report (2014)
10. Slotta, J.D., Najafi, H.: Supporting collaborative knowledge construction with web 2.0 technologies. In: Mouza, C., Lavigne, N. (eds.) Emerging Technologies for the Classroom: A Learning Sciences Perspective, pp. 93–112. Springer, Heidelberg (2012)

Towards Full Engagement for Open Online Education. A Practical Experience for a MicroMaster

Rocael Hernández(✉) and Hector R. Amado-Salvatierra

GES Department, Galileo University, Guatemala, Guatemala
{roc,hr_amado}@galileo.edu

Abstract. This work explores on the different phases of the student's participation in a MOOC. For this particular study three phases of a MOOC are defined: pre-MOOC, MOOC and post-MOOC. This work presents an innovative framework with the aim to create full engagement for the learners on massive open online learning environments. The proposed framework was prepared with the aim to increase the engagement and motivation of the student from the enrollment step to the start of the course, but the most important objective is to extend the interaction beyond the end of the course, the post-MOOC phase. This work explores the experience from two "MicroMaster" specializations in the edX platform: "Professional Android Developer" and one specialization taught in Spanish: "E-Learning for teachers: create innovative activities and content".

Keywords: MOOC experiences · Engagement · Motivation · Community · Lifelong learning

1 Introduction

For the particular case of massive online open courses MOOCs, there are interesting studies in literature [1–7] about the high drop-out and low approval rates from students. In terms of student engagement, Kuh et al. [8] defined the term as a two-fold condition. The first one is represented by the amount of time and effort students put into their learning activities and self-study. The second component of student engagement is represented on how the institution deploys its resources and organizes the learning activities in order to induce students to participate in the proposed activities that lead to the experiences and desired outcomes such as persistence, satisfaction, learning, and finally, course completion and certification. In this sense, there are studies in literature [9–12] that explore on different approaches to motivate and engage students to be persistent and complete a learning course. Nevertheless, it is not possible to find a conceptual framework proposing specific actions to be performed to involve students in all the phases of a MOOC.

In a MOOC context, it is possible to identify three phases related to the participation cycle for a student in a MOOC: pre-MOOC, MOOC and post-MOOC. In order to identify each of the aforementioned phases, the use case of a participant enrolled in a

C. Delgado Kloos et al. (Eds.): EMOOCs 2017, LNCS 10254, pp. 68–76, 2017.
DOI: 10.1007/978-3-319-59044-8_8

course is presented. In the pre-MOOC phase, the student was enrolled to the course two months before the beginning of the learning experience. During this waiting time several scenarios can happen, including a loss of interest from the student in the course topics or the incursion of new time-consuming tasks that will hinder the participation of the student in the course, leading to a potential drop-out. In this sense, it is important to mention the high amount of students that enroll on a course and actually never log-in to start the learning experience. The second phase of the participation cycle is the learning experience within the MOOC, this phase involves the specific duration of the course and the different activities planned by the teaching staff.

The post-MOOC phase begins after the end of the course and it is important to highlight that nowadays a good part of the students that are enrolled in MOOC courses are looking to improve their careers or learn new competencies to apply to a new job. It is interesting to mention that Jennings and Wargnier [13] explored on the so-called 70:20:10 rule [14]. This rule states that only 10% of relevant knowledge and expertise is acquired through formal training and education (e.g., MOOC courses), 20% through coaching and mentoring (e.g., from team-workers and bosses), and 70% via on-the-job learning, learning by doing, and other actual experience-building activities. This rule is well-accepted and used in the corporate training world, at the same time this could be interpreted that students need to continue learning, apply the content of the courses in their jobs and get feedback from peers. This fact gives a potential opportunity to create a community from the participants of a course interested in a common subject. At the same time the idea to be part of a long-lasting and active community could engage participants after the end of a course.

This paper proposes an innovative conceptual framework with the aim to create full engagement for learners on massive open online learning environments. The proposed framework relies on the importance of creating engaging experiences before, during and after the finish of a course to increase students' participation and reduce drop-out rates. This paper presents a compelling idea in the universe of MOOCs: It intends to expand the efforts of the learning design team to achieve pre and post-course engagement, where post-course engagement take the form of an ongoing community of learners. This work presents the first successful experience results from two "Micro-Master" specializations in the edX platform: "Professional Android Developer" and one specialization taught in Spanish: "E-Learning for teachers: create innovative activities and content". For this, the paper is organized as follows: Sect. 2 presents a literature review related to virtual communities and MOOC frameworks. Then Sect. 3 describes the proposed Full Engagement Educational Framework (FEEF), complemented with a first validation of the proposal in Sect. 4. Finally, in Sect. 5 conclusions are presented with a lookout for future work.

2 Related Work

The creation of virtual communities around a common topic, but especially in the context of e-Learning, is a well explored topic in literature [15–18]. In this sense, the work by Barab [17] clearly identifies that there is an evident gap between a real community of learners and a group of students learning collaboratively, enrolled in a common virtual space but without a genuinely sense of belonging. In terms of engaging activities during the second phase of the participation cycle, the MOOC itself, it is interesting to mention the experiences from the "EdTechX: Educational Technology XSeries Program" and the "U.lab: Leading From the Emerging Future course" taught through the edX platform using external forums to enable different communication channels and a closer relationship with the students. Overall, the learning experiences have been improved through the creation of a community of learners. In this sense, this concept is related to the term "communities of practice" that was introduced by Wenger as: *"... are groups of people who share a concern or a passion for something they do and learn how to do it better as they interact regularly*" [19]. This concept is particularly important in MOOCs because in general, a good amount of the participants of MOOC courses are professionals that are looking to update their knowledge and improve their career. It is important to highlight that although the above courses used external forums and channels to improve the learning experiences, it is not possible to identify a live community after the end of the courses.

In terms of engaging content, the work by Malthouse and Peck [20], highlights that the most engaging experiences in media content, that can be applied to a learning scenario, are related to prepare content that fulfills some of the following characteristics: "The content makes me smarter", "It looks out for my interests", "It is convenient" and "It gives me something to talk about". Complementarily, it is possible to affirm based on literature [21–23] that the interaction among participants is the cornerstone to achieve valuable learning experiences and that at the same time, the participants are using several ways of communication using social networks. This affirmation is particularly true based on the work of Bolton et al. [21] explaining the new generations and their use of social media and how Davis et al. [22] highlights the use of online media to increase engagement. In this sense, Irving [24] also explores on the multi-access learning using different communication channels.

In terms of conceptual frameworks related to MOOCs, it is possible to find in literature interesting proposals for conceptual frameworks intended for educators to describe and design MOOC courses [25], to improve the learning outcomes in MOOCs based on different learning strategies [26], and a framework to take into account the accessibility in the different phases of a virtual learning project [27]. However, there are no proposals related to the different actions that need to be taken to motivate and involve students to maintain and increase the engagement in MOOCs.

3 Framework Proposal

The aim of this work is to propose and validate a Full Engagement Educational Framework (FEEF) in the context of virtual learning but especially for MOOCs. The definition of the proposed Conceptual Framework (FEEF), is based on three building blocks: The concept of the FEEF, the components and the expected results. In this section the three building blocks will be presented.

3.1 The FEEF Concept

The aim of the Full Engagement Educational Framework (FEEF) is to create an holistic learning experience that will last before, during and especially after a MOOC course is finished. The proposal is intended to tackle the motivation and engagement in Self-paced courses where there are no specific cohorts with starting and ending dates, aspects that require special attention in order to give students appropriate automatic or personal follow-up. This conceptual framework is composed of different strategies to identify specific target audiences in order to drive engagement through valuable and interesting content based on the premises identified from [20]: "The content makes me smarter", "It looks out for my interests", "It is convenient" and "It gives me something to talk about".

3.2 The Components of the FEEF

The proposed Full Engagement Educational Framework (FEEF) is composed by the following components:

- An online active community
- A blog to publish valuable content to targeted audience
- An email marketing tool to distribute content to enrolled learners and create engagement
- Configuration and update of search engine optimization (SEO) in order to increase exposure to targeted audiences and general public awareness
- Social media channels for content distribution with the purpose of increasing the reach to targeted audience
- Specific segmentation of the different types of enrolled learners with the aim of providing targeted communication to take them to the next level of engagement and course participation
- The process
- Production of edutainment content to create engaging experiences
- Use the network effect to increase the reach of the content distribution
- Execution of appropriate communication according to the student's level of engagement and course participation.

3.3 The FEEF Expected Results

The expected results from the Full Engagement Educational Framework (FEEF) are detailed as follows:

- Metrics related with the engagement perception
- Identification of at least three main levels: non-participant, low to moderate participation, high participation
- Identification of the following stages: potential user stage, enrollment phase, pre-MOOC, becoming active user, MOOC, post-MOOC

- Generation of a sense of belonging materialized with the enrollment in the next courses of a proposed series of courses from the same institution
- Increased awareness and enrollment
- Generation of positive influence in order to have new learners continually
- Maintain a long-term relationship with the learner, independently of her current engagement and participation level.

4 Framework Validation and First Results

This work explores the experience of the validation of the Full Engagement Educational Framework (FEEF) within two "MicroMaster" specializations, one was titled: "Professional Android Developer" and one specialization was taught in Spanish: "E-Learning for teachers: create innovative activities and content". The experiences were prepared by Galileo University within the edX platform. Figure 1 presents the main page of the "Professional Android Developer" specialization. This specialization has five courses and the first cohort had more than 30,000 enrolled participants. It is important to notice that both specializations are offered as a self-paced modality, a fact that allows to validate the framework through time.

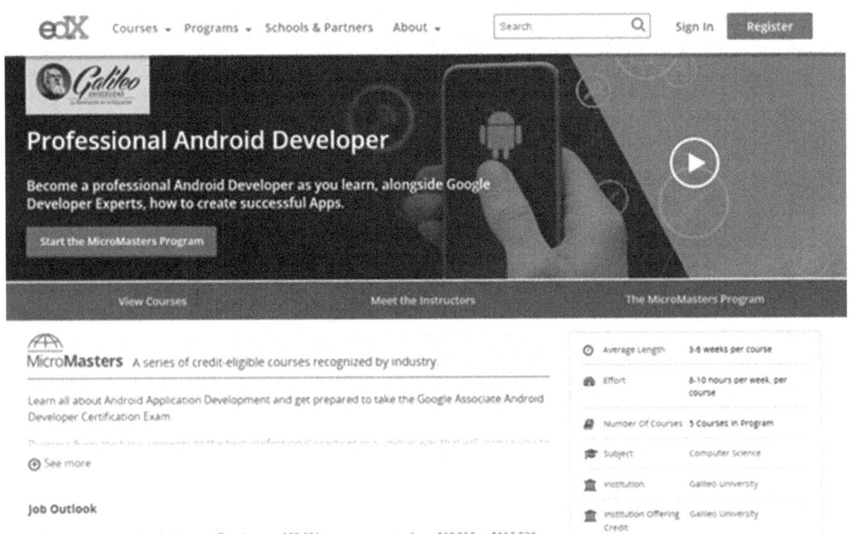

Fig. 1. Professional Android Developer MOOC. Available at: https://www.edx.org/micromasters/galileox-professional-android-developer

For the proposed innovative framework two engaging communities for each of the aforementioned specializations were prepared. The name of the communities are: Android Developers and e-Learning Masters. Figure 2 present the home page of one of the communities to enhance the learning experience of the students in all phases. The

Fig. 2. Android XCommunity. Available at: http://androiddeveloper.galileo.edu/

communities, part of the full engagement educational framework, were prepared following the seven principles proposed by Wenger et al. [28]:

1. The communities are designed for evolution with dynamic and updated content.
2. Facilities for an open dialogue between inside and outside perspectives.
3. Participation is encouraged at all levels, from starters to professionals in the specific topic.
4. The interaction was developed with public and private community spaces.
5. The communities have a focus on value.
6. There is a combination of familiarity and excitement.
7. The communities have a rhythm related to the publication of contents and interaction.

For this innovative framework, specific engaging actions were identified for each of the three phases: pre-MOOC, MOOC and post-MOOC. The proposed engaging experiences are intended to take the participants from a very low interest in pursuing the course at a specific time, to an increased level of engagement that will enable the learner to gain real interest in the topic and invest more time to learn in the near future.

Related to the pre-MOOC phase, the teaching staff part of the proposed educational framework prepared engaging and informative content to periodically send e-mail messages to keep the students interested and informed even if they enrolled in the course three months before the start of the course.

For this full engagement educational framework a real community is built around each MOOC specialization. The aim is to create a community that persists after the learner finished the course through the post-MOOC phase. While nurturing a sense of belonging, sharing knowledge and increase skills, the community also serves as a place where participants can ask for help with real job questions and problems. The discussion forums are the heart of the community, thus all questions and answers are done through the community. The communities provide blogs, high quality content and videos related to the topic of the courses. It is important to mention that the community resides outside of the MOOC platform, but is fully integrated with it. In terms of the expected results from the FEEF, Table 1 presents the results related to the communication metrics, showing interesting results, highlighting the high open rates of email notification and the low bounce rates from the external blog/communities prepared for each of the courses.

Table 1. Identified metrics for the FEEF validation phase

FEEF metric	Result
Blog/community bounce rate from SEO	41.18%
Blog/community bounce rate from email marketing	18.79%
Blog/community bounce rate from social media	85.92%
Blog/community returning visitors rate	36.10%
Mailing engagement open rate	59.79%
Mailing engagement click rate	5.26%

Additionally, it is important to mention that the discussion forums that are used during the MOOC course provide enhanced and easy tools to foster collaboration, and increase visibility of community leaders and major contributors, providing means for community recognition. Gamification instruments are introduced as part of this process. An important fact is that the community is fully open, and will remain open after the end of the course so the students are able to browse through it without login, and also is possible to participate into it without being member of a MOOC in order to create a live and growing community to enhance the post-MOOC phase.

5 Conclusions and Future Work

Nowadays the MOOC movement brings together thousands of students around a common topic for a short period of time. However, the student's experience may last up to three to four months since the enrollment, creating a long waiting time that should be filled with engaging content. On the other hand, for self-paced MOOC courses the students are starting the learning experience every day, and they could feel alone or without attention if they do not get the appropriate follow-up.

This paper presents a thought-provoking work to evolve the MOOC conception to a wider scope through the use of engaging experiences within an external community. The authors explore on the three phases related to the participation cycle for a student in a MOOC: pre-MOOC, MOOC and post-MOOC with the aim to reduce the high drop-out rates and propose actions to engage students from the enrollment steps. This experience paper proposes a Full Engagement Educational Framework (FEEF) in the context of virtual learning but especially for MOOCs. The definition of the proposed

Conceptual Framework (FEEF), is based on three building blocks: The concept of the FEEF, the components and the expected results. The FEEF is based on the use of communities of learners, active interaction and high quality content to motivate the students to start, finish and approve a MOOC course, while at the same time giving the student the opportunity to be part of a strong and long-lasting community.

This work presents the experience of the validation phase, showing the first FEEF expected results, highlighting the high open rates of email notification and the low bounce rates from the external blog/communities, prepared within two "MicroMaster" specialization in edX platform. As a future work, the metrics and best practices of running the FEEF in different context will be prepared, showing how the students perceived, interacted and engaged with the communities, serving as a motivation mean to conclude the courses and being part of a learning community. The final aim is that MOOC administrators for educational institutions will be able to adopt the proposed FEEF and engagement strategies in their own courses. Complementarily, the external communities will be expanded as a showcase for Portfolios and Job Market Place to be evolved into a strong professional network for the post-MOOC phase. The professional networks will be enhanced with external applications like LinkedIn [29] and regional face-to-face meetings and workshops with Meetup [30].

Acknowledgments. This work is partially supported by European Union through the Erasmus +programme - projects MOOC-Maker and ACAI-LA.

References

1. Rivard, R.: Measuring the MOOC dropout rate. Inside High. Educ. (2013). http://www.insidehighered.com/news/2013/03/08/researchers-explore-who-taking-moocs-and-why-so-many-drop-out
2. Kloft, M., Stiehler, F., Zheng, Z., Pinkwart, N.: Predicting MOOC dropout over weeks using machine learning methods. In: Proceedings of the EMNLP 2014 Workshop on Analysis of Large Scale Social Interaction in MOOCs, pp. 60–65 (2014)
3. Onah, D.F., Sinclair, J., Boyatt, R.: Dropout rates of massive open online courses: behavioural patterns. In: EDULEARN 2014 Proceedings, pp. 5825–5834 (2014)
4. Liyanagunawardena, T.R., Parslow, P., Williams, S.: Dropout: MOOC participants' perspective (2014)
5. Halawa, S., Greene, D., Mitchell, J.: Dropout prediction in MOOCs using learner activity features. In: Experiences and Best Practices in and Around MOOCs, p. 7 (2014)
6. Gütl, C., Rizzardini, R.H., Chang, V., Morales, M.: Attrition in MOOC: lessons learned from drop-out students. In: Uden, L., Sinclair, J., Tao, Y.-H., Liberona, D. (eds.) LTEC 2014. CCIS, vol. 446, pp. 37–48. Springer, Cham (2014). doi:10.1007/978-3-319-10671-7_4
7. Hernández, R., Morales, M., Guetl, C.: An attrition model for MOOCs: evaluating the learning strategies of gamification. In: Caballé, S., Clarisó, R. (eds.) Formative Assessment, Learning Data Analytics and Gamification, Chap. 14, pp. 295–310. Elsevier (2016)
8. Kuh, G.D., Kinzie, J. Buckley, J.A., Bridges, B.K., Hayek, J.C.: Piecing Together the Student Success Puzzle: Research, Propositions, and Recommendations: ASHE Higher Education Report, vol. 32, no. 5. Jossey-Bass, San Francisco (2007)

9. Quaye, S.J., Harper, S.R.: Student Engagement in Higher Education: Theoretical Perspectives and Practical Approaches for Diverse Populations. Routledge, Abingdon (2014)
10. Clark, R.C., Mayer, R.E.: E-learning and the Science of Instruction: Proven Guidelines for Consumers and Designers of Multimedia Learning. Wiley, Hoboken (2016)
11. Muntean, C.I.: Raising engagement in e-learning through gamification. In: Proceedings of 6th International Conference on Virtual Learning ICVL, pp. 323–329 (2011)
12. Hernández, R., Guetl, C., Amado-Salvatierra, H.R.: Facebook for e-moderation: a Latin-American experience. In: Proceedings of the 11th International Conference on Knowledge Management and Knowledge Technologies, p. 37. ACM (2011)
13. Jennings, C., Wargnier, J.: Effective learning with 70:20:10. The New Front. Ext. Enterp. CrossKnowledge **1**, 9–21 (2011)
14. Eichinger, R., Lombardo, M.: The Career Architect Development Planner. Lominger Limited, Minneapolis (1996)
15. Hagel, J.: Net gain: expanding markets through virtual communities. J. Interact. Mark. **13**(1), 55–65 (1999)
16. Ardichvili, A., Page, V., Wentling, T.: Motivation and barriers to participation in virtual knowledge-sharing communities of practice. J. knowl. Manag. **7**(1), 64–77 (2003)
17. Barab, S.: An introduction to the special issue: designing for virtual communities in the service of learning. Inf. Soc. **19**(3), 197–201 (2003)
18. Chiu, C.M., Hsu, M.H., Wang, E.T.: Understanding knowledge sharing in virtual communities: an integration of social capital and social cognitive theories. Decis. Support Syst. **42**(3), 1872–1888 (2006)
19. Wenger, E.: Communities of Practice: Learning, Meaning, and Identity. Cambridge University Press, Cambridge (1998)
20. Malthouse, E.C., Peck, A. (eds.): Medill on Media Engagement. Hampton Press, New York (2011)
21. Bolton, R.N., Parasuraman, A., Hoefnagels, A., Migchels, N., Kabadayi, S., Gruber, T., Solnet, D.: Understanding generation Y and their use of social media: a review and research agenda. J. Serv. Manag. **24**(3), 245–267 (2013)
22. Davis, R., Malthouse, E.C., Calder, B.J.: Engagement with online media. J. Media Bus. Stud. **7**(2), 39–56 (2010)
23. Fischer, G.: Understanding, fostering, and supporting cultures of participation. Interactions **18**(3), 42–53 (2011)
24. Irvine, V., Code, J., Richards, L.: Realigning higher education for the 21st century learner through multi-access learning. J. Online Learn. Teach. **9**(2), 172 (2013)
25. Alario-Hoyos, C., Pérez-Sanagustín, M., Cormier, D., Kloos, C.D.: Proposal for a conceptual framework for educators to describe and design MOOCs. J. Univ. Comput. Sci. **20**(1), 6–23 (2014)
26. Fidalgo-Blanco, Á., Sein-Echaluce, M.L., García-Peñalvo, F.J.: Methodological approach and technological framework to break the current limitations of MOOC model. J. Univ. Comput. Sci. **21**(5), 712–734 (2015)
27. Amado-Salvatierra, H.R., Hilera, J.R., Tortosa, S.O., Rizzardini, R.H., Piedra, N.: Towards a semantic definition of a framework to implement accessible e-learning projects. J. Univ. Comput. Sci. **22**(7), 921–942 (2016)
28. Wenger, E., McDermott, R., Snyder, W.M.: Seven principles for cultivating communities of practice. Cultiv. Communities Pract.: Guide Manag. Knowl. **4**, 49–64 (2002)
29. LinkedIn Social Network. https://www.linkedin.com/
30. Meetup. https://www.meetup.com/

From Low-Scale to Collaborative, Gamified and Massive-Scale Courses: Redesigning a MOOC

Alejandro Ortega-Arranz[1(✉)], Luisa Sanz-Martínez[1(✉)], Susana Álvarez-Álvarez[2], Juan A. Muñoz-Cristóbal[1], Miguel L. Bote-Lorenzo[1], Alejandra Martínez-Monés[1], and Yannis Dimitriadis[1]

[1] GSIC-EMIC Research Group, Universidad de Valladolid, Valladolid, Spain
{alex,luisa}@gsic.uva.es
[2] ITNT-ITAST Group, Universidad de Valladolid, Soria, Spain

Abstract. Despite the success of MOOCs to promote open leaning, they are usually criticized for their high drop-out rates and behaviorist pedagogical approach. Some active learning strategies, such as collaboration and gamification, have shown their potential to overcome some of these problems at low scale. However, the design and implementation of such strategies in MOOCs is still a challenge, which is being studied by several researchers, who tend to focus specially on the enactment of MOOCs. Therefore, there is a need for research studies exploring the design processes of MOOCs including active strategies. In this paper, we describe a co-redesign process in which an economic translation course conceived as a MOOC but finally implemented in Moodle for blended learning, was redesigned to include collaboration and gamification to implement it in Canvas Network (a MOOC platform). During the redesign process we found severe difficulties related to the scale, which were mainly caused by the initial implementation in a typical LMS.

Keywords: MOOC · Redesign · Co-design · Active learning · Collaboration · Groups · Gamification

1 Introduction

Massive open online courses (MOOCs) are arising as a new and global form of education that extends learning all over the world. The popularity and the number of MOOCs offered is increasing over the last years [1]. Nowadays, higher education institutions, companies and public entities aim to share their knowledge through MOOCs. There is a growing effort in creating new learning resources (*e.g.*, self-contained videos) or MOOCifying the existing ones. However, the MOOCs success is not only about the resources employed, but also about the pedagogical strategy of the course.

Currently, most MOOCs follow a behaviorist pedagogical approach where the instructors add the educational content to the course stream and the students auto-assess their learning with questionnaires [2,3], limiting the interaction

C. Delgado Kloos et al. (Eds.): EMOOCs 2017, LNCS 10254, pp. 77–87, 2017.
DOI: 10.1007/978-3-319-59044-8_9

between participants and instructors to forums and peer reviews. As a consequence of this pedagogical approach, the research community has perceived several shortcomings in MOOCs: (i) the role of the students as passive receivers of learning contents [2,4] and (ii) the high drop-out rates [5,6].

Strategies promoting the students' active learning at low scales have shown encouraging outcomes that could help to overtake the aforementioned shortcomings [7]. Bonwell and Eison define active learning as *the instructional activities involving students in doing things and thinking about what they are doing* (*e.g.*, read, write, discuss, or be engaged in solving problems) [8]. Bonwell and Eison also performed a literature review identifying common strategies to promote active learning in which collaborative learning and games are included [8].

Collaboration enriches learning with social and cognitive dimensions that maintain student motivation and elicit verbal communication [9]. There are many forms for implementing collaboration such as discussions or study groups, where the group formation represents one of the main features to put in practice collaboration [10]. Second, gamification is defined as the inclusion of elements and structures that frequently appear in games (*e.g.*, narrative, badges, missions). Gamification can help increase the students' engagement and interaction [11]. Thus, gamification is also posed as a potential mechanism to enhance interaction among students and group members, and to reduce the course drop-outs in MOOCs.

Due to the benefits of collaborative learning and gamification, there have been some efforts to include them in MOOCs, typically using simple approaches (such as forums and badges), as a consequence of the difficulties imposed by the massive scales. Thus, the generic underlying research question that leads this study is *how to design and implement MOOCs that involve active pedagogies.*

We decided to start addressing this question by exploring the redesign process of an existing MOOC (sparing monetary and effort costs) which had been initially conceived as a MOOC, but finally implemented in a common LMS (*i.e.*, Moodle) and only enacted at low scale in formal education. The goals of the redesign process were to include active learning strategies in the course, and to deploy it in a typical MOOC platform. In order to explore the redesign process, we decided to use co-design, forming a co-design team composed of a teacher, researchers and a MOOCs instructional designer. However, during the redesign process, we found severe difficulties, beyond the inclusion of active learning strategies, related to the scalability and platform constrains of the original MOOC. In this paper, we describe the redesign process, all the difficulties that we found and how we solved it to implement the original course, including active pedagogies (*i.e.*, collaborative activities with groups and gamification), in a typical MOOC platform (*i.e.*, Canvas Network).

The next section presents the whole redesign process. Section 3 discusses the main outcomes of the study and highlights some conclusions and future directions of this work.

2 Co-redesign Experience

This section describes the context and settings of the initial MOOC; the research methodology; and the main issues, decisions taken and findings regarding the platform selection, the scale and the inclusion of active learning that were encountered during the redesign process.

2.1 Initial Context and Settings

The course was initially designed by two teachers and one undergraduate student of the Faculty of Translation at University of Valladolid (UVa) who previously had never worked with MOOCs. The course design was intended to be used as a 7-week instructor-led MOOC. However, the course had only been implemented as part of an undergraduate subject taught by the teachers, in a blended learning modality. The topic of the course is an introduction to the translation in the business and economic field from English to Spanish.

The course was initially designed by the teachers, bearing in mind that it would be implemented in Moodle since it was the only e-learning platform they had access to. Subsequently, they followed a bricolage approach (*i.e.*, a continuous refinement of the design) during the implementation in Moodle [12].

The course was provided with a title (*i.e.*, "Por los Mares de la Traducción Económico-Financiera (EN-ES)"), weekly structured activities, self-contained recorded videos and peer reviews (common elements in MOOCs). Nevertheless, although the course was conceived as a MOOC, it was only used in formal blended learning. Table 1 summarizes the type of resources and activities included in this original course design. Further description of the activities and structure of the implemented MOOC can be found in Álvarez-Álvarez and Arnáiz-Uzquiza [13].

The course was successfully implemented in Moodle during the 2015–2016 academic year as a support tool for the subject *Traducción Especializada B (inglés) (EN-ES Specialized Translation)* taken in the fourth year of the Degree in Translation and Interpreting of the University of Valladolid. Most of the content videos, activities and readings initially included in the MOOC were used by students as supplementary material for the subject, although they were not evaluated from a summative perspective.

2.2 Methods

A co-design team was formed to explore the design process. Co-design is defined as a highly-facilitated, team-based process in which different stakeholders work together in defined roles for addressing a specific educational need [14] (in this case, how to redesign a MOOC including active pedagogies). The team was composed of (i) a designer of the initial course who took the final redesign decisions; (ii) six researchers experts in technology; and (iii) a Canvas Network instructional designer who advised and provided information based on her experience on a large set of MOOCs. The following technological tools were employed for

Table 1. Summary of the type of resources and activities included in the original course design.

Resources	
Recorded videos	There are 3 types of videos in each module: (i) Introduction videos summarize the content and the activities of the module; (ii) Content videos describe the theoretical content included in the module; and (iii) Test videos assess that students learned the content at the end of the modules
Readings	Some modules include compulsory and recommended readings through external links
Activities	
Glossaries	In the first module, students are expected to complete a glossary of business terms and definitions extracted from different specialized sources
Terms extractions	In modules 3 and 5, students should extract a number of key terms from a set of short documents in order to identify the most representative terms of a certain field
Text translations	Some modules include translation activities in which students are expected translate from English into Spanish different texts belonging to a number of fields
Questionnaires	The main aim of questionnaires, which are integrated in three different modules, is to develop in students a better understanding of the contents tackled during the course. A pre-questionnaire and a student satisfaction questionnaire are also included at the beginning and at the end of the MOOC
Forums	Students are encouraged to post their impressions, doubts, comments and answers in the different course forums. There are one general forum for off-topic discussions, and one forum per module for content-relation discussions

the redesign process: (i) *Google Drive* for shared documents, meeting reports, outcomes and research tools (*i.e.*, questionnaires), (ii) *Skype* for online meetings, (iii) Emails for scheduling meetings, asking doubts, reporting decisions, etc., and (iv) Two *Canvas* instances (one for the trials and one for the final implementation).

In order to explore the general research question that guides our work, we conducted an anticipatory data reduction process (see Fig. 1) inspired in Miles and Huberman [15]. We defined an issue as a conceptual organizer of the research process: *How to redesign a Moodle MOOC incorporating active learning (collaborative activities with groups and gamification)?* We divided this issue into three more concrete topics to help illuminate the issue. The three topics were: (i) platform features and constraints, (ii) scale and (iii) active learning. Finally, each topic was explored through several informative questions which guided the data collection during the course redesign.

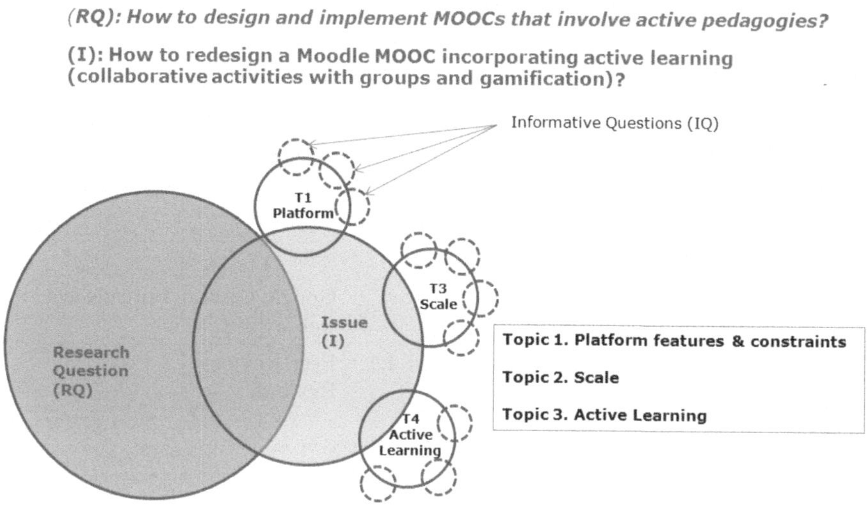

Fig. 1. Anticipatory data reduction diagram including research question, issue, topics and informative questions.

We used different data gathering techniques in the research process: (i) Questionnaires to know the designers' background about MOOCs, collaboration and gamification, the original course design, activities and contents, and the designers' preferences for including collaboration and gamification in the course. Such questionnaires were formed by open, multiple choice and weight assignment questions. (ii) Collection of designers' generated artifacts (*i.e.*, meetings reports and emails) to summarize the progress of the course design. (iii) Recording of meetings (*i.e.*, videos, audios and chats) to analyze the issues found and the decisions taken during the meetings.

2.3 Towards an Active and Scalable MOOC

This subsection describes the issues and decisions the team took to overcome the design and implementation shortcomings regarding the platform selection, the scalability and the inclusion of active pedagogies (see Table 2).

Platform Selection. Moodle is the official platform for the virtual campus in the university in which the course was developed. Although Moodle is able to support a relative high scale of students [16], it is generally intended to low scale courses. Therefore, we decided to implement the MOOC in other platform better adapted to high scales, in order to reduce the potential technical risks caused by the scale, and to achieve higher audience. After a MOOC platform analysis, Canvas Network was selected for the implementation of this course due to its capability to support massive-scale courses, collaborative activities in groups and gamification. Moreover this platform provides an instructors' dashboard and an

Table 2. Edited course features in the redesign and implementation processes.

Features	Original MOOC	Redesigned MOOC
Platform		
Bricolage Approach	Moodle	Canvas Network
Course front page	No	Yes
Course listing page	No	Yes
Scale		
Third-party tools	Google Docs	Google Form + Spreadsheet web exportation
Assessment	Manual Assessment 1:1 Peer Reviews	Peer Reviews 1:2 Peer Reviews
Collaboration		
Collaborative design	No	Yes
Group formation	No	Criteria-based groups
Open enrollment dates	Yes	No
Open activity dates	Yes	No
Restriction-date content	No	Yes
Gamification		
Badge criteria	No	Yes
Badge visual design	No	Yes

open API to analyze the course outcomes. As a consequence, a front-page and a coursing listing page were designed to advertise the course in the Canvas Network platform.

The original course was implemented in Moodle following a bricolage approach, and therefore, using many of the Moodle ad-hoc internal tools (see Fig. 2). Although we used the Canvas importation feature, which imported automatically the Moodle course into a Canvas platform, the team was forced to manually implement and edit some activities in the new platform. For example, the *glossary* activity (see Table 1) was implemented in the glossary module that Moodle provides to teachers. However, many MOOC platforms (including Canvas Network) lack this tool. Therefore this activity was implemented through two external tools: Google Forms to insert the terms and the Google Spreadsheets web exportation function to show the resulting sorted list. Other tools such as Canvas forums were considered as alternatives for implementing the glossary, but they were finally rejected because of the lack of shorting capabilities.

Scale. The team detected two main issues regarding the scale. First, the *terms extraction* activity (see Table 1) was implemented in the original course with Google Docs. However, Google Docs limits the maximum number of concurrent users to fifty people (*i.e.*, non-scalable for massive-scale activities). Due to this fact, this activity was re-implemented using Google Forms and the Google Spreadsheets web exportation function. Also, other implementations were considered such as the use of forums or the creation and configuration of many Google Docs instantiations but they were either not useful enough or more complex solutions.

Second, the assessment of the *glossary* and *terms extraction* activities was designed to be rated by instructors following a rubric. However, the high number of resulting activity terms would increase the instructors' workload within the course. Therefore, the instructor-based assessment of such activities was replaced by peer-review assessment. Also, the original design included some peer-review assessments in which each student had to assess the work of another student (*i.e.*, text translations). Since one of the most common problems in MOOCs is the student drop-out, we decided to increase the number of revisions of each student from one to two, in order to reduce the possible students' products without any review.

Active Learning. The course redesign aimed to include collaborative activities in groups and gamification in order to promote active learning. The course design decisions related to the collaboration were: (i) Selecting (based on pedagogical reasons) the *term extraction* activities as those to include collaboration. (ii) Developing an external semi-automatic tool to support instructors in the creation of criteria-based groups for such collaborative activities; (iii) Fixing concrete dates for completing the group activities. The self-paced character of MOOCs can led student to perform the collaborative activity in different time periods avoiding the collaboration. (iv) Disabling the openness of the course resources and content. Thus, the team tries to avoid grouping students that only enroll in the course to download the contents without interacting. (v) Setting an enrollment closing date (*i.e.*, the previous week to the first week with a collaborative activity) to avoid regrouping problems caused by late enrollments as shown in Cooch et al. [16].

The goal of including gamification in this course is to promote students' social interaction and activity submission by rewarding these actions with badges. To do so, ten badges were designed and configured to be automatically issued when students participate in the general and group forums, contribute to the collaborative activities (*e.g.*, glossary), and submit the small-group and peer review activities. Five more badges were also added to keep students engaged during the individual course activities. Moreover, a badge leaderboard was enabled to let students see their gamification progress during the course.

3 Discussion, Conclusions and Future Work

The original course design included many features common in MOOCs: online, title, content divided in modules, self-contained videos and peer reviews. However, other common MOOC features were not considered in the original design, and hampered the course implementation in a real MOOC context: non-scalability of third-party tools, manual assessments, course completion criteria, etc. These limitations and the introduction of active learning forced to redesign the course. We can extract some lessons learned from the experience gained in the redesign process.

The existence of a co-design team highly affected the design, since specific gamification and collaboration strategies feasible in a MOOC context were proposed to the instructor (*e.g.*, the gamified small-group activities).

It is already known that video production is one of the most demanding elements in MOOCs. The instructors should pay attention to video contents trying to avoid dates, tools and activities references to ease future redesign processes. If a MOOC has been created directly in an enactment platform following a bricolage approach, there is a challenge for reusing the design in other platform. In our redesign process, we found that it is specially challenging if the MOOC was designed in a typical LMS, due to the multiple decisions taken based on the LMS features (such as the internal or external tools included). Further work is needed to check whether a learning design approach can help reuse the contents and activities in MOOCs. In addition, some tools included in LMS-based or online courses can be limited by the scale. For example, as the team tested in our course, Google Docs is limited up to fifty people concurrently working, forcing the team to change the implementation tool.

We also confirmed the known issue that massive contexts hinder the form of assessing the activities. Albeit the instructor feedback can ensure the quality of the assessment, the massive scale of MOOCs makes manual assessment unfeasible. Despite the fact that peer review is a scalable solution for assessment in MOOCs, it does not guaranty the quality of reviews, which is a relevant aspect to take into account. Another aspect to consider in MOOCs is to increase the number of artifacts reviewed by each student, to assure that all artifacts will have at least one review. The instructor manual assessments included in the original design were changed by peer reviews, and peer reviews were configured for performing more reviews than submissions (2:1).

We verified that simple collaborative and gamification mechanisms can be implemented in a MOOC platform (*i.e.* Canvas Network, see Fig. 2). However, any introduction of complexity in the gamification or collaboration (such as allowing instructors to select the grouping criteria) might require the implementation of additional tools not included in the default MOOC platform features. Moreover, in order to encourage students to complete these collaborative activities, the redesign team decided to set concrete dates for group activities, to enable weekly course resources and content, and to set an enrollment closing date. Further work is needed to analyze if finally these factors affected to the activities completion and if there are other course factors that can also influence in the completion of such collaborative activities.

Initially, the co-design team expected to include more collaborative and gamified features in the course. However, the problems found during the redesign process (*i.e.*, scalability problems and platform constraints), limited the focus

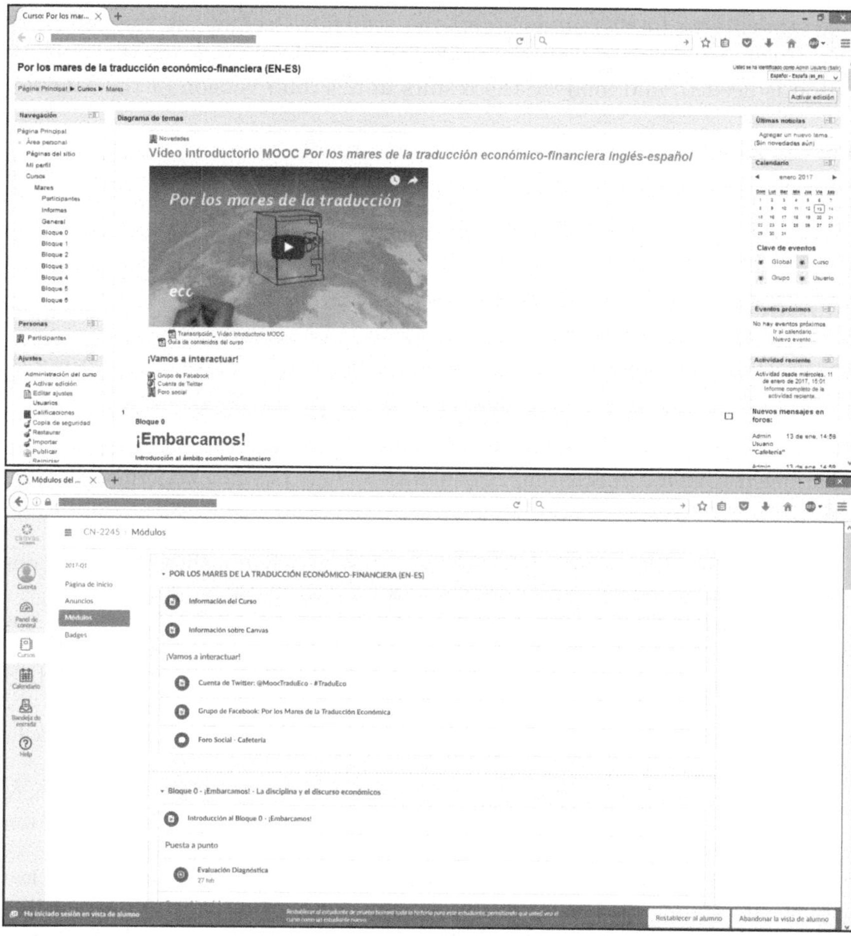

Fig. 2. Screenshots of the initial course design implemented in Moodle (top) and the redesigned course implemented in Canvas Network (bottom).

on active learning. As future work, we aim to analyze the design and implementation process of more complex collaborative and gamified activities such as the use of inter- and intra-group leaderboards and its integration through CSCL scripts.

The redesigned course is already listed in the upcoming Canvas Network course list and it is intended to be enacted by the beginning of 2017[1]. The results and analysis of the course will allow us to check if the decisions taken during the redesign and implementation processes had a positive effect in the course enactment (*e.g.*, the assessments, the collaborative activities and the gamification elements). Moreover, the team already designed a questionnaire for the

[1] MOOC available at: https://learn.canvas.net/courses/1343/.

course students to further understand the students' feelings at the end of the course. Such feedback will provide evidence to check whether another redesign iteration is needed, and analyze the results in a second version of the MOOC.

Acknowledgements. This research has been partially supported by the Junta de Castilla y León, Spain (VA082U16) and Ministerio de Economía y Competitividad, Spain (TIN2014-53199-C3-2-R). The authors thank the rest of the GSIC-EMIC research team as well as the Canvas team for their valuable ideas and support.

References

1. Shah, D.: By the numbers: MOOC in 2015. How has the MOOC space grown this years? Get the facts, figures, and pie charts (2015). https://www.class-central.com/report/moocs-2015-stats/. Accessed Nov 2016
2. Ferguson, R., Sharples, M.: Innovative pedagogy at massive scale: teaching and learning in MOOCs. In: Rensing, C., Freitas, S., Ley, T., Muñoz-Merino, P.J. (eds.) EC-TEL 2014. LNCS, vol. 8719, pp. 98–111. Springer, Cham (2014). doi:10.1007/978-3-319-11200-8_8
3. Margaryan, A., Bianco, M., Littlejohn, A.: Instructional quality of massive open online courses (MOOCs). Comput. Educ. **80**, 77–83 (2015)
4. Dillenbourg, P., Fox, A., Kirchner, C., Mitchell, J., Wirsing, M.: Massive open online courses: current state and perspectives (Dagstuhl perspectives workshop). Dagstuhl Manifestos **4**, 1–27 (2014). Schloss Dagstuhl–Leibniz-Zentrum fuer Informatik
5. Jordan, K.: Initial trends in enrolment and completion of massive open online courses. Int. Rev. Res. Open Distrib. Learn. **15**(1), 133–160 (2014)
6. Alario-Hoyos, C., Pérez-Sanagustín, M., Delgado-Kloos, C., Muñoz-Organero, M.: Delving into participants' profiles and use of social tools in MOOCs. IEEE Trans. Learn. Technol. **7**(3), 260–266 (2014)
7. Hew, K.F.: Promoting engagement in online courses: what strategies can we learn from three highly rated MOOCS. Br. J. Educ. Technol. **47**(2), 320–341 (2016)
8. Bonwell, C.C., Eison, J.A.: Active Learning: Creating Excitement in the Classroom. ASHE-ERIC Higher Education Reports No. 1. The George Washington University, School of Education and Human Development, Washington, D.C. (1991)
9. Roschelle, J., Teasley, S.D.: The construction of shared knowledge in collaborative problem solving. In: O'Malley, C. (ed.) Computer-Supported Collaborative Learning, vol. 128, pp. 69–97. Springer, Heidelberg (1995)
10. Isotani, S., Inaba, A., Ikeda, M., Mizoguchi, R.: An ontology engineering approach to the realization of theory-driven group formation. Int. J. Comput.-Support. Collab. Learn. **4**(4), 445–478 (2009)
11. Dicheva, D., Dichev, C., Agre, G., Angelova, G.: Gamification in education: a systematic mapping study. Educ. Technol. Soc. **18**(3), 75–88 (2015)
12. Berggren, A., Burgos, D., Fontana, J.M., Hinkelman, D., Hung, V., Hursh, A., Tielemans, G.: Practical and pedagogical issues for teacher adoption of IMS learning design standards in Moodle LMS. J. Interact. Media Educ. **2005**(1), Article no. 3 (2005). doi:http://doi.org/10.5334/2005-2
13. Álvarez-Álvarez, S., Arnáiz-Uzquiza, V.: Próxima estación, MOOC: diseño de un curso masivo abierto para la enseñanza de la traducción. In: Proceedings of the XIII Jornades de Xarxes d'investigació en Docència Universitària. Universidad de Alicante, pp. 521–536 (2015)

14. Penuel, W.R., Roschelle, J., Shechtman, N.: Designing formative assessment software with teachers: an analysis of the co-design process. Res. Pract. Technol. Enhanc. Learn. **2**(01), 51–74 (2007)
15. Miles, M.B., Huberman, A.M.: Qualitative Data Analysis. An Expanded Sourcebook. SAGE Publications Inc., Newbury Park (1994)
16. Cooch, M., Foster, H., Costello, E.: Our MOOC with Moodle. Position papers for European cooperation on MOOCs (2015). http://research.moodle.net/6/1/Our%20MOOC%20with%20Moodle.pdf. Accessed Jan 2017

Innovation in EU Communication: MOOCs from the European Committee of the Regions

Martin Gosset(✉) and Wolfgang Petzold(✉)

European Committee of the Regions,
Rue Belliard/Belliardstraat 101, 1040 Brussels, Belgium
{martin.gosset,wolfgang.petzold}@cor.europa.eu

Abstract. Towards the background of its political work and communication activities, the European Committee of the Regions (CoR), the EU's assembly of regional and local representatives, became in the last two years the first EU institution having developed two MOOCs to contribute to capacity-building of regional and local authorities with regard to EU affairs, helping them to navigate their way through the EU's complex legal and institutional set-up, and multi-faceted decision-making process. This experience paper briefly presents the two online courses developed by the CoR in 2015 and 2016, and focuses on the production process, design and delivery, as well as student evaluation and survey results. It aims to show how the reflection of the CoR has evolved regarding the development of online courses, and which lessons can be learnt from the past to improve the offer of MOOCs in the future.

Keywords: MOOCs · Local and regional authorities · EU affairs · Capacity-building · Course design · Evaluation

1 Introduction

The first MOOC of the CoR on 'Regions, EU Institutions and Policy-Making' was launched in October 2015, and ran for eight weeks [1]. This project was part of the 2015 communication plan of the CoR, which notably focused on increasing digital and online communication.

This eight-week MOOC focused on EU policies and their impact on regions and cities. It involved around 50 EU and regional/local experts, and reached 8,500 participants from over 70 countries. Around two-thirds of the MOOC followers were representatives of local, regional, national or EU authorities, as well as NGOs. The content of the course was delivered by video interviews, factsheets, infographics, live debates and quizzes. The MOOC page was the most visited one of the CoR website in 2015 (13% of all page views). In total, 17% of the followers completed the course (with a pass mark of minimum 80%), a rather high completion rate compared to MOOCs offered by HEIs or the private sector.

At the end of the course, a final ex-post evaluation was conducted among participants. 83% of them indicated that they were satisfied with the course, and would be interested to follow a subsequent course on EU affairs.

C. Delgado Kloos et al. (Eds.): EMOOCs 2017, LNCS 10254, pp. 88–94, 2017.
DOI: 10.1007/978-3-319-59044-8_10

The positive feedback received from the participants of the 2015 MOOC highlighted the potential of the online course to contribute to strengthening the administrative capacity at a local level, as well as raising awareness of the EU policies and their impact to a wider audience. Building on this, a second MOOC was developed in 2016 with more specific content on the 'EU budget and funding for regions and cities' [2]. The course was developed with three partners: the European Investment Bank and two Directorates-General from the European Commission (Regional and Urban Policy, and Budget). An ex-ante survey conducted among potential followers helped the CoR to design the course according to the existing knowledge, needs and expectations of these stakeholders. The 2016 MOOC attracted a high number of followers: over 5,145 registered participants from over 105 countries; over 5,184 web-streaming views of the live debates.

2 Course Design and Delivery

2.1 2015 MOOC on 'Regions, EU Institutions and Policy-Making'

The design of the first MOOC started in March 2015, with an online survey conducted by the CoR among its key contacts and clients' databases. The survey received 1,200 responses within five working days, confirming the interest in a course on regions, EU and policy-making among stakeholders with limited experience of online learning. The responses received highlighted the necessity to concentrate on eight main topics:

- EU Institutions and legislation;
- The role of regions and cities in EU affairs;
- EU Cohesion Policy and Structural and Investment Funds;
- Research and innovation for regions and cities;
- Environment, climate change and sustainable development policies;
- Free movement and migration;
- EU competition policy and state aid;
- The EU budget, programmes and projects.

Based on these results, the MOOC was designed as an eight-week modular course. It was delivered in English and included several learning tools, for instance video interviews with experts and practitioners, infographics, fact-sheets, web streamed live debates, as well as learning resources, e.g. web-links to relevant sources of information. Besides, a weekly quiz assisted the MOOC followers to assess their knowledge and monitor their learning progress.

The production of the learning tools and course materials started in May 2015. In June, four expert panels composed of 2 to 3 speakers and one moderator were organised and filmed. Between June and November 2015, four other experts were interviewed and filmed for the different chapters of the course. Besides, a series of eight infographics and eight factsheets were designed for each module. Eventually, eight expert panels were organised for the live debates, which took place at lunchtime every Friday throughout the course. Over 50 experts contributed to this MOOC, including EU and regional/local politicians, practitioners, technical experts and academics.

During the production process, a communication campaign was implemented to keep key stakeholders, partners and the targeted audience aware about the launch of the MOOC. The campaign included a specific webpage on the CoR website, electronic and printed leaflets, promotional videos, targeted email campaigns, a social media campaign on LinkedIn, Facebook and Twitter, as well as event-specific advertising.

The course was hosted on Iversity, a German-based e-learning platform. Registration opened on 1 August 2015, and the course started on 19 October 2015. Around 7,000 participants enrolled at the start of the course and, eventually, 9,500 had signed up. The last module was concluded on 11 December 2015, but the course remained accessible online until the end of February 2016. At the course closure, in December 2015, 8,500 students had registered. A statement of participation – subject to a pass mark of minimum 80% – was issued to 17% of them (1,500 participants).

Slightly more women than men followed the course. Most followers were in the 31–40 age group (25%), followed by the 26–30 age group (23%) and the 41+ age-group (22%). The majority of participants came from Belgium (10%), Spain, Germany and Italy (9% each), Greece and the UK (5% each), as well as France and Romania (4% each). Overall, the course had followers from over 70 countries. The ex-post evaluation conducted by the CoR showed high satisfaction levels towards both the course content and the Iversity platform. No specific difficulties were mentioned by the participants who used the online platform.

2.2 2016 MOOC on the 'EU Budget and Funding for Regions and Cities'

The success of the first MOOC and the positive feedback received from participants highlighted the potential of the online course to contribute to strengthening the administrative capacity at a local level as well as raising awareness of the EU policies and their impact to a wider audience. On this basis, the CoR decided to launch a second edition with both an introduction on local aspects of EU policy-making, and more specific content to enhance the knowledge of participants on the EU budget and funding for regions and cities.

The main themes of the MOOC were developed around the knowledge about the EU budget and access to EU funding for regions and cities. It was agreed to reduce the number of modules compared to the first edition, and the following six topics have been identified as being of particular relevance:

- The role of regions and cities in EU affairs;
- How the EU budget works;
- Implementation of the European Structural and Investment Funds (ESIF);
- The Investment Plan for Europe and a range of EIB instruments;
- Other EU programmes relevant for regions and cities (e.g. Horizon 2020, Erasmus+, IPA/ENI, COSME);
- The debate on the mid-term review of the EU budget 2014–2020 and the post-2020 prospects.

Another innovation of the 2016 MOOC is that it was co-created with three partners, namely the European Investment Bank and two Directorates-General of the European

Commission (Regional and Urban Policy, and Budget). In June 2016, a first meeting was organised with the partners to take stock on the first edition, and present the key results of the online survey conducted among potential participants for the new MOOC. This online was opened between 25 May and 10 June 2016, and received 1,069 responses. It showed that respondents were mostly new followers (77% did not follow the 2015 MOOC), had some experience with EU funding (70% had at least two years of relevant experience), were interested in both introductory and advanced content, and wanted to acquire useful professional skills.

Therefore, the second MOOC of the CoR was designed as a six-week modular course based on the topics listed above. It was delivered in English and included the same variety of learning tools as in the first edition. Due to several reasons, the course was provided on a different e-learning online platform, namely the French-based France Universite Numerique (FUN-MOOC).

The production of the course materials and learning aids started in July 2016. Between July and October, over 50 experts were interviewed and filmed to cover the different modules. This included individual interviews, as well as four expert debates. In parallel, a series of six factsheets and various infographics were developed for each module. Finally, six expert panels were organised for the live debates, which took place at lunchtime every Friday throughout the course.

Similarly to what was implemented for the first course, the CoR launched a dedicated communication campaign to inform and update interested stake-holders about the development of the course. Registration opened on 1 August 2016, and the course started on 31 October 2016. The course material is still available online until July 2017, so participants can still register. The latest figures indicate that this MOOC attracted over 5,145 participants from over 105 countries. Besides, there were more than 5,184 web-streaming views of the live debates. A statement of participation – subject to a pass mark of 80% – was issued to 13% of all MOOC followers them (655 participants).

Two-thirds of the MOOC participants come from six countries: France (26%), Italy (12%), Belgium (9%), Spain (8%), Greece (7%) and Romania (6%). There were more female (58%) than male followers (42%). Over 70% of the MOOC participants belong to the 25–45 age group, while 18% are below 25. Most MOOC followers (35%) work for a regional or local authority, or a representation/association of regional or local authorities. Many followers also come from the private sector (22%). The three main goals for participating in this MOOC were: (i) Increasing knowledge about the EU (24%); (ii) Acquiring useful professional skills (21%); (iii) Gaining a broad overview of the subjects (18%). Here again, in the ex-post survey conducted by the CoR, there were no particular complaints from participants about using the FUN-MOOC platform. However, from the course designer's point of view, the Iversity platform was more attractive visually and more user-friendly. Besides, the technical support provided was slightly better and more responsive, and the fact that Iversity launched its own evaluation at the end of the course was also useful for data analysis.

3 Student Evaluation and Survey Results

3.1 2015 MOOC

Two surveys were conducted by the CoR and the Iversity platform at the end of the course. Yet, with respectively 280 and 400 responses, the representativeness of the findings remains limited.

The survey from the CoR focused on the organisational affiliation of course followers and on their satisfaction regarding course content and delivery. Among the 280 respondents, 48% worked for a public authority, mostly at regional or local level (28%), but also at national (14%) or EU level (6%). 24% of the respondents were students and 12% held a teaching position. In addition, 13% worked for an NGO. Gender distribution indicated that there were more female (58%) than male followers (42%). Most respondents had followed all the course chapters.

The large majority of respondents (77%) found that the course satisfied their expectations. Regarding the different learning tools, the factsheets were considered the most interesting (83% 'very interesting'), followed by infographics (76%) and video interviews (74%). Around 10% of the course followers made contact(s) with others, for instance in the course discussion forum, during the Q&A sessions of the live debates or through the Facebook group formed by the most active followers. Eventually, 86% of the respondents indicated their interest in following another course on the EU and its regions.

The Iversity platform also conducted an ex-post satisfaction survey among the MOOC followers. 83% of the respondents said they were very satisfied with the instructor's (the CoR) performance (61% very satisfied, 22% somewhat satisfied) and with the platform (71% very satisfied, 16% somewhat satisfied). Most respondents said they were likely to take another course by the same instructor (53% very likely, 30% somewhat likely) and recommend the CoR to a friend (50% very likely, 28% somewhat likely).

The content of the course was evaluated as factually accurate (66% agree, 26% somewhat agree), well-structured and organised (65% agree, 25% somewhat agree). The most common objectives for participating in the MOOC were 'to gain a broad overview of the subject' (37%) and to 'acquire professionally useful skills' (34%), followed by 'to study the subject in-depth' (16%). The majority of the respondents indicated that the course enabled them to achieve their original goal (55% agree, 38% somewhat agree). The main obstacle in achieving the goal was the lack of time (40%), followed by quality of content (12%). Most respondents found they had the necessary prior knowledge for the course (52% agree, 30% somewhat agree). They spent three hours per week on the course on average.

3.2 2016 MOOC

One survey was conducted by the CoR at the end of the course. Yet, with 180 responses, the results must be looked at carefully.

On average, 78% of the respondents followed the course completely. The module which had most followers was Module 1 on ‘the role of regions and cities in EU affairs’ (85% followed completely), while Module 6 on ‘the debate on the mid-term review of the EU budget 2014–2020 and the post-2020 prospects’ was only followed completely by 65% of the respondents. A very large majority of the respondents (90%) found the course either ‘very interesting’ (64%) or ‘somewhat interesting’ (26%). Module 2 on the ‘EU budget’ was the most appreciated (70% of ‘very interesting’, 24% of ‘somewhat interesting’). In total, the large majority of respondents (82%) found that the course fulfilled their expectations.

Factsheets and infographics were considered by far the most interesting learning aids (80% ‘very interesting’), followed by introductory animated videos (66%) and interview videos (57%). The majority of survey respondents found the course workload and duration ‘just right’ (respectively 76% and 78%). More than two-thirds of the respondents were satisfied with the course difficulty (68%), while 18% found the course ‘somewhat easy’ or ‘too easy’. Besides, the large majority of the respondents is satisfied with the platform (62% very satisfied, 26% somewhat satisfied). 19% of the course followers made contact(s) with others. Finally, almost all respondents (99%) said they would like to follow another course from the European Committee of the Regions (56% on a different topic, 43% on the same topic).

Recommendations to improve the course include developing the course in other languages, subtitling the videos, showcasing more concrete examples and good practices from regions and cities, as well as providing a summary of the most relevant information.

4 Conclusions, Recommendations and Follow-Up

Feedback by and outreach to MOOC followers confirmed the potential of online courses to contribute to administrative capacity-building at local level and to enhance interest and understanding of EU affairs among regional and local authorities. MOOCs can be considered as relevant channels for targeted EU communication; they create synergies with other communication tools, such as social media, web-based information and events. The evaluation conducted showed that these MOOCs seemed to reach a relatively young (below 40) – and possibly distant – audience with regard to EU communication. Eventually, the cost-efficiency of both MOOCs suggests further developing this instrument and experimenting more with such interactive online tools, including the co-creation of their content.

Statistics from the web also showed that both MOOCs had a positive impact on the CoR’s institutional web communication: for instance in 2015, it was by far the most visited page of the year, with 13% of all page views [3]. While the MOOC itself was hosted on an external platform and the CoR’s dedicated webpage contained only static information about the course, the latter had a significant return rate, mainly from the MOOC’s Twitter account, which gathered over 800 followers.

As far as quality is concerned, it seems that the concept was successful, especially since both MOOCs were built on a variety of experts and sources – EU officials, academics, regional and local authorities, practitioners, etc. The satisfaction surveys conducted among the followers also confirmed the appreciated quality of the course.

For both MOOCs, improvements could be done in terms of using a more journalistic approach based on story-telling and co-creation of content with the help of potential users. Participants' feedback also indicated that debates could be more controversial, and that the course should be provided in more than one language (currently English). We are taking into account these different areas of improvement while reflecting on the development of a third MOOC. One of the ideas is to produce the course material in the languages of the majority of previous MOOC users (i.e. French, Italian, Greek, Spanish and Romanian). Another area for quality improvement relates to the preparation of speakers and the setting of interviews, which could be more carefully planned – this would require further preparatory work with the speakers and the audio-visual support team. It also came out of the evaluations that the combination of real stories (e.g. videos about concrete examples of local/regional projects) and practitioners' interviews is more appealing and more interesting for MOOC students than individual experts' interviews.

As a conclusion, it can be said that the MOOCs developed by the European Committee of the Regions are a communication tool with a strong leverage effect for the CoR communication. The development of the online course through an ex-ante survey with potential clients of CoR communication should be seen as a leading example on how to co-create content and formats of new communication tools. The ex-post surveys conducted among participants, which highlighted high satisfaction levels, can also be considered as good practice. In the future, a systematic promotion via the websites of other EU-institutions and other communal or regional bodies would be useful, as it would significantly step up this leverage effect. Currently, we are in the process of preparing the 2017 edition of the CoR MOOC and spend more time with our partners on the coherent development of the course content through initial brainstorming meetings and exchanges, the sharing of new ideas and good practices and the distribution of work between partners.

References

1. MOOC (2015). https://iversity.org/en/courses/eu-regions-and-cities-matter
2. MOOC (2016). https://www.fun-mooc.fr/courses/CoR/114001/session01/
3. MOOC webpage of the CoR. http://cor.europa.eu/en/events/Pages/CoR-online-MOOC.aspx

Does Gamification in MOOC Discussion Forums Work?

Matthias Reischer, Mohammad Khalil(✉), and Martin Ebner

Educational Technology, Graz University of Technology, Graz, Austria
matthias.reischer@student.tugraz.at,
{mohammad.khalil,martin.ebner}@tugraz.at

Abstract. Massive Open Online Courses (MOOCs) are a new form of learning environment aimed towards accessibility and openness using contemporary technologies. One of the MOOC's key features is the social interaction which usually takes place in discussion forums. This article focuses on reworking and analyzing the existing iMooX forum by enriching the new design with gamification elements. The intended objectives aim at refreshing the current style and improving its handling and usability. This article provides our experience of this implementation as well as examining whether or not the gamification elements can help increase the participation rate and the teacher-to-student and student-to-student communication exchange. Results of the new design showed a good user satisfaction and a slight positive impact.

Keywords: MOOCs · Gamification · Discussion forums · Learning Analytics · Evaluation

1 Introduction

Over the last decades, technology specifically the Internet has blended with most forms of traditional learning methods, opening up new possibilities for students and teachers alike. We are no longer bound by restrictions such as physical presence or fixed schedules, but can instead access knowledge and educational materials whenever and wherever we desire. MOOCs are a natural evolution of this circumstance. They offer open and free of charge courses requiring only the Internet and our own interest [9]. Mostly provided by institutes from the Higher Education, MOOCs include several types of content; for example, in form of lecturing videos, quizzes, documents, and discussion forums in order to support the holistic learning experience for online learners.

Following the strong emergence of MOOCs, The Graz University of Technology and Graz University have established the first Austrian MOOC platform called iMooX (http://www.imoox.at) in February 2014. iMooX has a registered user base of over 10.000 participants [6, 8]. The desired goals behind iMooX were introducing Open Educational Resource (OER) courses and keeping pace with lifelong learning tracks [4]. In fact, each offered MOOC at iMooX is held within a corresponding discussion forum instead of the old-fashioned classroom, which serves as the main communication tool between students themselves from one side and students and teachers from the other side. Although the intercommunication in MOOC platforms lacks the direct impact,

C. Delgado Kloos et al. (Eds.): EMOOCs 2017, LNCS 10254, pp. 95–101, 2017.
DOI: 10.1007/978-3-319-59044-8_11

discussion forums remain the central venue for teacher-to-student interaction [1]. Therefore, forums need to work in a fast and dependable manner as well as in a user-friendly atmosphere in order to support the larger number of participants [10].

The article at hands aims at redesigning the iMooX MOOC discussion forums. The new design implements the newest web technologies such as gamification and looked at leveraging students' desire for socializing. The research study will determine whether or not the gamification elements can help increase the participation rate as well as shed the light on users' feedback on the new design. The motivation of this work came from the idea of increasing the students' engagement within MOOC variables and increasing the forum interactivity based on the Salmon's [10] *five-stage* models.

2 Research Design

The research design includes two main methods: prototyping and quantitative evaluation. The prototyping approach follows four steps: "Determine the needs of users", "Build the prototype", "Evaluate the prototype", and "Determine when finished" [11]. Determination of user needs was accomplished by conducting interviews and evaluation of data accumulated from the old forum. Subsequently, multiple prototypes were built, evaluated and tested with the help of users. Finally, user satisfaction was achieved and the process was accomplished according to the required view. The new design of the discussion forums followed the "gamethinking" process that involves users to solve problems using gamification elements [12]. We implemented the following four main mechanisms of gamification [5]: (a) rewards, (b) badges, (c) points, and (d) leaderboard. To evaluate the new design, we examined a course called "*Lernen im Netz*" that was offered in 2014 and 2016 respectively. The quantitative summary and evaluation were carried out using Learning Analytics. The iMooX Learning Analytics Prototype (iLAP) is a tool that offers a complete logging system for all MOOC variables in iMooX [6].

3 Implementation

The interface was restructured as shown in Fig. 1. The old design of the discussion forum is shown on the top part of the figure. It is based on a tree view clickable threads. The design is basic and any usage of images or other interactions (like private messaging, profile pictures, emoticons, etc.) could not be possible. Nevertheless, the new design in the bottom of Fig. 1 offers several interactive features. The users have the ability to make likes, set a favorite thread, upload profile picture, set up their own profiles, or set their personal preferences. In addition, the new design provides various gamification elements (see Fig. 2) that are intended to increase user engagement, enhance the user-friendly environment, and add fun to the communication channels of the MOOC platform.

Forum users can now obtain badges as well as see their progress bar and level. For example, if a user likes a thread for the first time, they obtain the badge "Like." Upon reaching level 2 they are allowed to upload a profile picture and have a different username color. Another motivational example is the progress bar. The design of the

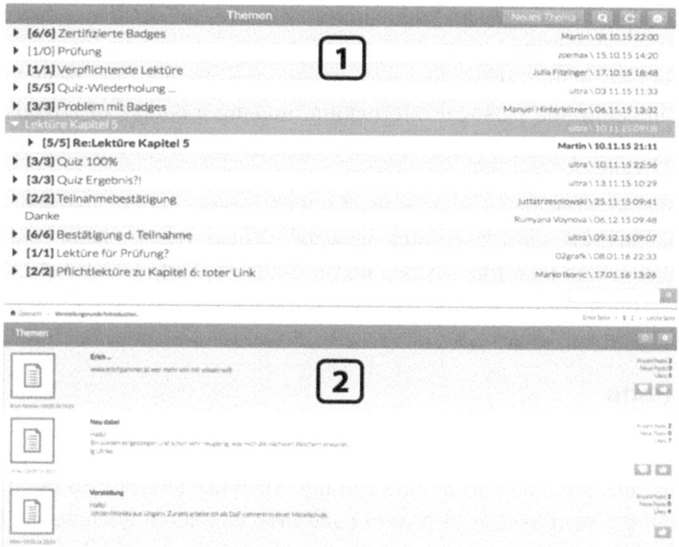

Fig. 1. iMooX MOOC platform discussion forum design. Top: the old design. Bottom: the new design.

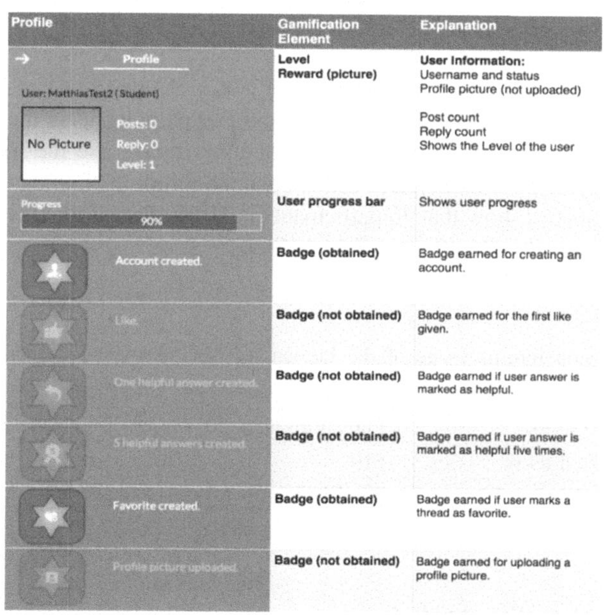

Fig. 2. A general overview of the available gamification elements that are offered in the new forum design of iMooX (profile view)

progress bar expresses a dynamic animation that shows the student's development to level up. The concept of the progress bar is to inform users on how convenient they are to completing tasks with a stamp of a percentage token. In this case, tasks like creating an account, updating the personal information, making a couple of threads likes, and having helpful answers. That is to say, each level gets harder and harder to reach and requires extra tasks to complete.

To encourage students to post in the MOOC forum, we created badges such as "One helpful answer" and "5 helpful answers". These badges label a student as a problem solver which therefore gives a hint to other students to ask help from. Other features are explained in Fig. 2.

4 Evaluation

We investigated two respectively offered courses "*Lernen im Netz 2014*" and "*Lernen im Netz 2016*" using the data from the Learning Analytics tool of iMooX (iLAP). Both MOOCs require a workload of (5 h/week) and they talk about learning on the Internet through the web in general, mobiles, social media, OER, and MOOCs. The courses lasted eight weeks and were offered in German language. Students who complete the MOOCs are credited with university European Credit Transfer and Accumulation System points (ECTS) and they get certificates at no cost.

4.1 General Stats

This part gives a general overview of both MOOCs. As described in Table 1, there were 605 registered users in the 2016 MOOC and 519 participants in the 2014 MOOC. In "*Lernen im Netz 2016*" MOOC, 39.83% of users didn't use the forum at all. In comparison, only 33.53% participants did not use the forum in "*Lernen im Netz 2014*". Furthermore, statistics show that 76 participants in 2016 were certified (12.56%) stands against 99 students (19.07%) in the 2014 MOOC.

Table 1. Discussion forums usage of the Lernen im Netz 2014 and Lernen im Netz 2016 MOOCs

Type of users	Lernen im Netz 2014	Lernen im Netz 2016
Registered users	519	605
Certified users (%)	99 (19.07%)	76 (12.56%)
Never used the forums (%)	33.53%	39.83%

4.2 Forum Interaction Analysis

We recorded user actions from the new forum of the "*Lernen im Netz 2016*" MOOC. As seen in Fig. 3, we recorded the following: there were 50 threads created, 67 answers written, 88 "Likes" given and 25 helpful answers posted. In total, there were 350 forum actions. Next, we compared both MOOC forum activities. In Fig. 4, we show a line plot of the average reading activity in both MOOCs subdivided into eight weeks long. While in Fig. 5, we show the average posting activity. Both figures are detailed in two line colors. The red line depicts the activities of "*Lernen im Netz 2014*" MOOC, while the blue line depicts the activities of "*Lernen im Netz 2016*" MOOC. Reading and writing activities are nearly identical for both MOOCs. However, there is a huge peak in the pre-MOOC of week1 credited to "*Lernen im Netz 2014*". Moreover, Fig. 4 shows that readings in the last week of the 2016 MOOC have nearly tripled the readings of the seventh week. Another key observation is that Fig. 5 shows the writing in the second and third week of the 2014 MOOC was high in comparison to the following weeks. In fact, our forum engagement results are in the line with a recent MOOC study by Coetzee et al. [2], where the authors found that 68% of students interact with videos or quizzes but never visited the MOOC forum.

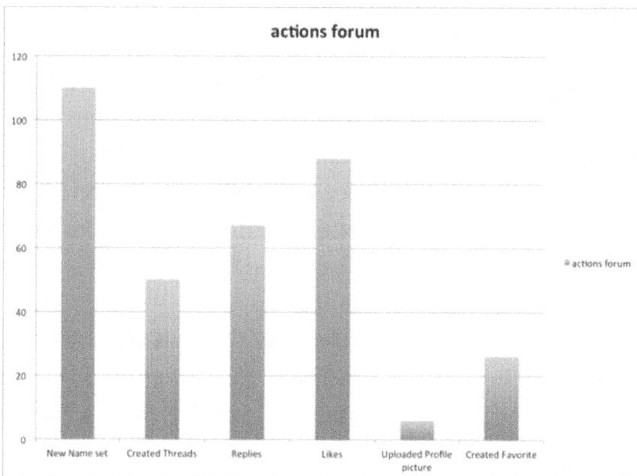

Fig. 3. The new discussion forum actions stats

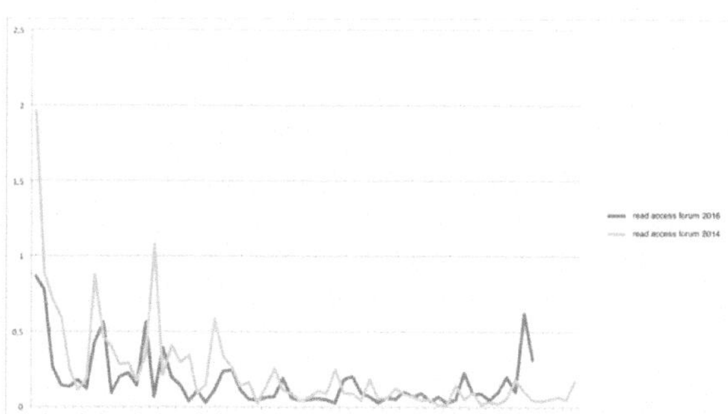

Fig. 4. Reading in forums of the 2014 and 2016 MOOCs (Color figure online)

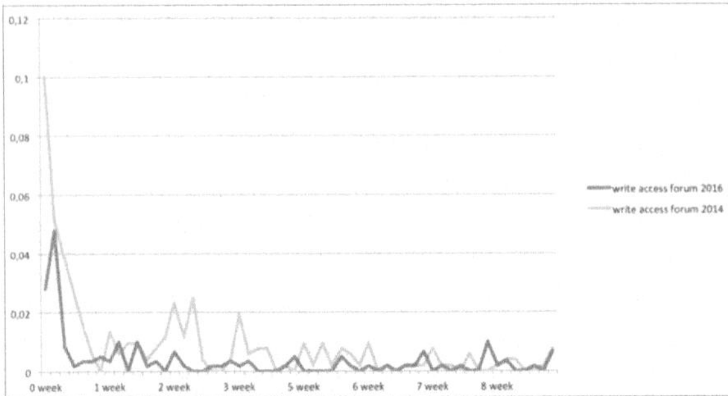

Fig. 5. Writing in forums of the 2014 and 2016 MOOCs (Color figure online)

5 Discussion and Conclusion

Discussion forums play a major role within MOOCs as a channel of communication between students and teachers. Recording students' interaction in forums could indicate an early dropout [3, 7]. Thus, there were several purposes that pushed us to redesign the discussion forums besides the above-mentioned reason. The old forum design of iMooX lacked personalization of preferences, usability, and interactivity. We looked at increasing student engagement through employing gamification elements in this educational context (MOOCs). Based on one of the offered MOOCs in 2014 and 2016, to our best, we tried to evaluate our new design.

The previous analysis showed that forum activity was nearly the same for both MOOCs. In fact, the difference of the rewarded ECTS points for both MOOCs might have left a psychological impact on the students' activity in the MOOC in general and in the forums in particular. Another explanation for the slightly lower involvement might belong to the reasons of the iMooX huge advertisement back in 2014 when iMooX was first launched. That is, Lernen im Netz 2014 MOOC was one of the few offered courses at that time. In addition, we saw that writing in forums in 2016 was, to some extent, lower than the 2014 MOOC. After a quick comparison of the content between the two forums, we saw that students of the 2014 MOOC were more active, however, by asking technical questions. As a matter of fact, this belongs to the dissatisfaction of use of the old forum. Although the results were not very promising, we believe that the new design is better than the older design since the students and the teacher of the examined MOOC agreed that the new design offers usability, flexibility, and is fun. They further said that the gamification elements of the new discussion forum have brought their motivation and proposed exciting features. However, further evidences of the new forum design can be collected in "*Lernen im Netz 2017*" MOOC.

References

1. Brinton, C.G., Chiang, M., Jain, S., Lam, H., Liu, Z., Wong, F.M.F.: Learning about social learning in MOOCs: from statistical analysis to generative model. IEEE Trans. Learn. Technol. **7**(4), 346–359 (2014)
2. Coetzee, D., Fox, A., Hearst, M.A., Hartmann, B.: Should your MOOC forum use a reputation system? In: Proceedings of the 17th ACM Conference on Computer Supported Cooperative Work and Social Computing, pp. 1176–1187. ACM (2014)
3. Ferguson, R., Clow, D.: Examining engagement: analysing learner subpopulations in massive open online courses (MOOCs). In: Proceedings of LAK 2015, pp. 51–58 (2015)
4. Fischer, H., Dreisiebner, S., Franken, O., Ebner, M., Kopp, M., Köhler, T.: Revenue vs. costs of MOOC platforms. Discussion of business models for xMOOC providers based on empirical findings and experiences during implementation of the project iMOOX. In: Proceedings of ICERI 2014, pp. 2991–3000. IATED (2014)
5. Gunawardhana, P., Palaniappan, S.: Gamification. J. Adv. Appl. Sci. (JAAS) **3**(02), 51–58 (2005). AROPUB
6. Khalil, M., Ebner, M.: What massive open online course (MOOC) stakeholders can learn from learning analytics? In: Spector, M.J., Lockee, B.B., Childress, M.D. (eds.) Learning Design and Technology. Springer International Publishing, Cham (2016). doi:10.1007/978-3-319-17727-4_3-1
7. Khalil, M., Ebner, M.: Learning analytics in MOOCs: can data improve students retention and learning? In: Proceedings of EdMedia 2016, pp. 569–576, AACE, Vancouver (2016)
8. Kopp, M., Ebner, M.: iMooX Publikationen rund um das Pionierprojekt. Druckerei, Verlag Mayer GmbH, and Co KG, Weinitzen (2015). ISBN 978-3-8533-259-7
9. McAuley, A., Stewart, B., Siemens, G., Cormier, D.: The MOOC model for digital practice. Research report (2010). http://www.davecormier.com/edblog/wp-content/uploads/MOOC_Final.pdf. Accessed 07 Jan 2016
10. Salmon, G.: E-Moderating. The Key to Teaching and Learning Online. RoutledgeFarmer, Abingdon (2007)
11. Vasylyna, N.: 4 Steps For Successful UI Prototyping. Article (2011). http://blog.qatestlab.com/2011/02/28/4-steps-for-successful-ui-prototyping/. Accessed 02 Dec 2016
12. Zichermann, G., Cunningham, C.: Gamification by Design, vol. 1. O'Reilly and Associates, Sebastopol (2011)

A MOOC-Based Flipped Class: Lessons Learned from the Orchestration Perspective

María Fernanda Rodríguez[1(✉)], Josefina Hernández Correa[1], Mar Pérez-Sanagustín[1(✉)], Julio A. Pertuze[1], and Carlos Alario-Hoyos[2]

[1] School of Engineering, Pontificia Universidad Católica de Chile, Av. Vicuña Mackenna, 4860 Macul, Santiago (RM), Chile
{mfrodri3, jmhernal, mar.perez, japertuz}@uc.cl
[2] Department of Telematic Engineering, Universidad Carlos III de Madrid, Av. Universidad 30, Madrid, Leganés, Spain
calahoy@it.uc3m.es

Abstract. This paper presents the results of a case study about the orchestration process of a MOOC-based flipped-class, and the students' adoption of this teaching practice. The study was conducted on a mandatory third-year course on Organizational Behavior in the School of Engineering at Pontificia Universidad Católica de Chile with 346 students. The analysis shows that students pay more attention in class and are more participative, even though this means more work and study. Also, implementing this strategy is much more work for the teacher than giving a traditional face-to-face lecture, but the students pay more attention in class and are more participative. Furthermore, up to 96% of the students were active in the MOOC under study before class, especially watching the video-lectures, and students who were more active in the MOOC showed better scores on the course exams than those less active, a difference that proves to be statistically significant. These findings suggest that a MOOC-based flipped class is a good solution to promote student's motivation and learning, but the implementation of this teaching strategy is delicate and must be very well planned. We provide a list of lessons learned about five key factors to be considered when orchestrating a MOOC-based flipped classroom: design, management, awareness, adaptation and role of actors.

Keywords: Orchestration · MOOC · Flipped class · Engineering

1 Introduction

The production of Massive Open Online Courses (MOOCs) has been on the rise [1], but producing them is complex and expensive for the institutions involved, since it requires new infrastructure, work teams, time and the coordination of several participants [2]. In order to obtain the maximum benefit of the MOOCs, one of the approaches that many Universities are following is incorporating MOOCs as part of their traditional curriculum and teaching practices through Blended Learning (BL) practices [3, 4]. BL refers to the combination of face-to-face (f2f) experiences with activities outside the classroom, generally offered in technological formats [5, 6]. One BL approach that became more popular because of its student-centered nature is

C. Delgado Kloos et al. (Eds.): EMOOCs 2017, LNCS 10254, pp. 102–112, 2017.
DOI: 10.1007/978-3-319-59044-8_12

the *flipped class*. This methodology presents two components: (1) individual instruction before classes, generally supported by technology; and (2) interactive group activities during class, focused on problem solving and brainstorming [7]. However, implementing these types of initiatives is not easy and involves both a methodological change for the teacher and a change of mindset in students.

In order to address these challenges, both practitioners and researchers have made an effort to report MOOC-based flipped classroom initiatives and their results. For example, authors in [3] present six strategies for combining f2f teaching time with work time in a MOOC. Also, authors in [4] present the results of using a MOOC in a f2f course as an effective mechanism to improve students' learning significantly. These initiatives are good examples for teachers' understanding of how MOOCs can be reused in flipped learning practices. However, they lack a systematic analysis on the factors that teachers need to orchestrate to succeed [8]. Therefore, there is a need of a more systematic analysis of current MOOC-based flipped classroom initiatives, as well as guides and models to support teachers in their orchestration process.

Orchestrating (technology-enhanced) learning has been defined as the coordination of a multiplicity of activities, contexts and media, as well as learning processes, technologies and the adaptation of activities to the classroom context [9]. Under this definition, authors in [10] define five key aspects to be considered for orchestrating an educational setting that involves the use of technology: (1) **Design**, understood as the preparation and organization of the learning activities before implementation; (2) **Management**, which refers to the coordination of activities developed during the class implementation (timelines, group work); (3) **Awareness**, understood as the perception of what happens in the learning situation (teacher monitoring, assessments, and awareness); (4) **Adaptation**, referred to how to deal with unexpected situations, and adapting the activity to students' progress; (5) **Role of the actors**, understood as having clarity about each of the above.

The objective of this study is to provide **a systematic analysis of a MOOC-based flipped class in order to gain insights about its orchestration process and the students' adoption of the initiative**. To meet this goal, this paper presents the results of a case study conducted at the Pontifical Catholic University of Chile (PUC) with a course of 346 students. Specifically, we describe lessons learned about the orchestration that was conducted to flip the course, as well as the students' adoption of the experience and their learning outcomes.

2 Case Study

2.1 Context

The study was conducted in the Organizational Behavior (OB) course taught to engineering undergraduate students at PUC. The OB course is mandatory for all engineering students and is one of the largest courses taught at the university (approximately 350 students per class). The course aims at providing general knowledge of organizational matters and thus content breadth, not depth, is sought. During the last two years, instructors of the course have tried different strategies to promote class participation. However, the results of these initiatives did not result in a significant increment of students' motivation, participation or learning outcomes.

To address these problems and make the classes more participative and student-centered, for the second semester of 2016 the instructor decided to implement a flipped class, making use of an existing MOOC named "*Gestión de Organizaciones Efectivas*" (Effective Organizations Management), which he had created and launched about a year earlier in Coursera. The objective of the existing MOOC is to provide general knowledge on the factors that guide the success of an organization. The MOOC aims at a broad audience, and no prior knowledge on management is required to enroll.

2.2 Activity Orchestration

A total of six OB classes were 'flipped', given that their contents were aligned with the MOOC modules. Each class lasted 90 min, and consists of a lecture (mostly videos), a formative quiz, a graded quiz (not available until the time of the f2f class), and supplementary materials (readings and cases).

The orchestration of each session was designed as a sequence of phases before, during and after the class (see Table 1). **Before the class** students had to read and watch the video lectures in the MOOC. The objective of this phase was to promote the students' self-study and get prepared for the activities of the second phase. **During the class**, sessions were structured into 3 parts: (1) *Evaluation*, where students had to answer a graded quiz to evaluate their work before class; (2) *Hands On*, where students were organized into groups and worked on activities prepared by the teacher, and (3) *Metacognition*, the phase where students had to reflect about what they had learned. Parts (2) and (3) varied from session to session. The *Hands On* phase was organized following two collaborative learning patterns: Pyramid and Jigsaw. In the Pyramid, students start working individually on a case study and propose an initial solution. Then, they are grouped to compare and propose a final solution to share with the class. In the Jigsaw, the entire class is divided in 4 groups and each group is assigned a particular sub-problem of a big case that has to be solved individually. Then, students working in the same sub-problem are grouped in order to discuss and exchange ideas. Finally, students of each group (sub-problem of the case) are grouped with students from another sub-problem, and together, they must propose a final solution to the whole problem. In the Pyramid, groups were formed voluntarily by the students, and in the Jigsaw, they were formed randomly by the teacher. The *Metacognition* phase was organized in two different ways: (1) one or more general questions using *clickers*, and (2) *wrap up discussion* between the students and the teacher. **After class**, students were invited to review the work performed by their classmates (co-evaluations).

2.3 Research Questions

The main objective of this study was to gain insights about the orchestration of the flipped class intervention, as well as of the students' adoption of the initiative and its effectiveness in terms of learning outcomes; all this has the aim of extracting a set of lessons learned for future interventions. Accordingly, we defined two research questions:

Table 1. Orchestration and phases of class.

	Design	Management	Awareness	Adaptation	Role of actors
Phase: before class					
Self-study	MOOC materials	Students had access to the MOOC material of the whole course on demand	Students had the information about what activities they perform and some feedback from quizzes Teacher had the feedback of the students quizzes	Students could adapt their study according to their needs and interests	Students had access to the material Teacher organized the content
Phase: during class					
Evaluation	Quiz in the MOOC platform	Students had access to the MOOC quiz	Students: feedback from the platform Teacher: scores in real time	Teacher adapted the quiz format for students who could not access the platform	Teacher activated the quiz Students took the quiz
Hands On Case	Pyramid or Jigsaw. Groups were sometimes formed randomly by the teacher and sometimes by the students	Students had access to the case delivered through the MOOC or printed Teacher guided the workflow	*No awareness was provided*	Teacher adapted the class according to the students' interventions	Student analyzed case in groups Teacher managed the working time period.
Metacognition	Clicker activity or Wrap up	Students were facilitated with clickers when needed Teacher managed discussion and proposed general questions	Students answered the questions with the clickers Teacher received the answers in real time	Student argued through votes with clickers Teacher adapted the class according to the students' interventions	Student answered the questions Assistant coordinated the clickers Teacher coordinated the debate
Phase: after class					
Self-reflection	Peer review activity	Peer review activity that students access through the MOOC	Student peer reviewed the work performed by their group mates Teacher used and knew report of peer-review	Teacher generated questions for the peer-review activity from the workflow and the argument types	Student sent peer review Teacher received and used the information about peer review

- **RQ1. What are the teacher's orchestration actions before, during and after each class from the design to the enactment of the activity?** This question aims at extracting information about the phases of the orchestration process.
- **RQ2. What is the students' adoption of the flipped class teaching strategy?** This question aims at studying the students' use of the MOOC in terms of their interactions with the course content to better understand how and when they use it, and in terms of the learning outcomes.

2.4 Participants

The flipped class intervention took place between August 12th and September 5th, 2016. The OB course was taken by 346 students of different engineering majors. Students were generally in the 3rd year of their studies and approximately 21 years old. Classes took place in a large auditorium, with sufficient room for all students and WiFi Internet connection capabilities for a massive number of people.

2.5 Methods: Data Collection and Analysis

The data collection consisted of qualitative and quantitative data using different instruments. Table 2 shows the instruments used for collecting the data. The analysis uses a Mixed Method Approach, with emphasis on qualitative data [11]. For interpreting all the information, we used a Triangulation Method as verification technique and credibility of the data [12].

To address RQ1 about the orchestration process, three researchers participated in a qualitative analysis of the [T, AC-Interview], [S, A-Focus] and [T-Timeline]. The

Table 2. Data collection instruments and labels used to refer to them along the paper.

Instruments labels	Description
Qualitative data	
[T-Interview]	Semi-structured interview with the teacher of the OB course
[AC-Interview]	Semi-structured interview with the coordinator assistant of the OB course
[S-Focus]	Focus group with ten students of the OB course
[A-Focus]	Focus group with six teacher assistants of the OB course
[T-Timeline]	Timeline proposed by the teacher for each class
Quantitative data	
[MOOC Interactions]	The MOOC logs give information about all the movements each user does in the platform. We defined an interaction as each time a student reviewed or completed any activity (lecture, quiz or supplement) in the MOOC
[S-Grades]	Students' grades in the first course evaluation (Exam #1, taken between the 3rd and 4th flipped class). The exam contemplated a scale from 1.0 (Lowest grade) to 7.0 (Highest grade). Students pass the exams if they get a score of 4.0 or higher

analysis was carried out using an open coding technique supported by the NVivo software. To address RQ2 about the students' adoption of the flipped class experience and their behavior in the platform we analyzed two things. First, the number of interactions with the platform registered in each flipped class, before and after the class. Second, the students' activity with the course content: lectures, quizzes and complementary material. To study the students' learning outcomes, first we calculated the amount of interactions [MOOC Interactions] each student had during Modules 1, 2 and 3 (contents of Exam #1), and grouped them into three groups of equal size (1/3 of the sample), resulting in the "most-active", the "regular-active" and the "least-active" students according to their interactions in the platform in modules 1, 2 and 3. After classifying the students, we conducted a T-test analysis to statistically compare the students' scores and the group where they were classified in relation to their activity in the MOOC.

3 Results

This section reports on the results obtained from the analysis to address the two research questions (Subsects. 3.1 and 3.2). The results in each subsection are numbered as RX.Y, where X is the number of the research question addressed and Y the specific result. In the Sect. 4 we cross-analyze the results found in each of the questions to extract lessons learned about the whole orchestration process.

3.1 Orchestration Actions

We organize the results about the teachers' orchestration actions according to the 5 aspects of orchestration defined in the literature and based on the guiding questions for each of them.

We identified three results regarding **Design.** First, the structure of using videos before the class complemented with lectures and group activities during the class is motivating for the students [R1.1]. Evidence from students' focus group and assistants' interviews support this result: *"The MOOC lectures allow you to have a visual support while you are studying, since you are hearing, but also watching."* [S-Focus], *"The videos are interesting (…) they provide a summary of all the content."* [A-Focus]. Second, the design process is very demanding for the teacher, but not for the assistant professors [R1.2]. The teacher stated: *"You have to be motivated, because it is more work, much more work (than a traditional session)* [T-Interview; A-Focus]. And third, the characteristics of the physical space where the flipped class takes place conditions the design and should be taken into account [R1.3]. *"The classroom space (…) does not give the facilities for discussion, there is a lot of noise and it is not easy to speak face to face"* [A-Focus].

Regarding **Management** aspects, we identified two main results. First, the time assigned for discussion in the design phase was insufficient [R1.4]. *"The initial quiz is time consuming; there is only an hour or less for the discussion and a closure at the end. There was very little time"* [AC-Interview; T-Timeline]. In addition, the teacher and the assistants agreed that the time reserved for the quiz could be used for group discussion [T-Interview]: *"the quizzes (...) it would be good if the students could answer them before the class, to save time for discussion"*. Second, both students and assistants agreed that when assigning random groups for working in the class, the students the students tend to get prepare more [R1.5]: "*when the groups were random, more students come to class having watched the video-lectures and prepared the readings"* [AC-Interview].

Regarding the **Awareness**, two results were found. First, students are more motivated and active in these types of methodologies than in traditional ones [R1.6]. The teacher and the assistants agreed: *"I saw the students paying more attention than in other classes, more interested and participative in the discussion"* [T-Interview]; *"Compared with other semesters, students were more participative (...) this methodology encouraged them from the beginning to participate, at the end, they were used to it"* [A-Focus]. Second, for both the teacher and the assistants it was hard to monitor what students were doing while working in groups [R1.7] [T-Interview]: *"I did not have the details about what they were talking, I always had doubts"* [A-Focus]: *"had to go group by group, so we need many more assistants for each class"*.

Regarding **Adaptation** aspects, we identified three results. First, teacher motivation for innovation led him to transform his teaching [R1.8]: *"I like to vary (...) I am willing to innovate and do different things"* [T-Interview]. Second, designed classes were modified to follow a Jigsaw pattern because this was the model that the students preferred the most [R1.9] [S-Focus]. Third, the teacher decided to added a quiz at the beginning of each class, so that he could monitor what the students knew and to force them to arrive on time to the class [R1.10]. *"In my previous courses, I invited once a former minister of State, and students arrived 45 min late. This didn't happen in this new format"* [T-Interview].

Regarding the **Role of Actors,** we found that the teacher plays an essential role in structuring the classes before going to class, while the assistants are crucial to ensure the coordination of the activities during the class so that students follow the class [R1.11]. Also, we found that the students need to be responsible and follow the whole instructions effectively and follow the course [R1.12].

3.2 Students' Adoption of the Flipped Class Initiative

R2.1. 78% of students (on average) interacted with the course contents before the class and 63% interacted with the course contents during the class (Table 1)**. The first modules present many more interactions than the latter ones.** Students' interaction with the platform decreases as the course advances. Specifically, 95% of the students interacted with the course contents of Modules 1, 2 or 3 before class and only

Table 3. Number of students that interact with MOOC modules before and during class.

	Module 1	Module 2	Module 3	Module 4	Module 5	Module 6
Before class	332 (96%)	332 (96%)	320 (92%)	259 (75%)	188 (54%)	191 (55%)
During class	288 (83%)	305 (88%)	124 (36%)	275 (79%)	42 (12%)	274 (79%)

61% interacted before class with Modules 4, 5 or 6 (on average). Table 3 shows the number of students that interacted with each module before or during class.

R2.2. Although all the content of the course was available in the MOOC from day one, most of the students accessed this content sequentially, in parallel with the f2f course curriculum. Before class students accessed the MOOC content corresponding to the content that they were going to work on in the f2f class. Instead, during the class, the access to the content is more chaotic, accessing only the content in which they are interested in order to solve the activities in class (Fig. 1).

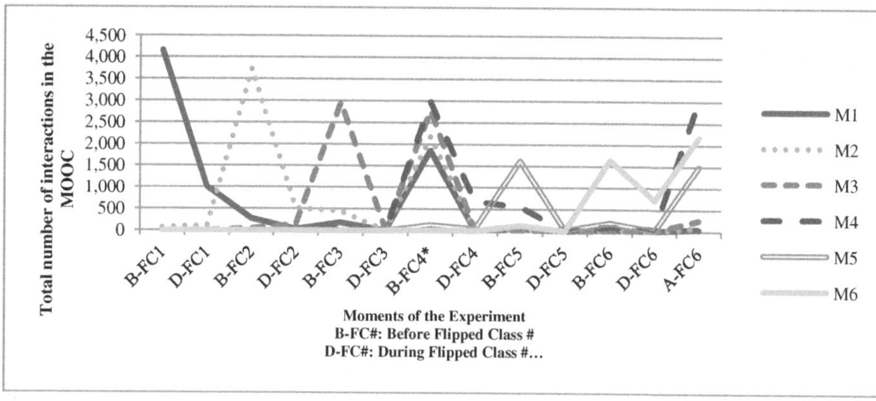

Fig. 1. Number of completed or reviewed course activities in the MOOC's different modules vs. the moment of the experiment.

R2.3. Students reviewed lectures much more than quizzes and supplements material, especially before the exams. As it can be seen in Fig. 2, the interactions with the video-lectures are more than three times the interactions with the other

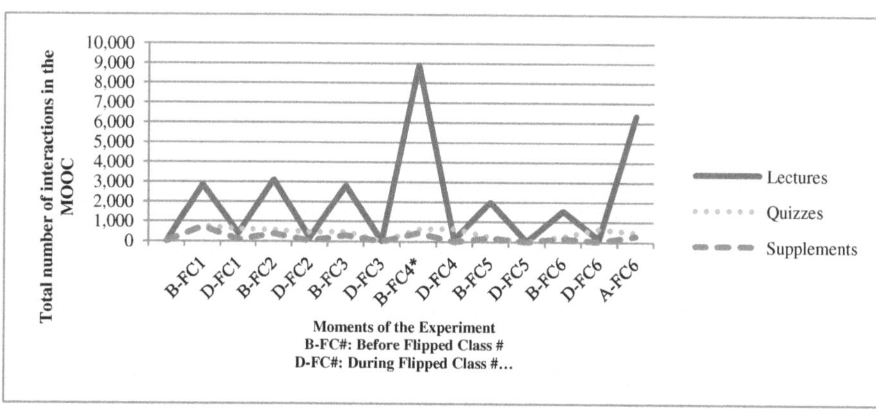

Fig. 2. Number of completed or reviewed course activities in the MOOC's different course items VS. the moment of the intervention

resources before each class (when the students were preparing for the lectures beforehand as should occur in a flipped class).

R2.4. Students who were more active in the MOOC showed better scores in their exam and this difference is statistically significant. Table 2 shows that the least-active students in the MOOC have an average exam grade of 4.39, whereas the regular-active and most-active ones have an average of 4.71 and 4.66 respectively. This differnce between the least-active group and the other two group is statistically significant (Table 4).

Table 4. Exam Grade differences regarding if the students were active or not in the MOOC.

Activity level	# of students	Interactions in modules 1–3 (average per person)	Exam grade (average)	Standard deviation of grade
Least-active	115	30.24	4.39	1.09
Regular-active	115	54.67	4.71	0.81
Most-active	116	99.88	4.66	0.70

T-student test

Comparison between	P-Value
Least-active & regular-active	0.01
Regular-active & most-active	0.06
Least-active & most-active	0.03

4 Lessons Learned and Conclusions

The lessons reported in this section were obtained from the cross-analysis of the qualitative and quantitative results. First, in the **Design** phase, we learned that (1) a well design flipped classroom based on a MOOC is well adopted by the students [R1.2], fosters their motivation in the course [R1.2], and promotes active participation through cases and practical activities [R2.3]. Similar results have been obtained in previous studies [13–15]. Moreover, our results show that those students who interact more with the MOOC earned better grades [R2.4]. This result is especially interesting, since only a few studies report learning outcomes from these experiences [4, 7]. (2) The classes should be designed to have the same workload each in order to keep high the levels of participation throughout the whole course [R2.2]. (3) Teachers need to set aside time to redesign a course like this, which involves much more work than a traditional one. Second, regarding **Management**, we learned that (1) it is necessary to schedule long periods for group discussions in the class (especially if classes are massive), and organize the individual quizzes to be done at home to save time for discussion [R1.4]. (2) Grouping the students randomly to perform the activities in class is more effective at keeping them more active and prepare the class better [R1.5]. Third, regarding **Awareness**, we learned that it is necessary to promote a culture of active participation from day one [R1.6; R2.1]. Fourth, regarding **Adaptation**, the teacher should be able to adapt the class to the timings of the students [R1.8], but also to the data obtained from quizzes conducted in-class [R1.10]. In fact, having constant evaluations is highly recommended to know about the students' progress [15]. In addition, to adapt the structure of the class, it is fundamental to consider the awareness of all actors involved [R1.6; R1.8; R1.9; R1.10]. As pointed out in previous studies [14], the implementation of BL experiences requires the teacher to be flexible in the design and management of the activity, and for the students to take an active role during the whole process. Fifth and finally, regarding the **Role of the Actors**, the teacher and the assistants have a fundamental role in the design and management of each class [R1.2; R1.4; R1.11], whereas the students will adopt an active role during them class if they follow the structure that is proposed [R1.1; R1.6; R1.12].

In conclusion, this paper has shown that the orchestration of a flipped class reusing MOOCs is a complex process that involves many variables and dimensions that need to be taken into account in order for each class to be a success. Also, teachers should be ready to spend more time in the preparation of the classes and face unexpected situations that would need to be solved in runtime. However, the benefits of this effort benefit include raising the motivation of the students, getting them more involved in their own learning process, and, in some cases, improving their grades. Some limitations we encountered were the difficulty to properly observe and analyze each group discussion given the number of students VS. the number of assistants, and that we did not have more MOOC modules to flip more classes of the course. This paper, however, is only the beginning of a set of works that aim at exploring which are the factors and main considerations that practitioners need to take into account to conduct MOOC-based flipped classroom experiences.

Acknowledgements. This work has been partially supported by the Fondecyt (11150231), the Clover 2030 Engineering Strategy (14ENI2-26862), the Erasmus+ Programme of the European Union, MOOC-Maker (561533-EPP-1-2015-1-ES-EPPKA2-CBHE-JP), SHEILA (562080-EPP-1-2015-BE-EPPKA3-PI-FORWARD) and COMPETEN-SEA (574212-EPP-1-2016-1- NL-EPPKA2-CBHE-JP), by eMadrid Excellence Network (S2013/ICE-2715), and the RESET (TIN2014-53199-C3-1-R) and FPDI-2013-17411.

References

1. Bras, I.: Los mooc en números, un análisis para comenzar la reflexión **17**, 1–16 (2016)
2. Kloos, C.D., Alario-hoyos, C., Pérez-sanagustín, M.: Tips and techniques for MOOC production, vol. 37, p. 28911 (2015)
3. Kloos, C.D., Muñoz-Merino, P.J., Alario-Hoyos, C., Estévez Ayres, I., Fernández-Panadero, C.: Mixing and blending MOOC technologies with face-to-face pedagogies. In: IEEE Global Engineering Education Conference EDUCON, pp. 967–971 (2015)
4. Rayyan, S., Fredericks, C., Colvin, K.F., Liu, A., Teodorescu, R., Barrantes, A., Pawl, A., Seaton, D.T., Pritchard, D.E.: A MOOC based on blended pedagogy. J. Comput. Assist. Learn. **32**(3), 190–201 (2016)
5. O'Flaherty, J., Phillips, C.: The use of flipped classrooms in higher education: a scoping review. Internet High. Educ. **25**, 85–95 (2015)

6. van Niekerk, J., Webb, P.: The effectiveness of brain-compatible blended learning material in the teaching of programming logic. Comput. Educ. **103**, 16–27 (2016)
7. Njie-Carr, V.P., Ludeman, E., Lee, M.C., Dordunoo, D., Trocky, N.M., Jenkins, L.S.: An integrative review of flipped classroom teaching models in nursing education. J. Prof. Nurs. **33**(2), 133–144 (2017)
8. Martinez-Maldonado, R., Martinez, R.: Seeing learning analytics tools as orchestration technologies: towards supporting learning activities across physical and digital spaces. In: CEUR Workshop Proceedings, vol. 1601, pp. 70–73 (2016)
9. Prieto, L.P., Dimitriadis, Y., Asensio-Pérez, J.I., Looi, C.-K.: Orchestration in Learning Technology Research: Evaluation of a conceptual framework. Res. Learn. Technol. **23** (1063519), 1–15 (2015)
10. Prieto, L.P., Holenko Dlab, M., Gutiérrez, I., Abdulwahed, M., Balid, W.: Orchestrating technology enhanced learning: a literature review and a conceptual framework. Int. J. Technol. Enhanc. Learn. **3**(6), 583–598 (2011)
11. Creswell, J.W., Clark, V.L.P.: Designing and Conducting Mixed Methods Research. Google Books (2011)
12. Santiago-Delefosse, M., Gavin, A., Bruchez, C., Roux, P., Stephen, S.L.: Quality of qualitative research in the health sciences: analysis of the common criteria present in 58 assessment guidelines by expert users. Soc. Sci. Med. **148**, 142–151 (2016)
13. Bekele, T.A.: Motivation and Satisfaction in internet-supported learning environments: a review. Educ. Technol. Soc. **13**(2), 116–127 (2010)
14. Spanjers, A.E., Könings, K.D., Leppink, J., Verstegen, D.M.L., de Jong, N., Czabanowska, K., van Merriënboer, J.J.G.: The promised land of blended learning: quizzes as a moderator. Educ. Res. Rev. **15**, 59–74 (2015)
15. Velegol, S.B., Zappe, S.E., Mahoney, E.M.I.L.Y.: The evolution of a flipped classroom: evidence-based recommendations. Adv. Eng. Educ. **4**(3), 1–37 (2015)

An International Collaboration in the Design Experience of a MOOC Series

Susanna Sancassani(✉), Paola Corti(✉), and Valeria Baudo(✉)

Politecnico di Milano – Servizio METID, Milan, Italy
{susanna.sancassani,paola.corti, valeria.baudo}@polimi.it

Abstract. Is it possible to accelerate didactical innovation processes by building new kinds of collaboration between different institutions in the Higher Education scenario? Using MOOCs as a lever to share experiences and co-design learning paths might be one effective way to it. The experience of Polimi Open Knowledge and the "MOOCs for Teachers" series about didactical innovation is the focus of this paper, which aims at giving evidence of the crucial role played by the collaboration among institutions and individual teachers in building new learning strategies for the Higher Education.

Keywords: Collaborative design · Knowledge sharing · Instructional design · MOOCs · Didactical innovation · Kolb's learning cycle · Experiential learning

1 Introduction

This paper gives an answer about how Massive Open Online Courses (from now on MOOCs) and Open Educational Resources (from now on OERs) could accelerate didactical innovation processes, by providing the opportunity of building new kinds of collaboration between different institutions in the Higher Education scenario able to overcome disciplinary and organizational boundaries.

We performed a literature search, in order to investigate the state of the art about the topic. Our focus was to find similar experiences about collaborative instructional design in MOOCs development. We went through the published literature (performing a search on Scopus Database, ISI Web of Science and Google Scholar using the keywords "collaborative design" AND MOOCs); we searched the grey literature, too.

The results do not focus on collaboration during the instructional design phase, but mainly on the collaboration among learners who are participating a course [2, 4, 6].

They don't focus on the collaboration among instructional designers during the creation of a new MOOC, either, and no literature seems to exist about international collaboration in the same phase among different universities.

So, the experience described in this paper seems to be at least one of the first examples focusing on international collaboration among Higher Education Institutions in the MOOC design process: it is about the experience Politecnico di Milano shares with different universities in the design of a series of MOOCs, and in the design of the first two MOOCs in it. The series is named "MOOCs for Teachers", the MOOCs are "To Flip or Not To Flip" and "Using OERs in Teaching".

C. Delgado Kloos et al. (Eds.): EMOOCs 2017, LNCS 10254, pp. 113–119, 2017.
DOI: 10.1007/978-3-319-59044-8_13

2 "MOOCs for Teachers" Series

May MOOCs in general represent a chance to foster collaboration between teachers and instructional designers, coming from different countries and different cultures?

"MOOCs for Teachers" series is the result of a partnership between METID, the service of Politecnico di Milano (Italy) devoted to e-learning and e-collaboration (http://www.metid.polimi.it) and Université Numérique Ingénierie et Technologie-UNIT (France), the national French institution in charge of the development of digital strategies for the Engineering Universities. The partnership is aimed at contributing to the design, production and dissemination of MOOCs about didactical innovation, whose main target are teachers of higher education institutions.

MOOCs for Teachers series represents an example of international collaboration during the design phase. This series is based on four MOOCs, two of them already online – "To Flip or Not To Flip", about flipped classroom methodology, and "Using Open Educational Resources in Teaching" – and two of them to be developed and launched during 2017. They will focus on active learning methodologies and new strategies for learning assessment. Polimi Open Knowledge - POK (www.pok.polimi.it) is the MOOCs platform designed by METID on the basis of Open edX. POK hosts this series of MOOCs, together with many others, organized in different series.

The MOOCs of this series are connected to each other. The flipped classroom methodology, in fact, takes advantage of OERs to be studied especially before class (but also to be suggested after class); active learning methodologies may be adopted during class time; a reflection about new assessment strategies (whether formative or summative) is needed, in order to support learning (during class time) and to measure learning outcomes achieved (both during and mainly after class time), in innovative teaching-learning settings (Fig. 1).

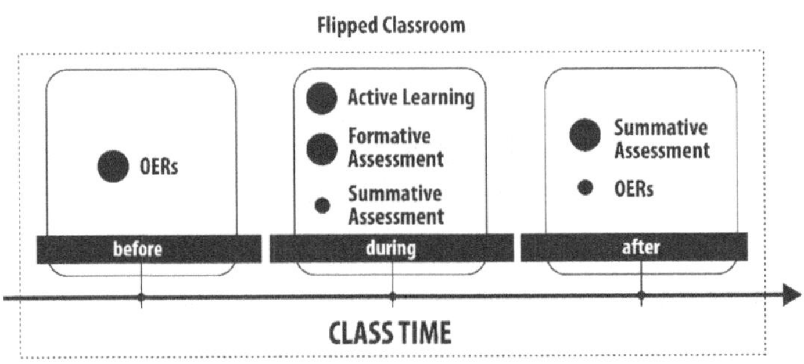

Fig. 1. A representation of the relation between the topics of MOOCs for Teachers.

Since the very generation of the series, Politecnico di Milano strongly believed in the opportunity to involve other Universities and individual teachers in order to discuss and design the pedagogical approach to be transversally applied in all the MOOCs of this series and to share ideas and approaches with professionals and experts coming from other academic contexts.

Politecnico di Milano thus invited UNIT consortium to join the project in order to work together at different levels, choosing between the mere endorsement of the project in itself, or a participation in the collection of digital contents, or the design of the MOOCs in themselves, as preferred.

Through some online and face-to-face meetings, Politecnico di Milano and UNIT reached the following expected results:

- to sign a Memorandum of Understanding between the partners, open to sharing and reusing contents in an OER perspective;
- to define a common strategy about the development of contents' structure, according to partners' different competencies;
- to share a pedagogical perspective, consistent both with the target users (teachers) and the innovative approaches to be focused, starting from experiences (coming from participants themselves and collected from testimonials by the staff involved in the MOOC design) in order to build knowledge and to enable practical didactical design skills.

After a discussion with the partners, the most consistent approach with this attitude was focused to be Kolb's Learning Cycle [3] which starts from concrete experiences, to reflective observation in order to review the experiences, then passes through abstract conceptualization in order to learn from experiences, and ends with active experimentation of the lesson learned.

The MOOCs in the series (two at the moment) are thus built in a collaborative way, counting on the contribution of experts and experimenters coming from all over the world. Their contributions are the core of the MOOC structure, which starts from experience and comes to experimentation, going around the entire Kolb's Experiential Learning Cycle Model.

It was agreed to let the participants free to choose their own path in the whole series of MOOCs. So these are the available paths: the informative path, which requires only a final test; the active path, which proposes different activities to support reflection and deep understanding; the collaborative path, in which participants are invited to share their experiences and their evaluations and reconstructions of meaning, and much more. Participants can shift from one path to the others whenever they want.

3 "To Flip Or Not To Flip" MOOC

The first MOOC of the series, "To Flip or Not To Flip", is about flipped classroom methodology. It was firstly released at the beginning of 2016.

We started with UNIT partners from a shared design scheme, applying the constructive alignment methodology [1]: for each general objective we defined specific learning objectives and suggested specific activities to achieve them. This scheme was built collaboratively and updated each time the design team focused on a specific section of the course and added (or slightly modified) something, so that all the team members might always be aware of what happened, even if changes were related to parts of the course they were not directly working on.

Since Kolb's experiential learning cycle starts with "experience", a team of professionals who already tried at international level the flipped classroom methodology was invited as contributor and asked to produce a video-interview to be shared in the MOOC. In order to develop this activity, we went through an online benchmarking activity, analysing paper presentations and asking all our contacts about relevant experiences in which the flipped classroom methodology was applied, better if at university level and on STEM subjects. This phase took around two months, while we were starting the design of the course content.

Since we wanted the storytelling of the experiences to be totally consistent with the pedagogical approach adopted, we wrote a set of questions for each step of the Kolb's Learning Cycle, to guide the narration. We checked for it with the pedagogical experts within the partnership, then we sent the list of questions to the invited testimonials who agreed in taking part to the project together with a technical document with some tips for the video recording (some easy and light requirements about lights, microphones, formats, etc.) they had to perform by themselves or with their staff.

We received video interviews from Penn State University (USA), École Polytechnique Fédérale de Lausanne (CH), Leiden University (NL), University of Zurich (CH) and École des Ponts ParisTech (F). The post-production of all collected experiences was made by METID.

To build the theoretical parts of the course with a strong practical attitude, the design team had the chance to involve an international expert in the field, Ariane Dumont, that developed a great collaboration with the design team by sharing sources, materials, papers, documents used for the preparation of the lessons, ideas, doubts.

The final revision of all storyboards involved the whole team in asynchronous activities, in order to check consistency of all parts and implement the best option for each choice.

The MOOC was online after six months of work, thanks to eight people involved in the design and implementation phases at different levels.

The first edition had around 2000 participants, with a 31% rate of completion (intended as the number of people who achieved the final certificate).

We included an initial survey for participants, in order to better investigate their background and their willing about the MOOC in itself, and a final one, in order to investigate the satisfaction of the users and to collect suggestions about possible areas of improvement.

Reading the answers to the initial questionnaire, it emerges that the participants, although the course is in English, are mainly Italian or French teachers at University level, at High School level or even at Elementary School level.

Their main interest is to better understand the Flipped Classroom Methodology and to try to experiment it in their working fields.

From the answers to the final questionnaire, it emerges a very good feedback from respondents, with most of them (68%) evaluating the experience as "definitely positive".

In the final questionnaire, we asked explicitly some suggestions about possible improvements, in order to further improve the user experience in the next editions. For example, we noticed that having six experiences narrated in parallel along the MOOC, may have been heavy to be followed step by step, and some users might have preferred to view each interview integrally. A new module with each interview given as a whole was then created and added to the MOOC index.

4 "Using Open Educational Resources in Teaching" MOOC

The evolution from the MOOC about Flipped Classroom to the MOOC about OERs is the focus of this paragraph. Starting from the analysis done at the end of the first one, we decided to make testimonies lighter but we strongly believed in maintaining experiences under the spotlight. So we searched for new guests willing to share their direct experiences, the challenges they encountered and the chances they offered to innovate didactic. But in this new MOOC we thought it would have been better to have inspiring videos about the concept of OERs, their history and the motivations we could bring to participants in order to raise their awareness about the theme and convince them to adopt OERs through the voice of relevant professionals of the sector. The adopted approach was, thus, slightly different from one adopted in "To Flip or Not To Flip", because of the intrinsic nature of the OERs themselves.

Collaboration with international experts was so important for us that we decided to participate to a very relevant congress on this theme, in order to get directly in contact with the most influential experts. More: we went through the program of the event (OE Global 2016) and searched for more information about all the presentations that might be more relevant for our objectives, and contacted the presenters before the event. In this way, since we received positive answers, we could meet some them directly in between the congress. We also had the chance to start recording video contributions on-site, thanks to the kind hospitality of AGH University of Science and Technology, which offered us the settings we needed.

So we started contacting some of the most relevant testimonials we could involve, and most of them were enthusiastic to take part in our project. Thanks to their kindness, their belief in the mission of OERs and their commitment, we now have a MOOC with Anant Agarwal (CEO at edX and Professor at MIT, USA), Jane-Frances Agbu (former Head of OERs Unit at NOUN, Nigeria), Ariane Dumont (Professor at Western Switzerland University of Applied Sciences, CH), Cable Green (Open Education Director at Creative Commons, USA), Rory McGreal (Professor and UNESCO/Commonwealth of Learning Chairholder in Open Educational Resources at Athabasca University, Canada), António Moreira Teixeira (former President of EDEN), Joseph Pickett (Publication Director at MIT OpenCourseWare, USA), Susanna Sancassani (Managing Director at Politecnico di Milano – METID, Italy), Robert Schuwer (Lector OER at Fontys University, Netherland), Katsusuke Shigeta (Associate Professor at Hokkaido University, JAPAN) and Andrea Zanni (former President at Wikimedia Italia). We also had the chance to add to the additional materials a valuable contribution from Martin Ebner (Graz University of Technology, Austria).

In order to collect all the videos with these guests, we sometimes tried to record them in contingent settings (in the corridor of a conference, in an office offered by the President of a Faculty at the last moment, from home using a web conferencing system…), sometimes succeeded in recording them taking care of all quality aspects (in a studio at our office).

After seven months of work, eight people involved in the design and implementation phases at different levels, notwithstanding all the problems encountered during the production phases, the MOOC was ready.

We launched this MOOC on Polimi Open Knowledge platform during Autumn 2016, with more than 450 participants coming from all over the world: from Italy to Malaysia, from Kenya to United States. Also in this MOOC we proposed an initial survey, in order to investigate the profile of participants and their expectations about the MOOC, and a final questionnaire aimed at investigating their perception about the MOOC after taking the course.

Most of participants are teachers at University or High School Level (65%); among the other participants we can find students, instructional designers or librarians. Their expectations about the MOOC was mainly to deepen their knowledge about the OER topic (63%) and to experiment it in practice (52%), since most of them are already familiar, in some way, with the OER world.

Since the whole series of MOOCs for Teachers was launched in order to strongly promote didactical innovation, we decided to introduce in the questionnaires a specific item about the perceived role of OERs in relation with didactical innovation itself. In the initial questionnaire it emerges that the participants consider OERs relevant for didactical innovation at a medium degree. After taking the course, in the final questionnaire it emerges that the perceived relevance of OERs to innovate didactics shifts to the higher levels of the scale. This is consistent with the main aim of the MOOC, which is to raise awareness.

5 Conclusion

The collaborative approach adopted at international level in the MOOCs For Teachers series is here described in order to be shared and, with due adaptations, to be reused in other academic contexts, if suitable. For Politecnico di Milano it is an ongoing meaningful experience, since it allows the international team of instructional designers and teachers, with their specific experiences in different contexts and cultures, to work together and to reciprocally enhance the chances to learn-on-the-job.

MOOCs are, from this perspective, a concrete "educational resource", also for the design team in itself; they foster teachers and instructional designers to rethink:

- their role in this specific context
- their contribution to the design activities
- their ability to learn from each other while reaching a better-shared result.

Thus, the one described is not only a shared design experience: it becomes a reciprocal teaching experience, and an enlarged international collaboration experience, which are high objectives in the evolution of the academic scenario, and are consistent both with the growing need of internationalization of Universities and the sharing knowledge perspectives promoted by the third mission of Universities.

We look forward continuing this international collaboration in the next years, in order to enhance as much as possible our attitude to effective innovative design.

According to this approach, we are going to complete these first two steps of MOOCs for Teachers series with the other two MOOCs planned, about active learning and assessment.

References

1. Biggs, J., Tang, C.: Teaching for Quality Learning at University. McGraw-Hill and Open University Press, Maidenhead (2011)
2. Claros, I., Garmendia, A., Echeverría, L., Cobos, R.: Towards a collaborative pedagogical model in MOOCs". Paper Presented at the IEEE Global Engineering Education Conference, EDUCON, pp. 905–911 (2014). doi:10.1109/EDUCON.2014.6826204
3. Kolb, D.: Experiential learning: Experience as the source of learning and development. Prentice-Hall, Englewood Cliffs (1984)
4. Guàrdia, L., Maina, M., Sangrà, A.: MOOC design principles: a pedagogical approach from the learner's perspective. eLearn. Pap. (33) (2013)
5. Sancassani, S., Corti, P., Brambilla, F.: From MOOCs to knowledge sharing. In: Proceeding of EADTU Conference Transition to Open and On-Line Education in European Universities, Paris, 24–25 October 2013
6. Zheng, S., Rosson, M.B., Shih, P.C., Carroll, J.M.: Designing MOOCs as interactive places for collaborative learning. In: Proceedings of the Second ACM Conference on Learning@ Scale, pp. 343–346. ACM (2015)

Research Track

Measuring the Degree of Innovation in Education Through the Implementation of an Indicator Based on Analyzing MOOC-Related Activities

Jose María Alvarez-Rodríguez(✉), Antonio de Amescua, Javier García-Guzman, and Maribel Sánchez-Segura

Computer Science and Engineering Department,
Carlos III University of Madrid, Leganés, Spain
{joalvare,amescua,jgarciag,misanche}@inf.uc3m.es

Abstract. Nowadays, the digital transformation is affecting any task, activity, process that is done in any organization or even in our daily life activities. The education sector, considered as one of the leading sectors in terms of innovation through technology, is also facing a transformation in which digital technology is rapidly evolving. In this context, the Massive Open Online Courses (MOOC) phenomenon has gained a lot of attraction due to the capability of reaching thousands or even millions of students from all over the world. However, the activities related to MOOCs are not yet being evaluated or quantified as a driver of change. Since the creation of MOOCs requires support and institutional commitment to deliver high-quality courses on technology-based platforms, it seems reasonable to measure the degree of innovation in education through the definition of an indicator that collects the commitment of an institution or a person to this new environment of digital education. That is why, in this paper, authors present the definition of a novel indicator and several potential metrics to represent and quantify the degree of innovation in education in universities. Furthermore, a case study is conducted to evaluate 3 different metrics on 36 European universities in the context of the edX and Coursera platforms.

Keywords: Innovation · Indicator · Performance · MOOC · University · Digital education

1 Introduction

The selection of the proper university is a cornerstone decision in the education and career development of any person. Universities offer a large catalogue of degrees, masters and doctorate programs with the aim of providing new career opportunities while students perceive education as a mean to reach better job positions, to get higher salaries and to experience a kind of cultural exchange. The chance of finding a perfect university can be a challenge due to the huge number of universities, program of studies, language, duration, location, funding and many other subjective factors such as students opinion, historical and on-line reputation or prospects for the future. On the

C. Delgado Kloos et al. (Eds.): EMOOCs 2017, LNCS 10254, pp. 123–133, 2017.
DOI: 10.1007/978-3-319-59044-8_14

other hand, universities are continuously seeking for innovative ways to improve their performance in terms of academic and research activities to attract the best students and researchers, to get private and public funding, to create and disseminate knowledge and to become an essential driver for the welfare society.

Taking into account these two main aspects it is necessary to establish methods for ranking higher education institutions and to provide insights that can quantitively reflect in just one number the value of a university. In this sense, some worldwide university rankings such as the ARWU (Academic Ranking of World Universities) ranking (also known as Shangai Ranking), the QS World University Rankings or the Ranking Web of Universities (Webometrics) are published every year to classify universities according to some criteria. As an example, the ARWU ranking considers a set of weighted criteria: "(1) Quality of education: alumni of an institution wining Nobel Prizes and Field Medals (10%), (2) Quality of faculty: staff of an institution winning Nobel Prizes and Fields Medals (20%) and highly cited researchers in 21 broad subject categories (20%), (3) Research Output: papers published in Nature and Science (20%) and papers indexed in Science Citation Index-expanded and Social Science Citation Index (20%) and (4) Per Capita Performance: per capita academic performance of an institution (10%)".

Although this type of rankings are perfectly supported by the opinion of experts and the scientometrics behind, there is also a lot of criticism [1, 2] due to their reproducibility, transparency, economic interests, selection or weight of criteria. Furthermore, it seems that an important variable is not usually considered: the degree of innovation. To do so, last times have also seen the creation of new indexes to collect information about university innovation. Thus, the "Times Higher Education"[1] has compiled a set of observations about four different criteria: "Resources from industry", "Industry Collaboration", "Patent Citations" and "Industry Contribution". Reuters[2] has also defined other ranking considering again indicators related to the creation of patents ("Patent Volume", "Patent Success" or "Global Patents") and industry collaboration ("Percent of Industry Collaborative Articles"). Recent approaches[3] are also trying to measure innovation in universities through the establishment of a degree of entrepreneurship what is a quite good measure to classify industry-oriented institutions. However, after this brief review of university rankings there is a missing or not fully covered variable: the innovation in education [3].

Nowadays, the digital transformation is affecting any task, activity, process that is done in any organization or even in our daily life activities. The education sector, considered as one of the leading sectors in terms of innovation through technology, is also facing a transformation in which digital technology is rapidly evolving. Institutions and teachers are trying to take advantage of this new digital environment to bring students new learning methods and digital resources providing new opportunities for specialization, continuous education or flexibility at a worldwide scale. The use of

[1] https://www.timeshighereducation.com/features/which-universities-are-the-most-innovative.

[2] http://www.reuters.com/most-innovative-universities/methodology.

[3] https://www.timeshighereducation.com/blog/most-innovative-universities-alternative-approach-ranking.

emerging technologies must serve to fulfill the new needs but also to create new technology-driven business opportunities. However, institutions must not focus only on technology but people: consumers, workers and partners. The first step to become a leading digital educational institution will rely on changing the corporate culture to incorporate technology as a key driver to empower people and to drive the change and disruption in this sector. In this context, the Massive Open Online Courses (MOOC) phenomenon [4] has gained a lot of attraction due to the capability of reaching thousands or even millions of students from all over the world. From facilitators, such as the edX, Udacity, Coursera or XuetangX platforms, to course generators, there is a tremendous interest in becoming part of this new learning environment mainly based on interactive multimedia objects such as videos. MOOCs are considered the future of higher and corporate education. Taking into account that the creation of MOOCs requires support and institutional commitment to deliver high-quality courses (implying the need of a policy, budget, training for teachers, creation of new contents, application of new learning methods, etc.) on technology-based platforms, it seems reasonable to measure the degree of innovation in education through the definition of an indicator that collects the commitment of an institution or a person to this new environment of digital education.

That is why, in this paper, authors present the definition of a novel indicator and several potential metrics to represent and quantify the degree of innovation in education in institutions. The following section reviews the main works in regards to the creation of quantitative indexes, innovation in education and an overview of the main works related to MOOCs. Afterwards, a definition of an indicator, the MI-KPI (MOOC Innovation Key Performance Indicator), and a set of potential metrics are provided. In the case study section, an experiment is carried out to evaluate the MI-KPI in the European universities. Finally, some conclusions and future work are also outlined.

2 Related Work

Public and private bodies are continuously seeking for new analytical tools and methods to assess, rank and compare their performance based on distinct indicators and dimensions with the objective of making some decision or developing new policies. In this context, the creation and use of quantitative indexes and key performance indicators (KPI) is a widely accepted practice that has been applied to domains such as Bibliometrics and academic performance/research quality (the Impact Factor by Thomson-Reuters, the H-index or the aforementioned university rankings: ARWU, QS Top Universities and Webometrics), the Web impact [8] (the Webindex by the Webfoundation or the Open Data Index by the Open Knowledge Foundation) or cloud computing (the Global Cloud Index by Cisco, the CSC index, the VMWare Cloud Index, the Service Measurement Index, etc.) or Smart Cities (The European Smart Cities ranking) to name a few (apart from the traditional ones such as the Gross Domestic Product).

In the frame of university rankings, some key performance indicators have been defined in existing indexes, as Table 1 shows. In all of them, data and information is gathered every year to finally aggregate the different observations in just one value through an ordered weighted averaging (OWA) operator. The output ranking gives us an insight of the performance of universities providing useful information for decision makers, researchers and potential students. As we have previously introduced, university rankings have also generated a lot of discussion [1, 2] due to the reproducibility, transparency, economic interests, selection and weight of criteria and, one, could even argue about the completeness of the information gathered and selection of criteria but in practice, they provide a realistic ranking of universities.

Table 1. Quality indicators of the main university rankings.

ARWU		QS Top Universities		Webometrics	
Indicator	Weight	Indicator	Weight	Indicator	Weight
Quality of Education	10	Academic peer review	40	Activity-Presence	50/3
Quality of Faculty	40	Faculty/Student ratio	20	Activity-Openness	50/3
Research Output	40	Citations per faculty	20	Activity-Excellence	50/3
Per Capita Performance	10	Employer reputation	10	Visibility-Impact	50
–	–	International student ratio	5	–	–
–	–	International staff ratio	5	–	–

However, the current digital environment is maybe not well reflected in their indicators. On-line social network engagement or the degree of innovation represent two kind of indicators that are being relevant for other industry sectors such as marketing, electronic commerce or banking and they are not directly covered in existing indicators.

In the field of MOOCs, it is possible to find a good number of works addressing: (1) learning or pedagogical aspects, classification of MOOCs; (2) design and planning of MOOCs including operational environment: technological, logistics and financial aspects. In the first case, MOOCs has been organized and classified using different criteria. As an example, an early classification made a distinction between CMOOCs (focus on knowledge creation) and xMOOCs (focus on knowledge duplication). Downes [9] created a four criteria classification: autonomy, diversity, openness and interactivity. Clark [10] also provided a taxonomy of MOOCs based on pedagogy. Colen [11] argued against such classifications to describe the nature of a MOOC and created a set of dimensions to classify and map MOOC courses. Other works are currently discussing the relevant pedagogical aspects of MOOC design [12], how the contents will be delivered to learners [13] and how the interaction between learners will be [14].

Secondly, a good number of best practices, methodologies and on-line guidelines created by main universities and institutions can be found in [15, 16]. Some of the main works in design and planning of MOOCs are available in [7, 17, 18] where authors present a conceptual framework for designing on-line courses and introduce the "Business Model Canvas" technique to gather the main issues of logistical, technological, pedagogical and financial nature of MOOCS. There is also a large body of research trying to analyze students' behavior in MOOCs (e.g. learning analytics [5]) to figure out the main reasons of the drop outs or to analyze the perceived quality of a MOOC. However, the study of MOOCs from other perspectives such as economic impact or as a measurement of innovation in education is still an open challenge.

Finally, the innovation in education has been subject of study in different works such as the report entitled as "Measuring Innovation in Education" [3] published by the OECD (Organization for Economic Co-operation and Development) in 2014. In this work, authors focus on the degree of innovation in education assessing the role of technology, institutions and people in the creation of one of the most innovative sectors, education. Furthermore, they also defined a set of indicators (and a composite index) to assess the innovation in different areas such as: teaching styles, instructional practices, class organization, the use of textbooks in classrooms, the methods of assessment used in classrooms, the availability of computers and the internet in the classroom, the use of computers in the classroom, the provision of special education in schools, the extent of teacher collaboration in schools, feedback mechanisms in schools, evaluation and hiring in schools and schools' external relations.

Although the use of open online educational resources is partially mentioned under the indicator "the use of textbooks in classrooms", there is not a direct reference to the use of MOOCs as an indicator of innovation in education. Besides, the report is mainly focused on schools and results may vary in the case of evaluating higher-education institutions. Some gray literature can also be found[4,5] assessing the role of innovation in education but, in both cases, the focus lies on technology, pedological and learning challenges.

3 MI-KPI: Definition of an Indicator to Measure the Degree of Innovation in Education

Th present work is focused on defining a new indicator: "The degree of innovation in education in higher-education institutions". This indicator can be measured by different metrics (inspired by similar metrics used in existing composite indexes) as the next table shows. Thus, it is possible to quantify innovation and to define further strategies to become part of the digital education environment. In Table 2 a set of metrics to measure the indicator MI-KPI (MOOC Innovation Key Performance Indicator) are presented. Each metric is identified by an unique identifier represented by m_k. It is then defined through a mathematical formula to obtain a quantitative value. The metric has also a scope that can be a course (C), degree (D), university (U) or country (Co) and a set of possible values (or range).

Following a brief description of this preliminary set of metrics to measure the MI-KPI indicator is provided:

- Metrics $m_1, m_3, m_4, m_5, m_6, m_7, m_{11}$ provide a ratio value between the number of courses or degrees that have been published as MOOCs in regards to the courses or

[4] http://oecdeducationtoday.blogspot.com.es/2016/09/educating-for-innovation-and-innovation.html.

[5] http://www.oecd.org/edu/skills-beyond-school/EDIF24-eng(2014)EN.PDF.

Table 2. Initial set of metrics to measure the MI-KPI.

Metric ID	Definition	Scope
m_1	$\frac{number\ of\ courses\ published\ as\ a\ MOOC}{total\ number\ of\ courses}$	D,U
m_2	$\frac{number\ of\ courses\ published\ as\ a\ MOOC}{e^{Size\ of\ the\ university}}$ The size of a university could be defined according to different criteria. Here, the size is defined as the number of enrolled students (a well-accepted metric of size for universities) being: • 1 if size <=5000 • 2 if size is between 5000 and 15.000 • 3 if size is >15.000 • 4 if size is >25.000 • 5 if size is >35.000	U
m_3	$\frac{number\ of\ instructors\ participating\ in\ MOOCs}{total\ number\ of\ teachers}$	C,D,U
m_4	$\frac{number\ of\ degrees\ having\ at\ least\ 1\ MOOC}{total\ number\ of\ degrees\ in\ the\ university}$	U
m_5	$\frac{number\ of\ universities\ having\ at\ least\ 1\ MOOC}{total\ number\ of\ universities}$	Co
m_6	$\frac{number\ of\ unique\ shares\ of\ MOOCs\ in\ online\ social\ networks}{number\ of\ published\ MOOCs}$	C,D,U, Co
m_7	$\frac{number\ of\ microdegrees\ as\ MOOCs}{total\ number\ of\ degrees}$	U
m_8	$\frac{number\ of\ microdegrees\ as\ MOOCs}{e^{Size\ of\ the\ university}}$	U
m_9	$e^{-\frac{number\ of\ courses\ or\ microdegrees\ published\ as\ a\ MOOC}{e^{Size\ of\ the\ university}}}$	U
m_{10}	$value^{University}_{ranking_k} = \frac{position\ of\ University\ in\ ranking_k}{size\ of\ ranking_k}$ $\frac{number\ of\ courses\ published\ as\ a\ MOOC\ -\ value^{University}_{ranking_k}}{e^{-value^{University}_{ranking_k}}}$	U
m_{11}	$\frac{number\ of\ universities\ having\ at\ least\ 1\ MOOC}{number\ of\ universities\ in\ ranking_k}$	Co

degrees that are available in a university or degree. Thus, it is possible to assess to what extent the university is engaged with digital education through MOOCs. The range of these metrics is between 0 and 1 being 0 the total absence of MOOC activities and 1 the maximum engagement in MOOC-based education and technology (which would represent a complete virtual university). Furthermore, these metrics can take as an input argument the topic or category in which online resources are being published.

- Metrics $m_2, m_8\ and\ m_9$ represent a relative value of the number of courses or degrees that have been published as a MOOC in regards to the size of the university.

These metrics follow a kind of power law distribution rewarding the publishing of MOOCs depending on the size of the university and, by extension, its resources.

- Metric m_{10} represent a relative value of the number of courses published as a MOOC in regards to the size and position of a university in a certain ranking. Thus, it is possible to reward universities that although they cannot have a good position in existing rankings they are keeping a quite good activity in terms of digital education through MOOCs.

In general, most of these metrics can take as an input argument the topic or category in which the MOOC course is being published. Furthermore, they can have different scope if they can be applied to just a course, a degree or an institution. Besides this set of metrics could also be aggregated to get a measure by university and/or country. Finally, it is important to remark that metrics do not reflect other parameters that could be generated by applying learning analytics or social network analysis techniques. Thus, values are just descriptive and are not impacted by other type of strategies for dissemination and engagement in on-line networks that could imply a more complex calculation and interpretation.

4 Case Study: Applying the MI-KPI to the European Universities

To illustrate the applicability of the MI-KPI to measure the degree of innovation in education, a case study based on calculating different metrics by country and European universities have been conducted.

4.1 Research Design

In order to design the experiment, a stepwise method has been defined to semi-automatically collect, analyze and calculate the MI-KPI indicator.

1. Selection of the MOOC platforms. In this case, edX, Coursera, Udacity and Udemy were initially selected as target platforms to gather information about MOOC courses and universities. However, the public API of Udacity did not provide information about universities (just two American universities were available). In the case of Udemy, a request was done to access the public API but it was not approved. That is why, the final selection only includes the edX and Coursera platforms.
2. Selection of metrics. In this case, metrics m_2, m_9, m_{10} were selected after checking the information available in the target platforms.
3. Selection of universities. The experiment is only focusing on European universities since all of them share similar characteristics and policies. The inclusion criteria were quite simple, just those universities that have at least 1 MOOC published in the target platforms.
4. Access to data and information. To do so, a Python program has been coded to access and format data according to the needs of metrics calculation. Furthermore,

an external service "Shared Count" has been used to get the shares in social networks (Facebook, Twitter and Linkedin) of every MOOC course. More specifically, two different scripts were created to access the REST API of Coursera and the RSS of edX. However, the RSS of edX only contained information about the last course so a manual gathering of data was done. In regards to the size of universities, the Wikipedia was used to get the number of students. Finally, the ARWU Ranking 2016 (Alumni) was also scrapped from the web.

5. Calculate metrics and analysis. In this case, the MSExcel tool was selected to analyze the data gathered from the MOOC platforms and to calculate metrics. A process for reconciling data was semi-automatically doing to unify university names. Furthermore, a decision was done to assign a ranking value to universities when the ARWU Ranking places a university in a range. The left-value was taken as ranking value. E.g. (101–150)->101. A value of 501 was assigned to those universities that are not part of the ARWU Ranking.
6. Publish of results. Both code and the output results are publicly available in a Github repository[6].

4.2 Results and Discussion

Table 3 shows the number of universities having at least 1 MOOC and the number of universities in the ARWU Ranking by country. In general, it seems that just a few universities in Europe have already MOOCs but according to the number of MOOCs that have been published, this set of universities is quite active. It is also relevant to remark that just 11 European countries and 36 universities have MOOC-related activities while the ARWU Ranking contains 25 different European countries and 209 universities. Furthermore, the European universities have participated in just 255

Table 3. Ratio between the number of universities having MOOC activities in comparison to the number of universities in the ARWU ranking 2016.

Country code	#Universities having at least 1 MOOC	#Universities in the ARWU ranking 2016	m_{11}
CH	5	8	0.63
ISR	2	5	0.40
DK	2	5	0.40
BE	2	6	0.33
RU	1	3	0.33
FR	7	22	0.32
SE	3	11	0.27
NL	3	12	0.25
ES	3	12	0.25
UK	5	36	0.14
DE	3	39	0.08

[6] https://github.com/sa-mooc-uc3m/mooc-research-public/tree/master/trunk/papers/emooc2017.

Table 4. The MI-KPI metrics for 36 European Universities.

University	Country code	Size of the university	ARWU ranking 2016*	#MOOCs in Coursera	#MOOCs in edX	m_2	m_9	m_{10}
Swiss Federal Institute of Technology Lausanne	CH	10124 (2)	92	8	25	4.47	0.01	39.67
Delft University of Technology	NL	19613 (3)	151		51	2.54	0.08	68.98
Centrale Superior Paris	FR	1394 (1)	501	3		1.10	0.33	8.17
Chalmers University of Technology	SE	11000 (2)	201		8	1.08	0.34	11.96
Swiss Federal Institute of Technology Zurich	CH	10851 (2)	19		8	1.08	0.34	8.31
Universidad Carlos III de Madrid	ES	18676 (3)	501		17	0.85	0.43	46.30
University of Notre Dame	FR	12179 (2)	501		6	0.81	0.44	16.34
Karolinska Institute	SE	5978 (2)	44		6	0.81	0.44	6.55
Ecole Normale Superieure - Lyon	FR	2000 (1)	301	2		0.74	0.48	3.65
Ecole Polytechnique	FR	2888 (1)	301	2		0.74	0.48	3.65
Catholic University of Louvain	BE	29711 (4)	151		24	0.44	0.64	32.46
University of Geneva	CH	14489 (2)	53	3		0.41	0.67	3.34
IESE Business School	ES	2081 (1)	501	1		0.37	0.69	2.72
HEC Paris	FR	4000 (1)	501	1		0.37	0.69	2.72
IsraelX	ISR	0 (1)	501		1	0.37	0.69	2.72
Institut Mines-Télécom	FR	0 (1)	501		1	0.37	0.69	2.72
Technical University of Denmark	DK	11190 (2)	151	2		0.27	0.76	2.71
Leiden University	NL	24270 (3)	93	5		0.25	0.78	6.02
ITMO University	RU	12000 (2)	501		1	0.14	0.87	2.72
Eindhoven University of Technology	NL	9711 (2)	201	1		0.14	0.87	1.49
University of Lausanne	CH	13500 (2)	201	1		0.14	0.87	1.49
The University of Edinburgh	UK	35582 (5)	41	14	3	0.11	0.89	18.45
University of Zurich	CH	25732 (4)	54	6		0.11	0.90	6.68
The Hebrew University of Jerusalem	ISR	23000 (3)	87	2		0.10	0.91	2.38
Autonomous University of Madrid	ES	36118 (5)	201		8	0.05	0.95	11.96
The University of Manchester	UK	38590 (5)	35	8		0.05	0.95	8.58
University College London	UK	161270 (5)	17	8		0.05	0.95	8.28
Copenhagen Business School	DK	22829 (3)	501	1		0.05	0.95	2.72
University of Oxford	UK	22602 (3)	7		1	0.05	0.95	1.01
KU Leuven	BE	55484 (5)	93		7	0.05	0.95	8.43
Ludwig-Maximilians-University of Munich (LMU)	DE	50542 (5)	501	5		0.03	0.97	13.62
Sorbonne University System	FR	57800 (5)	501		5	0.03	0.97	13.62
Technical University Munich	DE	40000 (5)	47	2	3	0.03	0.97	5.49
RWTH Aachen University	DE	42000 (5)	201		4	0.03	0.97	5.98
Sapienza University of Rome	IT	112564 (5)	151	1		0.01	0.99	1.35
Lund University	SE	41000 (5)	101	1		0.01	0.99	1.22

MOOCs out of 1679 (413 in Coursera + 1266 in edX) representing a 15% of the current courses available in these platforms. This situation implies that MOOC activities are just starting in Europe.

On the other hand, Table 4 shows the results for each university that has been included in this case study. More specifically, each row contains the name of the university, the country code (ISO 3166-1 alpha-2 code), the size of the university, the current position in the ARWU Ranking 2016, the number of MOOCs published in Coursera and edX and the values for the selected metrics. The table has been sorted according to the first metric (m_2) to show the impact of MOOC activities in the selected platforms. In this first top 10 of universities, one can realize that only 7 out of 10 institutions are also in the ARWU Ranking what it can imply that considering the proposed indicator (and this metric) results about the degree of innovation could change the position of several institutions. In the same manner and taking the value for the last metric (m_{10}), the top 10 of universities changes a bit the position of some universities in regards to the first classification but the percentage of those in the ARWU Ranking is a bit lower (60%). However, if metric m_9 is used to sort institutions it seems that the ranking is more similar to the ARWU Ranking meaning that this metric is more conservative. According to these results, it seems reasonable to think that metric m_2 is affected by the size of the university while in m_{10} the number of published MOOCs seems to be more relevant. It is also remarkable that some important universities in terms of size and international reputation are having a very few MOOC-related activity.

Some key limitations of the presented work must be outlined. The first one relies on the sample size; our research study has been conducted in a closed world and more specifically, just 36 European universities, 2 MOOC platforms and 3 metrics have been considered. That is why, results in a broad or real scope could change having more up-to-date data directly from the universities. Nevertheless, the research methodology, the design of experiments and the creation of a kind of indicator and a preliminary set of metrics to measure innovation in education seem to be representative and informative.

Building on the previous comment, we merely observe and re-use existing public and on-line data sources to provide a quantitative value for a quality indicator. Finally, we have also identified the possibility of adding some new variables to the experiment regarding the quality of MOOCs or on-line social network analysis techniques. Thus, it should be possible to state that the higher quality the MI-KPI is, the stronger commitment and level of innovation in education in some institution is.

5 Conclusions and Future Work

Digital technology is impacting every sector and activity of our society. Education as a critical sector, is being dramatically affected by the digital transformation. The rising MOOC phenomena seems to be one of the main drivers of change that higher-education institutions and corporations are facing. On the other hand, once MOOCs clearly represent a disruptive innovation in education it is necessary to benchmarking and provide metrics of the impact of this technology. In this work, a novel indicator and a set of potential metrics have been proposed to measure the degree of innovation in institutions. On the other hand, future work may include a review of the metrics including analysis of the robustness and accuracy, mapping to existing Scientometric foundations, and evaluation of the presented approach at a world-wide level.

References

1. Billaut, J.-C., Bouyssou, D., Vincke, P.: Should you believe in the Shanghai ranking? Scientometrics **84**(1), 237–263 (2010)
2. Docampo, D.: Reproducibility of the Shanghai academic ranking of world universities results. Scientometrics **94**(2), 567–587 (2013)
3. OECD: Measuring Innovation in Education. OECD Publishing, Paris (2014)
4. Christensen, G., Steinmetz, A., Alcorn, B., Bennett, A., Woods, D., Emanuel, E.J.: The MOOC phenomenon: who takes massive open online courses and why? SSRN Electron. J., 1–25 (2013). https://papers.ssrn.com/sol3/papers.cfm?abstract_id=2350964
5. Leony, D., Muñoz-Merino, P.J., Ruipérez-Valiente, J.A., Pardo, A., Kloos, C.D.: Detection and evaluation of emotions in massive open online courses. J-JUCS **21**(5), 638–655 (2015)
6. Rizzardini, R.H., García-Peñalvo, F.J., Kloos, C.D.: Massive open online courses: combining methodologies and architecture for a success learning. J-JUCS **21**(5), 636–637 (2015)
7. de Amescua, A., Alvarez-Rodríguez, J.M., Sanchez-Segura, M.-I., Medina-Domínguez, F.: An agile framework definition for creating an engineering massive open online course from scratch A case study. Int. J. Eng. Educ. **35**(5(B)), 2360–2373 (2016)
8. Alvarez-Rodŕiguez, J.M., Clement, J., Gayo, J.E.L., Farhan, H., Ordoñez De Pablos, P.: Publishing statistical data following the linked open data principles: the web index project. In: Cases on Open-Linked Data and Semantic Web Applications, pp. 199–226. IGI Global (2013)
9. Downes, S.: The quality of massive open online courses. In: Khan, B.H., Ally, M. (eds.) International Handbook of E-Learning. Theoretical Perspective, vol. 1. Routledg, 22 March 2015
10. Clark, D.: MOOCs: taxonomy of 8 types of MOOC (2013)
11. Conole, G.: MOOCs as disruptive technologies: strategies for enhancing the learner experience and quality of MOOCs. RED Rev. Educ. Distancia **39**, 1–17 (2013)
12. Guàrdia, L., Maina, M., Sangrà, A.: MOOC design principles: a pedagogical approach from the learner's perspective. ELearning Pap. **33**, 1–6 (2013)
13. Mackness, J., Waite, M., Roberts, G., Lovegrove, E.: Learning in a small, task–oriented, connectivist MOOC: pedagogical issues and implications for higher education. Int. Rev. Res. Open Distrib. Learn. **14**(4), 140–159 (2013)
14. McAndrew, P.: Learning from open design: running a learning design MOOC. ELearning Pap. **33**, 1–4 (2013)
15. Scott, I., Kendra, L., Woodgate, A.: How to Grow Your Own MOOC with Coursera. University of Edinburgh, Edinburgh (2014)
16. Kerr, J.: Building and Executing MOOCs. University of Glasgow, Glasgow (2015)
17. Alario-Hoyos, C., Pérez-Sanagustín, M., Cormier, D., Kloos, C.D.: Proposal for a conceptual framework for educators to describe and design MOOCs. J-JUCS **20**(1), 6–23 (2014)
18. Alario-Hoyos, C., Pérez-Sanagustín, M., Kloos, C.D., Muñoz-Merino, P.J.: Recommendations for the design and deployment of MOOCs: insights about the MOOC digital education of the future deployed in MiríadaX, pp. 403–408 (2014)

Toward a Typology of MOOC Activity Patterns

Learners Who Never Rest?

Rémi Bachelet[1(✉)] and Rawad Chaker[2]

[1] Centrale Lille, 59651 Villeneuve d'Ascq Cedex, France
remi.bachelet@ec-lille.fr
[2] Université Lumière Lyon 2, ISPEF, ECP, 69365 Lyon Cedex 07, France
rawad.chaker@univ-lyon2.fr

Abstract. This paper aims at understanding MOOC learners' activity patterns, taking into account factors like personal schedule, traditional working hours, domestic time, nighttime and their relation with MOOC course opening hours, live sessions, essay submission deadlines… Are MOOC learners adopting nonstandard learning schedules? Does the MOOC schedule determine the connection patterns of the learners? Four search topics and findings emerge from our research A/Observations related to the density of learning activity B/A weekly typology of learning days, C/Attraction for a "live" contact point, D/The "21:00 effect". Finally, we suggest a series of best practices for MOOC design.

Keywords: MOOC · Platform connection patterns · Live Q&A · Learning schedule

1 MOOC, Professional Education and Learners' Schedule

MOOCs are increasingly used to improve existing occupational skills as well as to acquire new skills [1]. They are perceived by students as a way to improve their employability [2], and by potential recruiters as professional development means [3]. As a matter of fact, today, "self-development and employability (…) is the long-term project that underpins all others" [4]. Taking into consideration that professionals have standard working hours, how do MOOC learners manage their connection and training schedules? Does the MOOC determine the connection rhythm of the learners, or is it their personal and professional rhythm that determines when do they connect to the MOOC?

As time flexibility is one of the most appealing options offered by elearning [5], that of learners is determined by their capacity to allocate time to learning activities and the quantity and quality of time they can spend on these activities [5]. Apart from professional schedule, adult e-learners have personal and family constraints [6, 7]. The time they can allocate to their learning activities is often "the time left over once their professional, social, and family commitments have been fulfilled" [5]. According to Romero and Barbera [5], "for adult learners who work during the day, the time when most are available for learning activities is in the evening and on weekends" [8]. In

C. Delgado Kloos et al. (Eds.): EMOOCs 2017, LNCS 10254, pp. 134–139, 2017.
DOI: 10.1007/978-3-319-59044-8_15

other words, we would like to find new evidence related to learners' behaviors, in order to improve the good practices thesaurus related to MOOC design, especially the scheduling and planning part.

2 Research Methodology

Both the data analysis and the implementation attempts described in this paper use data collected on a French project management MOOC: MOOC GdP. The first session of MOOC (GdP1) was the first xMOOC to be opened in France [9] and experience of running a distance learning course [10]. Enrollment opened January 11, 2013. The course offers two individual tracks: Basic and Advanced. After the "common core course", 13 specializations are available. Thus MOOC duration is 4 + 2 weeks. A "Team project" track is also proposed, with around 100 projects realized since GdP1.

This paper puts in use data recently collected during 4 sessions: MOOC GdP5, 6, 7 and 8. These sessions took place between March 2015 and October 2016. Attendance/Attrition was as follows (Table 1):

Table 1. Detailed session stats: https://goo.gl/MVVEpy

Session	Enrolled	Active basic track	Graduating basic track
GdP5	17,579	4,842	2,282
GdP6	23,315	7,537	3,900
GdP7	19,392	5,951	2,393
GdP8	24,603	7,998	4,526

Our first data source is Google Analytics, filtering out server data activity for each session. We get server-side raw connection data, not individual sessions. Our second data source is YouTube Analytics. For each live "Q&A" video, we extract: live views, video views after live session (our data consists in 5 * 4 = 20 live sessions).

2.1 Weekly Connection Patterns Are Regular and Stable

Our first finding is the regularity of connection patterns for weekdays. After normalizing sessions as a percentage of total attendance, and plotting average hourly activity for each weekday, we observe a very similar pattern for each session (Fig. 1).

Peaks on Wednesday (sessions 5 and 6) and Thursday (sessions 7 and 8) match our live "Q&A" videos.

2.2 Q&A Live Sessions: Convergence of Deferred and Live Attendance

Each session features five live "Q&A" videos at 21:30: Wednesdays (GdP5 and 6) or Thursdays (GdP7 and 8). As seen in Fig. 4, Youtube attendance analytics reveal a similar decreasing pattern along each session. Furthermore, these events are more

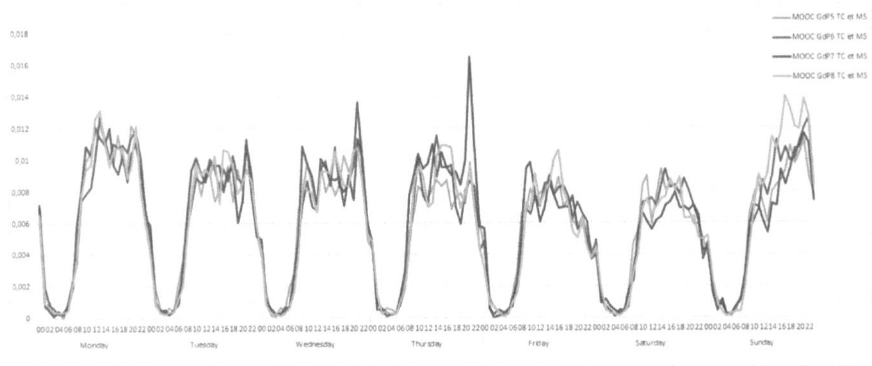

Fig. 1. Normalized hourly and weekly connection patterns

affected by technical glitches and ad hoc communication. Attendance pattern is one of convergence: live attendance is quite stable along the MOOC (−50%), while deferred attendance shows a sharp −300% decrease.

As a result, the last live "Q&A" attendance converge to 50–50 live/deferred in attendance. The live connection rate is around 10% of active learners. We hypothesize there is a category of "hardcore learners" who attend the live "Q&A" not matter what. Thus, live "Q&A" would be a major attractiveness factor for hardcore learners. The 20 live "Q&A" took place on Youtube and not on the MOOC platform. However, they still coincide with a greater number of platform connections. Our multi-platform MOOC arrangement is not detrimental to the main MOOC platform.

2.3 Daytime, Evening and Night Hours Work: Higher Density for Evening Time

Although our analytics are limited to server-side data, we can plot the aggregated connections during 3 time slots.

- time slot 1 (8 a.m. – 6 p.m.): daytime
- time slot 2 (7 p.m. – 10 p.m.): evening
- time slot 3 (11 p.m. – 7 a.m.): night

If we only take into account the number of hours into each plot, daytime work would of course appear dominant. Hence, were-ploted out data, taking into account hourly connections instead of total connections (Fig. 2):

It appears that evening hours represent a much higher density of work than traditional working hours.

2.4 Four Types of Daily Patterns

Finally, we isolate five typical weekdays, in order to study their daily pattern (Fig. 3).

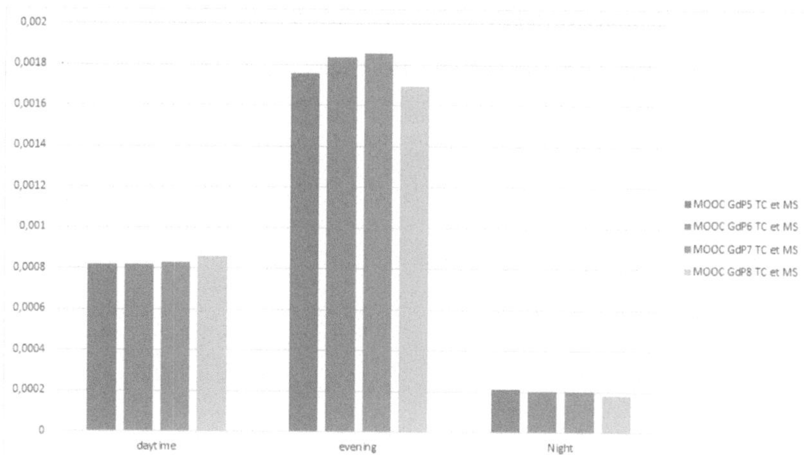

Fig. 2. Platform connections per hour on daytime, evening and night slots

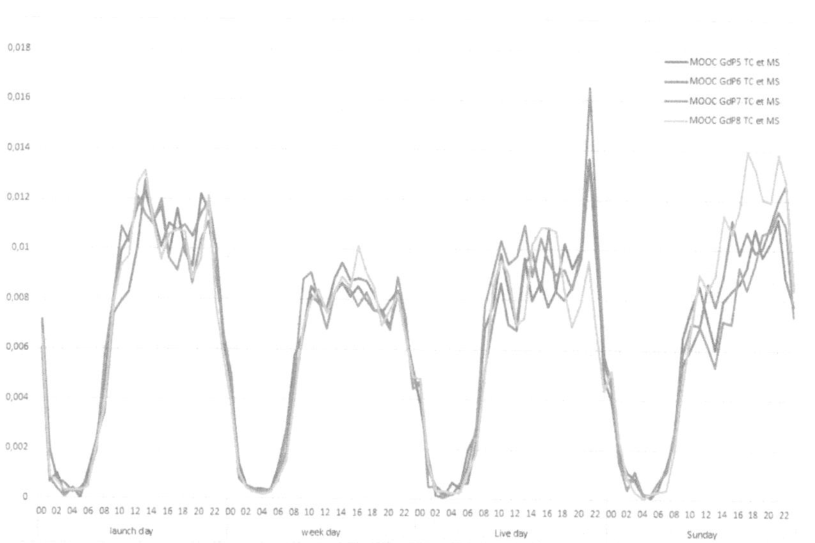

Fig. 3. Four types of daily patterns

1. **Launch days**: each weekly module opens Monday at 12:00
2. **Live days**: live "Q&A" session is held on the evening of that day
3. **Weekdays + Saturdays**: "normal" week day with no live "Q&A".
4. **Sundays**: essay submission is due Sunday midnight week 1–3

We observe in fact not five, but four daily patterns: Saturday does not seem a special day as it lies in the continuity of the slow decrease of weekdays. Once more, a traditional working hours model does not seem to fit.

2.5 Longitudinal Study of Daily Patterns: The "9 P.M. Effect"

Compiling all our data from all sessions we observe a recurring pattern with three typical time slots (Fig. 4):

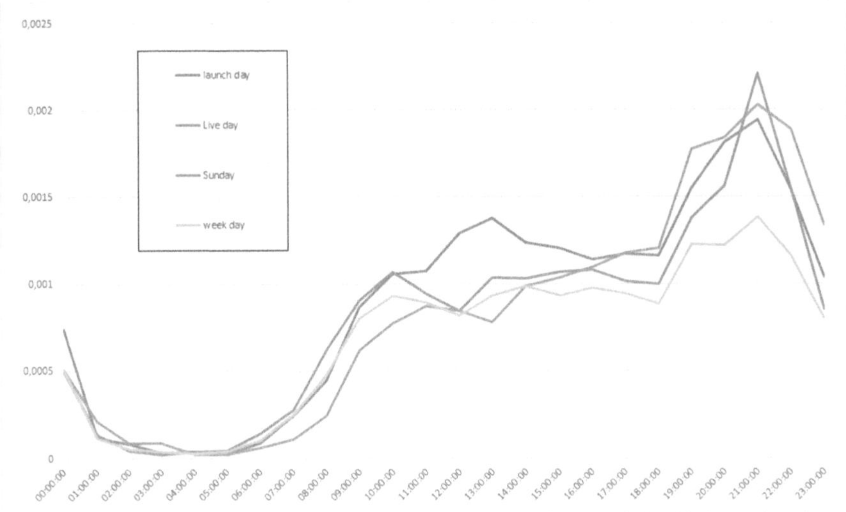

Fig. 4. Longitudinal connection density: the 9 p.m. peak

- Nighttime (steady and very few connections),
- Day 9 a.m.–5 p.m. (steady and around 1% connection density every hour)
- Evening 7 p.m.–10 p.m. (variable connection density: 1.5–2%)

Most interestingly, a connection peak appears on the 9 p.m.–10 p.m. slot every day. This peak is a recurring phenomenon: even though it's partly induced by MOOC organization (on the evening of live "Q&A" at 9:30 p.m. and to a lesser extent essay submission deadline at midnight) we still observe this peak when there is no specific trigger factor every day (except Saturday).

3 Conclusions and Recommendations

A series of results and search topics emerge from our research:

1. Learning on a MOOC occurs with a double density on evenings compared to daytime and nighttime.
2. We propose a typology of 4 types of days, each displaying a specific hourly pattern: 1/Launch days; 2/Live days; 3/Weekdays and Saturdays; 4/Essay submission days
3. A recurring "live" contact point has a lasting attraction on some hardcore learners, while other learners are less and less retentive. The two populations ("hardcore" and "standard") exhibit a specific mode of attrition. Thus, the first live session of particular importance to final attrition.

4. The "9 p.m. effect": there is a recurring peak on activity between 9 p.m. and 10 p.m. This peak appears every day but Saturdays.

Both instructional time flexibility and students' perception of this flexibility are considered indicators of e-learning quality [5] and an expectation of e-learners [11].

From this, we draw two best practices for MOOC design:

- Understand the importance and role of weekly live sessions in creating and maintaining hardcore learners.
- Preferential timeslot for working learners: 9 p.m.–10 p.m. is the best timeslot to set up events and work.

References

1. Milligan, C., Littlejohn, A.: Supporting professional learning in a massive open online course. Int. Rev. Res. Open Distrib. Learn. **15**(5) (2014)
2. Santandreu Calonge, D., Shah, M.: MOOCs, graduate skills gaps, and employability: a qualitative systematic review of the literature. Int. Rev. Res. Open Distance Learn. **17**(5), 67–90 (2016)
3. Radford, A.W., Robles, J., Cataylo, S., Horn, L., Thornton, J., Whitfield, K.E.: The employer potential of MOOCs: a mixed-methods study of human resource professionals' thinking on MOOCs. Int. Rev. Res. Open Distrib. Learn. **15**(5) (2014)
4. Boltanski, L., Chiapello, E.: Le nouvel esprit du capitalisme. Gallimard, Paris (1999)
5. Romero, M., Barberà, E.: Quality of e-learners' time and learning performance beyond quantitative time-on-task. Int. Rev. Res. Open Distrib. Learn. **12**(5), 125–137 (2011)
6. Diaz, D.P.: Online drop rates revisited. The Technology Source, pp. 93–106, May/June 2002
7. Palloff, R., Pratt, K.: The Virtual Student: A Profile and Guide to Working with Online Learners. Jossey-Bass, San Francisco (2003)
8. Kasprzak, J., Nixon, M.: Cheating in cyberspace: maintaining quality in online education. Am. Assoc. Comput. Educ. J. **12**(1), 85–99 (2004)
9. Bachelet, R., Cisel, M.: Evaluation par les pairs au sein du MOOC ABC de la Gestion des projets: une étude préliminaire. Atelier MOOC, EIAH, Toulouse (2013). http://goo.gl/6JHYOv
10. Bachelet, R., Zongo D., Bourelle A.: Does peer grading work? How to implement and improve it? Comparing instructor and peer assessment in MOOC GdP. In: Third European MOOCs Stakeholders Summit, 18–20 May 2015, Université catholique de Louvain (2015). https://halshs.archives-ouvertes.fr/halshs-01146710
11. Lorenzetti, J.P.: How e-learning is changing higher education: a new look. Distance Education Report, pp. 4–7, 1 August 2005

Improving MOOC Student Learning Through Enhanced Peer-to-Peer Tasks

Borja Bordel(✉), Ramón Alcarria, Diego Martín, and Diego Sánchez-de-Rivera

Universidad Politécnica de Madrid, Madrid, Spain
{bbordel,diegosanchez}@dit.upm.es, {ramon.alcarria, diego.martin.de.andres}@upm.es

Abstract. In the context of MOOCs, activities that imply a deeper learning are, undoubtedly, P2P tasks. However, the traditional MOOC structure makes very difficult to evaluate the learning level obtained by students when performing these activities. This situation is especially problematic as students increasingly demand the universities to certify the knowledge acquired by means of MOOCs, so higher education institutions must guarantee their learning. In order to address this challenge, in this paper it is proposed a new type of P2P activity, designed to automatically provide students a valuable feedback about their work. This new type of activity is supported by a module, including a coordination engine and a formal revision component communicating by means of the LTI protocol with an automatic revision assistant, which allows differentiating a genuine contribution from the simple repetition of ideas. Moreover, and experimental validation is carried out. Results show first evidences that most students (up to 82%) improve their learning when employed the new proposed technology.

Keywords: P2P activity · Revision assistant · LTI protocol · Learning improvement

1 Introduction

In its origin, Massive Online Open Courses (MOOCs) were only collaborative technological learning events, organized as an experience for innovational education [1]. Shortly after, online educational platforms to offer public and free MOOC appeared. The objective of these courses was to acquire certain competencies with the sole motivation of extending the own knowledge [2]. Thus, students with a strong intrinsic motivation enrolled in MOOCs. This model has been maintained from 2008 (when the concept was defined by Cormier and Alexander [3]) to practically today.

Nevertheless, since, approximately, two years ago most important MOOC platforms have incorporate certification procedures (each time more official, providing a document including the university name and logo, the professors' signature, etc.), which response to the students' claims for universities to consider the successfully finalized MOOCs with full academic effects. In that way, academic recognition of MOOCs has increased from no recognition, to virtual budgets, simple non-academic

C. Delgado Kloos et al. (Eds.): EMOOCs 2017, LNCS 10254, pp. 140–149, 2017.
DOI: 10.1007/978-3-319-59044-8_16

certificates and the current university-supported certificates (which, in some institutions, even may be used to obtain official European Credits –ECTS- [4]). The main obstacle the universities face in order to certificate the acquired competencies in MOOCs it is the difficulty of evaluating the student learning [5]. Competencies based on low learning levels of Bloom's taxonomy (remembering, understanding, etc.) may be evaluated using traditional quiz activities (similar to which employed by universities in official eLearning programs). However, competencies related to high learning levels (such as evaluating or creating) are very complicated to evaluate due to, mainly, the extraordinary high number of students per MOOC.

Although some instruments have been already integrated in MOOC platforms in order to address this challenge, they are focused on mathematical-like courses (such as mathematics or programming) [6]. In that way, open problems with non-unique solutions or creative compositions are not covered by these proposals and must be evaluated using traditional Peer-to-Peer (P2P) tasks. Nevertheless, various problems have been detected in the use of traditional P2P tasks: from plagiarism (intentional or unintentional) to the provision of useless feedback to students (by their partners) [7]. This situation, at the end, causes the student not to reach the expected learning level.

Therefore, the objective of this paper is to propose a new technology for P2P tasks, being able to automatically provide students with a valuable feedback about their works and learning. This new type of task is supported by a module (which can be integrated into most current MOOC platforms) including a coordination engine, a formal revision component and a revision assistant, which enables students to know the originality and elaboration level of their products. Moreover, this module puts the obtained results in relation to the recommendations of professors (who, moreover, might stablish minimum required values for these parameters in order to accept a product as valid). Finally, feedback provided by other students may be also evaluated using this new P2P module.

The rest of the paper is organized as follows: Sect. 2 describes the state of the art on learning evaluation in MOOCs; Sect. 3 includes the proposed new technology and module; Sect. 4 presents an experimental validation based on a research experience; Sect. 5 contains the experimental results and Sect. 6 concludes the paper.

2 State of the Art

Nowadays, different strategies related to learning certification are followed by different MOOC platforms. While some of them now even include the concept of "degree" (as a collection of MOOCs around a certain topic which has a special associated certification) [8], other continue composing courses, basically, with quizzes and P2P activities.

Making a review about MOOCs it is a complicated task, as (probably) the scene has changed when the review work gets published [9]. However, some global tendencies may be described.

Although various types of MOOCs have been defined (such as cMOOC or xMOOC), the claims of students to obtain a certification about the acquired competencies, as well as the origin of MOOCs (most times adaptations of classroom courses), have caused the MOOCs to be focused on a traditional learning based on different video-lessons, quizzes and development exercises [10]. Then, learning evaluation methods and pedagogy approaches follow higher education principles, rather than distance learning ones [11]. In particular, Bloom's taxonomy is usually employed to discuss about MOOCs [12] (although as time passes, it is being substituted by more modern proposals such as the constructivist approach of FutureLearn [13]).

Various works have proved that MOOC only consisting on quizzes do not promote a deep learning [7]. Thus, these courses only act on the first two levels of Bloom's taxonomy (remembering and understanding), and mostly on the cognitive dimension (sometimes also on conceptual knowledge). With these ideas, various new technologies to evaluate cognitive learning in MOOCs not only considering quizzes (adding, for example, forum comments) have been described [14].

However, most MOOC stakeholders are much more interested in deep learning. In particular, some authors propose that P2P activities are the only type of tasks which may allow students to work on higher levels of Bloom's taxonomy such as apply or creating [7]. Additionally, the feedback provision phase requires "evaluation" competencies and works the metacognitive learning [15] (the most deep).

Thus, many researchers have investigated the role of students in P2P tasks [16], founding some interesting phenomena such as clusters of students committing plagiarism (many times is an unconscious way) or that proper training on assignment evaluation should be provided to MOOC students [17]. Works about peer assessment can be also found [18]. In order to address both aspects, automatic feedback generators have been proposed, informing students about the fulfillment degree of the proposed competencies in the MOOC [19].

Our work continues this research line (tool design), proposing a module to feedback students about the quality of their contributions in P2P tasks (detecting false submissions, plagiarism, a low-level of elaboration, etc.), so they may know if it is required continuing working on the product. Our proposal employs a commercial revision assistant (Turnitin [20]) in order to support these functionalities, which communicates with the MOOC platform and a coordination engine using the Learning Tools Interoperability (LTI) protocol.

3 A New Module Supporting Enhanced P2P Activities

The proposed new module for MOOC platforms in order to include enhanced P2P tasks into courses may be seen on Fig. 1. As it is shown, two big blocks are distinguished: a plug-in which must be installed in the MOOC platform, and an external revision assistant (the commercial service, Turnitin). The proposed plug-in, moreover, contains two different functional components. First, a *coordination engine* managing the communications among the different elements, supporting the core of the new services and offering a uniform interface to the MOOC platform is considered. Second, a *formal revision module* is included. This component is in charge of analyzing the meta-information of the submitted product (not the content) in order to detect inadequate submissions: empty documents, corrupted files, non-allowed file formats, etc.

The coordination engine implements four different interfaces. The first one is based on web services (commonly REST services, but also SOAP protocol if the MOOC

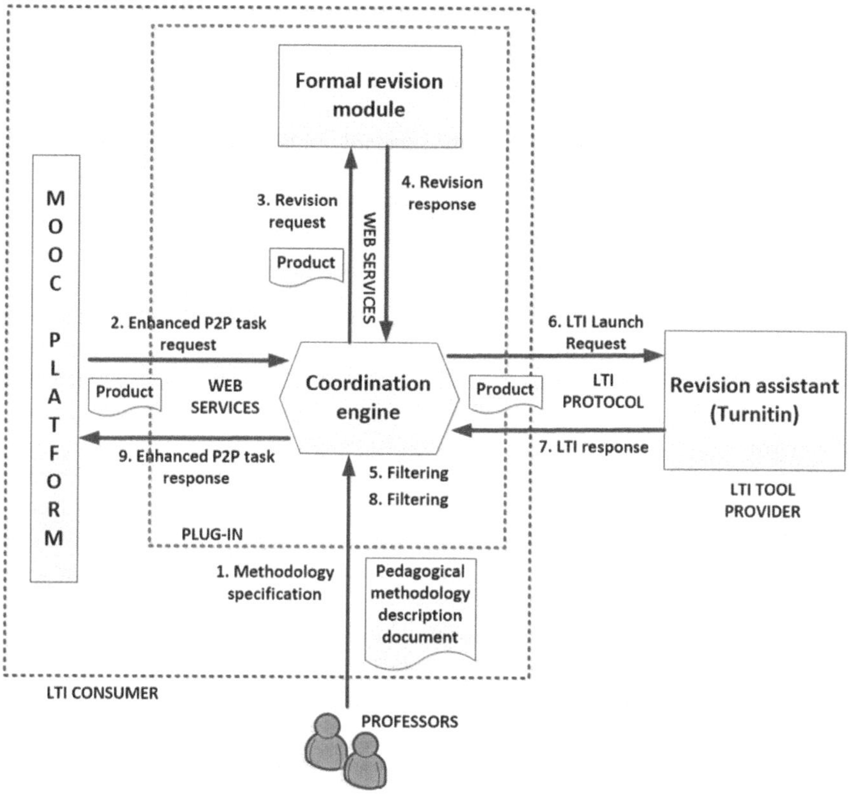

Fig. 1. Block diagram of the proposed technology

platform implements this technology). The use of Representational State Transfer (REST) interfaces allows us to obtain and send data directly employing the HTTP protocol (which makes easier to integrate the proposed module into current MOOC platforms). On the other hand, Simple Object Access Protocol (SOAP) requires modifying the programming of the MOOC platform which may be a complicated issue. The engine offers the enhanced P2P task service to the MOOC platform. Basically it receives a product (in this first work we are only considering textual compositions) and generates the adequate feedback to allow students to improve their work and learning.

The second one, in order to improve the modularity of the proposed technology and enable the creation of new versions in an easier way, it is also based on web services (in this case, it implements the REST ful interface -i.e. an interface which implements the REST design principles-). The third one, communicating with the assistant revision, it is based on the LTI protocol. The LTI protocol is the current standard mechanism to communicate educational online instruments, and (nowadays) it is employed in most eLearning platforms (e.g. Moodle). This solution for educational tools is based on the exchange of HTML forms using HTTP operations. Briefly, the coordination engine acts as *LTI consumer* and the revision assistant as *LTI tool provider*. Then, a LTI request sends the student's product and his identity to the assistant, which returns the results of the revision in a response message.

Finally, through a graphic interface professors may define the pedagogic methodology to be applied: maximum number of times students might employ the revision assistant, temporization, minimum quality standards to be fulfilled, etc. The provided methodology is organized as a XML description document which is employed by the coordination engine to manage the service operation.

As can be seen on Fig. 1, each time a product is submitted through an enhanced P2P task form, the message sequence is as described below:

1. Before the start of the submission period of the P2P task, professor should define the pedagogic methodology. The obtained description document will be employed during the future filtering phases. The proposed methodology highly influences the obtained improvement in the student learning. Thus, it must be very carefully designed.
2. Students submit their products to the P2P enhanced task service through the MOOC platform web interface. This submission generates a web service request (usually a HTTP POST operation) containing the student identity (typically his name, ID number, email and home country, as these parameters will be necessary later) and the submitted product.
3. The submitted product is sent to be evaluated in the formal revision module, using a new web service request. In order to protect the student identity, this operation is performed by means of a unique transaction number, so students' personal information remains in the coordination engine.
4. Results of the formal evaluation are sent to the coordination engine using the proper response message. Although many reviews may be developed in the formal revision module, in this first work we are only considering two: detection of corrupted files and detection of empty documents.
5. Considering the results of the formal revision and the methodology described by professors, the coordination engine decides if the revision process continues or if the submission should be discarded.
6. If the evaluation process continues, the product is sent to be deeply analyzed by the revision assistant. The product is sent in a LTI launch request, which consists of a HTTP POST operation containing an HTML form. This form describes all the parameters which must be considered in the revision process (in general, the same which are showed in the web interface, see Fig. 2). Additionally, the HTTP request contains other fields such as *remote_user*, *lti_message_type*, *lti_version* or *user_id* describing the student identity and some meta-information about the request. In order to protect the provided information, the LTI requests are always signed. Finally, the described HTML form contains a script which processes and sends the fulfilled form to the coordination engine.
7. Once fulfilled the received HTML form, the LTI tool provider executes the processing script which generates an LTI response (basically a JSON object with the evaluation results) which is sent to the LTI consumer (the coordination engine in this case).

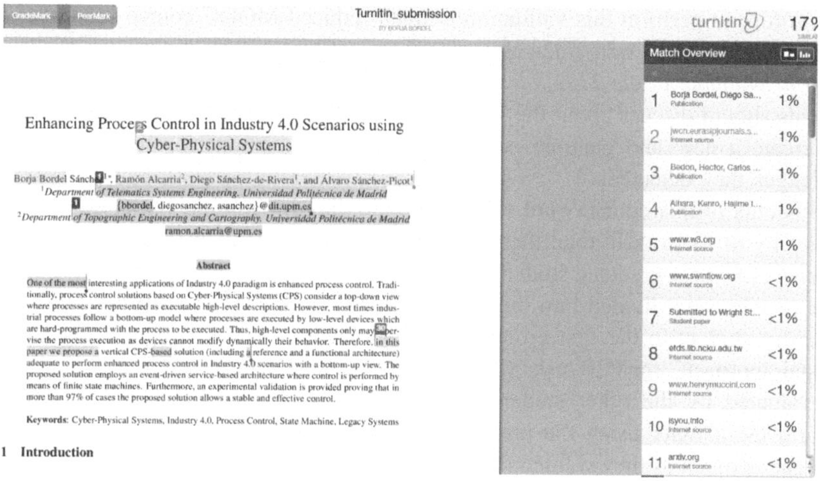

Fig. 2. Typical evaluation of a product with Turnitin

8. Considering the results of the revision process and the methodology defined by professors, the coordination engine performs a second filtering phase.
9. Finally, the coordination engine answers the original web service request indicating the results of the revision process: if the submission is accepted or rejected, if more opportunities to improve the product are available, etc. At this point, the showed parameters also depend on the interface of the MOOC platform. Any case, at least, two options should be offered to students: doing a preliminary submission (only the revision process is performed) and doing a final submission (the revision process is performed and, immediately, the product is sent to other students to be graded).

Although in this first work we are not considering this functionality, the proposed module may be extended in order to be able to analyze not only the products but also the feedback provided among the students (as a good grading work implies to improve learning, especially evaluation capacities).

4 Experimental Validation

In order to evaluate the performance of the proposed new technology, an experimental validation was planned and conducted.

As we said, the pedagogic methodology may greatly influence the learning improvement. As an important advantage, and contrary to traditional P2P tasks, this methodology may be described by professors in each P2P activity when employed the proposed technology. Thus, two different experiences were performed. During the first experience a group of selected MOOC students performed a P2P activity where they could employ the revision assistant as much as they wanted. During the second experiences, they could to employ this service as maximum three times. Then, only final submission was available.

In order to perform this validation a much reduced MOOC course was created. It consisted only on a 5 min video about the future of higher education (in particular this video is available in the *TED talks* repository [21]), followed of a P2P activity where students should discuss about the video, evaluate the current state of higher education and create a new and genuine educational approach answering some of the future challenges they detected.

Students of this course were selected among the different people at the Technical University of Madrid. In total there were forty five (45) of them, among pre-graduate students (15), post-graduate students (12), professors (9) and management staff (9). All these people were divided into three equal groups of fifteen (15) people.

Every student in the first group was asked to perform the activity using the "traditional approach" for P2P tasks (the product is created and immediately submitted to be evaluated by the other students). Students in the second group were asked to perform the activity using the proposed technology when they may use the revision assistant as much as they wanted (hereinafter called "free use approach"). And, finally, the third group developed the activity using the proposed enhanced technology but when only three attempts to use the revision assistant were allowed (hereinafter called "limited use approach").

Once all groups finished the activity, students answered a survey in order to know their opinion about their learning. Moreover, the authors corrected all the submitted final products and also evaluated the percentage of students which met the learning objectives and competencies of the proposed activity.

The MOOC test platform was developed using web technologies, and a very simple user interface.

5 Results

As we said, once all groups finished the activity, students answered a survey in order to know their opinion about their learning. In particular, they should answer if they considered that they had met a certain list of learning objectives. Survey was planned as a yes/no study. The results obtained from the group performing the activity in the traditional way were considered the ground true. Then, A Mann-Whitney U test was employed to compare the results obtained from the other groups and evaluate the learning improvement. Table 1 shows the results.

As can be seen, in general, low-level learning objectives (to know or to analyze) do not suffer a significant improvement when replaced the traditional P2P tasks by the proposed enhanced technology. However, as higher level learning objectives are considered the improvement gets more significant.

This result was expectable, as low-level objectives are completely met only listening in a comprehensive way the proposed video. Nevertheless, creation or evaluation competencies require working hard on the proposed topic. This work gets promoted if a system indicting students they should work a little bit more is implemented.

Moreover, created compositions and products were corrected by the authors, determining the fulfillment of the proposed learning objectives. Figure 3 shows the

Table 1. Results of the student surveys

Tool	Learning objectives			
	Knowing the current state and future challenges of the higher education	Analyzing the causes and possible solutions of the current problems of higher education	Evaluate the impact of the proposed solutions to the current problems of higher education	Create new and genuine educational proposals and approaches
Free use approach	*NS*	*	**	* * *
Limited use approach	*NS*	*NS*	**	**

*NS not significant; *significant at* $p < 0.05$*; **significant at* $p < 0.005$*; ***significant at* $p < 0.001$.

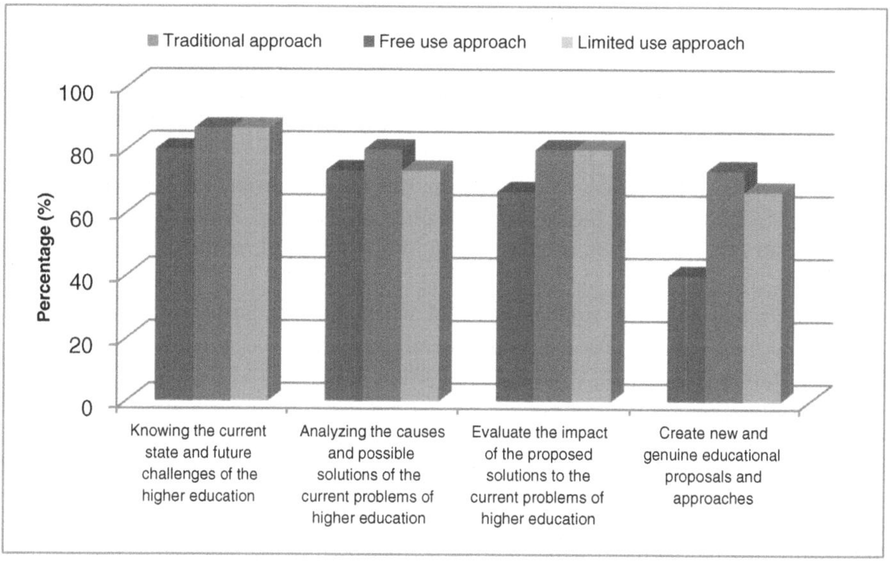

Fig. 3. Results of the professor corrections

percentage of students which met every learning objective depending on the P2P task technology employed.

As can be seen, in general, percentage of students meeting the proposed learning objectives increases for every learning objective and both pedagogic methodologies applied with the proposed enhanced P2P task technology.

This increase is especially important for the last learning objective (create new and genuine educational proposals and approaches) where up to 82% of students improve their learning (if considered the free use approach). In other cases, such as in the low-level objectives, the increase is much slighter (less than 1% of increasing, for example, if considered the objective "knowing the current state and future challenges of the higher education").

Results shown suggest that a free use methodology generates better results than a limited use approach. However, the differences between both methodologies are not very significant, so a more detailed analysis is required to confirm this hypothesis.

6 Conclusions and Future Works

In this paper we have described a new technology to integrate a new generation of P2P activities into MOOC platforms. The proposed enhanced P2P task technology consists of a module providing a report about the submitted product, so students may continue working on the composition if the quality level is not acceptable.

The module contains three functional components: a coordination engine, a formal revision module and an external revision assistant (in this case, the commercial Turnitin). Web services and the LTI protocol are employed to communicate all the components. In this first work, the proposed module only evaluates the submitted product, but future works will also evaluate the feedback provided by other students. Additionally, professors may describe the most adequate pedagogic methodology for each P2P task using the proposed technology.

An external validation it is also provided, showing the first evidences that a significant improvement in the learning level may be reached when considered the proposed technology. However, additional analyses to determine the impact of the pedagogic methodology in the obtained results are required. Any case, more robust statistical surveys should be performed in order to confirm these evidences and hypotheses.

Finally, results may be slightly different when massive groups of students (with different learning cultures, for example) attend the course and use the proposed technology. Future works should evaluate these variables.

Acknowledgments. Borja Bordel has received funding from the Ministry of Education through the FPU program (grant number FPU15/03977). Additionally, the research leading to these results has received funding from the Ministry of Economy and Competitiveness through SEMOLA project (TEC2015-68284-R) and from the Autonomous Region of Madrid through MOSI-AGIL-CM project (grant P2013/ICE-3019, co-funded by EU Structural Funds FSE and FEDER).

References

1. Pappano, L.: The Year of the MOOC. The New York Times, vol. 2, no. 12 (2012)
2. Dasarathy, B., Sullivan, K., Schmidt, D.C., Fisher, D.H., Porter, A.: The past, present, and future of MOOCs and their relevance to software engineering. In: Proceedings of the Future of Software Engineering, pp. 212–224 (2014)
3. Alexander, B.: Connectivism course draws night, or behold the MOOC. Infocult: Uncanny Informatics (2008)

4. Open Courses program, Granada University. https://abierta.ugr.es/. Accessed 16 Jan 2017
5. Abeer, W., Miri, B.: Students' preferences and views about learning in a MOOC. Procedia-Soc. Behav. Sci. **152**, 318–323 (2014)
6. EdPuzzle homepage. https://edpuzzle.com/. Accessed 16 Jan 2017
7. Bali, M.: MOOC pedagogy: gleaning good practice from existing MOOCs. J. Online Learn. Teach. **10**(1), 44 (2014)
8. Udacity Nanodegree program. https://www.udacity.com/nanodegree. Accessed 16 Jan 2017
9. Lakshminarayanan, S.: Ruminating about MOOCs. J. NUS Teach. Acad. **2**(4), 223–227 (2012). http://www.nus.edu.sg/teachingacademy/article/ruminating-about-moocs-2/. Accessed 16 Jan 2017
10. Kolowich, S., Newman, J.: The professors behind the MOOC hype: survey results. The Chronicle of Higher Education (2013). http://www.chronicle.com/article/The-Professors-Behind-the-MOOC/137905/#id=results. Accessed 16 Jan 2017
11. Anderson, S., Collier, A., Horii, C.V.: Designing and implementing MOOCs to maximize student learning. Online presentation delivered as part of the EDUCAUSE Learning Initiative Spring 2013
12. Krathwohl, D.R.: A revision of Bloom's taxonomy: an overview. Theory Pract. **41**(4), 212–218 (2012). doi:10.1207/s15430421tip4104_2
13. Constructivist learning in the FutureLearning platform. https://www.futurelearn.com/courses/blended-learning-getting-started/0/steps/7848. Accessed 16 Jan 2017
14. Wong, J.S., Pursel, B., Divinsky, A., Jansen, B.J.: Analyzing MOOC discussion forum messages to identify cognitive learning information exchanges. Proc. Assoc. Inf. Sci. Technol. **52**(1), 1–10 (2015)
15. Cook, E., Kennedy, E., McGuire, S.Y.: Effect of teaching metacognitive learning strategies on performance in general chemistry courses. J. Chem. Educ. **90**(8), 961–967 (2013)
16. Griesbaum, J.: Students as teachers in MOOCs? The double gain of MOOCs as an in-class teaching method experiences from a student-made MOOC. Int. J. Inf. Educ. Technol. **4**(1), 29 (2014)
17. Luo, H., Robinson, A.C., Park, J.Y.: Peer grading in a MOOC: reliability, validity, and perceived effects. J. Asynchronous Learn. Netw. **18**(2), 1–14 (2014)
18. Suen, H.K.: Peer assessment for massive open online courses (MOOCs). Int. Rev. Res. Open Distrib. Learn. **15**(3), 312–327 (2014)
19. Whitelock, D., Gilbert, L., Wills, G.: Feedback generators: providing feedback in MOOCs. In: Proceedings of the 2013 International Conference CAA. University of Southampton (2013)
20. Turnitin home page. http://turnitin.com/. Accessed 16 Jan 2017
21. Khan, S.: Let's use video to reinvent education. http://www.ted.com/talks/salman_khan_let_s_use_video_to_reinvent_education. Accessed 16 Jan 2017

Who Wants to Chat on a MOOC? Lessons from a Peer Recommender System

François Bouchet[1(✉)], Hugues Labarthe[1], Rémi Bachelet[2], and Kalina Yacef[3]

[1] Sorbonne Universités, UPMC Univ Paris 06, CNRS, LIP6 UMR 7606, Paris, France
francois.bouchet@lip6.fr,
hugues.labarthe@ac-creteil.fr
[2] Centrale Lille, University of Lille, Lille, France
remi.bachelet@ec-lille.fr
[3] School of Information Technologies, The University of Sydney, Sydney, Australia
kalina.yacef@sydney.edu.au

Abstract. Peer recommender systems (PRS) in MOOCs have been shown to help reducing attrition and increase performance of those who use them. But who are the students using them and what are their motivations? And why are some students reluctant to use them? To answer these questions, we present a study where we implemented a chat-based PRS that has been used during a MOOC session involving 6,170 students. Our analyses indicate that PRS-users are students unsatisfied by other means of interactions already available (forums, social networks…), and that they seem to use it more to share emotions than to learn together, or to assess their progression against their peers.

Keywords: Synchronous chat · Peer recommender system · Synchronous collaboration in MOOC · Social learning

1 Introduction

Recommender systems (RS) have become the key to industrial success in several sectors (e.g. online stores, music or movie services…) and many of us rely on them daily. They have also been used in the field of Technology Enhanced Learning, mostly to recommend resources or other classes relevant to follow [1, 2]. A specific kind of RS is those used to recommend other persons (persons to follow on social networks, potential mates on dating services…), which in a learning context can take the form of peer recommender systems (PRS) [3]. It is therefore logical to wonder what a PRS, a system allowing students to interact with each other while learning, could bring to an MOOC. Previous studies suggest that such a tool can not only help reducing students' attrition [4], as lack or loss of relationship is a good predictor of attrition [5], but also increase success and participation [6]. Beyond the issues relative to the identification of features to be used to make a good recommendation of a learner to another, we also need to better understand the users' motivations for using such a tool [7]: in our context, this means knowing whether MOOC learners would have an interest in a PRS and actually use it,

C. Delgado Kloos et al. (Eds.): EMOOCs 2017, LNCS 10254, pp. 150–159, 2017.
DOI: 10.1007/978-3-319-59044-8_17

and what distinguishes these learners from those who choose not to use it. This profiling would help us not only to improve the recommendation algorithms, but also to better understand what aspects currently missing in the MOOC experience these learners are seeking through the chat. It is even more interesting to study as reviews of the use of RS in education mention little to no use of RS as PRS [1, 2].

The question raised by a peer recommender is related to a more general issue, identified by researchers in Computer Supported Collaborative Learning (CSCL), since 1995. Social learning has been demonstrated to be, in many contexts, the best way to learn, as it allows students to identify and correct their misconceptions, as well as to improve their overall understanding by sharing it with others [8]. When dealing with thousands of students, it is obvious that some are not as involved as others for various reasons that may involve a combination of trust, confidence, shyness, willingness to share, willingness to help others… Social Learning researchers are interested in analyzing the different ways for somebody to be engaged through an analysis of the traces they leave when socializing.

In this paper, we aim at having a better understanding of this issue. To foster learners' discussions in MOOCs, we have designed, implemented and tested a PRS. Our recommender provides each student with a list of potentially relevant persons and a way to contact them directly through an instant chat system. This list is based on what the recommender knows about the student's profile and activities in the MOOC. We hypothesize that the students who have the keenest interest in social learning would make the most active use of the recommender. The remainder of this paper is organized as follows: in Sect. 2, we present the context and design of our chat-based PRS and give an overview of its functioning. In Sect. 3, we present the actual experiment, including the data collected, its preprocessing and the way it has been analyzed and the results provided by the statistical analyses performed to identify correlations between the expressions of interest for a peer recommender and its effective use. We then conclude the paper with a discussion on the lessons learned, their limits and the perspectives they open for future work.

2 Recommender in the GdP8 MOOC

2.1 Context of the Experiment

In a first controlled-study conducted during a Project Management MOOC, we observed a significant improvement of students' engagement, not only for those who interacted with the recommendations, but more largely, for all of those who accepted using the PRS [6, 9]. We also collected critical feedback from users and stakeholders concerning the design flaws of the widget (visual intrusiveness, difficulty to understand the recommendation mechanism, chat and recommendation system being two distinct elements of the interface…), the lack of interest for recommendation, and the potential features overlap with forums and social networks. Therefore, it appeared interesting to investigate the actual role of this peer recommender: who used it, who did not, and why.

This paper exploits data recently collected with a new version of our PRS implemented within the 8th GdP MOOC on project management, which took place between

September and November 2016. The MOOC relies on a proprietary modified version Canvas platform made by Unow. In this MOOC, two certification levels are available: basic and advanced. Both require students to follow and pass 2 specialization modules among 13 available. These modules are available on a separate specialization MOOC, which opens on the third week of the "common core course" (cf. Fig. 1 for a timeline). The peer recommendation widget was only available on the specialization platform, from its opening on week 3 to the MOOC end on week 10. On this platform, students learn and take quizzes individually, and no social interaction is encouraged through the pedagogy (e.g. no collaborative task or need to network with others). Not giving access to the widget on the core MOOC allowed us to ask participants if they were lacking interactions from the regular MOOC experience.

The GdP MOOC has a special place in the French MOOC ecosystem, as its first session (GdP1) was the first xMOOC (i.e. not run on connectivist principles) opened in France (Jan–Mar 2013). It was developed from an existing Open Course Ware (OCW) website [10] as an experience of running a distance learning course. It benefits from high enrolment, with over 130,000 distinct students having participated in the 8 sessions ran so far – some of them even returning several times [11] as the content evolves with each edition. Only the latest edition (GdP8 – Sep–Nov. 2016) is studied in this paper.

2.2 The Peer Recommender System and Chat Widget

The PRS and chat appear as a single widget visible on every page of the specialization module platform. It appears as minimized by default in the bottom right hand corner of the interface (cf. Fig. 2a), and can be expanded with a click. When minimized, a red cross allows users to opt out, which hides the button for the rest of the learning session. Once expanded, it consists of 3 main panels (Fig. 2c) accessible through tabs at the bottom of the interface. The first tab gives access to a list of discussion threads the student has created or has been added to. Each discussion is identifiable by the avatar of its creator and an excerpt of the first message. A click on a thread opens it (Fig. 2e), allowing the user to read the messages posted in it and to contribute by sending a message. Each student was added by default into an initial thread providing information about how the system worked. The second tab is used to initiate a discussion with a group of 20 persons chosen according to one of three sets of criteria: (1) randomly, (2) based on the student's demographics (age, location, socio-professional category…) or (3) based on the student's progression in the specialization modules (which modules they are following and how far they progressed, based on quizzes taken so far). Once a type of recommendation is chosen, students have to type their first message in the thread (Fig. 2d). The third tab gives access to a list of favorite contacts – initially empty, it can be filled by adding persons met through group chats (Fig. 2f). These persons can then be contacted individually. To ensure the widget was seen by everyone, a warning bubble (Fig. 2b) popped out after the first 3 pages visited. It disappeared forever after the student either opened the chat or ignored it for 5 pages.

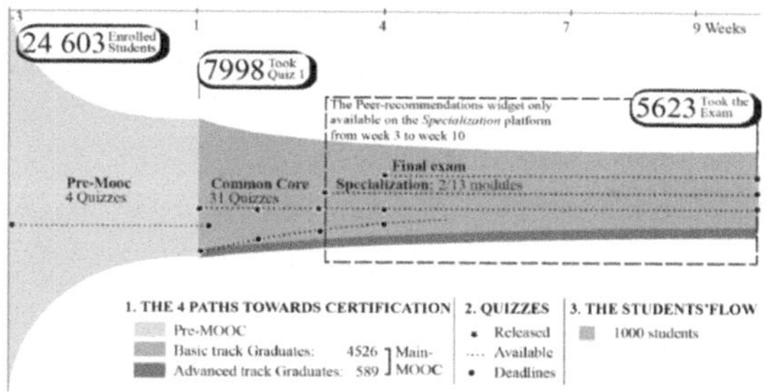

Fig. 1. An overview of the timeline for the GdP MOOC (8th edition)

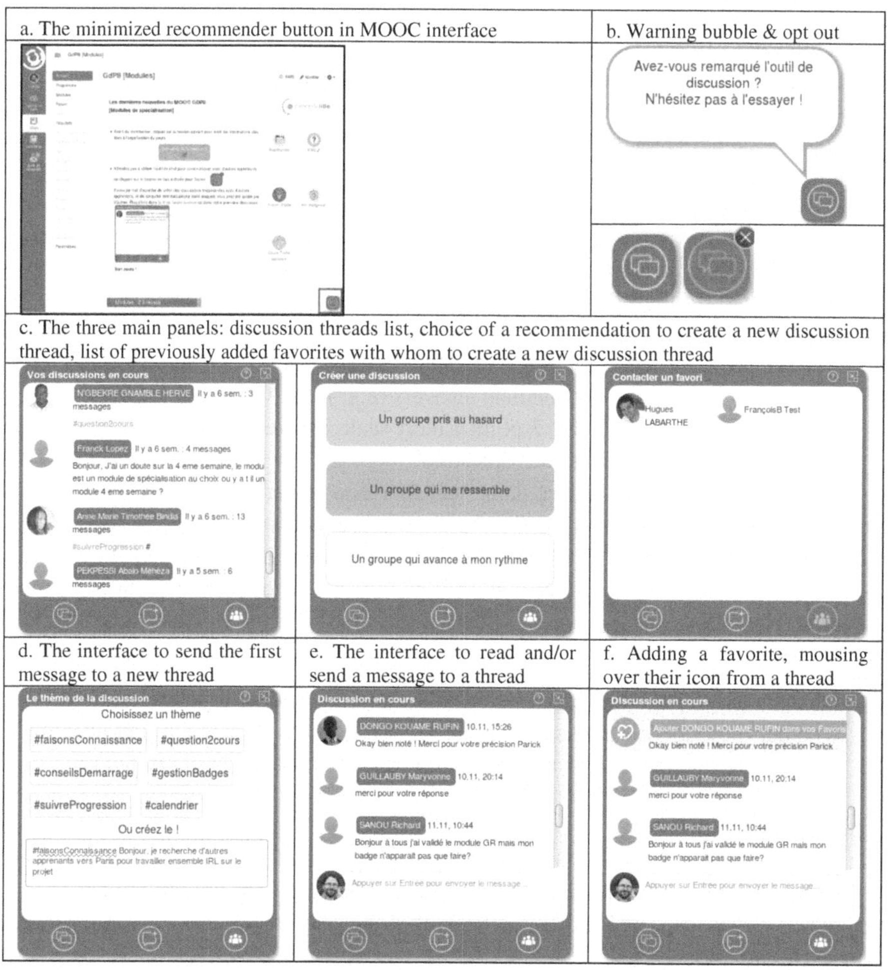

Fig. 2. The peer recommender and chat widget: implementation and design

Each panel also benefited from a distinct help page, accessible through a question mark icon on the top right hand of the interface. A dedicated forum thread was also opened to answer to specific questions regarding the PRS.

3 Experiment

3.1 Methodology

Participants. 24,603 persons registered to the MOOC, among which $N = 6{,}170$ logged at least once on the specialization modules platform (i.e. were still active in the MOOC by the time this platform opened in week 3) and were therefore exposed to the chat system and its associated PRS in the interface.

Data Collected. Before the start of the MOOC and in week 3, before the start of the specialization modules, students were invited to fill in two questionnaires which included questions relative to their will to interact with others and socialize, as well as the issues encountered so far with the GdP MOOC. The questions relevant to this paper are summarized in Table 1. These questionnaires provided a few bonus points (less than 1% of the final grade) to encourage students to answer to them, but they were not mandatory, which explains a reduction of the sample size when considering students who filled them. To increase the reliability of the questionnaire, the same concept was sometimes tested through different questions: we therefore merged these questions by calculating the average answer value (between 1 and 7) for all questions corresponding to the same concept (cf. column "variable extracted"). Then the answers were dichotomized by excluding intermediate answers (e.g. if the value was between 3.5 and 4.5 for an aggregation of several 7 point Likert scale answers), which led to different sample sizes when considering each question.

In addition to this self-report data, we also considered log data collected in a database tracking the use of the PRS during the specialization modules session. We tracked whenever the MOOC participants were opening the widget, opening a discussion thread within that interface and sending a message to an existing thread or to a new one. This allows us to separate our sample of 6170 participants according to 3 criteria:

(1) whether they opened (N_{open}) or not ($N_{not\text{-}open}$) the widget at least once,
(2) whether they opened a discussion thread (N_{thread}) or not ($N_{no\text{-}thread}$) at least once,
(3) whether they sent at least 1 message to a discussion thread (N_{msg}) or not ($N_{no\text{-}msg}$).

Experimental Procedure. To compare PRS users from non-PRS users, we performed multiple Pearson's chi-squared tests for statistical independence between the 3° of use of the chat (opening, reading a thread, sending a message) and the aforementioned 7 variables, i.e. we made the null hypothesis that the use of the chat was independent from each variable.

Table 1. List of variables extracted from research questionnaires

Question (translated)	Answers	Variable extracted
- It is important for me to succeed more than other students	7 point Likert scale	GoalBetterThanOthers
- It is important for me to succeed well compared to others in this MOOC		
- My goal in this MOOC is to have a better grade than most of the other students		
- I'm not concerned by what others might think of me	7 point Likert scale	FearOfBeingJudged*
- I'm not concerned by the judgment of others		
- I don't worry about what others think of me		
- When I think of the MOOC activities, I feel an emotion I want to share	7 point Likert scale	WillToShareFeelings*
- I went to the forums to share my issues with other students	7 point Likert scale	WillToInteractToLearn*
- When I am stuck in the course, I seek advice from other students		
- I talk with other students about parts of the course that appear unclear		
- I interact with other students to know if we have understood the same thing		
- I go to social networks to share my issues with other students		
- I interact with other students to know how to handle the online courses		
- For you, how useful are the forums in this MOOC?	5 point Likert scale	PerceivedSocializationUsefulness
- How useful are social networks (Facebook, Google Plus, Twitter, blogs…) to help you learn?		
- I have contributed to the discussion forums	5 point Likert scale	PerformedSocialization
- I have shared on social networks to ask or answer to questions, share my experience…		
- One of the problems I face with this MOOC is that I lack being in contact with other learners	Yes/No	LackContactWithOthers

*for these variables, one or several attention filters were used, i.e. a fake question asking participants not to answer anything was used to filter out those who answered anything to it.

3.2 Results

Use of the Chat with the Recommender System. When separating the different participant samples based on the type of use of the widget, we found the following results:

- N_{open} = 3025 (49.03%) participants opened the widget at least once
- N_{thread} = 570 (9.24%) participants opened a thread at least once
- N_{msg} = 206 (3.34%) participants sent at least one message in a discussion thread (84 of which created at least one thread).

Although they represent a minority of the participants in the specialization modules, these figures are similar to the percentage of learners who tend to use social features in MOOCs – usually from 3 to 15% according to a literature review from [12], higher in platforms explicitly encouraging conversational learning (e.g. 24 to 45% of FutureLearn's learners post at least one comment [13]). But more importantly, the sample sizes are large enough to allow us to perform a more detailed study in order to identify the features that distinguish these learners from the ones who did not use the PRS.

Comparing PRS Users and Non-users. The results (cf. Table 2) reveal that PRS users and non-users differ according to numerous characteristics. In particular, participants interested in doing better than others were more likely to send a message (although they opened the widget and threads in equal proportion to others). Conversely, being afraid of others' judgment was negatively correlated with the likelihood of opening a thread (moderately, $p = .043$) and sending a message (strongly, $p = .002$). Participants who expressed interest in sharing how they feel about the MOOC were more likely to welcome the PRS, opening it and using it very significantly more. The will to interact with others to learn was less correlated with the chat use, as only the action consisting in sending a message was significantly more performed by those who liked learning with others. Finally, learners who consider socialization to be useful, those who already socialized either through the forum and/or through social networks as well as those who declared not having enough contact with others were all very significantly more likely to engage with the PRS (by opening it, reading the threads and sending messages).

Why Don't Some People Want to Use a PRS in a MOOC? Until now, we have focused on students who used the PRS, but in order to get a complementary perspective, we also asked the 1,631 participants who did not use the recommender system but who noticed it to explain their decision not to give it a try (surprisingly, despite the warning bubble, 718 students declared not having noticed it, and 406 did not remember whether they had seen it or not). Participants were allowed to choose one or more options (or none, if none fitted their situation). Results are summarized in Fig. 3. Overall, it appears that the main reason was the lack of a relevant question to ask, followed by a preference for the forums (although it is unclear whether it is to reach more persons or simply because the interface was more familiar to them as it was already accessible in the main section of the MOOC). Around 8% of them mentioned issues, either technical (e.g. the recommender might have not worked well on some exotic devices or browsers) or practical (e.g. difficulties to understand how to use the chat, despite the provided help system). Finally, a few participants mentioned they did not think others could help them with the issues they were having. No participants felt intimidated by the widget, which was the case in a previous version [9] where chat users had to choose individually the persons they wanted to interact with, based on

Table 2. 3 × 7 Chi-squared test results: contingency table and p-values

		Opened the chat		Opened a thread		Sent a message		*n*
		0	1	0	1	0	1	
GoalBetterThanOthers	0	1222	1375	2323	274	2514	83	3748
	1	511	640	1008	143	1090	61	
		$p > 0.05$		$p > 0.05$		$p < 0.01$**		
FearOfBeingJudged	0	230	315	471	74	513	32	3098
	1	1177	1376	2283	270	2474	79	
		$p = 0.097$		$p = 0.043$*		$p = 0.002$**		
WillToShareFeelings	0	596	589	1114	71	1176	9	2701
	1	596	920	1271	245	1425	91	
		$p = 0.000$***		$p = 0.000$***		$p = 0.000$***		
WillToInteract ToLearn	0	1069	1300	2105	264	2295	74	2844
	1	201	274	415	60	450	25	
		$p = 0.261$		$p = 0.352$		$p = 0.020$*		
PerceivedSocialization Usefulness	0	691	695	1266	120	1359	27	3176
	1	674	1116	1521	269	1667	123	
		$p = 0.000$***		$p = 0.000$***		$p = 0.000$***		
Performed Socialization	0	1176	1236	2208	204	2368	44	3799
	1	457	930	1126	261	1264	123	
		$p = 0.000$***		$p = 0.000$***		$p = 0.000$***		
LackContact WithOthers	0	1921	2250	3733	438	4023	148	4506
	1	105	230	267	68	300	35	
		$p = 0.000$***		$p = 0.000$***		$p = 0.000$***		

*$p < 0.05$; **$p < 0.01$; ***$p < 0.001$

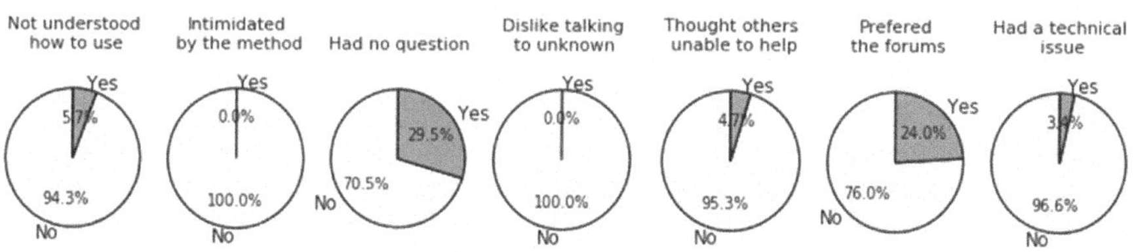

Fig. 3. The identified causes for not using the chat interface

their avatar and short bio (if available). This result is confirmed by the fact that nobody reported having issues about being in contact with unknown fellow learners.

3.3 Discussion

Chat users differed significantly from learners who chose not to use it. In particular, many were already users of other interaction media (forums, social networks…) and apparently were not fully satisfied by the interactions offered – as opposed to the non-users who stated that forums were enough for them. Moreover, combining the fact that a quarter of the non-users had no relevant question to ask and the fact that chat users needed to share feelings more than learning with others (which is consistent with [14]), it appears that chat users are mostly seeking a way to track other students' progress and emotions to reassure themselves. This seems even more crucial for those who like performing better than others, as MOOCs rarely provide mechanisms to benchmark oneself against others the way classrooms do. It suggests the chat was used by participants who feared being late compared with others: it would explain why the fear of being judged is highly correlated with the chances of sending a message.

It is interesting to confront the benchmark hypothesis with another observation: participants fearing judgment of others opened discussion threads in proportions similar to participants who did not, although they sent less messages. As we know from the questionnaire filled by people who did not use the chat, the fear to talk to unknown persons is not a valid explanation of this behavior. It could therefore be consistent with the aforementioned hypothesis, indicating a form of lurking behavior: they wanted to check how well others were doing, without necessarily sharing their own progress – either because they were doing better and it was enough for them to know it, or because they were lagging behind and feeling too ashamed to let others know about it.

4 Conclusion

In this paper, we have reported the results of the use of a peer recommender chat system in a MOOC, showing that participants interested in interacting with recommended peers differed significantly from those who did not. The chat seemed to fill a gap experienced by some of the MOOC participants who complain about the lack of interaction with others despite the tools already available (forums, social networks…). A detailed analysis of the answers also suggests the tool was mostly used to share emotions more than to actually learn together, and that it seemed interesting even to the eyes of some participants who did not want to post a message, as a way of reassurance on how well or not the others are doing.

Although implementing the PRS only in the second half of the MOOC allowed us to measure what participants felt was lacking, the fact it was not a feature available on day 1 may have reduced the overall use of the tool. In particular, as we know it may be used as a way to keep social links and not to drop off, we have probably lost participants who might have stayed around longer with this tool, but who had already dropped off by the time it became accessible in week 3. Another limitation of this work, relative to the analysis, is that we did not consider the final grade obtain by students, which could be an additional indication for explaining some of the observed behaviors. An analysis of the sequences of actions could also be relevant to confirm some of the hypotheses we are making here. Finally, the actual content of the discussion between participants would also need to be analyzed and maybe compared to the content of the forums.

In future work, we intend to use a similar version of the PRS in a new session of this MOOC that would be accessible from day 1 and to possibly encourage its use for learning activities (since it did not appear to be the most common use this time). We also wish to make our PRS system an open source plugin so that it can easily be embedded in any MOOC; we do not foresee any issue as it relies on information that is not specific to the GdP MOOC. The results of this experiment also raise questions about the interest of having an embedded tool to better keep track of other participants' progress.

Acknowledgments. The authors would like to thank Unow, and in particular Régis Millet for their technical assistance.

References

1. Manouselis, N., Drachsler, H., Vuorikari, R., Hummel, H., Koper, R.: Recommender systems in technology enhanced learning. In: Ricci, F., Rokach, L., Shapira, B., Kantor, P.B. (eds.) Recommender Systems Handbook, pp. 387–415. Springer, New York (2011)
2. Klašnja-Milićević, A., Ivanović, M., Nanopoulos, A.: Recommender systems in e-learning environments: a survey of the state-of-the-art and possible extensions. Artif. Intell. Rev. **44**, 571–604 (2015)
3. Tang, T.Y., Daniel, B.K., Romero, C.: Recommender systems in social and online learning environments. Expert Syst. **32**, 261–263 (2015)
4. Ferschke, O., Yang, D., Tomar, G., Rosé, C.P.: Positive impact of collaborative chat participation in an edX MOOC. In: Conati, C., Heffernan, N., Mitrovic, A., Verdejo, M. (eds.) AIED 2015. LNCS (LNAI), vol. 9112, pp. 115–124. Springer, Cham (2015). doi:10.1007/978-3-319-19773-9_12
5. Yang, D., Wen, M., Rosé, C.P.: Peer influence on attrition in massive open online courses. In: Proceedings of the 7th International Conference on Educational Data Mining, London, UK, pp. 405–406 (2014)
6. Labarthe, H., Bouchet, F., Bachelet, R., Yacef, K.: Does a peer recommender foster students' engagement in MOOCs? In: Barnes, T., Chi, M., and Feng, M. (eds.) Proceedings of the 9th International Conference on Educational Data Mining. pp. 418–423. International Educational Data Mining Society (IEDMS), Raleigh (2016)
7. Zheng, S., Rosson, M.B., Shih, P.C., Carroll, J.M.: Understanding student motivation, behaviors and perceptions in MOOCs. In: Proceedings of the 18th ACM Conference on Computer Supported Cooperative Work & Social Computing, pp. 1882–1895. ACM, New York (2015)
8. Kirschner, F., Paas, F., Kirschner, P.A.: A cognitive load approach to collaborative learning: united brains for complex tasks. Educ. Psychol. Rev. **21**, 31–42 (2009)
9. Labarthe, H., Bachelet, R., Bouchet, F., Yacef, K.: Increasing MOOC completion rates through social interactions: a recommendation system. In: Khalil, M., Ebner, M., Kopp, M., Lorenz, A., and Kalz, M. (eds.) Proceedings of the European Stakeholder Summit on Experiences and Best Practices in and Around MOOCs, Graz, Austria, pp. 471–480 (2016)
10. Bachelet, R.: Cours et MOOC de gestion de projet : formations en vidéo, ppt, pdf et modèles de documents. http://gestiondeprojet.pm
11. Bouchet, F., Bachelet, R.: Do MOOC students come back for more? Recurring students in the GdP MOOC. In: Proceedings of the European MOOCs Stakeholders Summit 2015, Mons, Belgium, pp. 174–182 (2015)
12. Alario-Hoyos, C., Perez-Sanagustin, M., Delgado-Kloos, C., Munoz-Organero, M.: Delving into participants' profiles and use of social tools in MOOCs. IEEE Trans. Learn. Technol. **3**, 260–266 (2014)
13. Measuring our first eight courses. https://about.futurelearn.com/blog/measuring-our-first-eight-courses/
14. Coetzee, D., Fox, A., Hearst, M.A., Hartmann, B.: Chatrooms in MOOCs: all talk and no action. In: Proceedings of the First ACM Conference on Learning @ Scale Conference, pp. 127–136. ACM, New York (2014)

Weekly Predicting the At-Risk MOOC Learners Using Dominance-Based Rough Set Approach

Sarra Bouzayane[1,3(✉)] and Inès Saad[1,2]

[1] MIS Laboratory, University of Picardie Jules Verne, Amiens, France
{sarra.bouzayane, ines.saad}@u-picardie.fr
[2] Amiens Business School, Amiens, France
[3] MIRACL Laboratory, Higher Institute of Computer Science and Multimedia, Sfax, Tunisia

Abstract. This paper proposes a method based on the Dominance-based Rough Set Approach (DRSA) to predict the learners who are likely to drop out the course during the next week of the MOOC (Massive Open Online Course) based on their demographic and dynamic data of the previous week. These are called "At-risk Learners". This method consists in two phases: the first aims at inferring a preference model while the second consists of classifying each learner either in the decision class Cl1 of "At-risk Learners" or in the decision class Cl2 of "Active Learners" based on the previously inferred preference model. The first phase is made of three steps: the first is to identify assignment examples of learners, the second is to construct a coherent criteria family for the learners' profiles characterization and the third is to infer a preference model resulting in a set of decision rules. The two phases should be weekly implemented throughout the MOOC broadcast. This method has been validated on real data of a French MOOC proposed by a Business School in France.

Keywords: Multicriteria decision making · Dominance-based Rough Set Approach · "At-risk Learner" · Preference model · Prediction

1 Introduction

As a product of the digital age revolution, MOOCs (Massive Open Online Courses) have become an alternative to the traditional higher education courses [14]. Since 2008, when the first MOOC has been coined by Downes and Siemens, the number of the MOOC platform providers and that of MOOCs has rapidly increased around the world, especially these last years where we note 4550 MOOCs in 2016 compared to 309 in 2013[1]. However, despite their popularity and proliferation, MOOCs still suffer from a big problem that is the high dropout rate that usually reaches 90% [13]. Researchers in this domain link the learners' dropout behavior to several factors such as the lack of instructor interaction and the course content difficulty [7] or the length of the MOOC

[1] http://www.onlinecoursereport.com/state-of-the-mooc-2016-a-year-of-massive-landscape-change-formassive-open-online-courses/.

C. Delgado Kloos et al. (Eds.): EMOOCs 2017, LNCS 10254, pp. 160–169, 2017.
DOI: 10.1007/978-3-319-59044-8_18

and the voluntary mode of participation [9]. This excessive dropout rate has encouraged researchers and experts to think of methods for early predicting learners who are at risk to dropout MOOCs in order to help them not give them up. Several prediction models were proposed in literature based on many learning machine techniques. In this paper we follow thus this same perspective. We propose a method based on Dominance-based Rough Set Approach (DRSA) [6] in order to weekly predict the learners who are likely to drop out the course during the next week of the MOOC based on their demographic and dynamic data of the previous week. To the best of our knowledge, rough theory was never used in the literature to a prediction purpose within the MOOCs. This method consists of two phases. The first phase aims to construct a preference model and comprises three steps which are: First, the identification of a training sample of "At-risk learners of reference", then, the construction of a coherent family of criteria to characterize the learner's profile, and finally, the inference of a preference model resulting in a set of decision rules. The second phase consists of the classification of the new learners called the "Potentially At-risk Learners" based on the previously inferred preference model. The method has been validated on real data coming from a MOOC proposed by a Business School in France.

The remainder of this paper is organized as follows: Sect. 2 shows the related work. Section 3 describes the method of weekly predicting the "At-risk Learners". Section 4 is dedicated to the application of this method. Section 5 concludes the work and advances some prospects.

2 Related Work

In this section, we present the prediction models that were proposed to early identify learners who are at risk of dropping out the MOOC.

The commonly adapted principle when addressing the dropout prediction issue within the MOOCs is to apply one or more machine learning techniques on a set of static and/or dynamic attributes. Balakrishnan [1] proposed a model to predict the students' retention in MOOCs using two kinds of Hidden Markov Model (HMM) techniques; HMM with a single feature and HMM with multiple features. Prediction is based on the cumulative percentage of the available lecture videos watched, the number of threads viewed on the forum, the number of posts made on the forum and the number of times the course progress page was checked. This model has the goal of predicting the dropout of a student for the next week of the MOOC on the basis of his data for the current week. Experiments showed that the multiple features HMM gives more reasonable results than the single feature one. In addition, the percentage of the available lecture videos watched is the most efficient when using the single feature HMM. Authors in [5] proposed a model based on the Neural Network to predict a student's attrition in MOOCs. And other than the classical attributes, such as the number of clicks made by the learner and the weekly number of the forum and the course pages viewed, authors integrated a sentiment score attribute. This is calculated using a lexicon-based sentiment analysis of the forum posts. Authors proved that the analysis of the sentiment expressed by students during their forum posts is an important indicator of the dropout behavior intention. Authors in [8] proposed a model to predict what they called the "leader learners" in the MOOC. To do this, they used the Support Vector Machine as well as the language accommodation measure. Their method is based on the lexical analysis of the forums posts in order to identify the students by whom the language of the struggling students is influenced. The students whose language influences positively the other students are called "leaders of the struggling students" and will be mobilized to answer their questions on the forums to encourage them not to drop. Authors in [12] proposed a temporal modeling approach to predict students who are at risk to dropout the MOOC using the General Bayesian Network and the Decision Tree. The used features are the number of discussion posts, the number of forum views, the number of quiz and module views, and the degree of the social network. Authors showed the importance of using the appended features input. This model permits to predict in a chronological order over weeks the dropout behavior of students.

In this context of MOOCs, the models based on machine learning techniques are usually faced to the problem of imbalanced data which can degrade the prediction performance. In effect, because of the weekly dropout rate that is relatively steep, the data used when training the prediction model are highly imbalanced towards the negative class. Thus, the method based-DRSA that we propose in the reminder of this paper overcomes this problem.

3 Method for Weekly Predicting the MOOC "At-Risk Learners"

The approach DRSA has been proposed by Greco et al. [6] for the objective of supervised learning, and inspired from the rough sets theory [10]. It allows comparing objects through a dominance relation and takes into account the preferences of a decision maker, to extract decision rules.

In this section we detail the method based DRSA for the weekly prediction of the "At-risk learners" in a context of MOOCs. We call an "At-risk Learner", the one who tends to leave the course in the next week of the MOOC and an "Active learner", the one who is still active and so does not have the intention to leave it. Prediction is based on the learner's demographic and dynamic data of the previous week. The method consists of two phases: (i) constructing a preference model resulting in a set of decision rules, and (ii) exploiting the preference model for the learners' classification.

First, we introduce some new notations. Let $W = \{W_1, \ldots W_i, \ldots W_n\}$ be the set of weeks making up a MOOC such that $n \geq 2$ is the number of weeks a MOOC holds and W_i is the ith week of the MOOC. We note $S_i = \langle K_i, F_i, V_i, f_i \rangle$ the information table build at the end of the week W_i such that K_i and F_i are respectively the non-empty finite set of reference objects selected during the ith week and the non-empty finite set of criteria and $f_i : K_i \times F_i \rightarrow V_i$ is the information function defined such that $f_i(x, g) \in V_{i,g}$ for each object $x \in K_i$ and attribute $g \in F_i$.

3.1 Phase 1: Preference Model Construction

This phase has the objective of inferring a set of decision rules permitting to weekly classify the learners enrolled in the MOOC. It is made of three steps: the first is to identify assignment examples of learners, the second is to construct a family of criteria for learners' profiles characterization and the third is to infer a preference model.

Step 1.1: Definition of a set of "At-risk Learners of Reference".

Given the massive number of learners involved in a MOOC, it is difficult to analyze and evaluate all of them. Hence, it is necessary to define a training sample including an adequate number of representative examples for each decision class; the decision class Cl1 of "At-risk Learners" and the decision class Cl2 of "Active Learners". In order to comply with the terminology used in the DRSA approach, we call the training examples, "At-risk Learners of Reference". However, since the learners within a MOOC can enter or drop it at any time while it is running, this training sample K_i can not be stable over many weeks. Thus, at the end of each week W_i, the pedagogical team has to define a new set K_i of the "At-risk Learners of Reference".

Step 1.2: Construction of a family of criteria.

The criteria family would permit to characterize the learners' profiles within a MOOC. Thus, to construct a family of criteria, we use a constructive approach based on a deepened literature review related to the issue of dropout prediction in the MOOCs context. The criteria can be either static, so strongly inhibit and catalyze the dropout behavior, or dynamic, where the variation indicates the dropout intention. In this work, we have retained eight static criteria that are the study level, the level of technical skills, the level of proficiency in MOOC language, the motivation for MOOC registration, the previous experience with MOOCs, the mastery level of the subject of the MOOC, the probability to finish the MOOC and the weekly availability. The four dynamics criteria are the weekly number of forum posts, the weekly number of forum questions, the weekly number of viewed resources and the weekly score. However, compared to an attribute, a criterion must allow the measuring of the decision maker preference according to a personal viewpoint [11]. To this end, direct meetings have to be conducted, at the beginning of the MOOC, with the pedagogical team in order to elicit his ordered preferential information for each criterion. For example, for the attribute "Study level" four increasing ordered scales are defined: 1: Scholar student; 2: High school student; 3: PhD Student; 4: Doctor. The criteria family remains stable throughout the MOOC broadcast. The construction process of the criteria family is detailed in [2–4].

Step 1.3: inference of the decision rules.

This step is made of three sub-steps: (i) the construction of the information table, (ii) the construction of the decision table and (iii) the inference of a preference model. The information table is a matrix whose rows form the set of the "m" "At-risk Learners of Reference" identified in step 1.1, and whose columns represent the "p" evaluation criteria constructed in step 1.2. The content of this matrix is the evaluation function $f_i(L_{j,i}, g_{k,i})$ of each learner $L_{j,i} \in K_i$ on each criterion $g_{k,i} \in F_i$ such that i $\in \{1..n\}$, j $\in \{1..m\}$ and k $\in \{1..p\}$. Variables n, m and p are respectively the number of weeks a

MOOC holds, the size of the "At-risk Learners of reference" set defined in the ith week of the MOOC and the size of the criteria family built at the beginning of the MOOC. Analogously, variables $L_{j,i}$ and $g_{k,i}$ are respectively the jth "At-risk Learner of Reference" in the set K_i and the kth criterion in the set F_i. We recall that K_i and F_i are respectively the set of "At-risk Learners of Reference" and the family of criteria identified at the beginning of the MOOC and used in its ith week. Once the information table S_i is complete at the end of the ith week of the MOOC, we have to construct the decision table with the pedagogical team during some meetings. Thus, we only have to add a column to the end of the information table. The last column concerns the decision of the pedagogical team about the assignment of each "At-risk Learner of Reference" in one of the two decision classes: Cl1, the decision class of the "At-risk Learners" or Cl2, the decision class of the "Active Learners".

The decision table is thus composed of "m" rows and "p + 1" columns. The decisions made by the pedagogical team about the classification of each "At-risk Learner of Reference" should be based on his/her assessment values on the set of all criteria. We call $D_i = \{d_{1,i}, d_{2,i}, \ldots, d_{j,i}, \ldots, d_{m,i}\}$ the vector of the decisions of the assignment of each "At-risk Learner of Reference" in one of the two decision classes such that $d_{j,i} = \{Cl1, Cl2\}$ is the classification of the jth "At-risk Learner" $L_{j,i} \in K_i$ either in the decision class Cl1 or Cl2. Once the decision table of the ith week W_i of the MOOC is complete, it will be provided as input to the algorithm DOMLEM proposed by the DRSA approach. This algorithm outputs a preference model resulting in a set of decision rules. The preference model has the objective to classify learners at the beginning of the week W_{i+1} of the same MOOC.

3.2 Phase 2: Classification of the "Potentially At-Risk Learners"

The second phase aims to exploit the inferred decision rules in order to assign the "Potentially At-risk Learners" either to the decision class Cl1 of the "At-risk Learners"

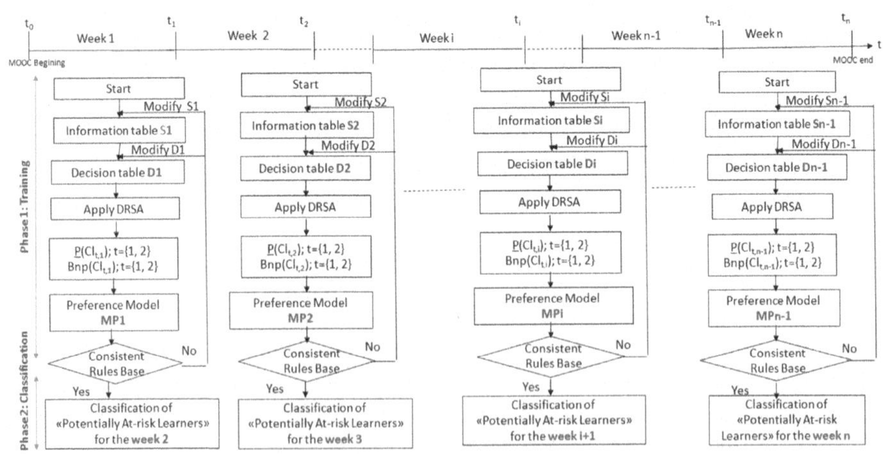

Fig. 1. Weekly prediction method of "At-risk learners" based on DRSA.

or the decision class Cl2 of the "Active Learners". We mean by "Potentially At-risk Learners", the learners who remain connected to the MOOC until the beginning of the week W_{i+1}. This method is weekly implemented: the first phase runs at the end of each week W_i of the MOOC while the second phase runs at the beginning of each week W_{i+1} of the same MOOC; for all i $\in \{1..n\}$. The second phase inputs the output of the first one (cf. Fig. 1).

4 Case Study

This section first provides a brief description of the MOOC used to validate the proposed method and then presents the weekly application of the two phases. Finally, it discusses the obtained results.

4.1 Application Field

The application field is a French MOOC offered by a Business School in France. For reasons of anonymity, we were discreet about its name. The MOOC started with 2360 learners and lasted "n = 5" weeks. The first, the second and the fourth weeks were closed with a quiz while the third and the fifth were ended with a peer-to-peer assessment. Data was saved in a CSV (Comma-Separated Values) file. However, only data about 1535 learners are used in these experiments. Learners who have been neglected are those who have not completed the registration form. Results were obtained using the JAVA language coupled with 4eMka2[2], which is a decision support system for multicriteria classification problems based on DRSA.

4.2 Method Application

Phase 1: At the end of each week W_i such that i $\in \{1..4\}$: First, the pedagogical team selected a sample K_i of "m = 30" representative examples of learners for each decision class Cl1 of the "At-risk Learners" and Cl2 of the "Active Learners". Second, with the pedagogical team we constructed the family of "p = 12" criteria that remained stable over weeks. Third, we constructed the information table S_i and determined with the pedagogical team the decision vector D_i that classifies each learner in K_i either in the decision class Cl1 or in the decision class Cl2. An extract of the decision table built at the end of the first week W_1 is shown in the Table 1. Finally, we applied the algorithm DOMLEM and inferred a set of decision rules.

Table 2 shows an extract from the obtained decision rules over weeks. For example, the first rule can be translated as follows: If the learner's motivation to participate in the MOOC is "at most" to discover the MOOC concept and the score that he obtained in the end of the week 1 is "at most" 6, then the learner is at-risk to drop the course in the week 2 of the MOOC.

[2] http://idss.cs.put.poznan.pl.

Table 1. An excerpt from the decision table built at the end of the first week

$L_{j,i}$	$g_{1,1}$	$g_{2,1}$	$g_{3,1}$	$g_{4,1}$	$g_{5,1}$	$g_{6,1}$	$g_{7,1}$	$g_{8,1}$	$g_{9,1}$	$g_{10,1}$	$g_{11,1}$	$g_{12,1}$	D_1
$L_{2,1}$	2	1	3	2	1	2	4	2	1	1	2	1	*Cl*1
$L_{3,1}$	2	1	3	1	1	0	5	2	1	1	5	4	*Cl*2

Table 2. Extract of decision rules inferred throughout the MOOC broadcast

Week	Examples of decision rules extracted over weeks	Force
Week 1–2	If $g_{4,1} \leq 1 \bigwedge g_{12,1} \leq 1$ then $L_2 \in Cl1^{\leq}$	28.57%
	If $g_{3,1} \leq 2 \bigwedge g_{11,1} \leq 1$ then $L_2 \in Cl1^{\leq}$	14.29%
Week 2–3	If $g_{5,2} \leq 0 \bigwedge g_{9,2} \leq 1 \bigwedge g_{11,2} \leq 3$ then $L_3 \in Cl1^{\leq}$	40%
	If $g_{2,2} \leq 1 \bigwedge g_{5,2} \leq 0$ then $L_3 \in Cl1^{\leq}$	20%
Week 3–4	If $g_{6,3} \leq 0 \bigwedge g_{11,3} \leq 1$ then $L_4 \in Cl1^{\leq}$	40%
	If $g_{7,3} \leq 3 \bigwedge g_{10,3} \leq 1 \bigwedge g_{12,3} \leq 2$ then $L_4 \in Cl1^{\leq}$	40%
Week 4–5	If $g_{4,4} \leq 1 \bigwedge g_{6,4} \leq 1$ then $L_5 \in Cl1^{\leq}$	27.27%
	If $g_{11,4} \leq 1$ then $L_5 \in Cl1^{\leq}$	45.45%

Phase 2: At the beginning of each week W_i such that that i $\in \{2..5\}$, we applied the previously inferred decision rules to classify each learner of the MOOC either in the decision class Cl1 or the decision class Cl2.

4.3 Results and Discussion

In this work, experiments showed that the obtained decision rules were strong, characterized by a high force (force reached 85%). Moreover, to measure the performance of the preference model defined by the approach DRSA we calculated the precision, the recall, the F-measure and the accuracy measures. The obtained results are summarized in Fig. 2.

The quality of the preference model is tested in two ways depending on the training sample ("Learners of Reference") construction. In fact, this sample can be non-incremental, so based only on the sample defined in the current week of the MOOC so as to make predictions concerning the next week during this same MOOC (Cf. Fig. 2, curve (a)). Likewise, it can be incremental if we add to the training sample of the current week, samples of all the previous weeks (Cf. Fig. 2, curve (a)).

The results analysis will focus only on the F-measures and the accuracy values because the F-measure already represents the harmonic mean of the precision and the recall measures.

We note so, that the incremental model (Curve (b)) gives the highest prediction F-measure. In effect, as we mentioned, the DSRA approach focuses rather on the quality of the training sample and not on its size. Thus, to meet the cognitive capacity of the decision maker, we generally select training samples of a limited size. However, the size is also important to diversify the examples to consider when predicting. Thus,

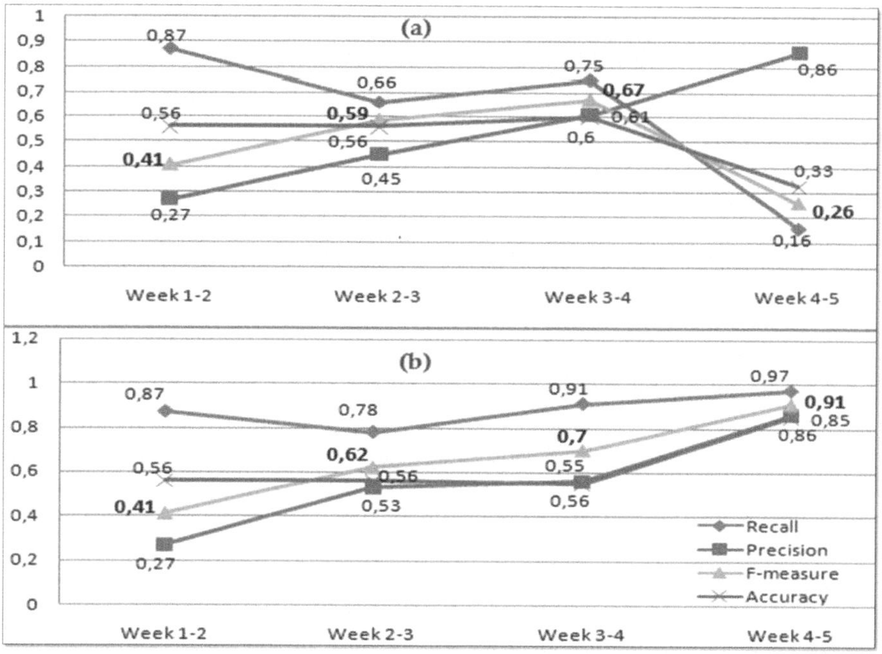

Fig. 2. Preference model performance measures

the incremental approach has addressed this limitation relative to the training sample size and therefore led to better results compared to the non-incremental one (Curve (a)).

Focusing now on the incremental model (Curve (b)), the F-measure corresponding to the decision class Cl1 of the "At-risk learners" is satisfying and it increases from a week to another. In effect, a MOOC is known by the presence of what we call "lurkers". These are the participants who register just to discover the MOOC concept and who leave it at the first evaluation. And even though they remain active during the first week of the MOOC, they have a prior intention to abandon it. This type of learners degrades the quality of the prediction model which is based on the profile and the behavior of the learner and not on his intention. Consequently, the more the number of lurkers decreases, the higher the prediction quality is improved. Moreover, this improvement is due to the increasing size of the training sample over weeks, which explains the large difference between the fourth week F-measure of the non-incremental model (0.26) and that of the fourth week of the incremental one (0.91). Concerning the accuracy, we note also that it increases over weeks especially for the fourth week of the incremental model. It is also influenced by the size of the training sample. This method is increasingly interesting in the case of MOOCs of longer duration since the results improve over time. Finally, it is important to say that the use of DRSA permitted to overcome the imbalanced data problem because of the human intervention in the decision making process and in the choice of the training set.

This method can be experienced either on similar MOOCs, that is to say on MOOCs with the same pedagogical team and the same subject, or on different MOOCs.

In the second case, we must mobilize the new pedagogical team to adapt the criteria family to his preferences and to the features of the new MOOC.

5 Conclusion

In this paper, we have proposed a method based on the multiple-criteria decision making for the weekly prediction of the "At-risk Learners" in a MOOC. This method is based on the DRSA approach and consists of two phases; first, the construction of a preference model resulting in a set of decision rules. Second, the classification of the MOOC learners that is based on this preference model. The DRSA approach relies on the expertise of the human expert decision makers which would permit to infer a set of decision rules of good quality and to overcome the issue of imbalanced data. This method has to be applied periodically at the end of the current week of the MOOC in order to predict the "At-risk Learners" of the next week. The prediction is based on both the static and the dynamic data. This method has been validated on real data provided to us by a French MOOC proposed by a Business School in France. That is obvious that the objective when predicting the "At-risk Learners" is to help them not to drop the MOOC. Thus, the future work will focus on the integration of a third decision class which is that of "Leader Learners". These will be mobilized to support the "At-risk Learners" by offering them an accurate and an appropriate knowledge that satisfies their needs. The aim is to strengthen the pedagogical team that is unable to conduct a support process because of the massive number of learners in the MOOC which causes their attrition.

References

1. Balakrishnan, G.: Predicting student retention in massive open online courses using hidden markov models (Technical report No. UCB/EECS-2013-109). University of California at Berkeley, May 2013. http://www.eecs.berkeley.edu/Pubs/TechRpts/2013/EECS-2013-109.html
2. Bouzayane, S., Saad, I.: A preference ordered classification to leader learners identification in a MOOC. J. Dec. Syst. **26**(2), 189–202 (2016). http://dx.doi.org/10.1080/12460125.2017.1252233
3. Bouzayane, S., Saad, I.: Prediction method based DRSA to improve the individual knowledge appropriation in a collaborative learning environment: case of MOOCs. In: Proceedings of the 50th Hawaii International Conference on System Sciences, pp. 124–133, January 2017
4. Bouzayane, S., Saad, I.: Multicriteria decision aid approach to "referent learners" identification within a MOOC. In: EMOOCs-2016, Research Track, pp. 237–250 (2016)
5. Chaplot, D., Rhim, E., Kim, J.: Predicting student attrition in MOOCs using sentiment analysis and neural networks. In: Proceedings of AIED 2015 Fourth Workshop on Intelligent Support for Learning in Groups (2015)
6. Greco, S., Matarazzo, B., Slowinski, R.: Rough sets theory for multicriteria decision analysis. Eur. J. Oper. Res. **129**, 1–47 (2001)

7. Hone, K.S., El Said, G.R.: Exploring the factors affecting MOOC retention: a survey study. Comput. Educ. **98**, 157–168 (2016). doi:10.1016/j.compedu.2016.03.016
8. Moon, S., Potdar, S., Martin, L.: Identifying student leaders from MOOC discussion forums thorugh language influence. In: Proceedings of the 2014 Conference on Empirical Methods in Natural Language Processing (EMNLP), pp. 15–20 (2014)
9. North, S.M., Ronny, R., Max, M.: To adapt MOOCs, or not? That is no longer the question. Univ. J. Educ. Res. **2**(1), 69–72 (2014)
10. Pawlak, Z.: Rough sets theory for multicriteria decision analysis. Int. J. Comput. Sci. **11**, 341–356 (1992)
11. Roy, B., Mousseau, V.: A theoretical framework for analyzing the notion of relative importance of criteria. J. Multi-Criteria Dec. Anal. **5**, 145–159 (1996)
12. Xing, W., Chen, X., Stein, J., Marcinkowski, M.: Temporal predication of dropouts in MOOCs: reaching the low hanging fruit through stacking generalization. Comput. Hum. Behav. **58**, 119–129 (2016)
13. Yang, D., Sinha, T., Adamson, D., Rose, C.P.: Turn on, tune in, drop out: anticipating student dropouts in massive open online courses. In: NIPS Workshop on Data Driven Education (2013)
14. Yuan, L., Powell, S.: MOOCs and disruptive innovation: implications for higher education. eLearn. Pap. in-depth **33**, 1–7 (2013)

#MOOC Friends and Followers: An Analysis of Twitter Hashtag Networks

Eamon Costello[1(✉)], Mark Brown[1], Binesh Nair[1], Mairéad Nic Giolla Mhichíl[1], Jingjing Zhang[2], and Theo Lynn[1]

[1] Dublin City University, Dublin, Ireland
eamon.costello@dcu.ie
[2] Beijing Normal University, Beijing, China

Abstract. In this paper we present results of the initial phase of a project which sought to analyze the community who use the hashtag #MOOC in Twitter. We conceptualize this community as a form of networked public. In doing so we ask what the nature of this public is and whether it may be best conceived of as a social or informational network. In addition we seek to uncover who the stakeholders are who most influentially participate. We do this by using Social Network Analysis (SNA) to uncover the key hubs and influencers in the network. We use two approaches to deriving a network typology - one based on follows and on based on replies and compare and contrast the results.

Keywords: MOOCs · Twitter · Social network analysis · Networked publics

1 Introduction

Research into what the term "MOOC" means and how it has been used have been conducted with reference to the traditional media [1–3]. Other studies have looked at #MOOC hashtags in Twitter such as contrasting #MOOC with #OER [4]. Two pertinent works analysed #MOOC hashtag use among English [5] and Chinese [6] speakers. An aspect of these studies is that they may be susceptible to over stating the correlation of the hashtag #MOOC with learners and teachers.

We can conceptualize the network formed by users of the #MOOC hashtag in Twitter as one of stakeholders that may be connected in various ways or who remain isolated. An analysis of their connections and activity can lead us to determine how influential each is in this arena. A network can be conceptualized as having both social and informational aspects. We can use techniques from social network analysis to determine information flows and both derive and analyze networks according to how social or informational they are. Accordingly, we sought to examine this online community with reference to a network based on who replies to whom; and one based on who follows whom. The case for generating social networks based on replies, as opposed to follows, has been posited as one that is more "social" rather than "informational" [7]. However, there are few actual case studies and examples that contrast follow versus reply based network representations. This study sought to address this gap through two targeted research questions. RQ1: What can *follow* based network topologies tell us about key hubs and influencers using the hashtag #MOOC? RQ2:

C. Delgado Kloos et al. (Eds.): EMOOCs 2017, LNCS 10254, pp. 170–175, 2017.
DOI: 10.1007/978-3-319-59044-8_19

What can *reply* based network topologies tell us about key hubs and influencers using the hashtag #MOOC?

1.1 Methodology

The data for this study comprised of tweets extracted from the Twitter GNIP API for the period of September–December 2015. The API produces large volumes of data so we used cloud computing data, extraction storage and processing techniques to handle it. The hashtag '#MOOC' was used to as a keyword filter in extracting the data following the example of [6]. The API provides a file of data for each 10 min interval of the specified time. Analytics on the data were performed in R BigQuery, and Gephi. The methodology follows established approaches for Twitter analytics [8, 9].

1.2 Results

32,309 tweets were extracted, 17,910 of which were original and 14,399 of which were retweets. Replies constituted 8% (1,434) of the tweets. We conducted several analyses of the dataset using natural language and other text corpus analysis techniques customized for Twitter datasets. This analysis of frequent words, n-grams, hashtags, urls and sentiment is reported elsewhere [10].

Network analytics, based on graph theory, represents a way to examine networks through statistics such as average degree, network density, diameter, average path length etc. A network is represented by nodes (user screen names) and edges (relationships represented by either follows or mentions). We used Gephi to generate and analyse the networks. We generated the network based firstly on follows and then on replies (mentions).

The follow based network had 16,966 nodes and 18,035 edges. The average degree of the network was 2.126. The average degree is on the lower end and this can be attributed to the presence of many users who are engaged less in the network. The network diameter was 6. Network diameter measures the largest distance between any two nodes. A small network diameter is an indication of the presence of powerful hubs. The network density, the ratio of actual connections and potential connections, is 0; mainly due to less connected users. In other words, users in this network are not utilizing potential connections.

The network of reply tweets had 1,389 nodes and 1,093 edges. Nodes correspond to users who received replies and edges the link between users who send and received replies. The average degree of this network was 1.574, network diameter 6 and network density 0,001. The average path length, measuring the average distance between any two nodes, was 1.773.

Centrality Analysis in the #MOOC Follow Network

Hubs represent the backbone of a network as they facilitate connections between users. There are key hubs in the #MOOC follower network as evident from small values for network statistics like average path length and network diameter. Key hubs were identified via the network statistic Betweenness Centrality (BC). BC measures how often a node falls in between the path of communication between any two nodes in the network. Key hubs tend to have a higher BC score. @mooc24 was found to be the most critical hub in the #MOOC follower network with a BC score of 66,620, followed by @NutritionMOOCs (52,116.67). Other key hubs in the network were @EUmoocs (24,171), @tleerwerk (14,182.17), @juandoming (4,141.67) and @Mirimi (3,043.67). Table 1 lists the key hubs.

Table 1. Key hubs in the #MOOC follow network

Screen name	BC	Screen name	BC	Screen name	BC
mooc24	66,620	Nancyrubin	1,614	CircularX	330
NutritionMOOCs	52,116	MOOCFactory	900	ColumbiaScience	325
EUmoocs	24,171	openSAP	842	KristerSvensson	192
Tleerwerk	14,182	UCTMOOCs	689	Drchuck	167
Juandoming	4,141	openHPI	499	CourseBuffet	118
Mirimi	3,043	MIT	443	PythonDaily	106
Iversity	2,715	Plusacumen	435	OpenClassrooms	74
FutureLearn	1,844	Hubert_edu	390	EducationDive	64
				Acumen	50

Influencers (users who attract many inward connections) were identified by In-degree and PageRank. In-degree is defined by the number of connections coming into a node. In the follow network, it defines the number of followers a user has i.e. users with many followers have higher In-degree. PageRank considers the link propensity of the linkers and the centrality of the linkers. Hence, it can be considered as a more robust measure to determine the centrality of the nodes. A list of top 25 key influencers in the #MOOC follower network is given in Table 2. @edXOnline (having an in-degree of 1,088) was found to be the most influential user in the network. Other influential users

Table 2. Key influencers in the follower network

Screen name	In degree	PageRank	Screen name	In degree	PageRank
edXOnline	1,088	0.0304 (1)	Esri	115	0.0030 (14)
Coursera	243	0.0053(4)	Esa	112	0.0029 (15)
Wharton	235	0.0062 (2)	openSAP	105	0.0038 (9)
Iversity	207	0.0054 (3)	MOOCsNews	103	0.0023 (27)
Classcentral	207	0.0047 (6)	EUErasmusPlus	101	0.0028 (18)
eu_schoolnet	194	0.0047 (7)	UNEP	97	0.0027 (20)
Kdnuggets	183	0.0051 (5)	SkillsetSSC	96	0.0028 (17)
DU_Press	160	0.0038 (8)	SalilShetty	95	0.0026 (21)
IMFNews	136	0.0037 (10)	mooc24	91	0.0013 (38)
thew3cx	120	0.0032 (12)	ASteiner	90	0.0025 (22)
WorldBank	119	0.0033 (11)	JimKim_WBG	88	0.0024 (23)
ESA_EO	119	0.0032 (13)	FutureLearn	86	0.0019 (29)
MIT	117	0.0029 (16)			

included @coursera (243), @Wharton (235), @iversity (207), @classcentral (207), @eu_schoolnet (194). It can be observed from the table that the most influential users are very similar in their rankings with respect to both in-degree and PageRank.

Centrality Analysis in the #MOOC @Reply Network
After calculation of BC for the reply network @CraigTaylor74 was found to be the most critical hub with a BC score of 261, followed by @LearnKotch scoring 209. Some of the other key hubs were @NUsocialmktg (173), @kiwirip (168), @RandyHlavac (138) and @LHTL_MOOC (109). Table 3 shows the top 25 key hubs in the reply network.

Table 3. Key hubs in the #MOOC @Reply network

Screen name	BC	Screen name	BC	Screen name	BC
CraigTaylor74	261	edXOnline	34	KR_Barker	4
LearnKotch	209	diando70	16	Mbrownz	4
NUsocialmktg	173	Yishaym	15	Judyfranks	3
Kiwirip	168	AleksejHeinze	12	Juandoming	3
RandyHlavac	138	TESSIndia	10	AdrianaGWilde	3
LHTL_MOOC	109	DarcoJansen	9	catspyjamasnz	3
Zaidlearn	80	Esrimooc	6	culturalprovoca	3
MdCplus	55	ECOmooc	6		
MGCleve	48	EUmoocs	4		

Indegree and PageRank were used to identify the key influencers. Table 4 shows the 25 top influencers. @edXOnline (in-degree 14) is the most influential. Other influencers are @coursera (13), @Ignatia (11), @RandyHlavac (6) and @eu_schoolnet (6).

Table 4. Key influencers in the @Reply network

Screen name	In degree	PageRank	Screen name	In degree	PageRank
edXOnline	14	0.0048	AleksejHeinze	3	0.0018
Coursera	13	0.0056	TESSIndia	3	0.0010
Ignatia	11	0.0056	EUmoocs	3	0.0016
RandyHlavac	6	0.0026	Judyfranks	3	0.0014
eu_schoolnet	6	0.0028	Mkalz	3	0.0017
NUsocialmktg	4	0.0022	Gsiemens	3	0.0016
Kiwirip	4	0.0019	FutureLearn	3	0.0014
MIT	4	0.0019	R3beccaF	3	0.0010
CourseTalk	4	0.0009	stylianosm2	3	0.0009
HarvardBiz	4	0.0016	MOOCNewsReviews	3	0.0010
Mentiveco	4	0.0023	pryme_ent	3	0.0018
LHTL_MOOC	3	0.0016	CraigTaylor74	2	0.0012

Community Analysis
Lastly, we conducted analysis of sub-networks within our two networks. The Blondel algorithm was used for this community detection. In the follow network the largest sub-group had 973 members. The second largest community had 674 members. The biggest influencer in the largest community was @edXOnline (in-degree 1088). @EcoShapeBwN (8), @katelockwood77 (7) and @mcd80x (6) were the other influencers. @KristerSvensson (BC 192), @EcoShapeBwN (8), @dongguangming (2) were the top hubs in this community.

The same analysis of the reply network found the biggest influencer to be @NutritionMOOCs (out-degree 226). Investigation of the tweets revealed that the majority promoted courses e.g. NutritionMOOCs is a strong disseminator. There were no hubs in the largest community.

The second largest community had 76 members (5% of the network). The average degree was 2.132, network diameter was 3 and average path length 1.445. A density score of 0.014 indicates that the network has been better utilized by its members than those in the largest community. This difference was observed in the topologies of the communities. The biggest influencers in terms of out-degree were found to be @jimjamyahauk (out-degree – 45), @diando70 (7) and @yishaym (6). Like the largest community, the key influencers are strong disseminators. The key BC hubs in the network are @diando70 (15.5), @yishaym (15) and @DarcoJansen (9).

Discussion and Conclusion
In seeking to determine what *follow* and *reply* based network topologies could tell us about key hubs and influencers of the hashtag #MOOC two distinct pictures emerged. Unsurprisingly the *follow* network was larger than the *reply* network. Users amongst the top 25 key hubs of the follow network were more likely to be marco level organizations. As per Tables 2 and 3 these were characterized by platform providers including Coursera, EdX, Iversity, OpenSAP, OpenHPI, FutureLearn; or media outlets and aggregators such as MOOCS24, Classcentral etc. The reply network by contrast contained many more named individuals as influencers and key hubs. Tables 3 and 4 for example include Ignatia, RandyHlavac, Kiwirip, Judyfranks, Mkalz, Gsiemens, mbrown, diando70, Yishaym, catspyjamasnz and DarcoJansen. These all directly correspond to individuals who are well known academics, MOOC researchers or MOOC teachers. This confirms the suggestion of other research that the term "MOOC" is not synonymous with teachers and leaners per se. Rather, those setting the agenda at this social layer of the #MOOC community are a mixed group including teachers, researchers, commentators and opinion leaders. Thus we contribute an example case study of the contrast between follower and reply based networks with real world data.

References

1. Bulfin, S., Pangrazio, L., Selwyn, N.: Making "MOOCs": the construction of a new digital higher education within news media discourse. Int. Rev. Res. Open Distance Learn. **15**, 290–305 (2014)
2. Kovanovic, V., Joksimovic, S., Gavsevic, D., et al.: What public media reveals about MOOCs: a systematic analysis of news reports. Br. J. Edu. Technol. **46**, 510–527 (2015)

3. Brown, M., Costello, E., Donlon, E., Giolla-Mhichil, M.: MOOCs in the news: the 'real' story behind the irish story. In: Global Learn, vol. 2016, no. 1, pp. 337–345 (2016)
4. Abeywardena, I.S.: Public opinion on OER and MOCC: a sentiment analysis of Twitter data (2014)
5. Shen, C., Kuo, C.-J.: Learning in massive open online courses: evidence from social media mining. Comput. Hum. Behav. **51**, 568–577 (2015)
6. Zhang, J., Perris, K., Zheng, Q., Chen, L.: Public response to "the MOOC movement" in China: examining the time series of microblogging. Int. Rev. Res. Open Distrib. Learn. **16**, 144–160 (2015)
7. Myers, S.A., Sharma, A., Gupta, P., Lin, J.: Information network or social network?: the structure of the twitter follow graph. In: Proceedings of the 23rd International Conference on World Wide Web, pp. 493–498 (2014)
8. Chae, B.K.: Insights from hashtag# supplychain and Twitter analytics: considering Twitter and Twitter data for supply chain practice and research. Int. J. Prod. Econ. **165**, 247–259 (2015)
9. Lynn, T., Healy, P., Kilroy, S., Hunt, G., van der Werff, L., Venkatagiri, S., Morrison, J.: Towards a general research framework for social media research using big data. In: Proceedings of 2015 IEEE International Professional Communication Conference (IPCC), pp. 1–8. IEEE (2015)
10. Costello, E., Binesh, N., Brown, M., Zhang, J., Nic Giolla-Mhichíl, M., Donlon, E., Lynn, T.: Social media #MOOC mentions: lessons for MOOC mentions from analysis of Twitter data. In: Barker, S., Dawson, S., Pardo, A., Colvin, C (eds.) Proceedings ASCILITE 2016 Adelaide, pp. 157–162 (2016)

Understanding Learning and Teaching in MOOCs from the Perspectives of Students and Instructors: A Review of Literature from 2014 to 2016

Ruiqi Deng[1(✉)], Pierre Benckendorff[1], and Deanne Gannaway[2]

[1] UQ Business School, The University of Queensland, Brisbane, Australia
{r.deng, p.benckendorff}@uq.edu.au
[2] Institute for Teaching and Learning Innovation (ITaLI), The University of Queensland, Brisbane, Australia
d.gannaway@uq.edu.au

Abstract. This article presents the results of a literature review on key learning and teaching dimensions in MOOCs. 95 studies published from January 2014 to October 2016 were selected for review. Four important learning and teaching dimensions were identified, and relationships between these dimensions were presented. The key dimensions and sub-dimensions reported in this literature review are student factors (education background, country of origin, age, gender, and motivation), teaching context (motivation, challenge, and pedagogical preference), student engagement (emotional, social, behavioural, and cognitive engagement), and learning outcomes (perception, retention, and grade). The review provides evidence of a relationship between student factors and engagement and a relationship between student engagement and learning outcomes.

Keywords: MOOC · Review · Student · Instructor

1 Introduction

The MOOC literature has grown dramatically over the last five years. Accordingly, a number of literature reviews have been conducted to provide an analysis of MOOC research trends, the academic backgrounds of MOOC scholars, MOOC users' motivations and challenges, and methodological approaches in MOOC research. Past reviews suggest that learning and teaching in MOOCs has received an increasing amount of scholarly attention and become a frequently researched area in MOOC scholarship. Despite its growing importance, there does not seem to be any synthesis of scholarly contributions on learning and teaching in MOOCs. This study aims to identify key learning- and teaching-related dimensions in MOOCs, and clarify the relationship between some of these dimensions.

C. Delgado Kloos et al. (Eds.): EMOOCs 2017, LNCS 10254, pp. 176–181, 2017.
DOI: 10.1007/978-3-319-59044-8_20

2 Literature Review

Past reviews suggest that the landscape of scholarship in the MOOC field has changed substantially in the last five years. Apart from becoming more interdisciplinary, it appears that recent studies are placing more emphasis on students' and instructors' characteristics and experience in using MOOCs. This is important, because the 'massive' and 'open' nature of MOOCs means that learning and teaching processes in MOOCs may differ from those in traditional online courses. Having a clear understanding of MOOC usage from the perspective of students and instructors can inform the design of pedagogies that produce more desirable learning outcomes.

In spite of the significance of learning and teaching, there does not seem to be any synthesis of studies on students' and instructors' characteristics and their use of MOOCs. Hew and Cheung's [1] review provided a useful account of MOOC users' motivations and challenges, but not all available papers were peer-reviewed, and a number of papers included in their sample were based on small sample sizes. More importantly, it is clear that other salient factors in the learning and teaching process, such as engagement and learning outcomes, have been neglected.

The extant reviews have provided evidence that research topics on MOOCs are diverse and the field is constantly evolving. The reviews conducted by Liyanagunawardena et al. [2], Raffaghelli et al. [3], and Deng and Benckendorff [4] presented a holistic picture of the MOOC scholarship from 2008 to 2015, outlining key research themes, trends, issues, and methodological approaches. However, existing reviews have failed to provide an in-depth analysis of learning and teaching dynamics in MOOCs. This study extends the scope of Hew and Cheung's [1] review by moving beyond motivations and challenges in the learning and teaching process. The core research question this study seeks to answer is: What do recently reported research findings suggest about learning and teaching in MOOCs?

3 Research Methods

A narrative analysis was conducted to synthesise the key themes. Biggs' 3P model was adopted to frame the discussion of learning and teaching dynamics in MOOCs (see Fig. 1). The 3P model describes the learning process as three stages. The presage stage

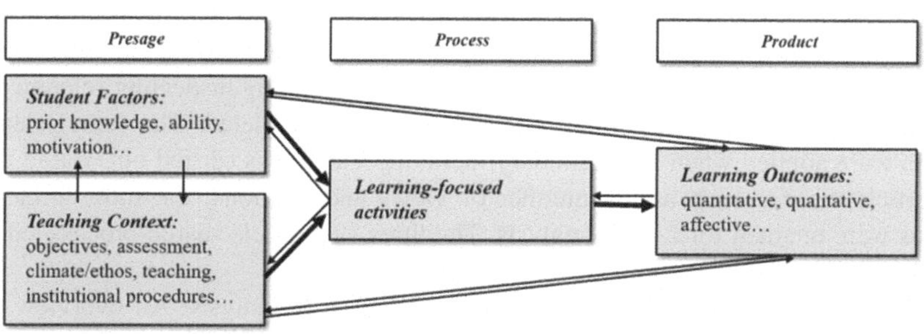

Fig. 1. 3P model of teaching and learning (Adapted from Biggs [5])

describes students' learning-related characteristics and teaching contexts prior to engagement that affects learning. Presage factors interact at the process stage to produce a particular learning and teaching mix which determines the student's learning-related activities. The interaction of these factors then affects learning outcomes. The heavy arrows mark the general direction of flow. The 3P model is heuristically useful for investigating learning and teaching in MOOCs because it includes any identifiable factors in the learning and teaching process.

Articles for inclusion in this review were limited to journal articles, book chapters, conference papers and proceedings, and theses and dissertations written in English. Article search strategies are displayed in Fig. 2. Several selection criteria were applied to ensure the selected articles were relevant. First, learning and teaching in MOOCs had to be the primary focus of the selected literature. The analysis was limited to studies that included learners with experience in studying MOOCs or instructors who taught MOOCs. Non-empirical observations of learning and teaching in MOOCs, such as conceptual and theoretical papers, were excluded. Additionally, the focus was on recent scholarly contributions from 2014 onwards because more recent MOOC studies generally employ methodologies that are more robust.

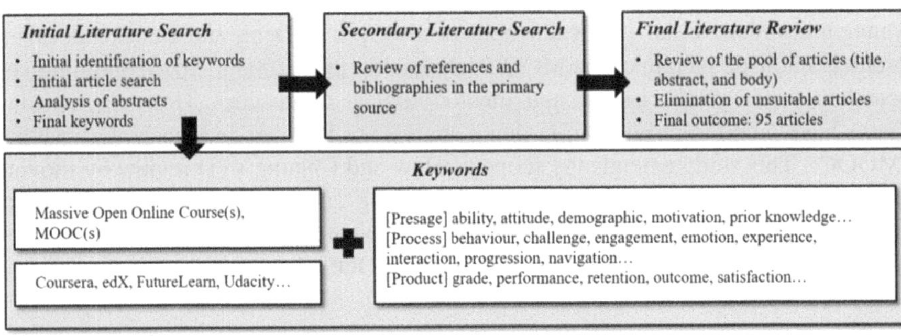

Fig. 2. Article search strategies

Firstly, primary literature was acquired by searching five scholarly databases - ERIC, Google/Google Scholar, ProQuest, Scopus, and Web of Science. Keywords were identified through screening titles, abstracts, and keywords of the literature. For this study, 'Massive Open Online Course(s)', 'MOOC(s)' and names of leading MOOC platforms were paired with learning- and teaching- related factors illustrated in Biggs' model. After that, secondary literature was obtained by inspecting references in the primary source after the initial article search was completed. The same selection criteria were applied when the secondary literature search was carried out. Based upon key article metrics such as the number of views and citations, the most influential articles were retained for further analysis. The three-step article search process led to a sample of 95 articles.

Each individual article was treated as a basic unit of analysis. An overview synthesis table was produced after reading all the articles eligible for review, containing key information such as author(s), year of publication, sample size, and major contributions. Based upon the research framework, all the selected articles were categorised into at least one of the four categories: student factors, teaching context, student engagement, and learning outcomes. These are discussed in more detail in the following section.

4 Research Findings

4.1 Student Factors

MOOC participants' education background, country of origin, age, gender, and motivation have been repeatedly investigated in the literature. This review suggests that MOOC participants tend to be well-educated members of society, irrespective of the types of MOOCs they studied or platforms used. The majority of MOOC participants hold a bachelor's degree. Research also shows that most of MOOC participants come from western, developed countries, such as the United States and France. In regard to age, research indicates that MOOC participants tend to be 45 years old or younger. While the education background, country of origin, and age of MOOC participants remain relatively stable, studies of gender are more inconclusive. Findings on the gender of MOOC participants are contradictory. A number of studies reported that most MOOC participants were male, but some studies found that there were more female participants in MOOCs. Studies have reported a variety of intrinsic, extrinsic, and social motivations for enrolling in a MOOC, but personal interest, career advancement, learning more about the current study field, finding resources, receiving a certificate, and socialising are frequently occurring motives.

4.2 Teaching Contexts

Several researchers have explored MOOC instructors' motivations, challenges, and pedagogical preferences, although this literature is not as well developed as the research on students. Key motivations for developing a MOOC are personal interest, personal desire to investigate innovative instructional approaches, reaching broader audiences, refining classroom teaching, and utilising MOOC data for research. Major challenges reported by instructors are a lack of time to produce MOOCs and engage with students, uncontrollable costs, and teaching MOOC participants of varying education and culture backgrounds. Additionally, research shows that instructors' pedagogical preferences and their conceptualisations of success in MOOCs can be very different.

4.3 Student Engagement

The learning dynamics of MOOCs have been observed from different points of view, but student engagement is a recurring theme. Studies typically examine behavioural, cognitive, emotional, and social engagement. *Behavioural engagement* is related to individuals' observable actions and participation in academic activities, such as patterns of navigation and use of course materials. *Cognitive engagement* is often conceptualised as students' mental investment in learning to comprehend complex ideas and master difficult skills, such as self-regulated learning. *Emotional engagement* refers to the emotional connections students are making with instructors, peers, and course content, such as non-achievement emotions and negativity. *Social engagement* is centred on individuals' social interactions with peers and instructors, such as communication patterns and face-to-face MOOC meetings. Researchers typically examined different aspects of engagement by having different focuses and using different terms. This makes it difficult to compare the findings of different studies. It could be useful to develop an instrument which allows MOOC instructors and practitioners to benchmark student engagement in MOOCs.

4.4 Learning Outcomes

Student learning outcomes in MOOCs have been explored from a number of perspectives, particularly perception, retention, and academic performance. In terms of perception, MOOC scholars have explored the level of satisfaction and helpfulness, students' positive and negative options, the most learner-perceived effective instructional method, and views about the educational values of MOOCs. The majority of such studies showed positive and satisfying study experience, with only a few studies reported negative experience. Student retention has been investigated under a number of terms by MOOC scholars, such as attrition, persistence pattern, completion, retention, dropout, and continuance. The pattern of retention across different courses and MOOC platforms is relatively consistent, featuring a steep drop-off at the start of the course which flattens out in the later weeks and stabilises to an almost negligible rate by the last module. In regard to academic performance, researchers have analysed students' assignment results, exam scores, and final marks.

4.5 Relationship Between Student Factors, Teaching Context, Engagement, and Learning Outcomes

MOOC scholars have also examined the relationships between the learning and teaching dimensions and sub-dimensions discussed above. In particular, student factors are found to be closely related to learning outcomes, but it should be highlighted that not all the relationships identified by researchers were positive. Negative effects were also identified in a few studies. From preliminary evidence, it appears that a range of student factors, such as education background, age, motivation, intended study behaviour, and self-directed learning skills, may be related to MOOC completion and students' academic performance in a MOOC.

MOOC scholars have also attempted to clarify the relationship between student engagement and learning outcomes. The existing evidence appears to suggest that students who displayed some planning skills, participated in more course activities, and actively contributed via social tools were more likely to perform well and retain in a MOOC.

5 Conclusions

A preliminary review of 95 articles published from 2014 to 2016 identifies a number of useful contributions and research gaps. First, the review indicates that the mainstream consumers of MOOCs tend to be under 45 years old, well-educated members of society, and individuals from western, developed countries. These findings confirm the results of existing studies that the majority of MOOC participants are already educationally advantaged. However, the characteristics of non-mainstream consumers of MOOCs, the ways in which they utilise MOOCs, and difficulties they might have are not yet clear. Future research should therefore shed light on these underserved MOOC populations. Second, the review shows that MOOC instructors had different motivations, challenges, and pedagogical preferences. However, little attempt has been made to understand the influence of these characteristics on MOOC participants. Future research could investigate how teaching contexts can shape patterns of student engagement in MOOCs. Third, this review indicates that researchers observed student engagement in MOOCs from behavioural, cognitive, emotional, or social perspectives. This variation in the conceptualisation of engagement has made it difficult to compare findings across studies. Future research could therefore attempt to develop and validate a theoretical driven, psychometrically sound instrument to measure student engagement in MOOCs. Fourth, the review suggests that MOOC scholars have attempted to clarify relationships between some of key learning-related factors. MOOC stakeholders should capitalise on these findings to create a more successful learning environment for students. At the same time, MOOC scholars should continue exploring relationships between key learning- and teaching-related factors to reveal what drives students to engage and succeed in MOOCs as well as the reasons behind disengagement, disaffection, and dropout.

References

1. Hew, K.F., Cheung, W.S.: Students' and instructors' use of massive open online courses (MOOCs): motivations and challenges. Educ. Res. Rev. **12**, 45–58 (2014)
2. Liyanagunawardena, T.R., Adams, A.A., Williams, S.A.: MOOCs: a systematic study of the published literature 2008–2012. Int. Rev. Res. Open Distance Learn. **14**, 202–227 (2013)
3. Raffaghelli, J.E., Cucchiara, S., Persico, D.: Methodological approaches in MOOC research: retracing the myth of Proteus. Br. J. Educ. Technol. **46**, 488–509 (2015)
4. Deng, R., Benckendorff, P.: A contemporary review of research methods adopted to understand students' and instructors' use of massive open online courses (MOOCs). Int. J. Inf. Educ. Technol. **7**, 601–607 (2017)
5. Biggs, J.B.: Teaching for Quality Learning at University. Open University Press, Maidenhead (2003)

Effect of Free Certificate Discontinuation in Completion Rates of MOOC

Ignacio M. Despujol[1(✉)], Carlos Turró[1], Linda Castañeda[2], and Jaime Busquets[1]

[1] Universitat Politècnica de València, Valencia, Spain
{ndespujol, busquets}@asic.upv.es, turro@cc.upv.es
[2] Universidad de Murcia, Murcia, Spain
lindacq@um.es

Abstract. Completion rates have been a controversial topic since Massive Open Online Courses (MOOCs) became mainstream in 2012. In January 2016, based in previous trials, edx.org discontinued the free honor code certificate for new courses, trying to increase the number of verified certificates sold. After one year we have studied the effects of this measure in completion rates and verified certification rates over enrollments for 24 UPValenciaX courses offered in 2015 and 2016 (199,278 enrollments in total), finding that there has been a modest global increase in verified certification rates and a strong decline in completion rates for all the courses. For exactly the same courses, the completion rate for all courses has practically halved going from 10.5% in 2015 to 5.6% and the total verified certification rate has been multiplied by 1.4 going from 0.7% to 1%, what is a significant relative improvement but it is not enough to achieve sustainability.

Keywords: MOOC · Massive Open Online Course · Motivation · Free certificate

1 Introduction

Completion rates have been a controversial topic since Massive Open Online Courses (MOOCs) became mainstream in 2012. Several studies have tried to establish a relationship between different parameters and course completion rates [1, 2], finding that course length, number of enrollments or type of exams have an influence in the completion rates and that a significant number of users enroll in the courses and never show up when the course starts, but, as during the first years of MOOCs almost all MOOC platforms offered a free certificate, these studies don't include the offering of a free certificate as a parameter that influences completion rates.

In January 2016, based in previous trials, edx.org discontinued the free honor code certificate for new courses, trying to increase the number of verified certificates sold, looking for revenue sustainability [3].

As members of UPValenciaX, the Universitat Politècnica de València MOOC initiative in edx, we feared that this measure could remove a strong motivator for course completion, so we asked for some kind of free or very cheap recognition of

C. Delgado Kloos et al. (Eds.): EMOOCs 2017, LNCS 10254, pp. 182–187, 2017.
DOI: 10.1007/978-3-319-59044-8_21

completion (like an electronic badge). We asked for something very different from a certificate (so it couldn't impact the number of verified certificates sold) but that was enough to motivate students to finish the courses. Based on the data they gathered on the trials, the edx team decided that it could create confusion with the verified certificates and that it was better not offering a free option.

There is one study [4] that shows that offering free badges on an edx course did not affect the completion rate of the course, but it was done when the free certificate was still being issued, so its conclusions do not contradict our hypothesis, as there was a free way to get recognition for course completion.

In the report published about the Curtin University MOOCs on edX.org during 2016 [5] there is no direct reference to the change in completion rates between 2015 (when free certificates where available) and 2016 (when they were discontinued), but we can see that completion rates fell down for the same course in the editions run during 2015 and 2016, going from 16.6% of total enrollments to 13.1% for their course TBOMX and from 7.5% to 5.4% and 4.5% for their course MKT1X. For TBOMX they gave digital badges to students in both editions, what could explain the lower decrease due to improved student motivation. For the course MKT2X, that they run twice during 2016, completion rates where 3.6% and 3.26%, very similar for the two runs.

A recent study by the joint research team from Harvard University and MIT about four years of MOOC initiative [6] shows that the number of certificates of their MOOCs grew steadily until free certificates where discontinued and then stayed almost flat (as the number of verified certificates issued is much lower than the number of free certificates), but has no information about the effect that the discontinuation of free certificates has had on the percentage of students that pass the courses.

So we decided that it was interesting to study how the discontinuation of free certificates has affected completion rate for our courses on edx and what has been its effect on the verified certification rate.

2 Initial Data

Universitat Politècnica de València (UPV) has been running MOOCs since 2013 using four different platforms (Google Course Builder, MiriadaX, a proprietary OpenedX instance called upvx.es and edx.org). At the moment of writing this article UPV is making MOOCs in upvx.es and edx.org. It has created 50 different courses, of which it has done a total of 220 editions so far with more than 637,000 enrollments.

UPV joined edx.org in November 2014 under the name UPValenciaX and since then it has run 36 different courses with 444,925 enrollments. 24 of these courses have been repeated in 2015 and 2016 under exactly the same conditions, except for the availability of a free certificate. With the data of the two editions of these courses (199,278 enrollments in total) we have studied the effects free certificate availability in completion rates and verified certification rates over enrollments.

In 2015 we had 112,333 enrollments for the 24 courses, with 11,812 students that passed the courses and 796 that paid for a verified certificate. In 2016 we had 86,945 enrollments for the same courses, with 4,892 students that passed the courses and 858 that paid for a verified certificate.

3 Discussion

We have found that there has been a modest global increase in verified certification rates and a strong descent in completion rates for all the courses. For exactly the same courses, the total completion rate has practically halved going from 10.5% in 2015 (an amount that was similar for previous editions of the same courses in other platforms) to 5.6% and the total verified certification rate has been multiplied by 1.4 going from 0.7% to 1% (Fig. 1 and Table 1).

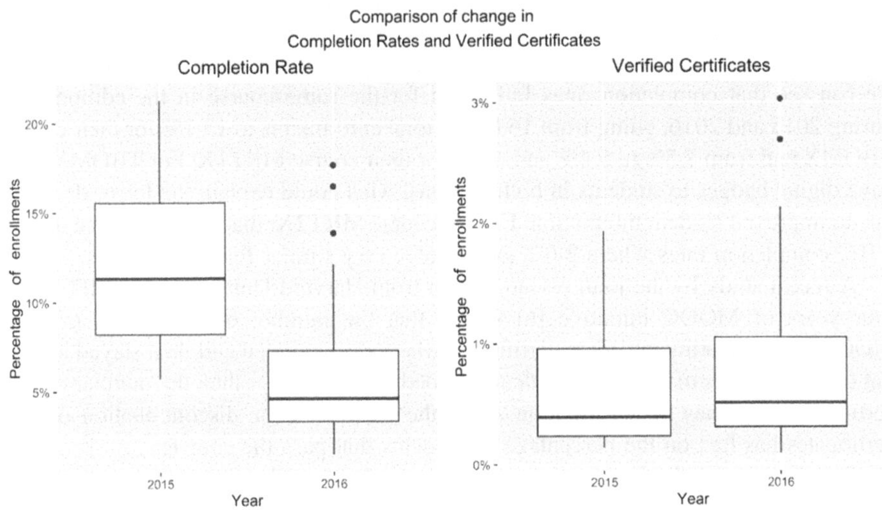

Fig. 1. Completion and verified certification rates over enrollments

Table 1. Completion rate over enrollments for individual courses

Course	2015	2016
Buscar en Internet BI101x	12.4%	6.7%
Valoración de futbolistas VF201x	15.8%	13.8%
Dispositivos Móviles: Aplicaciones a la ingeniería y la gestión del territorio DMT201x	15.3%	8.9%
Excel 2010 XLS101x	8.1%	5.0%
Android: Introducción a la programación AIP201x	5.7%	3.8%
Retos de la agricultura y la alimentación en el siglo XXI RA201x	21.3%	9.7%
Gestión participativa GP201x	8.1%	1.7%
Cómo implantar grupos de mejora de procesos GM201x	7.3%	3.3%
Tecnologías para la educación TE201x	15.6%	6.8%
Fundamentos de mecánica para estudiar ingeniería FFI101x1	11.6%	3.5%
El enlace químico y las interacciones moleculares IQ101.2x	15.8%	7.5%
Aplicaciones de la Teoría de Grafos a la vida real (I) TGV201x1	11.1%	5.4%

(continued)

Table 1. (*continued*)

Course	2015	2016
Bases Matemáticas: Números y terminología BMN101x	18.5%	12.1%
Fundamentos de comunicaciones ópticas FCO201x	8.2%	7.3%
Bases Matemáticas: Integrales BMI101x	9.9%	2.3%
Dynamics and Control DC201x	6.5%	4.4%
Bases Matemáticas: Derivadas BMD101x	15.4%	5.1%
Bases Matemáticas: Álgebra BMA101x	9.6%	4.8%
Fundamentos de Electromagnetismo para estudiar Ingeniería FFI101x2	6.9%	3.0%
Introducción a la estructura de la materia IQ101.1x	19.7%	8.6%
Formulación y nomenclatura de compuestos químicos IQ101.3x	8.4%	3.3%
Reacciones químicas y cálculos estequiométricos IQ101.4x	11.9%	4.6%
Introducción a la gestión de proyectos IGP101x	17.3%	7.3%
Aplicaciones de la Teoría de Grafos a la vida real (II) TGV201x2	11.3%	2.3%

We can see that all individual completion rates have fallen, with a couple of courses (Football player valuation VF201x and Fundamentals on optical communications FCO201x) that have modest decreases (completion rates in 2016 are around 90% of that of 2015), and courses in which completion rates in 2015 are between 20% and 30% of the completion rate in 2015 (High involvement management practices GP201x, Mechanics for engineers FFI101x.1, Integral calculus BMI101x, differential calculus BMD101x or graph theory applied to real life part 2 TGV201x2).

If we look at the median of both series of percentages we see that the difference is even bigger, as the median was 11.5% in 2015 and 5.1% in 2016, what indicates that, for the average course, the effect was even worse (Table 2).

Verified certification rates are bigger in general, but in 8 courses values are worse in 2016 than in 2015 (High involvement management practices GP201x, Chemical bond and molecular interactions IQ101.2x, Formulation of chemical compounds IQ101.3x, Chemical reactions IQ101.4x, Graph theory applied to real life part 1 TGV201x1, Integral calculus BMI101x, Differential calculus BMD101x or Algebra BMA101x). This makes that the median only changes from 0.4% to 0.5%, as the improvement for the average course is small.

Where does the improvement in total verified certification rate come from? We can see that for a group of courses that we can consider more career oriented (Mobile devices to manage land DMT201x, Excel XLS101x, Process improvement team management GM201x, Fundamentals on optical communications FCO201x and Introduction to project management IGP101x), verification rates have multiplied by around 2, and that for the more academic courses the verification rates have been maintained low (around 0.5%) of enrollments, descending in some cases.

As an anecdote, we can see that there has been a strong increase in the verified certification of the two Physics remedial courses, that have been multiplied by 2.6 and 3.1 but, given the low number of certificates awarded (between 5 and 7 for each course), this increase is not of any significance.

Table 2. Verified certification rate over enrollments for individual courses

Course	2015	2016
Buscar en Internet BI101x	0.2%	0.2%
Valoración de futbolistas VF201x	1.6%	1.7%
Dispositivos Móviles: Aplicaciones a la ingeniería y la gestión del territorio DMT201x	1.0%	1.9%
Excel 2010 XLS101x	0.3%	0.6%
Android: Introducción a la programación AIP201x	0.5%	0.7%
Retos de la agricultura y la alimentación en el siglo XXI RA201x	1.8%	2.0%
Gestión participativa GP201x	1.3%	1.1%
Cómo implantar grupos de mejora de procesos GM201x	0.9%	1.9%
Tecnologías para la educación TE201x	1.6%	2.1%
Fundamentos de mecánica para estudiar ingeniería FFI101x1	0.2%	0.5%
El enlace químico y las interacciones moleculares IQ101.2x	0.4%	0.3%
Aplicaciones de la Teoría de Grafos a la vida real (I) TGV201x1	0.9%	0.8%
Bases Matemáticas: Números y terminología BMN101x	0.2%	0.3%
Fundamentos de comunicaciones ópticas FCO201x	1.0%	1.5%
Bases Matemáticas: Integrales BMI101x	0.2%	0.1%
Dynamics and Control DC201x	0.3%	0.5%
Bases Matemáticas: Derivadas BMD101x	0.3%	0.2%
Bases Matemáticas: Álgebra BMA101x	0.2%	0.1%
Fundamentos de Electromagnetismo para estudiar Ingeniería FFI101x2	0.1%	0.4%
Introducción a la estructura de la materia IQ101.1x	0.3%	0.3%
Formulación y nomenclatura de compuestos químicos IQ101.3x	0.2%	0.1%
Reacciones químicas y cálculos estequiométricos IQ101.4x	0.4%	0.3%
Introducción a la gestión de proyectos IGP101x	1.9%	2.7%
Aplicaciones de la Teoría de Grafos a la vida real (II) TGV201x2	0.4%	0.5%

4 Conclusions

In conclusion, we believe that a means to recognize completion provides a strong motivation for students to pass the courses. By discontinuing the free certificate there is a gain in the number of paid certificates, mostly for career oriented courses, but it is not enough to achieve platform sustainability. For more academic courses (where the verified certification rate is low) this gain is negligible or even there is a loss.

It would be very interesting for student motivation to explore the use of different means of recognizing completion that are not equivalent to a certificate that can be used to apply for a job (to avoid losing income with verified certificates), like, for example, digital badges.

References

1. Jordan, K.: Massive open online course completion rates revisited: assessment, length and attrition. Int. Rev. Res. Open Distrib. Learn. [S.l.] **16**(3) (2015). ISSN 1492-3831. doi:http://dx.doi.org/10.19173/irrodl.v16i3.2112. http://www.irrodl.org/index.php/irrodl/article/view/2112/3340. Accessed 15 Jan 2017
2. Onah, D.F.O., Sinclair, J., Boyatt, R.: Dropout rates of massive open online courses: behavioural patterns. In: EDULEARN 2014 Proceedings, pp. 5825–5834 (2014). doi:10.13140/RG.2.1.2402.0009. http://www2.warwick.ac.uk/fac/sci/dcs/people/research/csrmaj/daniel_onah_edulearn14.pdf. Accessed 15 Jan 2017
3. Edx blog. http://blog.edx.org/news-about-edx-certificates. Accessed 15 Jan 2017
4. Ambrose, A.G., Anthony, E., Clark, C.: Digital Badging in the MOOC Space (2016). http://er.educause.edu/articles/2016/11/digital-badging-in-the-mooc-space. Accessed 15 Jan 2017
5. Curtin University: CurtinX Year in Review 2016 (2016). https://clt.curtin.edu.au/local/downloads/innovation/CurtinX_YearInReview2016_web.pdf. Accessed 31 Jan 2017
6. Chuang, I., Ho, A.D.: HarvardX and MITx: Four Years of Open Online Courses—Fall 2012 - Summer 2016, 23 December 2016. SSRN: https://ssrn.com/abstract=2889436. Accessed 13 Jan 2017

Challenges of Identifying Second Language English Speakers in MOOCs

Ismail Duru[1], Ayse Saliha Sunar[2(✉)], Gulustan Dogan[1], and Su White[2]

[1] Yildiz Technical University, Istanbul, Turkey
{iduru, gulustan}@yildiz.edu.tr

[2] The University of Southampton, Southampton, UK
{assla12, saw}@ecs.soton.ac.uk

Abstract. In this study, we aim to analyse English as a Second Language (ESL) and English as a First Language (EFL) MOOC participants' engagements in a MOOC. We aim to find out key points which directly effect learners' dropout and performance in MOOCs. We worked on a FutureLearn data which is provided by the University of Southampton. The course is Understanding Language: Learning and Teaching MOOC that was run between 2016-04-04 and 2016-05-02 is chosen for the analysis. According to the results, it is very challenging to identify who is a second language English speaker by using their location information. One of the important findings is that first language English speakers wrote longer comments. In order to identify strategies for ESL MOOC participants, which is one of the ultimate goal of our research, there is a need for much deeper analyses.

Keywords: Second language English speakers · MOOC · Online learning · Dropout · Predictive models · Learner behaviour

1 Introduction

Online platforms which offer online courses with free registration to any learners who would like to participate, become one of the trend implementations in technology enhanced learning and are investigated from many different perspectives [3, 7, 10, 12]. These courses are adverted as Massive Open Online Course (MOOC) and many institutions from all around the world have attempted to build MOOC platforms.

Even though these courses attract millions of learners from numbers of different countries, the mainstream MOOC providers are based on English speaking countries such as the US and the UK[1]. According to the 2015 statistics that *class-central* published, 75% of the MOOCs have been offered in English. This rate was 80% in 2014. The website published different kind of review analysis for 2016. They identified that around 25% of the new MOOC learners were attracted by the local providers that offer MOOCs in languages other than English[2].

[1] https://www.class-central.com/report/moocs-2015-stats.

[2] https://www.class-central.com/report/moocs-stats-and-trends-2016.

C. Delgado Kloos et al. (Eds.): EMOOCs 2017, LNCS 10254, pp. 188–196, 2017.
DOI: 10.1007/978-3-319-59044-8_22

Additionally, many researchers have identified that one of the reasons for the low completion rate, which is one of the main concerns in MOOCs, is their one- size-fits-all model [1, 5]. MOOC content does not change for individual students according to their needs such as language, difficulties, and learning approaches.

Some locally launched MOOC platforms provide courses in local languages for the targeted audience. For example, EMMA, a European MOOC platform, provides MOOCs in multiple European languages[3]. Japanese MOOC platform (JMOOC) stated on their website that since many Japanese are struggling with studying in English, they launched JMOOC to serve the Japanese speaking communities[4].

Nevertheless, ESL speakers continue to pay attention to MOOCs that are offered in English. In order to help these learners engage with the platform, some personalised services are provided. For example, Coursera asks their attendees to voluntarily contribute to translation of course content[5]. Herewith, learners may benefit from the course at a higher level.

However, to the best of our knowledge, there is not much studies available to investigate possible differences between engagements of first and second English language speakers in MOOCs. Therefore, our conducted research sought to address this problem. In this paper, we specifically focus on the identifying second language English speakers and their common engagement patterns. To follow up this study, we will research on (i) predicting participants' future participation and certificate earn using identified engagement patterns (ii) recommending specific identifiable strategies for the ESL speakers when working in a MOOC.

2 Related Works

Barak et al. [2] suggested that learners who have high motivation are likely to complete the course. Additionally, learners who study in their first language have higher confidence to finish the course and this increase their motivation level.

Eriksson et al. [4] put forward in their qualitative study investigating the reason of learners' dropouts that some learners had struggled with understanding the spoken language in the video and occasionally the instructors' accent. The MOOC participants also stated that subtitles in English were helpful.

There are numbers of studies that investigate how learners engage with MOOCs to identify and classify patterns of learner behaviours (i.e., [6, 8]). Researchers use leverage on statistical and learning analytics methods and machine learning techniques to classify learners' based on their behaviours predominantly based on activity logs data and click-stream data in courses. For example, Milligan et al. [9] conducted interviews and classified learners based on their statements and course activities. Gillani et al. [6] use participants' statements reflected by their comments in discussion threads for classification.

---

[3] https://platform.europeanmoocs.eu.

[4] http://www.jmooc.jp/en/about.

[5] http://www.coursera.community/#gtc.

Some researchers focus on different factors for identifying and predicting level of engagement and course completions, which is one of the common objectives in MOOC research. For example, Kizilcec et al. [8] mainly consider timely assessment submissions and identified learners' behaviour patterns as *auditing, behind, on track,* and *out*. Then, they group learners based on their level of engagement as *auditing, completing, disengaging,* and *sampling*.

However, to the best of our knowledge, there is not much many studies specifically emphasising on identifying ESL speakers and their engagement performance in MOOCs. Uchidiuno et al. [11] used browser language preferences of participants in a MOOC and analysed their video interactions. The authors found that using browser language preference is helpful to more accurately identify ESL speakers.

Our research also aims to contribute to the research in this area by identifying needs and behaviours of ESL participants in MOOCs. The finding of our research ultimately may help ESL speakers, and the instructors who may use MOOCs in foreign language as a material on their blended campus education.

3 Methodology

In order to identify second language English speakers, we first used the data about learners' location, which is generated from the pre-course survey on the platform. Then, we used participants' comments in the discussions to gather more information about their location and first language.

In this paper, we sought to do some investigation to find the best and most accurate method to group learners based on their first languages to analyse their behavior and predict their future performance. Further in the research, we will use machine learning techniques and natural language processing to automatically identify ESL speakers.

3.1 Datasets

We have used the forth run of the *Understanding Language: Learning and Teaching* MOOC (UL-MOOC) that was run between 2016-04-04 and 2016-05-02. We have chosen this course as a start since it has attracted many international English language teachers around the world. While dataset includes 25598 user records, only 3306 of them had location information.

Data files that we used in this study are as follows.

- Enrolments: Includes demographic information of participants, enroll and unenroll time, and purchased statement certificate information.
- Step Activity: *Step* is used for each learning unit in the course. Each week is consisted of numbers of steps. This dataset includes the visit and completion time information for each learner.
- Comments: Includes comment priorities related to course structure, comment text, commenting learner and time.

4 Results of Analysis

In order to identify ESL and EFL speakers in the MOOC, we took three different approach.

1. Divided into two groups as ESL and EFL speakers by using only their location.
2. Divided into three as primary ESL, not primary ESL, and EFL speakers by using only their location.
3. Updated the groups based on participants' comments.

4.1 Implementation of the First Stage

In this step, ESL participants are identified based on the country information only. In order to group countries by the country's official languages, we have utilised a Wikipedia article as a reference[6]. According to the languages, the groups are as follows: (i) English as a first language learners (EFL), (ii) English as a second language learners (ESL), and (iii) no country information presented in the database.

The results showed us that there is no statistically significant difference amongst the course performance of learners in each group. The reason could be the inefficient way of grouping learners by the countries' official languages. Therefore, we have conducted the second step for better categorisation.

4.2 Implementation of the Second Stage

In the first stage, India and the United Kingdom are in the same group. Even though English is very commonly used language in India, it is not the primary language. To have better understanding of the demographics of subgroups to identify their behaviours, we now divided the countries into: (i) English as official and primary language and (ii) English as official but not primary language, and (iii) English as second language. Here, we have again used the same Wikipedia article.

According to the country information of learners, 18% of participants join from a country of which English is an official and primary language, 11% of them join from a country of which English is an official but not primary language, and lastly 71% of them are English as a second language learners.

Figure 1 shows that what percentage of participants in each group completed at least one learning step in the course. There is no big difference between one- time-show-up ratio amongst the participant in each group.

Figure 2 presents the ratio of learners based on their course completion status. In the figure, A indicates a completion of less than half of the steps, B indicates a completion of more than half of the steps but less than 80% of the steps, and C indicates a completion of more than 80% of the total numbers of steps. Learners in the group of English as a official and primary language outperform in completing more than 80% of the steps.

[6] https://en.wikipedia.org/wiki/List_of_territorial_entities_where_English_is_an_official_language.

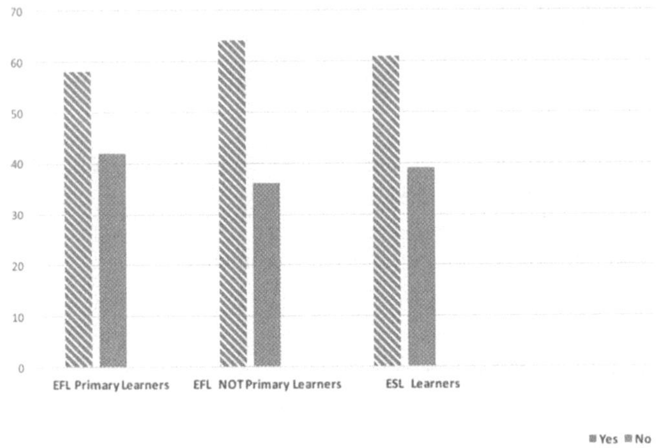

Fig. 1. Ratio of learners in each group who completed at least one step

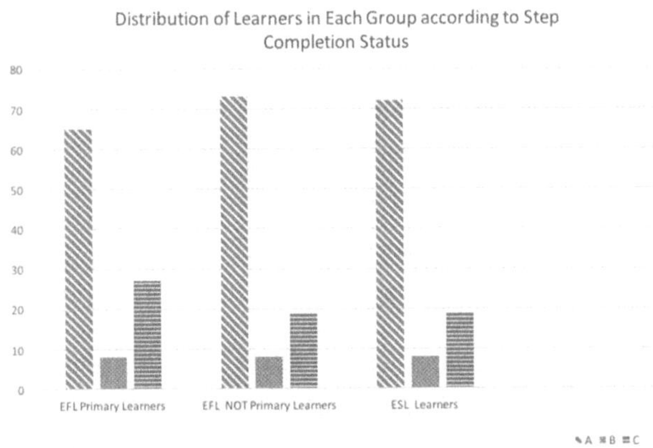

Fig. 2. Distribution of learners in each group according to step completion status

Figure 3 shows the percentage of learners in each group who contributed to the discussions with at least one comment. However, there is no big difference between groups in terms of presence in discussion forums. There is a need for a deeper investigation in forums. Therefore, we have checked the length of learners' comments in the discussion forums.

Figure 4 compares the length of comments written by learners in each group. The figure shows that higher percentage of the learners in the group English as a official and primary language wrote comments that contains at least 200 characters.

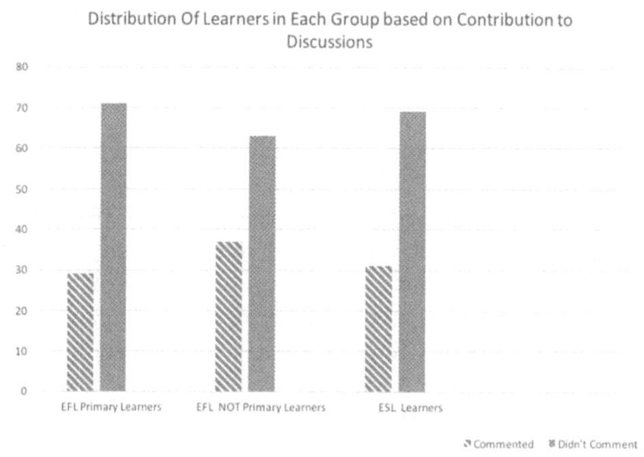

Fig. 3. Distribution of learners in each group based on contribution to discussions

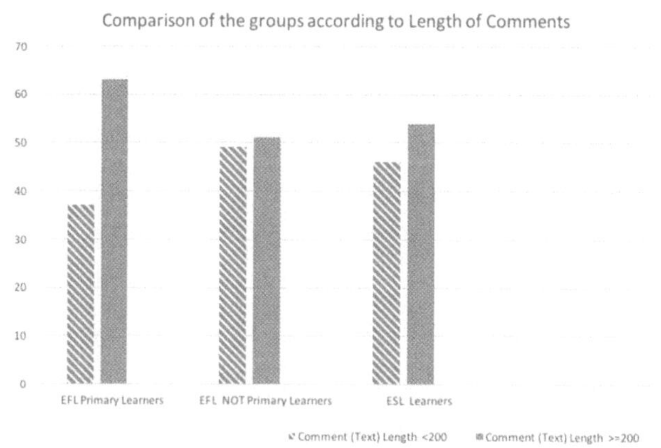

Fig. 4. Comparison of the groups according to length of comments

4.3 Implementation of the Third Stage

In the previous section, the results showed us there is not much difference between groups, especially between the learners in the English as official but not primary and the ESL learners. The reason could still be the inefficient way of grouping learners.

Indeed, when we group the learners according to where they live (which is the country information in the dataset), we sometimes miss the learners who speak a different language than the official/primary language of the country that they live in. Therefore, in the third step, we attempted to investigate comments that were posted to discussion forums.

The course instructors asked the participants how they use language in their daily life in the Step 1.5 of the first week. In the associated discussion forum to Step 1.5, participants gave information about where they live, what their first language is, and how fluent they are in English.

We updated the groups according to the additional information we acquired from learners' comments in Step 1.5.

We made the same analysis for the new updated groups. If we see different distributions than what we had in the first two stages of the analysis, we could say that the results for each group is mostly similar is not because this is the situation but there is a need for more precise grouping method. Number of the users gave information about their first language and had country information were 694. According to the comments on Step 1.5, we realised that 68 of the records were grouped in a wrong cluster in the previous stage, which is nearly 10% of the 694 records. Although some of other learners also commented in Step 1.5 they had no information about their location in the database. We have updated the groups according to the information we have acquired from the discussion thread. This stage indicates that a deeper and systematic analysis in learners' comments can help us to improve our grouping model with the aid of machine learning.

Figure 5 shows distribution of step completion status for participants who commented in Step 1.5 and have country information. According to Fig. 5, there is a huge increase in step completion rate.

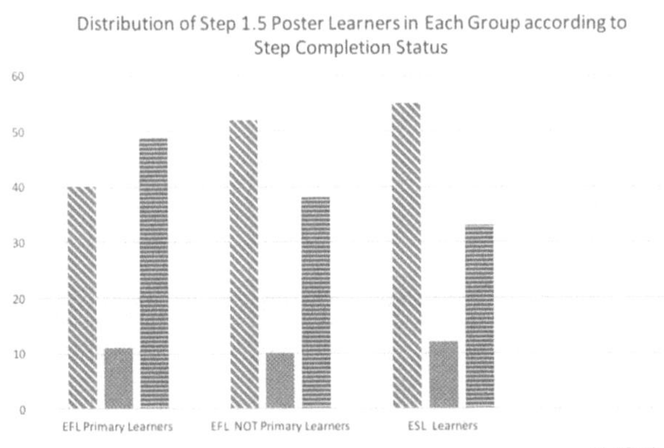

Fig. 5. Distribution of Step 1.5 poster learners in each updated group according to step completion status

Figure 6 shows distribution of the length of comments for learners who commented in Step 1.5 and have country information. The results indicates bigger difference than we have seen in the first two stages of the analysis. According to the new results, 80% of learners who commented in Step 1.5 and speak English as first language which is the primary and official language of the country they live in, wrote comments that are longer than 200 characters.

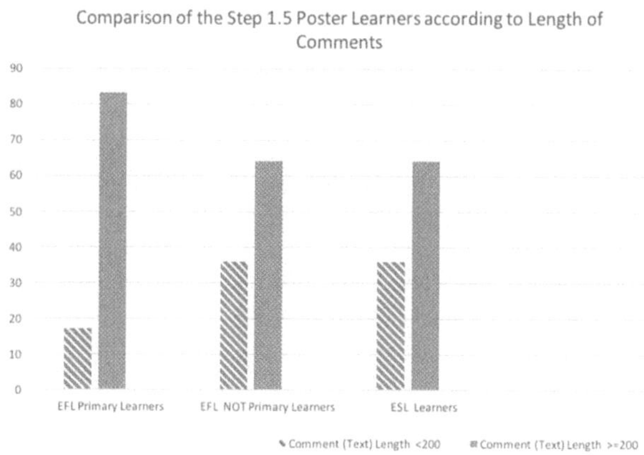

Fig. 6. Comparison of the Step 1.5 poster learners in each updated group according to length of comments

5 Discussion and Future Work

In this study we sought to (i) identify English as first and second language participants in a MOOC, and (ii) investigate and interpret differences between their overall course engagement.

Firstly, we grouped learners based on their country information as "English as a Official and Primary Language", "English as a Official but Not Primary Language", and "English as a Second Language" group.

Secondly, to have more accurate group separation, we investigated learners comment in the discussion forum of Step 1.5, where learners introduce themselves with country and language information. With this information, we have updated our groups.

However, the manual identification of ESL participants from their comments is time consuming and not reliable for implementing at massive numbers of learners in more than one MOOC. In the process of identifying ESL learners, the next step is to use a machine learning technique (a suitable technique has not determined yet) and natural language processing to accurately identify EFL and ESL participants in a MOOC. Additionally, we will take into account of fluency level of ESL learners in our future research.

We plan to do further data analysis to understand the characteristics of our data. In each group we will do outlier detection and will decide about how uniformly the groups behave. Then, we will run some correlation models to find out the highly correlated fields to determine a feature set and a prediction model. We will also analyse differences between social engagements of the learner groups. As a result of our studies, we aim to build a prediction model for the dropouts of the ESL learners.

We believe that our results can be a new perspective for MOOC personalisation. As we do not hold the source code for popular MOOC platforms, we cannot make direct changes to the platforms. However, these identification methods can be used by MOOC providers for identification of ESL students. An ESL student who uses any MOOC platform such as FutureLearn would be more engaged if they are given a more personalised experience.

Acknowledgments. This work has been done under the project numbered 2016-04-01-DOP05 in Yildiz Technical University (YTU). The dataset used in this paper is provided by the University of Southampton for the ethically approved collaborative study (ID: 23593). The authors would like to thank Prof. Dr. Banu Diri from YTU for her help in improving groups based on learner comments. Authors also want to thank Hatice Ata and Ali Demir who are undergraduate students in YTU for their help in analyses.

References

1. Bakki, A., Oubahssi, L., Cherkaoui, C., George, S.: Motivation and engagement in MOOCs: how to increase learning motivation by adapting pedagogical scenarios? In: Conole, G., Klobučar, T., Rensing, C., Konert, J., Lavoué, É. (eds.) EC-TEL 2015. LNCS, vol. 9307, pp. 556–559. Springer, Cham (2015). doi:10.1007/978-3-319-24258-3_58
2. Barak, M., Watted, A., Haick, H.: Motivation to learn in massive open online courses: examining aspects of language and social engagement. Comput. Educ. **94**, 49–60 (2016)
3. Brouns, F., Firssova, O.: The role of learning design and learning analytics in MOOCs. In: Conference Proceedings of the 9th EDEN Research Workshop, Oldenburg, Germany. EDEN, October 2016
4. Eriksson, T., Adawi, T., Stöhr, C.: "Time is the bottleneck": a qualitative study exploring why learners drop out of MOOCs. J. Comput. High. Educ. **28**, 1–14 (2016)
5. Fasihuddin, H.A., Skinner, G.D., Athauda, R.I.: Boosting the opportunities of open learning (MOOCs) through learning theories. GSTF J. Comput. (JoC) **3**(3), 112 (2013)
6. Gillani, N., Eynon, R., Osborne, M., Hjorth, I., Roberts, S.: Communication communities in MOOCs. arXiv preprint arXiv:1403.4640 (2014)
7. Guàrdia, L., Maina, M., Sangrà, A.: MOOC design principles: a pedagogical approach from the learner's perspective. eLearning Pap. **33**, 1–6 (2013)
8. Kizilcec, R.F., Piech, C., Schneider, E.: Deconstructing disengagement: analyzing learner subpopulations in massive open online courses. In: The 3rd International Conference on Learning Analytics and Knowledge, Leuven, Belgium. ACM, April 2013
9. Milligan, C., Littlejohn, A., Margaryan, A.: Patterns of engagement in connectivist MOOCs. J. Online Learn. Teach. **9**(2), 149 (2013)
10. Sunar, A., White, S., Abdullah, N., Davis, H.: How learners' interactions sustain engagement: a MOOC case study. IEEE Trans. Learn. Technol. (2016)
11. Uchidiuno, J., Ogan, A., Koedinger, K.R., Yarzebinski, E., Hammer, J.: Browser language preferences as a metric for identifying ESL speakers in MOOCs. In: Proceedings of the Third ACM Conference on Learning@ Scale, pp. 277–280 (2016)
12. White, S., White, S.: Learning designers in the 'third space': the socio-technical construction of MOOCs and their relationship to educator and learning designer roles in HE. J. Interact. Media Educ. **2016**(1) (2016)

MOOC Quality Evaluation System: Tomsk State University Experience

Victor Dyomin, Galina Mozhaeva, Olesya Babanskaya, and Ulyana Zakharova(✉)

National Research Tomsk State University, Tomsk, Russia
dyomin@mail.tsu.ru, {mozhaeva, babanskaya, zakharova}@ido.tsu.ru

Abstract. E-learning development comes with an increased attention to its quality that is managed via the control over not only the learners' knowledge but over the learning process, its organization and applied tools. This paper covers Tomsk State University experience in MOOC quality evaluation, in particular popular science MOOCs and specialized ones. The quality evaluation system implies the evaluation of the MOOC materials, the learning process and the results.

Keywords: Massive Open Online Courses · MOOCs · MOOC quality evaluation · Popular science MOOC · Specialized MOOC

1 Introduction

A rapid e-learning development goes along with an increased attention to its quality. The quality management is based on the control over the knowledge that learners acquire, the learning process, its organization and applied means. The quality of education should meet the unified requirements regardless its forms and technologies. Quality management in education attracts great attention in the research projects devoted to the methodological issues of quality management [1, 2] as well as to the challenges on different levels of education in various contexts including e-learning management [3] and managing the quality of massive open online courses (hereafter MOOCs) [4]. In the e-learning quality management system there are some important quality indicators: of educational content (of the course materials), of learning technologies, of the learning process organization and the quality of the learning outcomes. The choice of the certain quality indicators and their groups depends on the extent to which they influence the quality of the e-learning process and could be quickly estimated for practical usage in the quality management system.

This paper is devoted to the MOOC quality management system elaborated at Tomsk State University (hereafter TSU) that combines expert and learner evaluation, platform analytics, ways of managing the e-learning quality indicators, modification of the MOOC materials during the learning process and after it basing on the analysis of the learning outcomes. The study includes the empirical experience description, survey data processing, comparative analysis.

C. Delgado Kloos et al. (Eds.): EMOOCs 2017, LNCS 10254, pp. 197–202, 2017.
DOI: 10.1007/978-3-319-59044-8_23

2 MOOC Quality Evaluation System

In the previous studies we have analyzed and described the tools and mechanisms for the e-learning quality management at a university [5], and the e-learning organizational model based on MOOCs in a classical university and their integration into the system of lifelong education [6].

Starting from 2014 TSU has been working on the project producing MOOCs that are available on Russian and international e-learning platforms [7]. Nowadays there are more than 30 courses produced by 45 authors and the project team.

Performing the project we came to the point that quantitative indicators are not as important as the qualitative ones. Researchers from the Caledonian Academy and Glasgow Caledonian University found out that the quality evaluation of online courses in majority of cases is based on the learners' opinion while they can hardly be seen as experts in quality of education [4]. We involve diverse stakeholders to evaluating MOOCs at TSU such as university authorities, managers of e-learning platforms, experts in the subject field, the project team, and the course learners. Margaryan et al. have analyzed the quality of 76 MOOCs and revealed that they are of high organizational quality but their instructional quality is estimated at the level of 39% at best [4]. We pay special attention to teaching our faculty instructional design and MOOC management. For that purpose we regularly hold educational events, including annual Siberian MOOC Schools. This format implies lectures, workshops, training exercises, discussions and consultations on MOOC production, promotion and application. The School participants' final project is instructional design of their own future MOOC. When the School participants work on their final paper, we highlight that there are two major types of MOOCs, they are popular science and specialized. Depending on these types there are several parameters influencing course instructional design (see Table 1).

These characteristics that differ one type of a MOOC from another, to our mind, impact the quality requirements to their materials, learning process and outcomes.

Quality evaluation system for online courses that is used at TSU includes the same criteria as in the wide spread systems such as the Quality Matters [8] and the ECB-Check [9]. We will consider these criteria below in more details.

Table 1. Differences between popular science and specialized MOOCs.

Parameter	Popular science course	Specialized course
University objectives	University brand and promotion of the scientific school; enlightenment	Monetization; integration into the basic educational programs
Author's objectives	Building a new worldview that is aimed at reflecting on the learner's place and role in the world	Materials are aimed at learners who acquire professional knowledge and skills
Support of the learning process	Learning community is characterized with a higher level of independence from the instructor	Instructor's participation as an expert in the field is crucial, in some cases mentors are required
Required learning outcomes	Reflecting on the knowledge acquired; acquiring cognitive skills	Significant improvement of a learner in his/her professional position; relevance to the state standards (for the promotion or a credit shift)

Quality of MOOC Learning Materials

One of the effective ways of the learning materials quality evaluation is an expert evaluation provided by different specialists – both in the subject and in e-learning. MOOC expertise at our university includes two stages – when course is applied for production and when all the course materials are ready.

Step 1. Contest of applications for MOOC production.

All MOOCs produced at TSU have been winners of a special contest. Table 2 shows who evaluates potential courses and according to which criteria.

Table 2. Evaluation of MOOC applications.

Materials in the application	Expert	Evaluation criteria
The course instructional design including the course type, objectives and outcomes, target audience, curriculum, and promo video script Ideas on the MOOC integration into educational programs Information about chargeable services based on the MOOC Trial video lecture Open application presentation (oral report, answering the questions asked by the contest committee)	University authority	University branding potential Possible recover value (by means of services built on this MOOC) Potential to make the course in two languages
	Education program supervisor	Recruitment potential Potential for blended learning (it can be included into the educational program, the credit shift is possible, etc.) The MOOC is based on the results of the research performed at TSU The author's qualification in the subject and in e-learning
	Manager of the e-learning platform where courses are going to be launched	Novelty Meeting the needs of the platform target audience Potential income from the chargeable services based on the course Focus on practical activities
	TSU project team	Author's experience in taking MOOCs Well-written description of the course Particular goals and measurable learning outcomes Seeing one's target audience Diversified presentation of the learning material Diverse assignments Author's interest in one's subject, charisma in front of the camera and a pleasant narrative style

The contest winners get a grant for MOOC production. Our experience of four contests since 2014 proves that this selection system allows to significantly save costs in course production. The contest helps defining the authors who would develop campus e-learning, as far as those candidates who don't win the contest are suggested to make a SPOC first. If the SPOC is popular among learners it can be launched on a platform as a MOOC.

Step 2. Expertise of the MOOC materials.

After the contest the author and the project team starts working on the full pack of the MOOC materials (the course home page, video scripts, assignments, list of resources, additional materials and so on). We invite specialists in the subject field to evaluate the course materials. If the course receives a negative feedback, it comes back to the author for the improvement. If the author disagrees with the expert conclusion or the experts fail to reach consensus about the course we call for an additional expert evaluation to make a final decision.

If the course gets a positive feedback we continue our work with it and start recording and assembling the video lectures. Before launching the course we send 2–3 lectures and all of the course materials to the e-learning platform specialists to get their quality evaluation.

On uploading the MOOC material onto the platform, the course is subjected to the beta-testers evaluation who are students of the correspondent specialty at our university or volunteers.

Quality of the Learning Process

The quality indicators measuring the learning process and relevant pedagogical communications are the most difficult ones.

The analysis of MOOC quality during the process is aimed at defining weak course elements and correcting them before the course is over, so that the learning process goes on without interruption. The following data sources are used for such an analysis: (a) statistics retrieved from the course admin board, (b) feedback from the MOOC learners (messages to the course administrators, forum posts, course rating with a comment, learner success stories), (c) feedback from the MOOC authors who decide on the effectiveness of the course elements, methods, etc. This information helps us improving the quality of the MOOC only if the course author and the university MOOC team are highly professional. The main requirement at this stage is that the changes should not deprive the learners of the progress they have already achieved.

The most effective and frequently used course changes are: correcting tasks with a high percentage of learners' mistakes, uploading additional materials aimed to set lack of learners' knowledge off, posting new discussion forums to clarify troublesome issues of the material, updating the course information on the course home page.

We have several examples of changing the course during the learning process and improving it for the learners enrolled though they were not expected as the course target group. "Amazing World of Geography" has been made for schoolchildren but have attracted a lot of teachers. These learners have been invited for a new chargeable continuing teaching education program at the end of which they were awarded with a formal TSU certificate. 100 teachers out of 5241 learners have completed this program in two years. Another MOOC "Probability Theory – Science of Chance" showed that the assignments were not challenging for the learners. The reason for that has been found in the opening survey results – the background of learners was much higher than it was expected. The authors had to design new more difficult assignments for the course and upload it into the course immediately.

Quality of the Learning Outcomes
The third step in MOOC quality analysis takes place after the course is over and the results of learning process are available. For this purpose, we use statistical data collected from the platform and the results of the final survey.

Answering the survey is not a must. There are only 1499 replies out of 3238 of those who completed our courses as we write. But this data sample is representative enough, the confidence interval is 99.7%. This survey results are the following: 88.5% considers video lectures as the most useful MOOC elements, 75% rates tasks, tests and additional materials as helpful elements, 80% is satisfied with the depth of course content, 87% considers a high level of instructors' expertise, 83% plans to use the MOOC materials in one's professional activity, and 94% will recommend the MOOC to the friends.

The final survey also includes question about learners' recommendations on the MOOC quality. The learners' insights are discussed with the author and the project team, and it may be taken into account during the next changing session.

According to the survey results the following changes can be made: (1) the course description (e.g. target audience, required background, estimated engagement time), (2) tasks or the threshold, (3) promotion tools if it is found that the course is interesting and highly effective for a certain group of learners who haven't been taken into account earlier, (4) the course assistance regime.

Having analyzed the learners' replies for the final survey, we came to the conclusion that the average quality evaluation of popular science and specialized MOOCs are different. Lectures in popular science MOOCs are appreciated for easy language and artful videos, lectures in specialized MOOCs are evaluated for the instructor's expert opinion. Assignments for the first type of learners are optional activity, it is a quiz checking the basic concepts in the lecture, while learners of the second type consider them as a tool for checking professional knowledge and skills. The requirements to the instructor's level of competence and the depth of the material dramatically differ and influence the marks that those learners give to the course in the final survey. That is why the criteria for quality evaluation of MOOCs should not be unified. There should be at least two sets of criteria – for a popular science and a specialized MOOC.

3 Conclusion

Today MOOC evaluation systems are freely accessible in the web. The MOOC evaluation system used at TSU has been developed at the dawn of MOOCs in Russia on the basis of the system for assessing e-learning. The requirements to MOOC materials hardly differ from those for any electronic course. What is special about MOOCs is their "massive" characteristic. The data derived from the surveys completed by learners and data analytics provided by an e-learning platform can hardly be overestimated. The data sample is huge and difficult to analyze but it is representative enough to provide a foundation for data-driven decisions aimed at improving the quality of MOOCs. This sample data analysis performed by TSU revealed a significant difference between the quality evaluation of different MOOCs – popular science and specialized courses. This led us to the conclusion that the quality criteria for courses of diverse types should be different.

Acknowledgments. The project "Development of educational online projects at TSU" is being supported by the Ministry of Education and Science of the Russian Federation in the framework of Competitiveness Improvement Programme of the leading Russian universities (5–100 Programme).

References

1. Vasilkov, Y., Gushina, L.: Analysis of the effectiveness and efficiency of management systems based on system analysis methodology. Int. J. Qual. Res. **8**(3), 347–356 (2014)
2. Putnik, G., Ávila, P.: Mechanisms to promote continuous improvement in quality management systems. Int. J. Qual. Res. **9**(1), 1–8 (2015)
3. Moguš, A.M.: The use of quality management systems for e-learning. In: 6th International Conference on e-Learning (eLearning-2015) (2015). http://econference.metropolitan.ac.rs/files/pdf/2015/27-Ana-Mirkovic-Mogus-The-use-of-quality-management-systems-for-e-learning.pdf
4. Margaryan, A., Bianco, M., Littlejohn, A.: Instructional quality of Massive Open Online Courses (MOOCs). Comput. Educ. **80**, 77–83 (2014)
5. Babanskaya, O.M., Mozhaeva, G.V., Feshchenko, A.V.: Quality management as a condition for the development of e-learning in a modern university. In: EDULEARN16, Proceedings of 8th International Conference on Education and New Learning Technologies, 4–6th July 2016, Barcelona, Spain, pp. 4367–4373 (2016)
6. Babanskaya, O.M., Mozhaeva, G.V., Zakharova, U.S.: Integrating MOOCs into the system of lifelong learning: TSU experience. In: EDULEARN16, Proceedings of 8th International Conference on Education and New Learning Technologies, 4–6th July 2016, Barcelona, Spain, pp. 4353–4360 (2016)
7. Tomsk State University MOOC Project Website: http://mooc.tsu.ru/en
8. Quality Matters Website: http://www.qualitymatters.org/qa-resources/rubric-standards/higher-ed-rubric
9. ECBCheck Website: http://www.ecb-check.net/criteria-2/

The Drivers of Employer Support for Professional Skill Development in MOOCs

Monika Hamori(✉)

IE Business School, Madrid, Spain
monika.hamori@ie.edu

Abstract. This paper looks at the job-, employee- and organization-specific drivers of support from employers for MOOCs. A survey of 1481 employed learners is used to test the hypotheses. Results show that employers are more likely to support MOOCs if the MOOC content is more closely related to learners' job content and if learners plan to use the content in their current job or at their current employer. Learners lower in the organizational hierarchy are less likely to receive financial support. Organizations that invested more in employee development in the 12 months preceding the survey are more likely to support MOOC.

Keywords: Corporate training and development · Professional learners · Skill acquisition

1 Introduction

Despite the dominance of business MOOCs on the various MOOC platforms, there has been surprisingly little academic interest in analyzing how MOOCs may help corporate skill development or influence labor market outcomes [1, 2]. The research that addresses how MOOCs drive professional learning and corporate skill development represents a small body of literature, much of which is conceptual. The handful of empirical papers reveal that working professionals make up the majority of MOOC participants: 58% of the 52,000 respondents who completed a MOOC on one of the large platforms were employed full-time [3]. Another survey of 34,000 learners who enrolled in the MOOCs of a US university [4] finds that 62% were either employed full-time or were self-employed.

These studies also reveal that the acquisition of job-related skills is a primary motivation for employed participants to enroll in a MOOC: 44% of learners take MOOCs to gain specific skills to do their job bett [4]. The learning purposes of on-the-job and career development learning were rated the most highly by their 119 employed respondents who took MOOCs, more highly than the personal learning purpose [5]. Of those who had completed a MOOC more than four months before and

M. Hamori—This project was funded by the 2015 edition of the BBVA Foundation Grants for Researchers and Cultural Creators.

C. Delgado Kloos et al. (Eds.): EMOOCs 2017, LNCS 10254, pp. 203–209, 2017.
DOI: 10.1007/978-3-319-59044-8_24

whose primary aim was to gain skills for their current and future jobs, 62% reported that the MOOC enhanced their skills for the current job [3]. A downside of [3, 4] is that they do not differentiate between MOOCs that are appropriate for professional skill development at the workplace and other types of MOOCs and they do not go beyond reporting descriptive statistics. [3, 4] are contradicted by the results from thirty-five semi-structured interviews by Milligan and Littlejohn [6], which reveal that although many learners join MOOCs motivated by the challenges they face in their jobs, they end up focusing on course tasks and assignment completion, and fail to relate the course content to their job role or work tasks. Furthermore, Milligan and Littlejohn [6] suggest that the label "gain skills to do their job better" [4] or "enhance skills" [3] may be overly generic, because the job-related benefits that learners gain from MOOCs vary a great deal, from complementing existing knowledge to gaining new knowledge for a new job role.

Most employers are found to appear supportive of MOOCs. The eight HR managers see no obstacle in the MOOCs being open courses where learners from different organizations come together and have the chance to share employer-related information [2]. 83% of the HR managers surveyed and interviewed by Walton Radford et al. [7] reported positive views on using MOOCs as a professional development tool. While HR managers who had already heard of MOOCs had the most positive attitude to them, they represented only 31% of respondents. A mere 7% of them had started to use MOOCs for professional development at their corporation [7]. The interviews of Walton Radford et al. identify several benefits of MOOCs for professional development, which include engaging employees in their own development, expanding the breadth of training offerings organizations can provide, accommodating the development of a particular skill in a cost-effective manner and the overall low cost of MOOCs compared to other types of formal training.

Despite the positive views of HR managers on MOOCs in Walton Radford et al. [7], survey data of employed learners by Castaño-Muñoz et al. [1] show that 72% of them take MOOCs without their employer's knowledge. About 80% of the employers who are aware of learners' MOOC participation support MOOCs, although the bulk of their support involves encouragement, rather than cost reimbursement or providing time off to study. Informal employer support (encouragement) of employees who participate in MOOCs increases their likelihood of completing the course. Surprisingly, time off and cost reimbursement were found to have no effect, probably because of the very small number of employees receiving such support (8 out of the 376 salaried learners surveyed received financial support and 11 received time off to do their studies).

To sum, despite the fact that MOOCs represent an increasingly dominant way in which employees may gain job-related skills, we have fragmented evidence from a handful of empirical papers on how they are used for corporate skill development. Except for Castaño-Muñoz et al. [1], all of this data is descriptive. It addresses the incidence of employed individuals taking MOOCs, the frequency of learners who use MOOCs for job-related skill development and the incidence of employers supporting MOOCs. At the same time, it fails to identify the drivers of these outcomes.

Arguably one of the most important of these outcomes is employer sponsorship or support for MOOCs. While Castaño-Muñoz et al. [1] looked at the incidence of such sponsorship and linked sponsorship to course completion rates, the drivers of employer sponsorship, specifically, the type of courses and employees who receive support and the type of employers that sponsor MOOCs, have remained unexplored.

The research on employer support [1] also faced methodological challenges. The incidence of organizational sponsorship was so low in the dataset of employed learners used by Castaño-Muñoz et al. [1] that they were unable to find a significant relationship between employer sponsorship and learning outcomes. Finally, while the study by Castaño-Muñoz et al. contrasted learners supported by their employer with the rest of the learner population, no empirical study has made the important distinction in the group of employees who take MOOCs without employer support: between self-sponsored employees who pay for the MOOC themselves and whose objective is to gain knowledge as well as an official educational credential (certificate), and those whose primary goal is to obtain job-relevant skills without obtaining an educational credential.

To overcome these conceptual and methodological gaps in the extant literature, we look at the job-, employee- and organization-specific drivers of employers' support for MOOCs, in a larger sample of employed learners than the one in Castaño-Muñoz et al. [1]. Specifically, we test four hypotheses:

- Hypothesis 1: Employers are more likely to support MOOCs that impart knowledge and skills that are more directly related to learners' job content.
- Hypothesis 2: Employers are more likely to support learners who hold high value-added jobs.
- Hypothesis 3: Employers are more likely to support employees who have a stronger attachment to the firm.
- Hypothesis 4: Employers are more likely to support MOOCs if they have fewer resources for employee development in place.

2 Data and Methods

We surveyed 2490 learners who took any of the 14 different MOOCs offered on a range of topics (Brand and product management, Pricing, Channel Management, Integrated marketing communications, etc.) in the field of Marketing by one of Europe's top business schools between February and October 2016.

Over 13% of our sample were students, another 13% were self-employed individuals, 12% were unemployed, others retired (0.4%) or did not belong to any of these categories (1.7%). 53% of our sample were employed full-time, while 7% were employed part-time. Since we are interested in exploring the drivers of employer support, we focus on the 1481 full-time and part-time individuals, about 60% of the original sample. The survey was anonymous and voluntary.

To test our hypotheses, we run models with the dependent variable Support. Since this dependent variable is dichotomous, we run logistic regressions that enable us to report the coefficients as well as the odds ratios. For the purposes of robustness, we also ran the analyses as probit models, which led to identical results. Since the 1481 learners are nested in 14 different courses, we cluster the standard errors by course.

3 Results

Five percent of learners claim that they received financial support for the MOOC, 8% received time off to participate in it and 5% had the MOOC included in their performance evaluation. These percentages are higher than those reported by Castaño-Muñoz et al. [1], but they are still low considering that 60% of respondents report that they intend to use the knowledge gained in the MOOC in their current job. Table 1 displays

Table 1. Logistic regression predicting support

Variables	Model 1	
	DV = Support	
	Coeff.	S.e.
Age	0.08	1.30
Gender	−0.04	0.22
Years_school	−0.07*	1.65
Fluent	0.35**	2.21
Native	0.40*	1.66
No_MOOCs	0.50***	2.79
MOOCs1_5	0.20	1.29
GDP_capita	0.03	0.37
Marketing	0.12	0.67
Relevant_Current_Job	0.24***	3.08
Use_Job_Org	0.29**	2.31
Use_Other Org	−0.29**	2.20
Manager	0.06	0.29
Executive	0.63**	1.99
Part-timer	−0.15	0.68
Hours_Training1_10	1.03***	3.91
Hours_Training11_20	1.01***	3.66
Hours_Training21_50	1.01**	2.53
Hours_Training50	1.56***	5.30
Size_100	−0.61***	2.89
Size_250	−0.43**	2.37
Size_500	−0.52	1.60
Size_1000	−0.88***	3.46
Size_10000	−0.42*	1.88
Size_more than 10000	−0.61**	2.14
Employer_Training_Topic	0.68**	2.34
Constant	−3.57***	2.73
N	1309	
LR Chi2	121.1***	
Pseudo R2	.104	

Notes: *p < .1, **p < .05, ***p < .01

the logistic regression model. Hypothesis 1 states that organizations are more likely to support MOOCs that impart knowledge and skills that are more directly related to learners' job content. The evidence in Model 1 of Table 1 supports Hypothesis 1. Model 1 reveals that the more relevant is the course content to the job content, the more likely it is that it will receive support (Support) from the employer (Relevant_Current_job, $\beta = 0.24$, $p < .01$).

The odds ratio of 1.27 reveals that a unit increase in Relevant_Current_job increases learners' likelihood of receiving any type of support from their employer by 27%. Learners who are more likely to use the course content in their current job or during their career with the current employer are also more likely to receive Support (Use_Job_Org, $\beta = 0.29$, $p < .05$, odds ratio = 1.34). Marketing has the expected sign, but it is not significant. Finally, those who want to use the knowledge gained in the MOOC to find a new job at a different employer are less likely to receive employer support for the course (Use_Other Org, $\beta = -0.29$, $p < .05$, odds ratio = 0.75).

Hypothesis 2 states that organizations are more likely to support learners who hold high value-added jobs. This hypothesis receives support. Executives are 87% more likely to get support than non-managerial employees ($\beta = 0.63$, $p < .05$, odds ratio = 1.87). Managerial employees, however, show no difference from non-managerial ones.

Hypothesis 3 states that organizations are more likely to support MOOCs for employees who have a stronger attachment to the firm. Hypothesis 3 does not receive support.

Hypothesis 4 states that organizations are more likely to support MOOCs if they have fewer resources for training in place. Hypothesis 4 receives mixed support. Counter to Hypothesis 4, the results reveal that organizations that invested more in employee development during the 12 months preceding the survey are also more likely to support MOOCs: For the DV Support, all the dummies that signify various quantities of training are significantly different from the omitted category, no hours of training (Hours_Training 1_10: $\beta = 1.03$, $p < .01$, odds ratio = 2.80; Hours_Training 11_20: $\beta = 1.01$, $p < .01$, odds ratio = 2.75; Hours_Training 21_50: $\beta = 1.01$, $p < .05$, odds ratio = 2.74). The differences are largest for those learners who have received more than 50 h of training in the past 12 months (Hours_Training50: $\beta = 1.56$, $p < .01$, odds ratio = 4.75): these learners are almost five times more likely to be supported for MOOCs than those who received no training.

Counter to Hypothesis 4, the predictor Employer training on the topic increases learners' likelihood to receive Support for the MOOCs in Model 1 ($\beta = 0.68$, $p < .05$, odds ratio = 1.97). Employers who provide training on the topic of the MOOC probably train on a wide range of topics. Such employers are more likely to support MOOCs. At the same time, the results call in question the claim that those employers who offer no training on the topic of the MOOC may make up for their lack of training by exploring MOOC offerings and using them for corporate training purposes.

Nevertheless, consistent with Hypothesis 4, smaller organizations that have fewer resources to training are more likely to support MOOCs than their larger-sized counterparts. Larger size decreases the likelihood of getting Support (Model 1). All the size dummies have a negative coefficient and five out of the six dummies are statistically significant predictors of Support.

4 Discussion and Conclusions

This paper looks at an important facet of leveraging MOOCs for professional development at the workplace: employer support for MOOCs. It presents the first piece of empirical evidence on the job-, employee- and organization-specific drivers of employer support.

Employer support. Descriptive statistics show that employers provide little support for MOOCs. The logistic regression models reveal that when they grant support, they do it based on "traditional" considerations: namely, they support those employees who choose courses that are more relevant for their job content, who are in highly value-added jobs and who have greater attachment to the firm (full-time employees).

We find that small-sized organizations, those with 50 employees or fewer, are more likely to support MOOCs. These findings show that MOOCs may offer a training alternative to organizations that do not have the resources to offer in-company training courses or send their employees to external training providers.

We find that those employers that make larger investments in training their workforce are more likely to grant support for MOOCs, too. The number of training hours that employees received in the 12 months preceding the survey is a consistently significant predictor of employer support. Employers' likelihood of providing training on the topic area of the MOOC is also a significant predictor of support. MOOCs offer a low-cost, high-quality, accessible development alternative. Reasonably, then, employers without the scale or the resources to provide training on a certain topic are expected to turn to MOOCs in order to make up for their lack of training investment. The hope that MOOCs will be most likely to help organizations that failed to invest in workforce development because they lacked the resources to do so, however, is not supported by the data. We can only guess why this happens. One reason may be that it requires a learning culture and an openness to experiment with and capitalize on new models of learning delivery for workforce development. This is why organizations that have the mindset of investing in employee development on an ongoing basis are more likely to invest in MOOCs, too.

Non-employer-sponsored learning. Overall, the results reveal that MOOCs are bringing in a new paradigm of skill development at the workplace. Specifically, descriptive statistics show that while the majority of working professionals take MOOCs to gain knowledge and skills to do their job better, only one fifth of them gets support from their employer in any form, suggesting that employee efforts of professional skill development take place mostly without the employers' knowledge and support of these efforts. This phenomenon represents a completely different model of corporate skill development than in-company face-to-face training sessions where training efforts were planned and overseen by Human Resource (HR) or Learning & Development (L&D) managers. If employees opted for training content that was not sponsored by their employer, they faced considerable disruption at work to travel to and attend these courses. MOOCs, on the other hand, are offered by third parties, without control from employers. They pose no barriers: educational qualifications or financial investment, to join, and the lack of space and time constraints to access

MOOC content ("any time from any device") poses minimal disruptions at work. The entrance of MOOCs in the skill development marketplace changes how professional skill acquisition is done.

References

1. Castaño-Muñoz, J., Kalz, M., Kreins, K., Punie, Y.: Influence of employer support for professional development on MOOCs enrolment and completion: results from a cross-course survey. In: Proceedings of EMOOCs 2016, pp. 251–263. Books on Demand GmbH, Norderstedt (2016)
2. Olsson, U.: Open courses and MOOCs as professional development—is the openness a hindrance? Educ. + Train. **58**, 229–243 (2016)
3. Zhenghao, C., Alcorn, B., Christensen, G., Eriksson, N., Koller, D., Emanuel, E.J.: Who is benefiting from MOOCs and why (2015). https://hbr.org/2015/09/whos-benefiting-from-moocs-and-why
4. Christensen, G., Steinmetz, A., Alcorn, B., Bennett, A., Woods, D., Emanuel, E.J.: The MOOC phenomenon: who takes massive open online courses and why? (2013). http://ssrn.com/abstract=2350964
5. Egloffstein, M., Ifenthaler, D.: Employee perspectives on MOOCs for workplace learning. TechTrends **61**, 65–70 (2016)
6. Milligan, C., Littlejohn, A.: Supporting professional learning in a massive open online course. Int. Rev. Res. Open Distrib. Learn. **15**(5) (2014). http://www.irrodl.org/index.php/irrodl/article/view/1855
7. Walton Radford, A., Robles, J., Cataylo, S., Horn, L., Thornton, J., Whitfield, K.: The employer potential of MOOCs: a mixed-methods study of human resource professionals' thinking on MOOCs. IRR ODL **15**(5), 1–25 (2014)

To Change or Not to Change? That's the Question… On MOOC-Success, Barriers and Their Implications

Maartje Henderikx[1(✉)], Karel Kreijns[1], and Marco Kalz[2]

[1] Welten Institute, Open University of the Netherlands, Heerlen, The Netherlands
{maartje.henderikx,karel.kreijns}@ou.nl

[2] UNESCO Chair of Open Education, Faculty Management, Science and Technology and Welten Institute, Open University of the Netherlands, Heerlen, The Netherlands
marco.kalz@ou.nl

Abstract. This explorative study aimed to get an understanding of MOOC-success as seen from the perspective of the MOOC-taker and the types of barriers which might stand in the way of this success. Data of two MOOCs was used to illustrate MOOC-success from two perspectives and barriers encountered. Following the currently used approach to identify educational success, the success rate of MOOC-II was 5,6%. The success rates from the perspective of the MOOC-taker was 70%. In addition, data of MOOC-I and II showed that the encountered barriers were mainly non-MOOC-related. Work-place issues and lack of time were most frequently indicated. For MOOC-designers' decision making regarding redesign of a MOOC after evaluation, it is valuable to have insight in these matters to prevent unnecessary design interventions.

Keywords: MOOCs · Online learning · Success · Intention · Behaviour · Barriers

1 Introduction

When people start a MOOC their intentions are very diverse; some of them want to complete the MOOC and earn a certificate, others just want to freshen up on some specific knowledge or only browse to see what it is all about [1]. For this reason, it does not suffice to only look at the number of certificates earned by the MOOC-takers for determining success, even though this method is often transferred from the formal education context to the MOOC and is the most widely-used method of identifying educational success. As an alternative approach, we take the initial intention of the individual as a starting point for measuring success taking into account that MOOCs allow individuals to follow their own learning paths [2]. These intentions may vary from simply browsing through a MOOC to—indeed—getting a certificate. Studies on behavioural and cognitive psychology, however, showed that in general intention is not a perfect predictor for actual behaviour as there are many factors that can influence the

C. Delgado Kloos et al. (Eds.): EMOOCs 2017, LNCS 10254, pp. 210–216, 2017.
DOI: 10.1007/978-3-319-59044-8_25

process of acting out intentions [3]. Therefore, insight into the issues which hinder or prevent individuals from translating their intentions into actual behaviour is of great value when it comes to deciding whether course (re)design interventions are necessary. This paper is structured as follows: First we discuss the theoretical background. Next data from three MOOCs is analysed in line with the theoretical framework. Lastly, results of these analyses are discussed as well as implications for future research and limitations.

2 Theoretical Framework

The reasoned action approach (RAA) [3] serves as a theoretical framework to our study, as it pays attention to the intention-behaviour gap. The framework is centred around the formation of an intention and the translation of this specific intention to actual behaviour. Sheeran [4] described four different intention-behaviour patterns that can be distinguished: (1) *Inclined actors;* individuals who formed a certain intention and did act according to those intentions, (2) *Inclined abstainers;* individuals who formed a certain intention but fail to act according to this intention, (3) *Disinclined actors*; individuals who formed a certain intention but end up doing more than they intended to do and finally, (4) *Disinclined abstainers*; individuals who do not have any intentions and accordingly do not act. This latter group shall not be included in the context of MOOCs, for the reason that this group will never start a MOOC in the first place.

Figure 1 visually illustrates the three possible intention-behaviour patterns in a MOOC. As can be seen, many individual intentions are possible which may vary from only finishing the first three modules to completing the full course and getting the certificate. Following the intention-behaviour patterns, MOOC-takers who formed the intention to finish the first three modules of a MOOC and actually succeed in doing so, are identified as inclined actors and are considered successful MOOC-takers. MOOC-takers who only planned to browse through the course or download some interesting materials and who eventually finish three modules are also considered as successful.

However, an intention which is formed at the start of a MOOC does not always equal the actual behaviour [3]. This gap between intention and behaviour can be caused

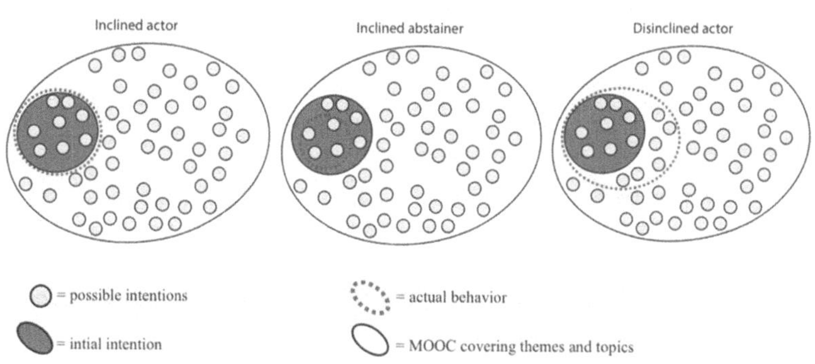

Fig. 1. Intention-behaviour patterns

by barriers; these barriers can be either MOOC-related (i.e. lack of interaction) or non MOOC-related (i.e. workplace issues) and may cause MOOC-takers to change their individual intention or even stop. An explorative, non-exhaustive, literature review on barriers encountered by students in MOOCs and online learning in general showed that lack of interaction [5–7], lack of time [8–10] and insufficient academic background [8, 10] are barriers students frequently encounter. Other barriers experienced by students were: family issues and lack of support family and friends [10], workplace commitments and lack of support from the workplace [10] and insufficient technology background [9]. Only a sub-set of these barriers can be addressed by redesign of the MOOC.

Thus, insufficient insight into the reasons behind success and failure rates in MOOCs could lead to negative evaluations and unnecessary interventions. To address this problem, the following two research questions will be addressed in this study:

1. What are implications of an intention-centric success measurement in MOOCs compared to a certificate-oriented success measurement?
2. What type of barriers do MOOC-takers encounter during the runtime of a MOOC?

3 Method

3.1 Participants

Participants were MOOC-takers of two MOOCs. The first MOOC (MOOC-I) was a Spanish MOOC about Business Intelligence and Big Data and was offered from February until April 2016, covering five modules for five weeks. The pre-questionnaire was unfortunately not distributed due technical problems with the platform but the post-questionnaire was completed by 143 MOOC-takers (37 women, 106 men, $M_{age} = 41{,}6$, age range: 25–64 years).

The second MOOC (MOOC-II) was a Dutch MOOC about The Adolescent Brain and ran from April until June 2016 in Dutch, covering seven modules for seven weeks. The pre-questionnaire was completed by 821 MOOC-takers (664 women, 157 men, $M_{age} = 45{,}1$, age range: 18–74 years). The post-questionnaire was completed by 126 MOOC-takers (unfortunately participant information was not available). In total 101 MOOC-takers completed both questionnaires (90 women, 11 men, $M_{age} = 37$, age range: 18–54 years).

3.2 Materials

To measure the intention of the individual MOOC-takers a self-constructed set of items was used aligned with the design of the respective MOOCs. Items covered increasing intentions from browsing, partial participation in one or more modules, up to participating in all learning activities and receiving a certificate. These items were included in the pre- and post-questionnaire of MOOC-II. In the post-questionnaire MOOC-takers were asked to indicate their actual behaviour on the same set of items as was used in the pre-questionnaire.

The post-questionnaire of MOOC-I and II included several questions on specific barriers MOOC-takers encountered. These barriers were derived from an explorative, non-exhaustive, literature review on barriers in MOOCs and online learning in general, including articles from 2008 until present. Figure 2 displays these barriers categorized into MOOC-related and MOOC. MOOC-takers could indicate multiple barriers.

MOOC-related		Non-MOOC related	
Design	Lack of support	*General*	Lack of information literacy
Problems with the site	Content was not appropriate	Workplace issues	Insufficient academic background
Lack of interaction	*Expectations management*	Lack of time	Lack of motivation
Lack of instant feedback	Course was too easy	Family issues	Lack of personal commitment
Lack of instructor presence	Course did not meet expectations	Lack of workplace support	*Technical*
Lack of useful feedback	Course was too difficult	Lack of family support	Technological problems pc
		Personal	Bad internet connection
		Lack of technological skills	

Fig. 2. Overview barriers arranged by type

3.3 Procedure

In the first week of MOOC-II, all the registered MOOC-takers received an invitation to participate in the pre-questionnaire. Due to technical difficulties, MOOC-takers of MOOC-I did not receive an invitation for the pre-questionnaire and therefore were not able to complete the pre-questionnaire. At the end of the last week of both MOOCs all the registered MOOC-takers received an invitation to participate in the post-questionnaire.

4 Results

4.1 Intention-Oriented vs Certificate-Oriented Success Measurement

Part one of this analysis focused on success measurement from the MOOC-taker perspective. We mapped the intention-behaviour on an individual level which follows the theory as discussed in the theoretical framework. In MOOC-II, 101 participants completed both the pre-questionnaire and the post-questionnaire.

In this MOOC, 49% of the MOOC-takers who completed both the pre-questionnaire and the post-questionnaire, can be regarded as inclined actors, 21% as disinclined actors, and 30% of the MOOC-takers as inclined abstainers (Fig. 3a).

Part two of the analysis focussed on comparing the intention-oriented with the certificate-oriented measurement of success. The certificate-oriented rates were calculated by taking the number of certificates earned by the MOOC-takers divided by the total number of registered MOOC-takers (Fig. 3b). MOOC-II had 1763 registered MOOC-takers, of whom 98 earned a certificate. which results in a success rate of 5,4%[1]. The intention-oriented rates result in a success rate of 70% and a failure rate of 30%.

[1] Calculation: (422/6452) × 100%.

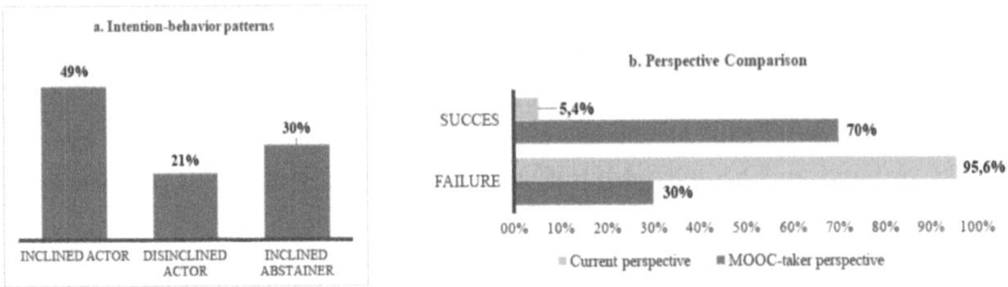

Fig. 3. a + b. Intention-behaviour patterns MOOC-II (a) and perspective comparison MOOC-II (b)

4.2 Barriers

The question which type of barriers were encountered during the runtime of MOOCs I and II was answered by 50 MOOC-takers of MOOC-I and 76 MOOC-takers of MOOC-II who completed both questionnaires. Figure 4a shows that in MOOC-I 75% and in MOOC-II 66% of the barriers are non MOOC-related. Figure 4b displays that 25% of the indicated barriers of MOOC-I are MOOC-related and 34% of the barriers of MOOC-II. Of the non MOOC-related barriers MOOC-takers mostly indicated general barriers; 50% in MOOC-I and 55% in MOOC-II.

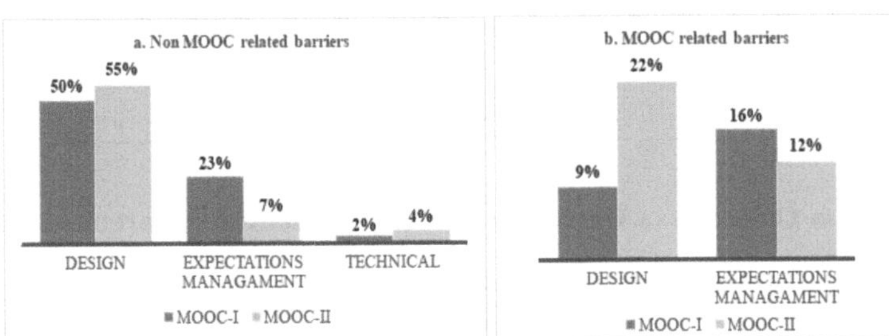

Fig. 4. a + b. Overview MOOC-related (a) vs non MOOC-related barriers (b)

The most important MOOC-related barriers were related to expectation management and design.

5 Discussion

This explorative study aimed to get an understanding of MOOC-success as seen from the perspective of the MOOC taker and the types of barriers which might stand in the way of transferring intentions into actual behaviour. Insight in these matters is valuable for MOOC-makers as the success measurement is often used as an indicator for the necessity of design interventions [2].

Data of MOOC-II was used to compare currently used certificate-oriented success measurement with our proposed intention-oriented success measurement. The results show that there is a big difference between success rates, which are respectively 5,4% and 70%. This finding demonstrates that merely looking at course completion as a measure for MOOC and individual success might not suffice. A small change in the way we look at determining MOOC-success might have a large impact on MOOC (re)design and strategic choices of the MOOC providers.

Furthermore, three intention-behaviour patterns were determined: inclined actors, disinclined actors and inclined abstainers [4]. After matching the intention-behaviour data from the pre- and post-questionnaire of MOOC-II, most MOOC-takers (49%) were identified as inclined actors. It can be expected that these MOOC-takers are content with their achievement. However, this does not necessarily imply that they were satisfied with issues like MOOC-content, design or learning experience. Quite a substantial group of 21% of the MOOC-takers were distinguished as disinclined actors. Reasons for this could be that they might have set low targets for themselves (just browse, or do some learning activities), or the course content might have unexpectedly interested them more than they anticipated. Further research is necessary to understand the reasons behind this behaviour. A third group of 30% was identified as inclined abstainers. These participants formed certain goal intentions but were not able to transform these intentions to actual behaviour. Did this group meet the most barriers? Did they set the highest targets? Future research should open this proverbial black box.

Lastly, in the post-questionnaire of MOOC-I and II, MOOC-takers could indicate multiple barriers they encountered during the course. An analysis of whether barriers encountered by MOOC-takers were MOOC-related or non-MOOC-related showed that most of the barriers can be considered as non-MOOC-related barriers. In MOOC-I and II 75% and 66% of the barriers were not related to the course itself. These results are important for MOOC-designers as they need to be well informed about the reasons behind success and failure rates.

This study had several limitations. First of all, the MOOC-takers who participated in the questionnaires are likely to belong to the group with higher intentions due to the survival bias that can occur in MOOCs. In addition, the samples are relatively small, especially to compare the intention-behaviour gap based on data from the pre-and-post questionnaire. Also, the way the respective MOOCs were designed might have had an impact on the type of barriers MOOC-takers encountered.

In conclusion, insight into individual intentions of MOOC-takers and types of barriers encountered by these MOOC-takers provides a richer knowledge base for MOOC-makers as it comes to deciding whether redesign is necessary. This explorative study is a first step into providing these insights and a first step towards further research into these matters to support MOOC-makers in their decision-making processes.

Acknowledgement. This work is financed via a grant by the Dutch National Initiative for Education Research (NRO)/The Netherlands Organisation for Scientific Research (NWO) and the Dutch Ministry of Education, Culture and Science under the grant nr. 405-15-705 (SOONER/ http://sooner.nu).

References

1. Koller, D., Ng, A., Do, C., Chen, Z.: Retention and intention in massive open online courses: in depth. Educ. Rev. **48**(3), 62–63 (2013)
2. Henderikx, M., Kreijns, K., Kalz, M.: Refining success and dropout in MOOCs based on the intention-behavior gap, submitted
3. Fishbein, M., Ajzen, I.: Predicting and Changing Behavior: The Reasoned Action Approach. Taylor & Francis, Milton Park (2011)
4. Sheeran, P.: Intention—behavior relations: a conceptual and empirical review. Eur. Rev. Soc. Psychol. **12**(1), 1–36 (2002)
5. Khalil, H., Ebner, M.: Interaction possibilities in MOOCs – how do they actually happen? In: International Conference on Higher Education Development, pp. 1–24. Mansoura University, Egypt (2013)
6. Levy, D., Schrire, S.: The case of a massive open online course at a college of education. Informally published manuscript. Kibbutzim College of Education, Technology and the Arts, Israel (2012). http://conference.nmc.org/files/smkbMOOC.pdf
7. McAuley, A., Stewart, B., Siemens, G., Cormier, D.: Massive open online courses: digital ways of knowing and learning. University of Prince Edward Island, Charlottetown (2010)
8. Belanger, Y., Thornton, J.: Bioelectricity: A Quantitative Approach. Durham, NC (2013). http://dukespace.lib.duke.edu/dspace/bitstream/handle/10161/6216/Duke_Bioelectricity_MOOC_Fall2012.pdf?sequence=1
9. Khalil, H., Ebner, M.: MOOCs completion rates and possible methods to improve rentention - a literature review. In: World Conference on Educational Multimedia, Hypermedia and Telecommunications, pp. 1236–1244. AACE, Chesapeak (2014)
10. Onah, D.F.O., Sinclair, J.E., Boyatt, R.: Dropout rates of massive open online courses: behavioural patterns. In: 6th International conference on Education and New Learning Technologies, pp. 5825–5834. EDULEARN14, Barcelona (2014)

Follow-Up of Learning Activities in Open edX: A Case Study at the University of Cauca

Daniel Jaramillo-Morillo[1(✉)], Mario Solarte Sarasty[1], Gustavo Ramírez González[1], and Mar Pérez-Sanagustín[2]

[1] Universidad Del Cauca, Popayán, Colombia
{dajaramillo, msolarte, gramirez}@unicauca.edu.co
[2] Pontificia Universidad Católica, Santiago, Chile
mar.perez@ing.puc.cl

Abstract. MOOCs are Massive Open Online Courses whose strategies have been used by higher education institutions for some years under the SPOC (Small Private Online Courses). However, MOOC technologies present some problems to support the personal relationships between tutor and students needed in a more traditional scenario. As a consequence, some types of activities, especially those that require more personal assessment and support from the tutor, become difficult to track. This article presents a tool and a set of indicators that facilitates the tutor to follow the learning activities of the students in SPOC. Specifically, a case study is presented, where the tool has been used to follow up the virtual course of "Astronomía Cotidiana" of the University of Cauca over Open edX instance.

Keywords: MOOC · Follow-up · Monitoring · Tracking

1 Introduction

Massive Open Online Courses (MOOC) are open courses to thousands of students covering topics ranging since technology to poetry [1]. Their size can range since hundreds to thousands of students, so the number of people who can benefit from learning is much higher than in traditional online courses.

The adoption of the MOOC model in universities and incorporating them into their training and educational programs represents a technological challenge that is being solved thanks to strategies such as Small Private Online Courses (SPOC) [2, 3], SPOCs are a variant of MOOCs that are characterized by being limited in access and therefore also in size but that have a wider scope of participation than in any conventional online course [2, 4].

Many advantages arise because of their massiveness, but also generate a number of disadvantages or challenges. One of the main difficulties to use SPOC is the lack of tools to maintain an adequate relationship between the tutor and the student, since it is difficult for the tutors to have a personalized treatment with each of the many active

C. Delgado Kloos et al. (Eds.): EMOOCs 2017, LNCS 10254, pp. 217–222, 2017.
DOI: 10.1007/978-3-319-59044-8_26

participants of a course. The lack of these tools makes it difficult for follow-up tasks, these being necessary in any learning process, and even more so when it comes to courses recognized academically by an institution of higher education and/or equivalent to academic credits [1, 5].

With the purpose of improve the tutor student relationship in a technological environment designed for massive amounts of students, this article presents a tool that facilitates the tutor to follow the learning activities of students in SPOC. Specifically, a case study is presented in which the tool has been used to follow up the daily astronomy course at the University of Cauca with a recognition of two academic credits. This tool is proposed as a support for teachers who guide courses deployed in Open edX and that are offered by institutions of higher education where a more personalized follow-up of the activities carried out by the students is required.

2 Related Work

This section presents some tools that currently offer a way to monitor the learning activities that students develop in a MOOC.

Halawa et al. [6] present an dropout predictor that uses characteristics of student activity to predict which students are at high risk of desertion in MOOC. The predictor analyzes the number of loginsto the learning platform, access to the contents, percentage of tasks performed, etc., and depending on the results marks him as a possible deserter or not. In this way the tutors are aware of who are the potential deserters and can provide assistance so that the student does not leave the course.

Chorianopoulos et al. [7] present learning analytics systems on video content in MOOC. The systems capture students' interactions with the video player (pause, replay, forward, etc.) using a YouTube API and at the same time collect information about students' performance in evaluations. Interaction data can be statistically visualized along with student assessment results helping tutors better understand student behavior. However, these works do not take into account interactions with other content, communication tools, or navigation on the platform.

Shi et al. [8] present VisMOOC, a visual analysis system to help analyze user learning behaviors by using video navigation data from MOOC platforms. The tool receives raw data of all events that are generated in the learning platform, then processes and filters them by selecting the video navigation data, the user's identification, date, time, video position, and type of event. The filtered data can be visualized using statistical graphs. The objective of the work is to provide a help for that the instructors can understand the behavior of the students and propose the designs of their courses.

ANALYSE [9] is a tool designed and developed for Open edX by the University Carlos III of Madrid and several members of the eMadrid network. Data are taken from low level and become indicators about the learning process. The indicators shown are: time distribution and course progress in terms of assessments and videos viewed, access to course content and the time spent on them. The presented visualizations are very useful for the students, however, there is no greater support for the teacher since the information that is shown is global (statistical data of the course). For the tutor, it is difficult to identify which of the participants perform poorly or which of the students have already reviewed all the content.

3 Indicators

The indicators identified are associated to the monitoring of massive learning environments and were taken as a reference in the implementation of the proposed tool. All these indicators are inspired by those extracted from the bibliographic analysis, and adapted to capture and distinguish between the different types of activities that students perform in a course. Table 1 presents the results obtained from the literature review.

Table 1. Indicators identified

Indicator	Commitment	Progress	Performance	Interest	Persistence	Constancy	Abandonment	Effectiveness	Capacity	Participation
Articles	[6, 10]	[6, 7, 9]	[7, 10]	[6]	[6]	[6, 11]	[6]	[6]	[6]	[8, 10, 11]
Students – assessments interaction										
Results	X	X	X	X	X	X	X	X	X	
Attempts	X				X			X		
Time taken	X			X			X			
Students – learning platform interaction										
Logins to the couse	X	X				X				
Access to course content	X	X				X				
Time taken	X						X			
Students - content interaction										
Viewed videos	X	X		X		X		X	X	X
Viewed videos completely	X	X		X				X	X	X
Time taken	X			X			X			X
Students – communication tools interaction										
Forums created	X			X		X			X	

4 Description of the Follow-Up Tool

The proposed tool is a web application to facilitate the teacher to follow up the learning activities of students in SPOC. A prototype implemented in the Open edX MOOC platform is presented below. This tool make the follow up the learning activities of the students in SPOC. Figure 1 presents the general architecture of the constructed mechanism.

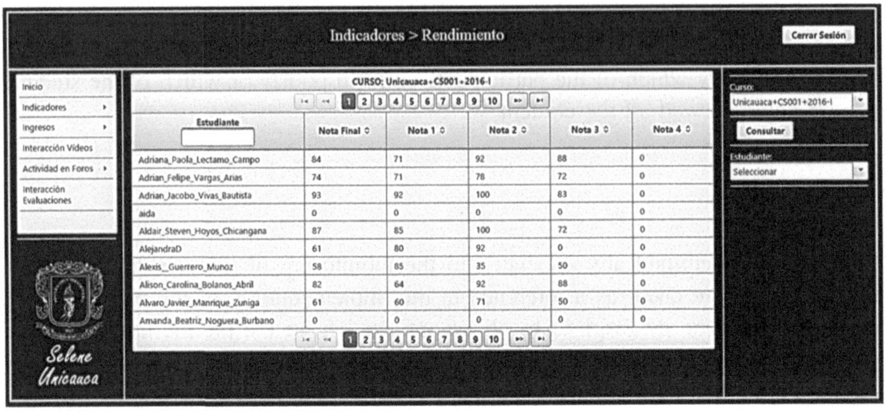

Fig. 1. Capture of the tool follow-up selene. Performance indicator - astronomía cotidiana course.

5 Results

As an example that the tool can provide support to the teacher to follow up the activities of students in SPOC a test was carried out in a real context. The follow up was made to the course "Astronomía Cotidiana" of the University of Cauca offered in virtual mode as elective of the Integral Social and Human Training component.

The objetive of the astronomy course is to introduce students to the principles, methods and tools of online education for the study of basic concepts of astronomy and its relationship with other earth and space sciences. The course was organized in three main themes and for each of them the students had to make an evaluation. The course lasted a period of 18 weeks beginning on February 15 and ending on June 10 of 2016 and counted with a participation of 403 students, ten times the number of students traditionally admitted to regular courses with academic recognition.

One of the concerns of the teacher of the course was to know the income of the students in the first days of the academic semester to know if the procedure defined for registration of students to the platform was correct and if the students had received the communications orienting at the beginning of the course, which took place through institutional communication mechanisms not yet integrated into Open edX. With the help of the tool it was obtained that the income for the course during the first month were 1508 from 401 students out of a total of 403. Figure 2 shows the income history obtained for that month (February 2016). In the first academic week (15th to 19th of February) was where higher income is presented due to the expectation generated by the course innovation, first in this modality at the University of Cauca.

A feature that stands out from the tool is that it allows the teacher to identify groups of students according to the indicators mentioned in Sect. 3. The Fig. 3 shows the screen capture of the tool where students can be identified according to their constancy in the course. It is possible to sort the results by the number of entries in the course,

Fig. 2. History of income in the pilot course for the month of February.

CURSO: Unicauaca+CS001+2016-I

1 2 3 4 5 6 7 8 9 10

Estudiante	Ingresos al Curso	Ingresos a los contenidos	Reproducciones de Videos	Participación en Foros	Intentos en evaluación
Edison__Torres_Medina	2	25	3	3	2
Julian_David_Moreno_Andrade	2	11	9	0	0
Ivan_Dario_Martinez_Martinez	2	9	0	0	1
Cristian_Fernando_Lopez_Ceron	2	8	5	0	0
Jackeline_Bolanos_Silva_	2	8	4	0	0
Johana_Andrea_Maca_Alemesa	2	8	23	1	0
YESSICA_PAOLA_GUERRERO	2	7	0	0	1
Carlos_Ferney_Ortiz_Alegria	2	6	8	0	0
Yinet_Viviana_Perez_Sotelo	2	4	0	0	1
Laura_Camila_Bermudez_Barcenas	2	4	2	0	0

1 2 3 4 5 6 7 8 9 10

Fig. 3. Results of the constancy indicator in the pilot course.

number of entries in the course contents, number of videos played, participation in the forums and number of evaluations made.

6 Conclusions

In recent years there has been a great interest to incorporate the MOOC strategy to universities and allow this type of courses to count as credits and be part of the professional programs offered. However, the current platforms for offering courses do not yet provide sufficient support for teachers to be used in a more traditional environment such as SPOCs, where it is necessary to have adequate processes of assessment, follow up and feedback.

During the development of the pilot course all the information provided by the tool was very useful for teachers of the course (Mario Solarte, plant teacher at the

University of Cauca), who based on the follow up was able to solve some of the problems presented. From these results it is possible to understand the potential of the tool, but also the work still to be done. It is highlighted that the tool offers predefined indicators that are very supportive for MOOC, especially for SPOC, where it is required that there be a follow up of student activities.

References

1. Chen, X., Barnett, D., Stephens, C.: Fad or future: the advantages and challenges of massive open online courses (MOOCs). In: Research-to Practice Conference in Adult and Higher Education (2014)
2. Kloos, C.D., Muñoz-Merino, P.J., Muñoz-Organero, M., Alario-Hoyos, C., Pérez-Sanagustín, M., G, H.A.P., Ruipérez, J.A., Sanz, J.L.: Experiences of running MOOCs and SPOCs at UC3 M. Presented at the 2014 IEEE Global Engineering Education Conference (EDUCON), 3 April 2014
3. Guo, W.: From SPOC to MPOC – the effective practice of Peking University online teacher training. In: 2014 International Conference of Educational Innovation Through Technology (EITT), pp. 258–264 (2014)
4. Cabero, J., Llorente, C., Vázquez, A.: MOOC's typologies: design and educational implications. Profesorado **18**, 13–26 (2014)
5. Claros, I., Garmendía, A., Echeverría, L., Cobos, R.: Towards a collaborative pedagogical model in MOOCs. Presented at the 2014 IEEE Global Engineering Education Conference (EDUCON), 3 April 2014
6. Halawa, S., Greene, D., Mitchell, J.: Dropout prediction in moocs using learner activity features. ResearchGate, pp. 58–65 (2014)
7. Chorianopoulos, K., Giannakos, M.: Merging learner performance with browsing behavior in video lectures. In: WAVE 2013 Workshop LAK 2013 (2013)
8. Shi, C., Fu, S., Chen, Q., Qu, H.: VisMOOC: visualizing video clickstream data from massive open online courses. Presented at the 2014 IEEE Conference on Visual Analytics Science and Technology (VAST), 25 October 2014
9. Gascon, J., Ruipérez, J., Muñoz, P., Pijeira, H., Ruiz, J., Kloos, C.D.: ANALYSE: A Learning Analytics Tool for Open edX. http://www.it.uc3m.es/pedmume/ANALYSE/
10. Guo, P.J., Kim, J., Rubin, R.: How video production affects student engagement: an empirical study of MOOC videos. Presented at the Proceedings of the First ACM Conference on Learning @ Scale Conference, 4 March 2014
11. Claros, I., Cobos, R., Guerra, E., Lara, J. de, Pescador, A., Sánchez-Cuadrado, J.: Integrating open services for building educational environments. Presented at the Global Engineering Education Conference (EDUCON). IEEE, 13 March 2013

Increasing Educational Value: The Transformation of MOOCs into Open Educational Resources

Michael Kopp[1(✉)], Ortrun Gröblinger[2], and Claudia Zimmermann[1]

[1] Academy for New Media and Knowledge Transfer,
University of Graz, Graz, Austria
{michael.kopp, claudia.zimmermann}@uni-graz.at

[2] New Media and Learning Technology Department,
University of Innsbruck, Innsbruck, Austria
ortrun.groeblinger@uibk.ac.at

Abstract. MOOCs (Massive Open Online Courses) have developed into one of the most prominent instruments of technology-enhanced learning, and their much-praised potential has often been connected to one of their core components: openness. In theory, this feature not only ensures free access to content, but also affects other aspects that enable participants to make the most of their learning experience, like re-using and copying materials or even creating derivative works. In practice, however, most MOOCs do not subscribe to these more advanced principles of openness, especially those provided by for-profit platforms.

In this paper, we would like to discuss one particular strategy to improve the current situation. OER (Open Educational Resources) generally adhere to higher standards regarding the meaning of openness, and we argue that this strong focus on the reusability of learning materials would present a tremendous improvement to the educational value of MOOCs. We conclude that the transformation of MOOCs into OER shows promising potential in the areas of financing, collaboration and usability, with a particular focus on benefits from the students' perspective.

Keywords: MOOCs · OER · Openness · Higher education

1 Introduction

At the end of their first decade in existence, MOOCs (Massive Open Online Courses) have already come a long way. They appear in various types (like cMOOCs, xMOOCs and mixtures of them [1, 2]) and have developed into an established component in the educational landscape that has gained much awareness from the public. A lot of research on MOOCs has been conducted [3–5], but several questions still lack comprehensive answers. Some of them concern the openness of MOOCs.

Generally, MOOCs are considered courses that can be accessed for free at anytime from anywhere. However, this is only partially correct. The availability, accessibility and affordability of MOOCs mostly depends on their providers, and they often tend to restrict the openness of MOOCs due to economic motives.

C. Delgado Kloos et al. (Eds.): EMOOCs 2017, LNCS 10254, pp. 223–232, 2017.
DOI: 10.1007/978-3-319-59044-8_27

These circumstances can be considered a growing disadvantage for (higher) educational institutions and learners because it affects the educational value of MOOCs. In this context, the concept of OER (Open Educational Resources) could provide a viable attempt at a solution. In this paper, we will discuss how MOOCs may (re)gain openness by transforming them into OER, and what impact on (higher) educational institutions and students might be associated with this approach.

2 The Meaning of "Openness" in MOOCs

Openness is an undisputed feature of MOOCs, but the defining criteria with regard to what does and does not constitute openness are still subject of debate [6]. After explaining the meaning of the term "openness" in the broader context of education, we will then discuss the use of the concept in the field of MOOCs.

2.1 Variations in Meaning

In (higher) education, openness has a broad range of meanings and many phrases like "open content", "open access", "open data" or "open science" contain the term "open". However, the term is interpreted in different ways. There are various definitions with regard to teaching and learning, depending on the respective context, which makes it impossible to formulate a consistent definition of the term. As early as 1975, MacKenzie et al. stated that "open learning is an imprecise phrase to which a range of meanings can be, and is, attached. It eludes definition" [7].

Nevertheless, some general statements can be made about the term "open" when it is used in the context of open education. Stewart [8] states that "open" "tend[s] to be tied in some way to the paths by which the Internet bypasses closed and traditionally monetized systems". In relation to data and content, the Open Group provides the following definition: "Open means anyone can freely access, use, modify, and share for any purpose (subject, at most, to requirements that preserve provenance and openness)" [9]. Weller [10] distills the following principles of openness: freedom to reuse; open access; free cost; easy use; digital, networked content; social, community based approaches; ethical arguments for openness; openness as an efficient model.

Even though "openness" can be defined in many different ways, there are some core aspects that most definitions have in common: availability, affordability, and accessibility. Openness in the sense of open education is also assumed to foster a supportive framework for teaching and learning. Thus, Groom [11] states that "[a]t its best openness is an ethos not a license. It's an approach to teaching and learning that builds a community of learners online and off."

2.2 Openness of MOOCs

Many aspects of openness mentioned above apply to MOOCs, but not all of them to the same extent. It is therefore appropriate to have a closer look at what is meant by "open" in connection with MOOCs.

Since at least 2012 – the year that was deemed "Year of the MOOC" by the New York Times [12] – MOOCs were celebrated as a promising branch of open education. However, at the beginning of the MOOC-hype the meaning of openness in MOOCs had already changed from a focus on open collaboration for creating new material towards an emphasis on the accessibility of course content.

In 2008, George Siemens and Stephen Downes introduced the course "Connectivism and Connective Knowledge" (CCK08), which is considered the first MOOC, and more specifically the first so-called connectivist MOOC (cMOOC). In 2005, Downes [13] had already mentioned openness as one of the main characteristics of connective knowledge in addition to autonomy, diversity and interactivity. Based on these principles, cMOOCs emphasize the learner′s autonomy, peer-to-peer-learning and social networking. They are "characterized by openness of criteria for participation. Since there is no central organizational structure, the credentialism, which tends to put limits in participation, does not exist in c-MOOCs" [14]. Therefore, the concept of openness in cMOOCs focuses on making connections, collaboration and the joint development of materials across the open Internet.

When Sebastian Thrun offered his online course on artificial intelligence in 2011 with about 160,000 enrollees, the era of so-called xMOOCs began. This was a turning point: the didactic model shifted from a constructivist to a behavioristic approach [15]. Based on a tutor-centric model that establishes a one-to-many relationship to reach massive numbers, xMOOCs can be viewed as learning management systems bundled with high quality content [14]. As a result, there is an increased need for professional institutions to ensure the efficient provision of xMOOCs. These providers can operate for profit (like e.g. Coursera, Udacity or the German platform iVersity) or as non-profit platforms (like e.g. edX or Future Learn). However, bundling courses within a central platform means that all these courses are subject to the terms of that specific platform. This restricts openness: first, because typical xMOOCs are not designed to encourage the extensive use of open collaboration tools (e.g. wikis), which means that enrollees are not well-equipped to work together on certain topics and/or to produce additional materials, and second, because legal conditions usually do not permit the re-use and modification of the provided materials.

Still, xMOOCs (the dominant MOOC type nowadays) are typically open in other ways. Courses are accessible with almost no temporal, regional or educational restrictions (as long as there is an Internet connection during use) and they may be attended without paying fees (although many MOOC-providers charge for certificates and in-depth offers). However, the conditions with regard to how long, to what extent and in which ways the materials may be accessed and/or used are set by MOOC providers and not by instructors and learners. This is where OER come into the game.

3 Expanding Openness – The Impact of OER on MOOCs

"Open" is the one term that MOOCs (Massive OPEN Online Courses) and OER (OPEN Educational Resources) have in common. However, there are significant differences with regard to the respective meanings of "openness", especially concerning the licensing of materials. This section provides a brief introduction of OER followed by arguments as to why and how MOOCs should be provided as OER, with special emphasis on the students' perspective.

3.1 OER – A Brief Outline

OER have a longer tradition than MOOCs. Originating in earlier work around "learning objects", the OER movement began in earnest when MIT announced its OpenCourseWare initiative in 2001. This allowed access to learning materials from 1,800 courses via the Internet, and these resources could be used and repurposed without charge [10]. Since then, the use of OER has steadily increased. Creative Commons states that 50 million OER objects were licensed in 2006. In 2015, this figure rose to 1.18 billion [16]. OER, however, never quite achieved the same popularity as MOOCs.

For a better understanding of the OER concept, it is helpful to clarify the eponymous terms, starting with "educational resource". The William and Flora Hewlett Foundation provides the following definition: "OER include full courses, course materials, modules, textbooks, streaming videos, tests, software, and any other tools, materials, or techniques used to support access to knowledge" [17]. UNESCO [18] proclaimed a similar definition within the Paris OER Declaration in 2012 [19]. This means that almost any learning object – including MOOCs – qualifies as an educational resource.

The more complex eponymous term is of course "open". In general, openness in the concept of OER has a more extensive meaning than it does with MOOCs. Many publications on OER [20–22] focus on the same issue: "open" must not only be understood in the way that learning materials are accessed for free, but that they must also be reusable. AsUNESCO states: OER "are any type of educational materials that are in the public domain or introduced with an open license. The nature of these open materials means that anyone can legally and freely copy, use, adapt and re-share them" [18].

Thus, licensing schemes are crucial to OER. A wide range of legal frameworks regulate the way in which OER are licensed. The most well-known among them is the Creative Commons licensing framework [23]. This framework "provides legal mechanisms to ensure that authors of materials can retain acknowledgement for their work while allowing it to be shared, can seek to restrict commercial activity if they wish, and can aim to prevent people from adapting it if appropriate" [24].

3.2 Arguments Why MOOCs Should Become OER

Based on the Gartner Hype Cycle, MOOCs have reached the slope of enlightenment and are heading towards the plateau of productivity rather quickly [25]. OER could be worthwhile companions in the future development of MOOCs, and there are many plausible reasons for transforming MOOCs into OER. As previously stated, OER contain a valuable feature that most MOOCs do not possess: an open licensing model in the form of the Creative Commons licensing framework. MOOCs are likely to benefit from the integration of this particular aspect in several areas, including MOOC business models, networks and collaborations as well as their educational value.

Business Models

It has been pointed out quite often that MOOCs – although they have been on the market for almost ten years by now – do not have efficient and sustainable business models [10, 26–29]. The leading MOOC platforms [29] are either funded by venture capital (e.g. Coursera) or by foundations (e.g. edX), at least for the most part. Refinancing models like charging for credentialing or individual support for participants are not profitable, most of the time they do not even cover their costs. By seeking to satisfy their venture capitalists, for-profit companies increasingly move away from an open access model. This means that enrolment is often restricted to certain periods and partnerships are limited to elite institutions. And – most important of all – the provided contents are not openly licensed [10]. In the end, it may well be that for-profit MOOC platforms will be fully commercialized. If this is the case, universities will no longer be able to offer free, accessible courses via these platforms.

Due to their different financing concepts, some open platforms like edX or Future Learn do not need to operate in a profit-oriented way. However, they too have to cover high production and implementation costs for their MOOCs. Currently these costs are often understood as marketing investments, which leads to the possibility that MOOCs might become "another form of broadcast controlled by a few" [10]. Thus, if MOOCs shall retain or even increase their value as tools for open education, universities (as non-commercial content providers) need to find solutions to distribute the share of costs.

Since OER are not oriented towards profit, they will not be supported by for-profit MOOC providers. Nevertheless, non-profit MOOC providers can benefit from offering their courses as OER: open licenses facilitate the sharing of resources, and an average university lacks the ability to employ an expert in every field [30]. In the long run, this will reduce the costs for both platform and content providers.

Cooperation and Collaboration

Stakeholders in the context of MOOCs are MOOC platforms and content providers on the supply side and students and the broad public on the demand side [29]. Platform operators do not cooperate much among each other, but they certainly cooperate with content providers. These in turn use various platforms to share their courses with formal and informal learners. The distribution and use of MOOCs therefore takes place based on networks on the supply side, whereby the operators usually specify the rules of use. This often prevents content from being interchanged between universities.

One way for content providers to make the system more open is to use a free and open source platform like Open edX [31]. If MOOCs or their individual parts are then provided as OER, collaboration between institutions would be more efficient: materials can be used and in some cases even modified without restrictions (license permitting). This way, content can be used by a larger number of students, and it can be adapted (e.g. as translations) leading to lower production costs.

If MOOCs become OER, collaboration between content providers as well as between enrollees will be fostered. When MOOC contents are openly licensed, enrollees get the opportunity to contribute their knowledge and experience to the provided materials, which not only improves collaboration but also the educational value of MOOCs.

Educational Value

Open access to knowledge, enhanced pedagogy and continuous improvement of teaching are the main reasons why universities decide to provide OER [32, 33]. These aims apply to MOOCs as well, with a few restrictions. Concerning open access, the terms "anywhere" and "anytime" are based on some prerequisites. In order to attend a MOOC, the participants need a broadband Internet connection, and courses may be attended only at anytime if they have a self-paced course structure (which is rarely the case). In contrast, OER may be downloaded and used on computers not connected to the Internet, so that they really are available anytime. For example, due to the insufficient technical infrastructure in Rwanda, MOOCs are only valuable if they can be used offline, which is possible when they are provided as OER [34].

MOOCs show great potential as parts of hybrid models combining online learning with classroom teaching. Again, their value increases when they are provided as OER: instructors may only use certain parts of a MOOC in their own lectures, and these parts must be available exactly at the time they are needed. MOOCs may also support innovative didactic models like the inverted classroom concept [35]. In this context, the integration of curriculum resources and teaching designs is only possible if lecturers and students have full access to MOOC material. Thus, the opportunity to re-use and re-mix – which is guaranteed by OER – is crucial to boost learning efficiency.

Of course, educational value is not only an issue for content providers, but also for learners. Therefore, the potential impact of OER on MOOCs from the students' perspective will be discussed in more detail.

3.3 How Students Benefit from MOOCs as OER

Weller states that MOOCs can be seen as a subset of OER [5]. As described above, this assumption is not true in every detail, because it heavily depends on the definition of "open", and because most MOOC providers do not use similar licensing models as specified for OER. It is, however, a useful categorization for the following contemplation, because it implies that most assumptions that apply to OER also apply to MOOCs.

Most MOOCs are designed to meet the demand of registered students, but in order to see the opportunities that come with OER, it is helpful to understand that a narrow focus on this particular target group is rather limiting.

In the context of OER use, Lane looks at three different groups of students: prospective students, registered students and alumni. Prospective students tend to use OER (in special open courses as well as MOOCs) for three main reasons: first, as a showcase, which functions as a window into the institutional ethos, second as a guide that helps them to decide if a topic is or is not of interest for long-term-studies, and third to build up a community, for example to approach potential fellow learners. Registered students use OER for different reasons. They strengthen what they have already learned, for example by watching a video lecture several times. They can use the material as a fallback when they miss a lesson. Some of the materials can be quoted as a primary source in an assignment. Since there are usually parts of a class that cannot be discussed in-depth, OER material can enrich the given information, or main study subjects can be enriched by using material from completely different courses. There is also the community factor, for example when students from different locations, maybe even different universities, are connecting in one open course. Often overlooked is the fact that OER can be seen as a public product that is not only composed by lecturers, but students too. This connects to another reason why registered students use OER according to Lane: as a training ground for publishing material, sometimes under their own name, sometimes under the name of their teachers. The use of open learning material by alumni is less complex, it is usually seen to act as a refresher or to enrich the daily professional practices [36].

As mentioned above, enrolled students should not be the only target group of MOOCs, but they can be seen as the pivot point of production and distribution. While there are regional differences in study conditions that can affect the possibilities of implementing MOOCs, there are also some aspects from the student's perspective that universities should always consider if they want to provide successful MOOCs, like credit systems, types of assessments and learning outcomes [37].

In 2013, the OER research hub project [38] proposed eleven hypotheses about the impact of OER. Four of them are directly connected to the students' interests: use of OER leads to improvement in student performance and satisfaction; use of OER is an effective method for improving retention for at-risk students; OER adoption at an institutional level leads to financial benefits for students and/or institutions; open education acts as a bridge to formal education, and is complementary, not competitive, with it. While there seems to be no clear evidence yet that OER and MOOCs lead to better student performance or higher satisfaction, one weakness of MOOCs has already been found to be improved by more openness, namely the typically high dropout rate, which has been established many times and is subject to a lot of debates and improvement efforts [6]. Alraimi et al. find that increasing openness in MOOCs – in addition to reputation – is an excellent way to "enhance an individual's intention for continued MOOCs enrollment" [30].

Investing in OER for MOOCs can lead to financial benefits for students, because supplementary material in conventional MOOCs are often subject to a charge (and this material might be indispensable in order to complete the final exam for the MOOC). As was mentioned above, current business models of MOOC production are not sufficiently sustainable, and the costs of producing new MOOCs from scratch are substantial. Without investments in OER, the worst-case scenario could be that the costs for production and distribution have to be taken on by the students themselves.

OER in general and MOOCs in particular are largely developed by lecturers and instructional designers. In addition to the possibility of feedback from their peers, open licensing changes the nature of the relationships between teachers and learners [21, 36], so that there is more room for contributions from students. Thus, OER can also be seen as an opportunity to rewrite the traditionally ascribed roles of teachers and students, with students becoming producers of knowledge themselves.

Summing up, what are the benefits for students when MOOCs become OER? First, they will probably develop a better understanding for the impact that producing, providing and sharing content can have on the educational sector, and with more responsibility for their own studying environment, they will likely get accustomed to a higher level of independence. Second, the increasing number of OER-MOOCs will probably lead to a higher number of "untypical" students at universities. These students might be no longer interested in getting a formal degree, but they may be keen on learning things that match their private interests and/or are useful for their vocational training.

4 Conclusion

In this paper, we argued that MOOCs are currently not as open as they are perceived to be. None of the leading MOOC platforms use open licensing models, which are also not common among content providers. However, some providers have already integrated the OER concept into their MOOC platforms [39], for example the Austrian platform iMooX [40] and the German platform mooin [41]. On these platforms, all courses and all course materials are released under a creative commons license.

In summary, OER can have a strong impact on MOOCs in several ways:

- Increasing collaboration among institutions and among students
- Improving efficiency in matters of cost and quality
- Transition to flexible educational content by the use of open licenses
- Enhancing pedagogy through the individualization of content
- Building reputation for institutions and individuals due to the wider distribution of educational materials

However, a transformation of MOOCs into OER will not happen in the short term, and it does not make sense for all MOOC providers. MOOCs as well as OER need conducive conditions on institutional, educational and economic levels [37, 42] for a prospering development, and particularly for their potential integration. As a start, and because of the associated benefits, more (higher) educational institutions should consider providing MOOCs as OER. This will establish a basis for further research, which would allow for a closer examination of the considerations presented in this paper.

References

1. Rosselle, M., Caron, P.-A., Heutte, J.: A typology and dimensions of a description framework for MOOCs. In: European MOOCs Stakeholders Summit 2014, eMOOCs 2014, pp. 130–139 (2014)
2. McGuire, W., Raaper, R., Nikolova, V.: Three perspectives on hybridising x and c MOOCs to create an online course on digital CVs. Int. Multidiscip. J. **3**, 20–33 (2016)
3. Yousef, A.M.F., Chatti, M.A., Schroeder, U., Wosnitza, M., Jakobs, H.: A review of the state-of-the-art. In: Proceedings of CSEDU 2014, 6th International Conference on Computer Supported Education, pp. 9–20 (2014)
4. Liyanagunawardena, T.R., Adams, A.A., Williams, S.A.: MOOCs: a systematic study of the published literature 2008–2012. Int. Rev. Res. Open Distrib. Learn. **14**, 202–227 (2013)
5. Veletsianos, G., Shepherdson, P.: A systematic analysis and synthesis of the empirical MOOC literature published in 2013–2015. Int. Rev. Res. Open Distrib. Learn. **17**(2), 198–221 (2016)

6. Zimmermann, C., Lackner, E., Ebner, M.: Facets of openness in MOOCs - a review. In: Beseda, J. (ed.): DisCo 2016. Towards Open Education and Information Society, pp. 193–203. Center for Higher Education Studies, Prague (2016)
7. MacKenzie, N., Postgate, R.S., Scupham, J.: Open learning: systems and problems in post-secondary education. Unesco Press, Paris (1975)
8. Stewart, B.: Massiveness + openness = new literacies of participation? J. Online Learn. Teach. **9**, 228–238 (2013)
9. The Open Definition - Open Definition - Defining Open in Open Data, Open Content and Open Knowledge. http://opendefinition.org/
10. Weller, M.: The Battle For Open: How Openness Won and Why It Doesn't Feel Like Victory. Ubiquity Press, London (2014)
11. Groom, J.: OSU Keynote. https://docs.google.com/presentation/d/1PZz2q3B5O5fPKv0isBbc0HZcxbOGc_3PfB0O43JOq8g/edit?usp=embed_facebook
12. Pappano, L.: The Year of the MOOC (2012). http://www.nytimes.com/2012/11/04/education/edlife/massive-open-online-courses-are-multiplying-at-a-rapid-pace.html
13. Downes, S.: An introduction to connective knowledge. http://www.downes.ca/post/33034
14. Rodriguez, O.: The concept of openness behind c and x-MOOCs (massive open online courses). Open Praxis **5**, 67–73 (2013)
15. Conole, G.: MOOCs as disruptive technologies: strategies for enhancing the learner experience and quality of MOOCs. Revista de Educación a Distancia **39**, 1–17 (2013)
16. State of the Commons. https://stateof.creativecommons.org/report/
17. Open Educational Resources. http://www.hewlett.org/strategy/open-educational-resources/
18. What are Open Educational Resources (OERs)? | United Nations Educational, Scientific and Cultural Organization. http://www.unesco.org/new/en/communication-and-information/access-to-knowledge/open-educational-resources/what-are-open-educational-resources-oers/
19. UNESCO: 2012 Paris OER Declaration. http://www.unesco.org/new/fileadmin/MULTIMEDIA/HQ/CI/WPFD2009/English_Declaration.html
20. Wiley, D.: Open education license draft. http://opencontent.org/blog/archives/355
21. Lane, A.: The impact of openness on bridging educational digital divides. Int. Rev. Res. Open Distrib. Learn. **10**(5), 1–12 (2009)
22. Commonwealth of Learning, UNESCO: Guidelines for open educational resources (OER) in higher education (2011)
23. When we share, everyone wins. https://creativecommons.org/
24. Butcher, N., Kanwar, A., Uvalic-Trumbic, S.: A basic guide to open educational resources (OER). Commonwealth of Learning, UNESCO, Vancouver, Paris (2011)
25. Bozkurt, A., Ozdamar Keskin, N., De Waard, I.: Research trends in massive open online course (MOOC) theses and dissertations: surfing the tsunami wave. Open Praxis **8**(3), 203–221 (2016)
26. Abeywardena, I.: The Role of OER in a New World of MOOC (2014). https://oerresearchhub.org/2014/07/08/the-role-of-oer-in-a-new-world-of-mooc-2/
27. Fischer, H., Dreisiebner, S., Franken, O., Ebner, M., Kopp, M., Köhler, T.: Revenue vs. costs of MOOC platforms. Discussion of business models for xMOOC providers, based on empirical findings and experiences during implementation of the project iMooX. In: ICERI2014 Proceedings, pp. 2991–3000. IATED, Seville (2014)
28. De Corte, E., Engwall, L., Teichler, U.: The hype of MOOCs. In: De Corte, E., Engwall, L., Teichler, U. (eds.) From Books to MOOCs? Emerging Models of Learning and Teaching in Higher Education, pp. xv–xxv. Portland Press, London (2016)
29. Peters, G., Seruga, J.: A supply sided analysis of leading MOOC platforms and universities. Knowl. Manag. E-Learn.: Int. J. (KM&EL) **8**, 158–181 (2016)

30. Alraimi, K.M., Zo, H., Ciganek, A.P.: Understanding the MOOCs continuance: the role of openness and reputation. Comput. Educ. **80**, 28–38 (2015)
31. Open edX Portal. https://open.edx.org/
32. McGill, A., Falconer, I., Dempster, J.A., Littlejohn, A., Beetham, H.: Journeys to open educational practice: UKOER/SCORE Review Final report. JISC (2013)
33. William and Flora Hewlett Foundation: White Paper: Open Educational Resources – Breaking the Lockbox on Education. William and Flora Hewlett Foundation (2013)
34. Bartholet, J.: Hype and hope. Sci. Am. **309**, 53–61 (2013)
35. Bishop, J.L., Verleger, M.A.: The flipped classroom: a survey of the research. Presented at the 120th ASEE Annual Conference & Exposition, Atlanta (2013)
36. Lane, A.: Design and development of OER: a student perspective. In: Glennie, J., Harley, K., Butcher, N., van Wyk, T. (eds.) Open Educational Resources and Change in Higher Education: Reflections from Practice, pp. 141–153. Commonwealth of Learning (2012)
37. Kopp, M., Ebner, M., Dorfer-Novak, A.: Introducing MOOCs to Austrian universities - is it worth it to accept the challenge? Int. J. Innov. Qual. Learn. **2**(3), 46–52 (2014)
38. OER Impact Map. http://oermap.org/hypothesis-list/
39. Ebner, M., Lorenz, A., Lackner, E., Kopp, M., Kumar, S., Schön, S., Wittke, A.: How OER enhances MOOCs—a perspective from German-speaking Europe. In: Jemni, M., Kinshuk, Khribi, M.K. (eds.) Open Education: from OERs to MOOCs. LNET, pp. 205–220. Springer, Heidelberg (2017)
40. iMooX. http://imoox.at/wbtmaster/startseite/
41. mooin. https://mooin.oncampus.de/
42. Ebner, M., Kopp, M., Freisleben-Teutscher, C.F., Gröblinger, O., Rieck, K., Schön, S., Seitz, P., Seissl, M., Ofner, S., Zimmermann, C., Zwiauer, C.: Recommendations for OER integration in Austrian higher education. In: Ubachs, G., Konings, L. (eds.) Enhancing European Higher Education "Opportunities and Impact of New Modes of Teaching", pp. 34–44. EADTU, Rome (2016)

Implementation Intentions and How They Influence Goal Achievement in MOOCs

Karel Kreijns[1(✉)], Marco Kalz[1,2], Jonatan Castaño-Muñoz[3], and Yves Punie[3]

[1] Welten Institute, Open University of the Netherlands, PO Box 2960, 6401 DL Heerlen, The Netherlands
{karel.kreijns,marco.kalz}@ou.nl

[2] UNESCO Chair of Open Education, Welten Institute & Faculty of Management, Science and Technology, Open University of the Netherlands, PO Box 2960, 6401 DL Heerlen, The Netherlands

[3] Joint Research Centre of the European Commission, Edificio Expo, Calle Inca Garcilaso, 3, 41092 Seville, Spain
{jonatan.castano-munoz,yves.punie}@ec.europa.eu

Abstract. Implementation intentions have been proven to be effective to help individuals reaching their goals in medical interventions. The current study investigated whether this is true as well for individuals who enrolled in MOOCs. Implementation intentions are concerned with planning where, when, and how learning will take place as well as planning how much time will be allocated to the learning and determining how potential problems will be resolved (referred to as shielding behavior). The current study investigated the relationship between the degree to which implementation intentions were formed and the degree to which goals were achieved, thereby taking the time spent for studying MOOCs and the number of barriers encountered into account. Goal achievement was taken relative to the intended goal achievement (more than intended, all as intended, less than intended).

The results, based on a small sample of MOOC learners enrolled a single MOOC, revealed that the two latent classes of implementation intentions (representing the group of MOOC learners with strong and the group with weak implementation intentions) were completely determined by whether these MOOC learners were time planning or not. The results also revealed limited influence of implementation intentions on relative goal achievement and no influence on the time spent for studying MOOCs. Implementation intentions negatively influenced the impact of the number of barriers on relative goal achievement but this finding was not significant which also means that there was no impact of the number of barriers on this relative goal achievement. But there was a direct effect of time spent for studying MOOCs on relative goal achievement, suggesting that the more time was spent on studying MOOCs the higher the probability was that intended goal achievement would be realized. In sum, we found some indications that implementation intentions can be as

C. Delgado Kloos et al. (Eds.): EMOOCs 2017, LNCS 10254, pp. 233–242, 2017.
DOI: 10.1007/978-3-319-59044-8_28

effective on relative goal achievement in MOOCs as they are in medical interventions. However, much stronger evidence is needed.

Keywords: Goal achievement · Implementation intentions · MOOCs

1 Introduction

Dropout in MOOCs is currently one of the most investigated subject in the MOOC research community [1]. Mostly, dropout rates are calculated based on the concept that a drop-outer is someone who did not receive a certificate after the MOOC run. MOOC providers mostly adhere to this concept and try to find ways to lower these dropout rates. This often meant changing the course design of the MOOC to increase engagement, persistence, and completion [2]. However, a growing group of researchers do not adopt this concept of dropout and argued that when the learner perspective is chosen as a point of departure the dropout rates will become much lower [3]. The learner perspective holds that dropout occurs when learners do not achieve their intended learning goals because there were reasons to stop premature such as time related problems [4, 12]. Using the learner perspective, three basic types of MOOC learners can be distinguished, namely those MOOC learners who have achieved more goals than intended, those who achieved exactly what they intended, those who achieved less than intended; we designated this latter group as the drop-outers [3]. We earlier proposed a research agenda on MOOCs based on the reasoned-action approach and the intention-behavior gap [5].

Gollwitzer [6, 7] proposed implementation intentions as a way to help individuals (here the MOOC learners) to act out their intentions. We interpreted his implementation intentions as being concerned with planning where, when, and how the learning will take place as well as planning how much time will be allocated to the learning and determining how potential problems will be resolved. The latter is referred to as shielding behavior. Previous research in medical interventions has shown that when implementation intentions were formed, acting out the goal intentions were more successful [8]. The research question in the current study was whether this is true as well for individuals who enrolled in MOOCs.

In order to answer the research question, the current study investigated the relationship between the degree to which implementation intentions were formed and the degree to which goals were achieved, thereby taking the time spent on learning and the number of barriers encountered into account. Goal achievement was taken relative to the intended goal achievement (more than intended, all as intended, less than intended). It was expected that the more time was spent on learning the MOOCs the higher the probability would be that the intended goal achievement would be realized. It was also expected that the more barriers were encountered the lower the probability would be that intended goal achievement would be realized but that the impact of the barriers would be reduced if plans for shielding behavior would exist. We also expected that, in general, formation of implementation intentions would reduce the impact of these barriers on the achievement of intended goals. The paper is structured as follows: we first present the research model. Then we present our research and the results. We discuss our results and draw conclusions of the approach.

2 Research Model

The research model of the current study is depicted in Fig. 1; the drawing follows the notations of Muthén and Muthén [8].

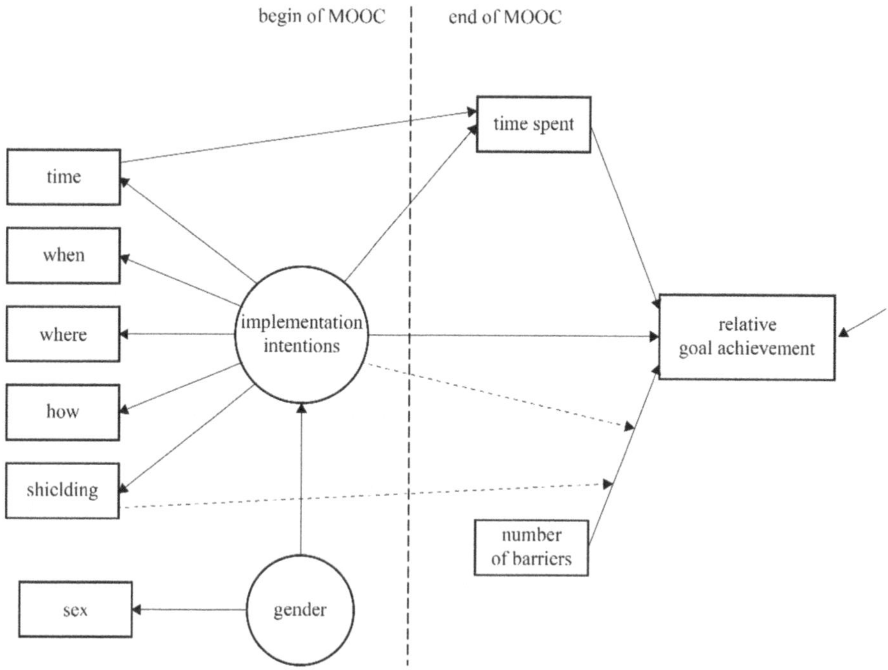

Fig. 1. The research model of the current explorative study

In this finite mixture model 'implementation intentions' is a categorical latent variable with binary latent class indicators 'time,' 'when,' 'where,' 'how,' and 'shielding.' The arrow from 'implementation intentions' to 'time spent' (continuous variable) indicates that the mean of 'time spent' may vary across 'implementation intentions' classes. The arrow from 'implementation intentions' to 'relative goal achievement' (continuous variable) indicates that the intercept of 'relative goal achievement' varies across 'implementation intentions' classes whereas the dotted arrow from 'implementation intentions' indicates that the slope in the regression of 'relative goal achievement' on 'number of barriers' (count variable) vary across classes of 'implementation intentions.' As we used a finite mixture model that identifies subpopulations within the overall population we treated 'gender' as a known categorical latent variable, determined by the single latent class indicator sex, rather than as a covariate. The arrow from 'gender' to 'implementation intentions' represents the multinomial logistic regression of 'implementation intention' on 'gender' when comparing the latent classes of 'implementation intentions.' The arrows from 'time spent' and 'number of barriers' to 'relative goal achievement' represent the linear regressions of 'relative goal achievement' on 'time spent' and 'number of barriers' respectively. Finally, the arrow from 'time' to 'time spent' indicates that the mean of 'time spent' varies between those of the overall population who made plans about time and those who did not. In a similar way, the slope in the regression of 'relative goal achievement' on 'number of barriers' is also varying between those who made plans about shielding behavior and those who did not.

3 Method

3.1 Participants and Procedure

Participants were the 1436 individuals who enrolled in the MOOC 'The Adolescent Brain.' This MOOC was offered in the Dutch language and ran from April until June 2016 covering seven modules for seven weeks. The weekly study load was estimated at three to five hours per week. MOOC learners who participated in all learning activities could request a certificate.

All participants received an invitation to fill in a pre-questionnaire before the start of the course and a post-questionnaire after course finalization. The pre-questionnaire assessed intended goal achievement and implementation intentions whereas the post-questionnaire assessed the time spent on learning, the number of barriers encountered, and actual goal achievement. The pre-questionnaire was completed by 821 MOOC-takers (664 women, 157 men, M_{age} = 45.1, age range: 18–74 years). The post-questionnaire was completed by 126 MOOC-takers (no demographic information available). In total 101 MOOC takers completed both questionnaires (90 women, 11 men, M_{age} = 37.0, age range: 18–54 years). However, only 40 respondents (4 men, and 36 woman) selected all items used in this study. This meant that the analyses for determining the number of latent classes for the categorical latent variable 'implementation intention' could only use these 40 participants.

3.2 Measures

The items to measure intended and actual goal achievement were designed according to guidelines by Sutton [10]. Intended and actual goal achievement were measured with a self-constructed single-choice scale with items of increasing intensity for participation ranging from 'browsing the course' up to 'finalizing all activities and requesting a certificate.' A new variable was constructed by subtracting actual from intended goal achievement leading to the new variable 'relative goal achievement.' This new variable 'relative goal achievement' is positive when more goals are achieved than intended, zero when all intended goals are achieved, and negative when less goals are achieved than intended.

The items to measure implementation intentions were taken from a study by Sheeran et al. [11]. Implementation intentions were assessed by five dichotomous items ('time,' 'when,' 'where,' 'how,' and 'shielding) with answering categories 'yes' and 'no.' These five items functioned as latent class indicators in the LCA analyses.

Number of barriers was measured by an optional multiple-choice item that presented a list of potential barriers and the option 'other' to participants. A new variable has been constructed based on the number of barriers selected for this list; this variable is 'number of barriers.'

Time spent was measured by one open entry item in the post-questionnaire.

3.3 Analysis

All latent class analyses (LCA) were performed in Mplus version 7.3 [9]. SPSS version 24 was used for some descriptive statistics. We first performed a series of LCA analyses for determining the number of classes of the categorical latent variable 'implementation intention.' After that the number of latent classes was determined, we performed LCA analyses on the structural model as depicted in Fig. 1. That is, we actually performed the LCA analyses on a simplified version of it—depicted in Fig. 3—for reasons explained in the result section.

3.4 Results

3.5 Number of Implementation Intentions Classes

The 40 respondents who completely filled in the surveys turned out to encompass only four men and thirty-six women. Therefore, it was decided to exclude the known categorical latent class 'gender' in our analyses. Because the latent class indicator 'where' was positively answered (i.e., a 'yes') by all respondents, this indicator was not included in these analyses as well.

The analyses on the measurement LCA model of 'implementation intention' revealed three classes of the categorical latent variable 'implementation intention;' more classes yielded values >.05 for the Vuong-Lo-Mendell-Ruben likelihood ratio test (LRT), the Lo-Mendel-Rubin adjusted LRT test, and the Parametric boot-strapped LRT (see Table 1).

Table 1. Fit indices for each solution of number of classes

	Number of classes		
	2	3	4
Akaike (AIC)	145.398	153.495	163.447
Bayesian (BIC)	160.598	177.139	195.536
Sample-size adjusted BIC	132.435	133.330	136.080
Entropy	1.000	1.000	0.573
Vuong-Lo-Mendell-Ruben LRT test	0.0238	0.0306	0.8163
Lo-Mendal-Rubin adjusted LRT test	0.0278	0.0345	0.8190
Parametric bootstrapped LRT	0.333	0.6667	1.0000

However, the three classes solution had one class (latent class 3) which has zero man and only one woman as class members. Therefore, it was decided to adopt the two classes solution. This choice also corresponds with the lowest values for AIC, BIC and adjusted BIC as well as for the Vuong-Lo-Mendell-Ruben likelihood ratio test (LRT), the Lo-Mendel-Rubin adjusted LRT test, and the Parametric bootstrapped LRT. The two latent classes differentiated between those who are strong on making implementations intentions (15 respondents; 1 man and 14 woman) and those who are weak on that (25 respondents; 3 men and 22 women). For each latent class the probabilities of answering positive on the latent class indicators were calculated, see the chart in Fig. 2. For example, those who belong to the class of weak implementation intention have an 86.7% probability of answering positive (i.e., a 'yes') on the latent class indicator 'where' whereas those who belong to the class of strong implementation intention have a 100% probability of answering positive on this indicator.

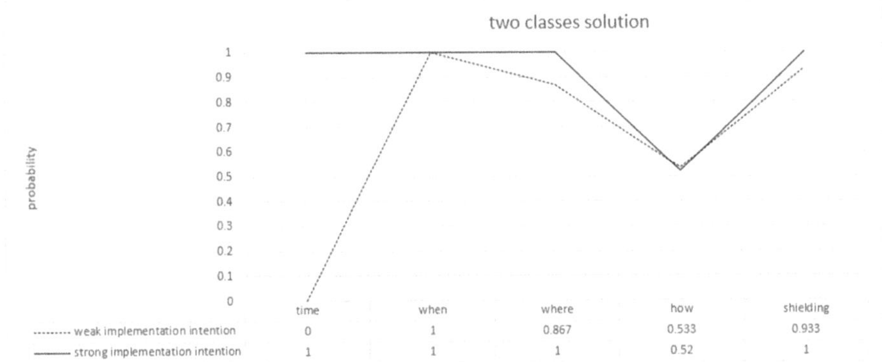

Fig. 2. The two latent classes of 'implementation intention'

Note that although the latent class indicator 'when' was not included in the analyses for the determination of the number of latent classes, it is included in this chart in Fig. 2 for completion reasons. Regardless to which latent class respondents belonged to, they would have a 100% probability of answering positive on this indicator; that is, the answer would always be 'yes.' As there were only 40 men and woman in the population, we must interpret the chart in Fig. 2 with care. Therefore, the extreme conditional probabilities (i.e., 100% or 0% conditional probability) should be interpreted with some relaxation.

Interestingly, the most important finding from these analyses was that the latent class indicator 'time' appeared to be completely responsible for the determination of who of the respondents belongs to the weak- or to the strong class of 'implementation intention.' By this finding, the categorical latent variable 'implementation intention' could be regarded as a known categorical latent variable with 'time' as it's only latent class indicator. As a result, the research model depicted in Fig. 1 was simplified to the model depicted in Fig. 3. An advantage of the finding was that a much larger group of respondents could be used for the analysis of simplified model as more respondents filled in answers for the latent class indicator 'time.' It turned out that actually all 101 respondents could be included in the analyses. As a result, the class representing MOOC learners with strong implementation intentions consisted out of 48 respondents (6 men and 42 women) whereas the class representing MOOC learners with weak implementation intentions consisted out of 53 respondents (7 men, 45 women, and one unknown).

3.6 Relationships

In Fig. 3, the known categorical latent variable gender was also excluded here from the LCA analyses for the same reasons we had when performing the LCA analyses on the population of 40 respondents; this time the population encompassed 13 men and 88 women. Note also that in Fig. 3 the results of the LCA analyses encompassing all 101 respondents are already depicted; these results are the unstandardized slopes (i.e., the path coefficients), the intercepts, and the explained variances (R^2) for each of the two latent classes of 'implementation intentions' in so far they were significant or are relevant for the presentation of the results below.

The results of the LCA analyses on the finite mixture model in Fig. 3 were a bit surprising. First, the intercept of 'relative goal achievement' did vary across the two latent classes of 'implementation intentions' but only for the latent class representing MOOC leaners with strong implementation intentions the intercept was significant. The mean of 'time spent,' however, did not vary across the two latent classes in contrast to

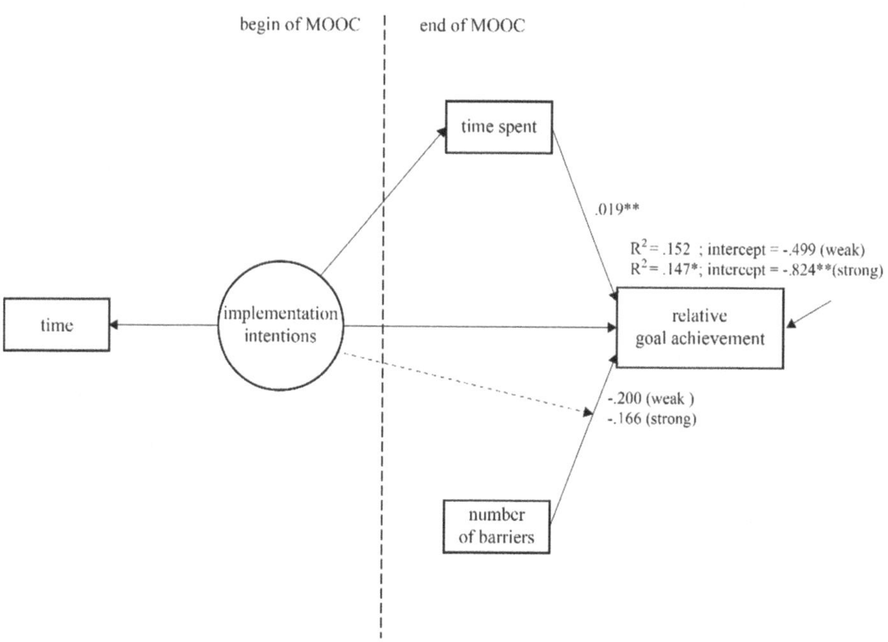

Fig. 3. The simplified research model of the current study.

what was expected. Second, though the latent class representing the group of MOOC learners with weak implementation intentions as well as the latent class representing the group of MOOC learners with strong implementation intentions had different slopes in the regression of 'relative goal achievement' on 'number of barriers,' these slopes were not significant, also in contrast to what was expected. Third, there was a significant direct effect of 'time' on 'relative goal achievement;' that is, the slope of the linear regression of 'relative goal achievement' on 'time spent' was significant which corresponded with what was expected.

3.7 Sample Statistics

MPlus provided as part of the LCA analyses estimated sample statistics for 'time spent,' 'number of barriers,' and 'relative goal achievement' for each latent class of 'implementation intentions.' These statistics are shown in Table 2 for the LCA analyses encompassing the 40 respondents and for the LCA analyses encompassing all 101 respondents.

Table 2 shows that the latent class representing the group of MOOC learners with weak implementation intention seemed to spent more time on studying MOOCs when compared to the latent class representing the group of MOOC learners with strong implementation intention. This was true for the first and second LCA analyses (see Table 2). However, a series of t-tests with Bonferroni adjustments[1] proved none of the differences in means of 'time spent,' 'number of barriers,' and 'relative goal achievement' between the two latent classes of 'implementation intentions' to be significant. The finding that there is statistically no difference in means of 'time spent' was already found when analyzing the relationships (in the previous section).

Table 2. Estimated sample statistics

	Estimated sample statistics for the 40 respondents in the first LCA analyses				Estimated sample statistics for all 101 respondents in the second LCA analyses			
	Weak (N = 15)		Strong (N = 25)		Weak (N = 53)		Strong (N = 48)	
	M	*SD*	*M*	*SD*	*M*	*SD*	*M*	*SD*
'Time spent'	38.80	26.46	28.48	14.32	36.04	29.81	26.83	16.20
'Number of barriers'	1.47	1.96	1.36	1.44	1.43	1.50	1.69	1.69
'Relative goal achievement'	−.67	1.68	−.40	−1.16	−.11	1.44	−.60	1.35

[1] The Bonferroni adjustment means that the normal alpha values of .05 and .01 were divided by three as there were three related variables: 'time spent,' 'number of barriers,' and 'relative goal achievement;' resulting in the values .017 and .0034 after rounding respectively.

4 Conclusions

The results, based on a small sample of MOOC learners enrolled a single MOOC, revealed that the two latent classes of implementation intentions (representing the group of MOOC learners with strong and the group with weak implementation intentions) were completely determined by whether these MOOC learners were time planning or not. It was not possible to determine whether men versus women had higher or lower probability to be members of one of two latent classes of implementation intentions due to the low number of male respondents.

The analyses also revealed that implementation intentions did have an influence on goal achievement in the sense that only for the group of MOOC learners with strong intentions a significant intercept could be calculated. Implementation intentions, however, did not have an influence on the time spent for studying the MOOCs.

Though implementation intentions negatively influenced the impact of the number of barriers on relative goal achievement, the finding was not significant. This finding also means that there was no impact of the number of barriers on this relative goal achievement. Nevertheless, implementation intentions tended to reduce the impact of the number of barriers on relative goal achievement.

Finally, there was a direct effect of time spent for studying MOOCs on relative goal achievement suggesting that the more time was spent on studying MOOCs the higher the probability was that intended goal achievement would be realized. Regarding the latter, slightly less goals were achieved than intended for both groups of MOOC learners meaning that relative goal achievement was a bit negative.

Overall, there was no difference between the number of barriers both group of MOOC learners encountered.

5 Discussion

First of all, we have to stress that because of the low number of participants completely filling in the survey both at the begin and at the end of the MOOC, all findings have to be taken with care. In fact, the MPlus analyses may have suffered from this low number.

We have also learned from this study that the assessment of implementation intentions was too simple and other ways should be investigated to construct a more reliable and valid instrument. Indeed, rather than that each latent class indicator has only two options (i.e., a 'yes' or a 'no') more options should be presented, for example, a 5-point Likert scale could be used in our future studies with answers like 'not at all,' 'very little,' 'somewhat,' 'to a great extent,' and 'completely' when respondents are asked whether they planned where, when and how they will study when enrolling in MOOCs as well as whether they planned the amount of time for studying these MOOCs and have thought about shielding behavior. A 5-point Likert scale will prevent us from getting such results as in the current study where only one latent class indicator is dictating the number of latent classes formed.

In sum, whether or not implementation intentions can be as effective on goal achievement in MOOCs as they are in medical interventions was not unambiguously answered in the current study although we found some indications in that direction. Our future studies will, therefore, be aimed at finding much stronger evidence.

References

1. Allione, G., Stein, R.M.: Mass attrition: an analysis of drop out from principles of microeconomics MOOC. J. Econ. Educ. **47**(2), 174–186 (2016). doi:10.1080/00220485.2016.1146096
2. Evans, B., Baker, R.B., Dee, T.S.: Persistence patterns in massive open online courses (MOOCs). J. High. Educ. **87**(2), 206–242 (2016). doi:10.1353/jhe.2016.0006
3. Henderikx, M., Kreijns, K., Kalz, M.: To change or not to change? That's the question on MOOC success, barriers and their implications. In: Delgado Kloos, C., et al. (eds.) EMOOCs 2017. LNCS, vol. 10254, pp. 210–216. Springer, Cham (2017)
4. Henderikx, M., Kreijns, K., Kalz, M.: Refining success and dropout in MOOCs based on the intention-behaviour gap (submitted)
5. Kalz, M., Kreijns, K., Walhout, J., Castaño-Muñoz, J., Espasa, A., Tovar, E.: Setting-up a European cross-provider data collection on open online courses. Int. Rev. Res. Open Distrib. Learn. (IRRODL) **16**(6), 62–77 (2015)
6. Gollwitzer, P.M.: Action phases and mind-sets. In: Higgins, E.T., Sorrentino, R.M. (eds.) The Handbook of Motivation and Cognition: Foundations of Social Behavior, vol. 2, pp. 53–92. Guilford Press, New York (1990)
7. Gollwitzer, P.M.: Implementation intentions: strong effects of simple plans. Am. Psychol. **54** (7), 493–503 (1999). doi:10.1037/0003-066X.54.7.49
8. Gollwitzer, P.M., Sheeran, P.: Implementation intentions and goal achievement: a meta-analysis of effects and processes. Adv. Exp. Soc. Psychol. **38**, 69–119 (2006). doi:10.1016/S0065-2601(06)38002-1
9. Muthén, L.K., Muthén, B.O.: Mplus User's Guide, 7th edn. Muthén & Muthén, Los Angeles (1998–2012)
10. Sutton, S.: Predicting and explaining intentions and behavior: how well are we doing? J. Appl. Soc. Psychol. **28**(15), 1317–1338 (1998). doi:10.1111/j.1559-1816.1998.tb01679.x
11. Sheeran, P., Webb, T.L., Gollwitzer, P.M.: The interplay between goal intentions and implementation intentions. Pers. Soc. Psychol. Bull. **31**(1), 87–98 (2005). doi:10.1177/0146167204271308
12. Eriksson, T., Adawi, T., Stöhr, C.: Time is the bottleneck": a qualitative study exploring why learners drop out of MOOCs. J. Comput. Hig. Educ. (2016). doi:10.1007/s12528-016-9127-8 (first online 24 Nov 2016)

A Social Learning Space Grid for MOOCs: Exploring a FutureLearn Case

Kalpani Manathunga[1(✉)], Davinia Hernández-Leo[1], and Mike Sharples[2]

[1] ICT Department, Universitat Pompeu Fabra, Barcelona, Spain
{kalpani.manathunga,davinia.hernandez-leo}@upf.edu
[2] Institute of Educational Technology, The Open University, Milton Keynes, UK
mike.sharples@open.ac.uk

Abstract. Collaborative and social engagement promote active learning through knowledge intensive interactions. Massive Open Online Courses (MOOCs) are dynamic and diversified learning spaces with varying factors like flexible time frames, student count, demographics requiring higher engagement and motivation to continue learning and for designers to implement novel pedagogies including collaborative learning activities. This paper looks into available and potential collaborative and social learning spaces within MOOCs and proposes a social learning space grid that can aid MOOC designers to implement such spaces, considering the related requirements. Furthermore, it describes a MOOC case study incorporating three collaborative and social learning spaces and discusses challenges faced. Interesting lessons learned from the case give an insight on which spaces to be implemented and the scenarios and factors to be considered.

Keywords: Collaborative learning · Social learning · MOOC

1 Introduction

The fact of putting students into groups does not ensure fruitful learning; rather effective collaborative learning must involve structured activities [1, 2]. Adapting from Social Learning theory, which states that continuous mutual interactions positively influence the way humans learn [3], many MOOC platforms are moving towards providing social learning opportunities [1]. Yet, forum discussions which are the most widely exercised collaborative or social learning approach in massive learning contexts [4], have not seen very effective due to the overwhelming amount of threaded discussions which are difficult to follow [5]. Researchers highlight the absence of enhanced collaboration opportunities for MOOC learners [6, 7]. In this paper, we look into different possibilities of implementing collaborative and social learning aspects in MOOCs along with an exploratory study using three such learning spaces with a MOOC launched on the FutureLearn platform.

Computer Supported Collaborative Learning (CSCL) is the process of knowledge creation by enabling fruitful interactions mediated by technology [1, 2]. Over decades CSCL activities have been applied at small scale in classrooms, but not widely used

C. Delgado Kloos et al. (Eds.): EMOOCs 2017, LNCS 10254, pp. 243–253, 2017.
DOI: 10.1007/978-3-319-59044-8_29

with large learning contexts, maybe because the scalability factor has not been properly considered in their design [4, 8]. Social Learning may bring a sense of community, avoiding isolation in online learning and providing possibilities to learn from others [3]. Studies highlight potential benefits of forming sub communities and learner networks with positive encouragement [7, 9] and understanding emergent social structures in MOOC sub communities [6]. Social learning elements, provoking conversational learning and CSCL enforcing rich interactions, are not so easily adaptable or applicable in MOOCs, as they have been in a traditional classroom.

MOOCs have shown the possibility of designing learning at scale and pedagogy that can be driven by discussion and social networking conceptions, where the more people joining, the richer the interactions [8]. Existing fruitful collaboration methods such as tutorial groups, project teams or action learning sets, that work well in small scale settings, are difficult to scale [7, 8]. Difficulties are mainly related to diversity in learner's motivations, expectations and differences in cultural expectations (e.g., how individuals should behave in social spaces) and therefore their behaviors when taking the MOOC [9, 10]. However, some initiatives offering collaborative and social learning opportunities are emerging within MOOCs other than discussion forums, given the concern of implementing novel pedagogies and learning theories [8, 11]. 'Study groups' provided by FutureLearn are local, private spaces for around 80 MOOC participants to discuss and share knowledge, 'cohort-specific discussion' by edX allows private group discussions visible only for a specific cohort, 'meet ups at learning hubs' by Coursera enable learners from nearby local to get-together for further discussions or project based learning and 'workspaces' from NovoEd support learning groups and project teams. Additionally, social networking spaces too provide scalable opportunities by allowing strangers to meet up and enhance connections which can be exploited in the context of education where social elements are complimented with learning [9, 12]. Learner-centered groups introduced within MOOCs harnessing the benefits of social media like Facebook, Twitter, Google+ or Hangout have been seen as fruitful while enhancing learner experience [9, 12, 13]. Meet-ups, proposed by Coursera, require physical spaces and high levels of facilitation. Cohorts from edX lack novel pedagogical approaches for further interactions. Social media groups such as Facebook Groups are easy to implement, yet very challenging to monitor since interactions are free to emerge and many such groups can exist. Educators require more effort and additional support to structure interactions in such online spaces. Hence, deeper understanding is needed regarding different social and collaborative learning possibilities, to explore challenges and consider options to design suitable learning scenarios. It is equally important to investigate, for massive learner communities, pedagogical methods that have been shown to work well in classrooms, by bridging existing technological challenges.

This paper presents a social learning space grid, organizing diverse social interaction possibilities with underlying rationale, to be used by the MOOC community. We explore the case of a MOOC on 3D Graphics for Web Developers offered on the FutureLearn platform by Pompeu Fabra University, Spain, in which three different collaboration spaces were presented to support collaborative and social learning. We describe these spaces situating them within a proposed framework, identify learning design associated and the motive behind the usage of each space, and discuss examples of use and perceived challenges. Section 2 of the paper describes social learning spaces and presents the social learning space grid followed by diverse particularizations found from literature. In Sect. 3, the MOOC case study is explained along with an analysis of the three collaboration spaces (Study Groups, PyramidApp, Conversational flows) adopted in the MOOC. The final section includes an accumulated discussion of lessons learned and challenges faced followed by concluding remarks and interesting future research directions as contributions from this exploratory study.

2 Social Learning Space Grid

2.1 Social Learning Space Grid: Categories and the Rationale

In order to lay a foundation to address collaborative and social learning aspects with their implications, this study proposes a collaboration space grid (Table 1), a social interaction framework, categorizing existing and prospective scalable collaboration techniques that can be offered within massive online courses. Apart from commonly picked collaboration spaces such as forums with multiple topic threads, dedicated discussion activities or cohort specific discussions in massive learning contexts [4], there can be other possibilities of implementing fruitful social interactions. Hence, the social learning space grid (Table 1) will be useful to study the dimensions of possible interactions, respective elements and how these can be used in open online courses. One important dimension is to study how far collaborations can be structured, using which elements. Unconstrained, long-lasting collaborations exist throughout the course lifetime and beyond. Also there exist ephemeral collaborations, constrained to an allocated task or for a given time period. Another dimension of the grid is the size factor affecting interactions. In a MOOC, all the course participants can interact in a common space, or it can be drilled down to small group level collaborations where 15 to 30 participants are grouped into one collaboration space. Moreover, the group sizes

Table 1. Social learning space grid

	Small	Increasing size	Whole cohort
Time and Task Unconstrained	Groups exist throughout the course. Participants are free to interact at any given moment, for any given task	Small groups can be joined based on certain criteria or behavior to interact at any time, for any given task	An open space for all course participants to interact regarding any topic at any time
Task constrained	Small groups formed to attend a given task	Small groups are combined based on task completion to attend another given task	All course participants attend given task in a common interaction space
Time constrained	Small groups formed to work during a specific time period	Small groups are combined based on time expiration to work together for another specific time period	All course participants attend in a common interaction space during a specific time period

can be incrementally growing over the constraints like time or task providing cumulative interactions enriching collaborations.

2.2 Particularizations of the Social Learning Space Grid

Table 2 illustrates several examples found in the literature and possible novel interaction mechanisms. Meet-ups at learning hubs by Coursera suggest local physical locations for learners to engage in collaborative learning activities or to clarify content related issues. Such meet-ups can be of varying size depending on the number of learners reaching the particular learning hub. Content-wide and course-wide cohorts on the edX platform, offer different types of interaction environments for MOOC participants where course designers can decide to allow unconstrained cohort experience by opening up cohort specific MOOCs or only certain content are made visible for specific cohorts. Most widely used general forums can attract all participants, leading to massive amounts of threaded discussions if forums are not constrained to tasks or time. In a massive community, small groups can be joined based on certain criteria (e.g., being active or time allocated or task allocated). Time-constrained weekly small groups or weekly forums accessible for all course participants are other possibilities of enabling interaction in MOOCs.

Table 2. Social learning space grid with examples

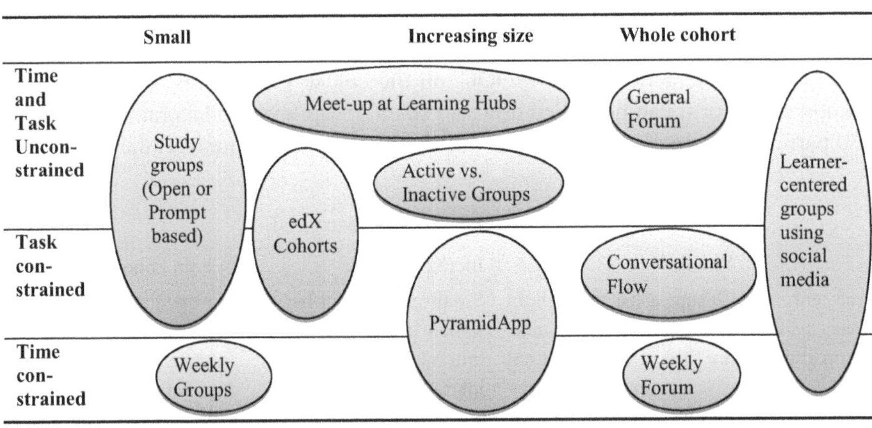

The FutureLearn MOOC platform has been developed on a social constructivist pedagogy that promotes effective learning through conversations [10]. FutureLearn MOOCs employ several levels of conversation flows including discussion steps for topic-related learner conversations, a space for comments and replies alongside every activity step for content clarifications and Study Groups to enable small group discussions or more focused group learning opportunities and such groups are consistent throughout the course. Participants are free to leave one group and join the next available, active group. Study groups can be implemented as either open group forums where up to a maximum of 80 MOOC learners are given the opportunity of sharing their learning experiences in a private local space, promoting free interactions that are not constrained by a particular topic, activity or time with no or very little intervention by the educator. Alternatively those can be educator instructions or prompts based, project-based or critique groups that differ from FutureLearn free-flowing discussion steps and focused discussions. FutureLearn's other conversation flows fall into the task-constrained forums category which provide a wider collaboration space for the whole cohort. Learners are able to comment on and reply to any activity step (task) since each step is associated with a conversation flow dedicated to it. Similarly, dedicated discussion steps available in the platform, are also in the same category since those are connected with tasks. PyramidApp [14] is another collaboration space instance that permits growing collaborations based on task and time constraints. PyramidApp is a scalable collaborative pedagogical method inspired by the Pyramid (aka Snowball) collaborative learning flow pattern [15] facilitating small group activity with cumulative collaborations. A Pyramid flow starts with individual proposals being discussed in small groups which are iteratively joined into larger-groups till a consensus is reached upon at the global level. Such scenarios foster individual participation and accountability (equal opportunity for all, yet with singular contributions) and balanced positive interactions (opinions of all members count). After situating diverse interaction options on the grid, we adopted Study groups, conversation flows and PyramidApp complementing the interaction spaces offered by FutureLearn in the following case study.

3 MOOC Case Study

3.1 Description

"3D Graphics for Web Developers" is a 5-week MOOC, especially for web developers to develop high quality interactive 3D applications to run natively on a browser. It completed two runs in 2016 (First run from February-March and the second run from July-August) on the FutureLearn platform. The MOOC is mainly aimed at web developers, who have existing knowledge of JavaScript, with the theoretical and practical knowledge to start programming 3D graphics applications to run natively in web browsers. There were around 6000 enrolments in the first run of the MOOC and around 4500 enrolments in the second. The MOOC had two lead educators and one mentor to mediate the course. In both runs, the course had more than 10% fully participating learners who had completed at least 50% of all course activity steps. As explained in the social learning space grid (Table 2), this exploratory study used three diverse collaboration spaces: task-constrained educator prompt based study groups (only in the second run of the MOOC); PyramidApp with both task and time constraints, promoting cumulative collaborations for small groups to study together and conversation flows linked to course step for the whole cohort.

As explained in the previous section, FutureLearn platform promotes learning through conversations where each video material or article is facilitated with a discussion thread alongside. Moreover, FutureLearn "Study Groups" were offered to interested learners that were added up to groups of 30 when they clicked on the study group tab available once they access the course content. In this specific course, task-constrained educator prompt-based study groups were offered where learners were expected to become active within the group when the educator sends a prompt and act accordingly. The prompts used were either to discuss a concept or to share artefacts created by learners within groups. To enable cumulative interactions causing collaborative knowledge building [5], PyramidApp [14] provided structured collaborations in a way that individuals proposed options (which can be a question, explanation or a 3D artefact) for a given task. Then, they teamed up to compare and discuss their proposals and, finally, propose a new shared 3D artefact or agree upon most relevant options. New larger groups were grown by iteratively combining previous groups in order to generate new agreed options. Provision of rating and discussing in a levelled structure ensured gradual exposure in a collaborative environment. Educators addressed or commented on the most highly rated options and learners are expected to improve knowledge in the critiquing and negotiation process. As pyramids are time and task constrained, once a set of pyramids reach the global level, another set of pyramids are initiated allowing late joiners to participate in the activity and emails are sent notifying about pyramid progression. Educators can easily monitor the activity progression, level by level along with the rated options and discussions happening within groups.

Table 3 shows example learning design of these collaborative and social learning spaces, how those were integrated in the MOOC and the steps along with the step identification to recognize the respective week that a particular learning step was offered (e.g., 1.10 represents week 1, step 10). Initially, there were only task constrained conversational flows for the whole cohort and PyramidApp for small group interactions. With the second run of the MOOC, the study groups feature was available in the platform and ephemeral small group interactions were expected through educator prompt-based study groups since those were dedicated to share course outcomes and created artefacts. More open-ended activities were allocated for conversational flows

Table 3. Step activity design of the 2nd MOOC run, across three collaboration spaces

Discussion steps	Prompt based study group	PyramidApp steps
1.2 Tell us about yourself!	1.4 Let's share what we know about 3D graphics creation	1.8 Pose questions about WebGLStudio
2.1 What makes a 3D scene look realistic?	2.6 Share your experiments in WebGLStudio	3.5 Pose questions about Three. js API and related utilities
4.7 Share your insights about your realistic earth scene	4.5 Share your final 3D earth scene	5.3 Do you have concerns or questions about advanced 3D concepts?
5.7 Your next steps in 3D graphics programming	5.6 Can you create it? (Share solar system)	

whereas PyramidApp was assigned for technical aspects discourse, in order to reduce educator's workload by filtering out the most interesting queries to attend to, rather than going through lengthy threads with specific technical issues as the course unveils. Study groups and conversational flows are built-in features of the FutureLearn platform whereas PyramidApp is an external application introduced as an external link within course activity step.

3.2 Results and Observations

Conversation flows were abundantly used in both runs, since every learner is familiar with this due to its presence at every educational step in the platform. Yet discussion steps get flooded easily with hundreds of comments/answers and suggestions, so for an educator or another learner, it can be challenging and time consuming to follow lengthy threads or to filter out relevant comments making knowledge building possibilities limited [5]. But the platform provides social networking concepts such as likes, following as filtering mechanisms and it was visible that some learners were using such features in the conversation flows. As the course content was very practical and programming oriented, some learners got lost and frustrated and they were seeking help from peers. Experts were offering help to novices by sharing their suggestions/ideas and experiences to solve technical problems they faced. For example, when *Grant* posted a DOMException error, *Ihor* stated that it was a local server issue, *Sheila* suggested to include images and *Fabien* suggested to try with own webserver to avoid the exception. Also they shared knowledge through programming code samples (e.g., what went wrong when they were trying to integrate the additional library, "Three.js" or which exceptions should be considered when configuring the localhost server) in the discussion steps. For late joiners' queries and comments, there were fewer interactions or support, maybe because by the time they join most learners had finished the course and left.

In task-driven educator prompt-based study groups, learners posted created artefacts and some learners encouraged others by using social features (likes, comments), positive critiques and suggestions. Study groups are consistent throughout the course and were mostly active upon receiving the educator's prompts at the beginning of each week (Fig. 1). From 16 groups formed, 12 groups had 30 members joined whereas

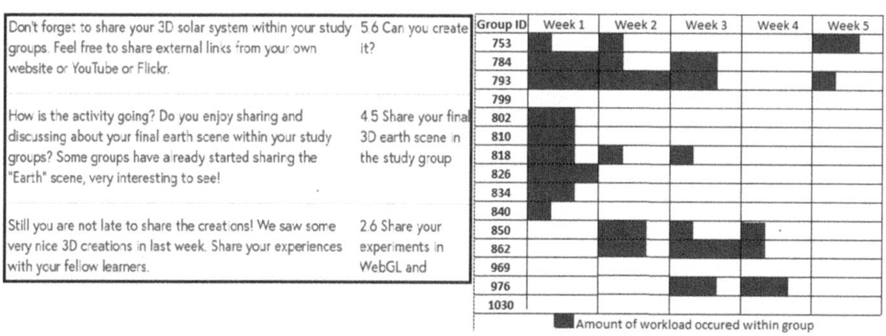

Fig. 1. Educator prompts (left-side view) and study groups behaviors (right-side view)

another two had 29 and 4 respectively. Just as in the overall MOOC, a decreasing trend of study group engagement was observed over the course lifetime. Figure 1 also illustrates the participation patterns in each group (shaded areas represent amount of activity) over the 5 weeks with respective group IDs issued by the platform. The lengths of the shaded boxes are proportionate to the number of days that group members were actively participating (sharing artefacts or commenting). Apart from the three groups that showed no activity in the Study group, other groups showed some interesting clusters of engagement patterns. Most common behaviour (5 out of 12 active groups) was to engage in activities for three weeks from the day the group was formulated.

PyramidApp was also presented as another social interaction space, via an external link embedded in three different 'Article' steps. It allowed learners to submit queries individually and then discuss and negotiate among themselves on more interesting queries for the attention of the educators, leaving behind the ones already addressed or solved at earlier stages or during the discussion process. Figure 2 shows how learners were curious and rate the questions. Those two questions were selected from the previous level (level 2) and participants in this level (top left hand corner in the screen) can rate then. In the discussion board, some had tried to answer these questions whereas others used it to discuss queries and state their opinions. In this way, the activity can be focused, narrowed down only to specific aspects targeted at specific situations that learners may require additional guidance related to the topic. As a different PyramidApp activity, learner artefacts were shared in groups to rate and critique and it shows that participants appreciated these artefacts and provided suggestions for further improvements like suggesting different materials to be used. PyramidApp used an email notification system to notify learners when subsequent levels were ready, notifying them about the timer values of that level to keep them updated about the activity. Learners who submitted emails received timely notifications. One final notification was sent informing about the selected options and where the answers for winning popular were available at the end of each pyramid.

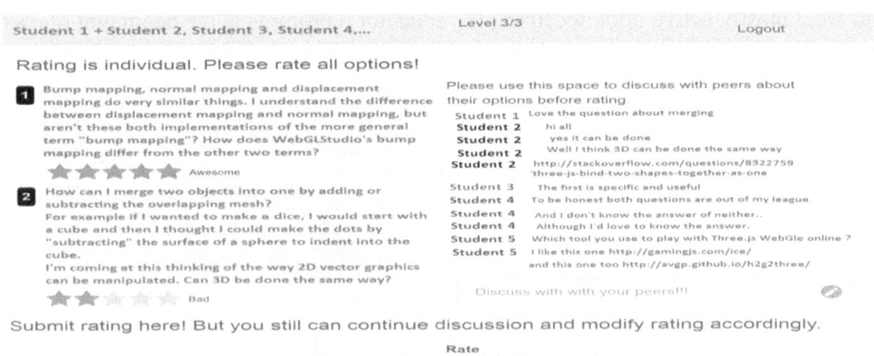

Fig. 2. Sample PyramidApp scenario with selected options and discussions occurred

4 Discussion on Challenges Faced

It is an interesting viewpoint to understand design and implementation challenges related with three interaction spaces explored in the case study and other aforementioned collaboration spaces (Table 2). In the educator prompt-driven study groups, prompts are required to be carefully designed, more structured and precise. A specific prompt such as, "Does your first 3D scene look "realistic", "artistic" and "imaginative"? Share links to the work you created using WebGLStudio (or other similar tool), within your study group. Also appreciate others' creations by liking or commenting on the aspects that you like about those 3D scenes", would be more meaningful than just asking them to discuss. Course facilitators should constantly monitor groups and interfere if required by sending reminders as mid-week prompts. A better design of activities can be to allocate specific tasks to be done within the study groups and share the resulting conclusions in a related discussion step where the whole cohort can access. Synchronous interaction mechanisms in a MOOC can be futile because not many learners are present at the same time in a platform. Yet, with task and time constraining, to a certain extent, PyramidApp tries to achieve a level of synchronicity, facilitating learners at similar paces to continue their learning experience enriched by social interactions. Activity monitoring is feasible using the PyramidApp monitoring view along with groups and levels information. Existing approaches like meet ups incorporate challenges such as a requirement for physical locations to enact collaborative activities, lack of novel pedagogical approaches and activity structuring to provoke further interactions. Activity monitoring is also demanding in small open groups, since interactions are free to emerge and many such groups can exist, the educator needs more effort to monitor, and require additional support to structure interactions. Though techniques addressing the whole cohort such as forums, conversational flows or large social media groups are easily facilitated, it is difficult to monitor and challenging for knowledge building process [5] due to overwhelming amount of messages. On the contrary, weekly forums can be comparatively easier because of the weekly structure. Hence, a better strategy is to allow small groups to increasingly grow, joined based on certain criteria (e.g., being active or time allocated or task allocated) in a way that reduces the number of groups and with provision of technological facilitation for regrouping and activity monitoring to reduce educator's workload.

5 Conclusion

Implementing scalable pedagogies and novel learning opportunities promoting more learner collaborations in MOOCs is essential and necessary for those to become a disruptive innovation in education. Making MOOCs more social can lead to enjoyable learning experience and the proposed social learning space grid shows potential social interaction methods applicable with examples. The three interaction spaces (conversation flows, study groups and PyramidApp) tested in this case study reveal possible practical challenges such as enabling more structured activities, well-thought out course design and more engaging tasks. Frequently study groups deviated from intended tasks to become help-seeking groups or spaces to get to know each other. Even the conversational flows were not populated equally and late comers were not receiving responses and help as early joiners. Though many learners accessed PyramidApp some were not really engaging in rating and discussing but it was coping with late-comers successfully as new pyramids were created for the same task. Based on these lessons learnt, the activity design for the studied MOOC (e.g., prompts for study groups) has been revised for a third edition of the course. Moreover, future research directions include implementing (quasi-)experimental or experimental designs to study the impact (learning, behaviors, facilitation and monitoring requirements) of different spaces for potentially effective scalable pedagogy considering the social learning spaces and options and combinations of social learning spaces expressed in the grid. The Social Learning Space Grid dimensions provide useful tips for learning technologists to implement social interaction spaces in MOOCs. Based on course requirements suitable social learning spaces can be embedded providing richer interaction opportunities for MOOC learners.

Acknowledgements. This work has been partially funded by the Spanish Ministry of Economy and Competitiveness under RESET (TIN2014-53199-C3-3-R), the Maria de Maeztu Programme (MDM-2015-0502) and the RecerCaixa CoT project.

References

1. Dillenbourg, P.: Orchestration Graphs. EPFL Press, Switzerland (2015)
2. Hernández-Leo, D., Asensio-Pérez, J.I., Dimitriadis, Y., Villasclaras-Fernández, E.D.: Generating CSCL scripts. From a conceptual model of pattern languages to the design of real scripts. In: Goodyear, P., Retalis, S. (eds.) Technology-Enhanced Learning, Design Patterns and Pattern Languages. Series Technology Enhanced Learning, pp. 49–64. Sense Publishers (2010)
3. Bandura, A.: Social Learning Theory. General Learning Press, New York (1971)
4. Manathunga, K., Hernández-leo, D.: Has research on collaborative learning technologies addressed massiveness? A literature review. J. Educ. Technol. Soc. **18**(4), 357–370 (2015)
5. Scardamalia, M., Bereiter, C.: Knowledge building: theory, pedagogy, and technology. In: Cambridge Handbook of the Learning Sciences, pp. 97–118 (2006)
6. Rosé, C.P., Carlson, R., Yang, D., Wen, M., Resnick, L., Goldman, P., Sherer, J.: Social factors that contribute to attrition in MOOCs. In: First ACM Conference on Learning @ Scale, pp. 197–198 (2014)
7. Siemens, G., Gasevic, D., Dawson, S.: Preparing for the digital university: a review of the history and current state of distance, blended and online learning (2015)
8. Ferguson, R., Sharples, M.: Innovative pedagogy at massive scale: teaching and learning in MOOCs. In: Rensing, C., Freitas, S., Ley, T., Muñoz-Merino, P.J. (eds.) EC-TEL 2014. LNCS, vol. 8719, pp. 98–111. Springer, Cham (2014). doi:10.1007/978-3-319-11200-8_8
9. Alario-Hoyos, C., Perez-Sanagustin, M., Delgado-Kloos, C., Parada, G., Munoz-Organero, M.: Delving into participants' profiles and use of social tools in MOOCs. IEEE Trans. Learn. Technol. **7**(3), 260–265 (2014)

10. Ferguson, R., Clow, D., Beale, R., Cooper, A.J., Morris, N., Bayne, S., Woodgate, A.: Moving through MOOCS: pedagogy, learning design and patterns of engagement. In: Conole, G., Klobučar, T., Rensing, C., Konert, J., Lavoué, É. (eds.) EC-TEL 2015. LNCS, vol. 9307, pp. 70–84. Springer, Cham (2015). doi:10.1007/978-3-319-24258-3_6
11. Saadatdoost, R., Sim, A.T.H., Jafarkarimi, H., Mei Hee, J.: Exploring MOOC from education and Information Systems perspectives: a short literature review. Educ. Rev. **67**, 505–518 (2015)
12. Knox, J.: Digital culture clash: "massive" education in the E-learning and Digital Cultures MOOC. Distance Educ. **35**(2), 164–177 (2014)
13. Beaven, T., Hauck, M., Comas-Quinn, A., Lewis, T., Arcos, B.: MOOCs: striking the right balance between facilitation and self-determination. MERLOT J. Online Learn. Teach. **10**, 31–43 (2014)
14. Manathunga, K., Hernández-Leo, D.: PyramidApp: scalable method enabling collaboration in the classroom. In: Verbert, K., Sharples, M., Klobučar, T. (eds.) EC-TEL 2016. LNCS, vol. 9891, pp. 422–427. Springer, Cham (2016). doi:10.1007/978-3-319-45153-4_37
15. Hernández-Leo, D., Villasclaras-Fernández, E.D., Asensio-Pérez, J.I., Dimitriadis, Y., Jorrín-Abellán, I.M., Ruiz-Requies, I., Rubia-Avi, B.: COLLAGE: a collaborative Learning Design editor based on patterns. J. Educ. Technol. Soc. **9**, 58–71 (2006)

The Double Classroom: Design Patterns Using MOOCs in Teacher Education

Anne-Mette Nortvig(✉) and Karsten Gynther

University College Zealand, Trekroner Forskerpark 4, 4000 Roskilde, Denmark
{ame, kgy}@ucsj.dk

Abstract. This paper presents findings from a study that used an archived MOOC as Open Educational Resources in teacher education in a hybrid learning setting. Using a design-based research approach created through collaboration with educators, two design patterns have been developed and tested to differentiate teaching and to enhance the feedback to students. The findings show that when MOOC resources are integrated, it 'doubles' the classroom, meaning it doubles the teacher's opportunities for being present in more places at once, both digitally on video and physically. Furthermore, MOOCs make it possible to parallelize the teaching, allowing some students to learn in MOOCs and others in a face-to-face manner on campus, as per their specific needs and situations. The paper also highlights some of the teachers' fears in relation to MOOCs, such as becoming residual in the classroom when the MOOC takes over the teacher's role.

Keywords: MOOC · Teacher education · Design-based research · Differentiation

1 Introduction

Student teachers in Denmark are a heterogenic group that includes recent graduates from high school, experienced middle-aged people re-educating themselves, singles with few responsibilities, family providers, bilinguals and dyslexics all in the same classroom. This group calls for differentiated teaching, and although the students tend to learn how to differentiate by imitating their educators [1], teacher education is criticised for not sufficiently preparing its students for differentiated teaching [2].

Differentiation is often handled at an organisational level, where students are grouped according to their abilities, which is more advantageous to the talented students [1, 3], or with more strategic approaches in relation to content, level, pace, interest or structure [4]. In this paper, we will focus on differentiation through pace, which can be defined as flexible lesson planning that enables those students who need more flexibility, time or repetition to understand a subject matter and to work with it for a longer time, while the students who need to progress faster can do so. Furthermore, we focus on differentiation through dialogue and feedback to the individual student. This is possible when the educator employs technology and digital learning resources to extend the classroom's teaching presence.

C. Delgado Kloos et al. (Eds.): EMOOCs 2017, LNCS 10254, pp. 254–262, 2017.
DOI: 10.1007/978-3-319-59044-8_30

Massive open online courses (MOOCs) are among the most debated educational designs in learning and teaching [5]. This way of learning is found to be more flexible and adaptable to the students' preferences and needs [6]. However, the limit between so-called 'traditional' education and MOOCs is blurring: MOOC elements can be integrated into face-to-face teaching and contribute to blended learning [7–9]. In this study, we have created and tested two learning designs developed in collaboration with educators in a teacher-training faculty. Thus, we wish to answer the research question: *How can learning design patterns that integrate MOOCs contribute to solving the central challenges of differentiation at different levels in teacher training?*

2 Theory and Methodology

Design-based research (DBR) has inspired our methodological framework [10–13]; thus, through iterative design experiments, we have developed two patterns for learning design that integrates MOOCs in teacher training [14]. In the project's initial phases, prototypes for blended learning designs with MOOCs were produced in collaboration with three educators and tested with their 73 student teachers [14]. During the final phases, these learning designs were redesigned and further developed into five designs, of which two were tested; these two tested designs will be presented in this paper. The other three designs were discussed among three educators and shared with all the faculty educators.

Design-based research speaks with many voices when asked about the role of users in the design process. Some argue that the design should be developed in a lab with researchers who have a hypothesis and an understanding of the problem the specific design is meant to solve [15, 16]. However, others find it necessary to include the users in several phases of the design process [10, 11, 17, 18], believing users are perceived as persons with important knowledge of the context; therefore, they should be active participants, both in the problem identification phase and in the design phase, as co-investigators [17] or co-participants [12] in a co-design [18] that grants them 'direct ownership of the design' [19]. In this project, the educators participated as co-participants in a series of co-designed experiments, even if it meant that our (the researchers') ideas were not tested as we wished.

The present project's overall goal has been to develop learning designs for use in teacher training. The learning designs used a special format of MOOCs - that is a Small Private Online Course (SPOC). Furthermore, it has been important to communicate the designs in a way that might inspire the faculty to use and further develop learning designs for their own teaching. For this purpose, we drew inspiration from the concept of design patterns [20–22] that aim to determine a pedagogically effective resolution for a critical problem [23]. Thus, a design pattern follows a template that focusses on problems, contexts and solutions (these concepts will be further elaborated below).

Our DBR phases consisted of an investigation/problem identification phase with three educators and a prototyping and testing phase with one of these educators and two others, followed by an observation and interview phase conducted by the researchers. The following semester, the phases consisted of a redesign and several tests with the same two educators, as well as further refinements and discussions of new designs with the three educators from our first semester; the developed design patterns were then shared with the entire education staff. Therefore, the educators have contributed to the development of the learning design patterns throughout the design-based research process of problem identification, prototyping, testing/redesign and final knowledge generation phases [24].

Our empirical materials, which consisted of observational and interview data, were analysed with inspiration from grounded theory [25–27]. All field notes from observing the 13 lessons and the transcriptions from the seven interviews with educators and students were analysed individually by the three educators and the two researchers in the project; afterwards, these analyses were compared and discussed among everyone at workshops in each of the two semesters.

3 Strategy for Data Analysis in Creation of Design Patterns

Our data analysis from the development, testing and redesign of learning designs with MOOCs has been based on three basic concepts for communication design knowledge: design patterns, design narratives and design scenarios [20]. We understand a design pattern in this context as a 'pedagogical pattern' [21], which is a semi-structured description of an experienced teacher's method to solve an educational problem. The aim of a design pattern is to externalise knowledge [28, 29] that can be shared in a community of teachers [21]. A design pattern is often created, shared, criticised and redesigned in a collaborative process between members of an educational community [30]. Design patterns can be deduced through analysis of 'design narratives' [20]. A design narrative structures, in narrative form, knowledge about how a design works in practice. A DBR project includes two different kinds of narratives: researcher narratives and participant narratives (educators and students) [31]. Based on analyses of numerous design narratives, one can thus deduce an abstraction described as a design pattern. Accordingly, design patterns can be deduced through research-driven design experiments that integrate analyses of design narratives from the initiated experiment; however, it is also possible to deduce design patterns through the analysis of collected design narratives from experienced teachers' ongoing practice [31].

In research projects working on the development of pedagogical design patterns, the concept 'design scenario' is used in different ways, as it can act both as a scientific category for analysis and as a practical design tool [20]. As a scientific category, a design scenario is used to validate the design statements that can be deduced from a design narrative that has subsequently been generalised in a design pattern. This is done through an analysis of whether a pattern is perceived as effective in numerous hypothetical scenarios in which a pattern can be included. The validity of a pattern increases if it is perceived as meaningful, not only to the practice that has already been experienced and described in a narrative but also to hypothetical future teaching practices. However, a design scenario also becomes a powerful tool for the learning designer. Like a design narrative and a design pattern, a design scenario constitutes a description of a context (a challenge), a solution and an expected result but is formulated as a postulate of the result or the effect. Design scenarios function well as a platform for organising a design experiment. The concept of 'design scenarios' has a double role in a DBR project, as it can both validate reflections on past success and be used to design the future [31].

4 Finding

The following section presents the project's three main findings: two design patterns and a study of the educational cultural mechanisms that influence whether the described patterns will be widely used.

4.1 Design Pattern A: The Parallel Classroom

Context: The educators teach campus classes that feature between 25 and 35 students. The students' study qualifications differ significantly. On average, two-thirds of the students attend classes and compulsory attendance is not required. Absences may be due to sickness, work, travel abroad, prioritising other scheduled classes on campus or simply a lack of commitment to training.

Problem: In a learning design, whose basic structure is an educator who meets facetoface with a larger group of students on campus, it is difficult to provide differentiated teaching to match the students' different learning needs, and it is impossible to comply with changing needs for flexibility in how students access education.

The Body of the Problem: In this case, there are two different problems that can be solved with the same pattern. The first is a differentiation problem. There is a need for a learning design that differentiates, individualises and personalises the teaching. The core of the second problem is that students can only access the program by attending classes on campus. On average, two-thirds of the students attend classes at the beginning of the semester and, as the semester progresses, participation declines. In lectures and class dialogues, approximately one-third of the attending students do not actively participate in class but are busy with other things, e.g. participation in social media (data from field notes). This traditional learning design is not resource-efficient, and a large group of enrolled students have no access to education for shorter or longer periods.

Solution: Establish a training design on a programme level that provides dual access to education. Create two parallel learning designs at the programme level with the same curriculum and the same division into modules, sequences and sessions (learning activities can, however, be different in the two designs). The first learning design must be 100% flexible in time and space (i.e. a MOOC). The second learning design takes place on campus. Learning designs on campus are re-designed at the session level to integrate the differentiation potential in the parallel MOOC. Students who do not attend classes on campus for a period (whatever the level of granularity) are guided to access the MOOC.

Prerequisites: Both the educator and the students are familiar with the contents in the MOOC and are used to navigating it. In addition, both educators and students must transform numerous conceptions of teaching and learning (see Sect. 4.3).

Design Narratives and Design Scenarios to Support the Pattern

An extract from a design narrative told by one of the students who tested this design illustrates the flexibility potential in 'parallel classrooms': Britt (student): *'The reason why I was studying in the MOOC, was that my lessons in another subject took place at the same time as the lessons in this subject, so I could not follow the regular class on campus.'* (Interview). In the same interview, Britt describes a design scenario for the potential of this design: *'When I was on maternity leave, I had my baby with me on campus. In this respect, I would have liked to take advantage of the MOOC instead of this or in addition.'* Regarding parallel classrooms' differentiation potential, several of the educators in the project formulated design narratives and design scenarios for this potential:

> Cindy (educator): *'I presented the students some videos in the MOOC and said: "You may see these when you have not understood what I said. Here it is explained in a different way by my colleagues". I think I will use it more for differentiated teaching, especially to students who are not so talented'.* (Interview).

The students' use of the MOOC supports this: *'I think it was nice that all the difficult words were explained'.* Another says: *'We find the spot in the video where the educator said something we did not understand in class'.*

Then they rewind, listen again and sometimes discuss it in their study groups. Both educators and students see the potential in the MOOC for either study preparation or repetition: Mary (educator): *'I will continue to use it for the students' study preparation or for them to revisit a lecture, e.g. when they are studying for the exam'* (Interview). And Paul (student) says: *'I will certainly use the MOOC for repetition. I wish I could insert bookmarks, because there is so much important information in there'* (Interview).

> Britt (student): *'For instance, my study group and I, we used the MOOC before the exam. You can just go in and refresh it and use the quizzes as a form of self-evaluation'* (Interview).

Differentiation in this learning pattern was thus found to a large degree at the programme level. However, as we shall see below, differentiation can be found at the session and activity levels as well.

4.2 Design Pattern B: The Double Classroom

Context: The educators teach subject-modules of 10 ECTS, which is equivalent to 270 study hours. The educators teach 76 face-to-face lessons of 45 min. Usually, there are between 25 and 35 students in the classroom, and the lesson is primarily used for lectures, exercises and dialogue with the students. In addition, students receive a small number of guidance sessions. Students study individually for the remainder of the period.

Problem: Both students and educators are experiencing a lack of time for differentiated feedback from the instructor, to either individuals or groups of students, in relation to the students' academic challenges and progression.

The Body of the Problem: Denmark's educational system is under pressure in terms of resources, and the number of face-to-face lessons has been reduced for several years. The educational institutions have attempted to solve the problem by creating a training design where students are studying in different ways without an educator presence; however, these activities have only been didactically scaffolded to a minor degree.

The Solution: A learning design on campus for a session (4–6 lessons) that starts with a common introduction, which describes the day's activities, objectives and organisation. The students are then to work in groups with several activities in the MOOC, which are affiliated to the day's academic theme. They are then to choose a theme in the MOOC, which forms a learning unit on the session level (2–4 lessons) and is structured to scaffold self-paced learning. Organised by an agreed schedule, the study groups alternately have a break within the MOOC study. During this break, the group gets feedback or guidance from the educator in relation to an assignment they have either filed or are about to deliver. The day ends with a joint session.

Prerequisites: Both the educator and the students are familiar with the contents in the MOOC and are used to navigating it. In addition, both the educators and students must transform numerous conceptions of teaching and learning (see Sect. 4.3).

Design Narratives and Design Scenarios to Support the Pattern

This design pattern operates at the session level. In our teacher-training program, we work with the following granularity: program, subject, module, course-sequences, session and learning activities [c.f. 32]. Therefore, the developed MOOCs also follow this structure. The research team first formulated the concept of the 'double classroom' as a design scenario for learning design with multiple differentiating and consecutive course-sequences.

The educators, however, found a greater need, first, to improve the activities relating to lectures and then to focus on differentiation in pace. Therefore, we undertook a series of design experiments that operated at the activity level instead. The students where then to watch and reflect on MOOC videos on campus instead of listening collectively to the lecture in the classroom at a common pace. These experiments made it evident that differentiation in students' activities and pace creates the educator's need for supplementary activities:

> *'The educator starts the lesson telling the students that they are going to watch a MOOC video in groups and that they are to work with a quiz based on facts from the video. They seem okay with that'* (Field notes).
> Astrid (educator): *'The first time, they watched a video lecture, and I walked around a bit after a while. But the next time ... I stood there and fluttered'* (Interview).

The students watched the videos and discussed on their own; however, it was difficult for the educator to find relevant activities to perform. She wandered around and answered questions, if the students had any:

> Cindy (educator): *'I find myself residual. I had much more time. When they began to do their assignments, they did not need me at all. They had seen the video and knew what to do. I thought I'd walk around and guide them more, but then I was afraid to disturb them'* (Interview).

In the field notes, one of the researchers wrote: *'The educator is not part of the learning design when the students watch a video in the MOOC on campus. Right now, the educator looks at her own PC and currently has no function in the learning design. The physical educator is represented/replaced by a video educator'.*

Our data showed that MOOC activities on campus do not work well for the educator if the learning design has not incorporated activities where the educator has a different function in relation to another learning activity that takes place simultaneously with the students' work in the MOOC. This requires longer coherent sequences with MOOC study work. Therefore, 'the double classroom' serves only as a design pattern on the session level, e.g. a sequence of 2–4 h. This is a challenge if educators only want to embed MOOC activities on the granularity level of learning activities.

4.3 Educators' Basic Understandings of the Purpose of MOOCs

As the above excerpt of design narratives and design patterns illustrate, both students and educators see the differentiation potential of parallel and double classrooms. However, educators do not see the flexibility and differentiation potential in the educators' activities. In this context, parallel classrooms are a student-centred learning design, which is not dependent on an educator being present on campus. Educators' concern about this design is the project's final finding.

The project has shown that educators are worried about design patterns that integrate MOOCs in a learning design at the granularity level of programs, modules, sequences or sessions. The reason for this can be found in the educators' general understanding of why an educational institution wants to implement MOOCs and in their self-understanding of themselves as educators.

> Mary: *'This is what concerns me: if I were replaced because all of a sudden they found out that it was much better, what happened in there [in the MOOC)... then one might say that the MOOC has replaced the educator. To be honest, I'm participating [in this project] to show that I am irreplaceable!'* (Interview).

Furthermore, Hillary expresses directly why she is worried about providing students with flexible access to education by allowing them to choose which design they prefer in the parallel classrooms:

> *'There are not so many [students in the classroom usually]. They slowly stop attending, so sometimes, only five students are present, and if I let them see the [entire] MOOC, I am afraid that they will all leave me... I am, of course, nervous that they will not show up if I say: 'The entire program is online now to study and for the exam'... I want to keep it this way: that they stay here [pause] ... with me'.* (Interview).

5 Conclusion and Further Research

The project shows that design patterns that integrate MOOCs in learning activities on campus, and at the same time maintain an educator-centred learning design, can be scaled up widely to the teaching staff. In contrast, the aforementioned worries about the educator's role in a student-centred learning design is common among the teaching staff. If parallel classrooms and other design patterns containing a learning design with MOOCs at the granularity levels from programmes to sessions are widely implemented in our institution, a professional development program for educators must support them. In relation to pace, it takes more than a few experiments to create learning designs that seriously consider differentiation at not only the activity level but at other levels too while focusing on differentiation in, for instance, content or structure. Therefore, we see a need for further research on how to support on-campus educators being included in the redesign and transformation processes of well-known learning designs, as well as their roles and identities as professional educators.

References

1. Ruys, I., Defruyt, S., Rots, I., Aelterman, A.: Differentiated instruction in teacher education: a case study of congruent teaching. Teach. Teach. **19**(1), 93–107 (2013)
2. Korthagen, F., Loughran, J., Russell, T.: Developing fundamental principles for teacher education programs and practices. Teach. Teach. Educ. **22**(8), 1020–1041 (2006)
3. Van Houtte, M., Stevens, P.A.: Study involvement of academic and vocational students: does between-school tracking sharpen the difference? Am. Educ. Res. J. **46**(4), 943–973 (2009)
4. Adami, A.F.: Enhancing students' learning through differentiated approaches to teaching and learning: a Maltese perspective. J. Res. Spec. Educ. Needs **4**(2), 91–97 (2004)
5. Bulfin, S., Pangrazio, L., Selwyn, N.: Making 'MOOCs': the construction of a new digital higher education within news media discourse. Int. Rev. Res. Open Distrib. Learn. **15**(5) (2014). http://www.irrodl.org/index.php/irrodl/article/view/1856/3072?
6. Doherty, I., Harbutt, D., Sharma, N.: Designing and developing a MOOC. Med. Sci. Educ. **25**(2), 177–181 (2015)
7. Bruff, D.O., Fisher, D.H., McEwen, K.E., Smith, B.E.: Wrapping a MOOC: student perceptions of an experiment in blended learning. MERLOT J. Online Learn. Teach. **9**(2), 187–199 (2013)
8. Najafi, H., Evans, R., Federico, C.: MOOC Integration into secondary school courses. Int. Rev. Res. Open Distance Learn. **15**(5) (2014)
9. Li, N., Verma, H., Skevi, A., Zufferey, G., Blom, J., Dillenbourg, P.: Watching MOOCs together: investigating co-located MOOC study groups. Distance Educ. **35**(2), 217–233 (2014)
10. Amiel, T., Reeves, T.C.: Design-based research and educational technology: rethinking technology and the research agenda. J. Educ. Technol. Soc. **11**(4), 29–40 (2008)
11. Anderson, T., Shattuck, J.: Design-based research a decade of progress in education research? Educ. Res. **41**(1), 16–25 (2012)
12. Barab, S., Squire, K.: Design-based research: putting a stake in the ground. J. Learn. Sci. **13** (1), 1–14 (2004)

13. Shattuck, J., Anderson, T.: Using a design-based research study to identify principles for training instructors to teach online. Int. Rev. Res. Open Distrib. Learn. **14**(5) (2013)
14. Nortvig, A.M., Gynther, K., Gundersen, P.: Blending MOOC in face-to-face teaching and studies. In: Proceedings for the 15th European Conference of E-learning (2016)
15. Brown, A.L.: Design experiments: theoretical and methodological challenges in creating complex interventions in classroom settings. J. Learn. Sci. **2**(2), 141–178 (1992)
16. DiSessa, A.A., Cobb, P.: Ontological innovation and the role of theory in design experiments. J. Learn. Sci. **13**(1), 77–103 (2004)
17. Collins, A.: Toward a design science of education. In: Scanlon, E., O'Shea, T. (eds.) New Directions in Educational Technology. NATO ASI Series (Series F: Computer and Systems Sciences), vol. 96, pp. 15–22. Springer, Berlin (1992)
18. Dede, C.: If design-based research is the answer, what is the question? A commentary on Collins, Joseph, and Bielaczyc; diSessa and Cobb; and Fishman, Marx, Blumenthal, Krajcik, and Soloway in the JLS special issue on design-based research. J. Learn. Sci. **13**(1), 105–114 (2004)
19. The Design-Based Research Collective: Design-based research: an emerging paradigm for educational inquiry. Educ. Res. **32**(1), 5–8 (2003)
20. Mor, Y.: SNaP! re-using, sharing and communicating designs and design knowledge using scenarios, narratives and patterns. In: Handbook of Design in Educational Technology, pp. 189–200 (2013)
21. Laurillard, D.: Teaching as a Design Science. Building Pedagogical Patterns for Learning and Technology. Routledge, New York (2012)
22. Alexander, C.: A Pattern Language: Towns, Buildings, Construction. Oxford University Press, London (1977)
23. Mor, Y.: A design approach to research in technology enhanced mathematics education. Ph.D. thesis, University of London, London (2010)
24. McKenney, S., Reeves, T.C.: Conducting Educational Design Research. Routledge, New York (2013)
25. Bryant, A., Charmaz, K.: The Sage Handbook of Grounded Theory. Sage, Thousand Oaks (2013)
26. Glaser, B., Strauss, A.L.: The Discovery of Grounded Theory: Strategies for Qualitative Research. Aldine Publishing Co., New York (1967)
27. Thornberg, R.: Informed grounded theory. Scand. J. Educ. Res. **56**(3), 243–259 (2012)
28. Goodyear, P.: Educational design and networked learning: patterns, pattern languages and design practice. Australas. J. Educ. Technol. **21**(1), 82–101 (2005)
29. Mor, Y., Winters, N.: Design approaches in technology-enhanced learning. Interact. Learn. Environ. **15**(1), 61–75 (2007)
30. McAndrew, P., Goodyear, P., Dalziel, J.: Patterns, designs and activities: unifying descriptions of learning structures. Int. J. Learn. Technol. **2**(3), 216–242 (2006)
31. Warburton, S., Mor, Y.: Double loop design. In: Maina, M., Craft, B., Mor, Y. (eds.) The Art & Science of Learning Design, pp. 93–104. Sense Publishers, Rotterdam (2015)
32. Dalziel, J., Conole, G., Wills, S., Walker, S., Bennett, S., Dobozy, E., Cameron, L., Badilescu-Buga, E., Bower, M.: The Larnaca declaration on learning design. J. Interact. Media Educ. **2016**(1), 7 (2016). doi:http://doi.org/10.5334/jime.407

Early Prediction and Variable Importance of Certificate Accomplishment in a MOOC

José A. Ruipérez-Valiente[1,3(✉)], Ruth Cobos[2], Pedro J. Muñoz-Merino[1], Álvaro Andujar[2], and Carlos Delgado Kloos[1]

[1] Universidad Carlos III de Madrid, Leganés, Spain
{jruipere, pedmume, cdk}@it.uc3m.es
[2] Universidad Autónoma de Madrid, Madrid, Spain
ruth.cobos@uam.es, alvaro.andujar@estudiante.uam.es
[3] IMDEA Networks Institute, Leganés, Spain

Abstract. The emergence of MOOCs (Massive Open Online Courses) makes available big amounts of data about students' interaction with online educational platforms. This allows for the possibility of making predictions about future learning outcomes of students based on these interactions. The prediction of certificate accomplishment can enable the early detection of students at risk, in order to perform interventions before it is too late. This study applies different machine learning techniques to predict which students are going to get a certificate during different timeframes. The purpose is to be able to analyze how the quality metrics change when the models have more data available. From the four machine learning techniques applied finally we choose a boosted trees model which provides stability in the prediction over the weeks with good quality metrics. We determine the variables that are most important for the prediction and how they change during the weeks of the course.

Keywords: Educational data mining · Learning Analytics · Prediction · Machine learning · MOOCs

1 Introduction

MOOCs are courses provided by online platforms that can be accessed by anyone with an Internet connection. These courses might have thousands of students at the same time taking a single MOOC. This massiveness and the fact that each student generates a large amount of events, provides the opportunity to analyze large datasets about the interaction of students with these online educational platforms with the objective of improving the learning process. MOOCs have many positive features and potential to be one of the main possibilities for learning, however many of the problems that were addressed since the beginning have not been resolved yet e.g. the easiness of students to perform academically dishonest behaviors [2].

One of the main identified problems in MOOCs is the high dropout rates. This issue was addressed since edX first MOOC on "Circuits and Electronics" where they reported a completion rate of only 5% with over 155.000 students registered for the

C. Delgado Kloos et al. (Eds.): EMOOCs 2017, LNCS 10254, pp. 263–272, 2017.
DOI: 10.1007/978-3-319-59044-8_31

course [4]. Most of the studies report very high attrition rates in MOOCs and it is commonly known as one of the main issues. Therefore, the early prediction of success in an educational course can be very important, since if we can predict which students are at risk of not passing the course, then we can take different decisions to try to change it. For example, adaptive systems can be implemented to adapt the contents based on this prediction and we can find in the literature different examples of adaptive systems in education [15].

In this work, we analyze how to predict early on which students are going to earn a certificate and which of them will not, with the purpose of enabling intervention that can alert students that they are in risk of not earning their certificate. This can be especially important for those students that have payed to obtain a verified certificate. In this study, we analyze data from "The Spain of Don Quixote" MOOC offered via edX platform and taught by instructors from Universidad Autónoma de Madrid (Spain, UAM). We use several indicators related to the learning process and different machine learning algorithms to predict which students are going to achieve a certificate. We evaluate and compare the different proposed algorithms and determine which variables are more important regarding the prediction of certification outcome. In addition, we discuss about the best moment for making the prediction and whether we can make accurate prediction with data of only the first weeks.

2 Related Work

One of the main identified problems with MOOCs is the high dropout rates. Recent reviews estimate the average completion rates in MOOCs around the 7% [13]. Regarding the prediction on student absenteeism in MOOC courses, several institutions have developed and designed models that focus on the detection and prediction of student dropout in MOOCs by making use of the indicators obtained from social interactions, the student activity with problems and the navigation within the course. For example, the study by Kloft *et al.* [14] proposes a model based on data from Coursera platform to predict which students are going to dropout the course, and analyzes how the accuracy of the model varies over the weeks; this approach is very similar to ours but our target prediction is certificate accomplishment and some of the variables used are different.

In this direction, The University of George Mason has carried out a task where they bring forward models to predict student performance for a determined assessment activity. It is a real time model that tracks student participation and predicts student performance in the following course evaluation; this model has been tested in Open edX [17]. Technology giant Samsung Electronics has worked towards the objective of being able to predict dropouts in MOOCs by extracting a wide variety of data related to the activity of students and applying different machine learning approaches [19]. The Abdelmalek Essaadi University from Tetouan in Morocco compared the proportion of students who complete the course with those who enrolled and reached the conclusion that some got even a rate lower than 2% [11]. Based on this data, they have created LASyM: A Learning Analytics System for MOOCs, a system based on Phil Hill's behavioral classification [10]. Students were classified in different categories: ghosts, observers, non-completers, passive participants and active participants. The objective was to identify students in risk by using two simple indicators based on interaction and persistence. These indicators are obtained by behavioral analysis and student activity, such as the number of visualized videos, exercises and other course content [20].

One of the most appealing topics in educational research is the prediction of learning outcomes. The study of this topic can help to improve knowledge regarding how students learn and what variables are important, to ultimately be able to improve the learning process of students. The target prediction and learning environment can vary from one study to another. For example we can find traditional settings such as high school education [1], but lately many studies are using data from different types of Virtual Learning Environments (VLEs) such as Intelligent Tutoring Systems (ITSs) [3, 12], and more traditional LMS environments [7, 16]. Furthermore, these studies target different learning outcomes such as graduation in high school [1], performance in course activities [7], learning gains [18] or end-of-the assessment scores [3].

We can find in the literature different studies that aim at the prediction of learning outcomes of students after interacting with ITS environments [3, 12]. MOOC environments are different to ITSs, e.g. the former usually contain more complex and specific exercise players that can provide different features (e.g. about hints) that usually MOOC environments do not have. Additionally, the interaction with videos and the context is different, thus we can expect that the variables that are used to predict learning outcomes in each educational environment differ a bit. We can find also different studies in this direction using MOOC environments, for example towards the prediction of learning gains after the interaction with a Khan Academy instance [18] and also to predict student knowledge status in MOOCs using Open edX [9]. Other works in the literature have approached the prediction of certificate accomplishment using different methods such as LDA [6]. In our work we focus on early prediction of certificate accomplishment, performance of different models and variable importance.

3 Methodology

3.1 Description of the MOOC

UAM offered the first delivery of their MOOCs at edX platform in February 24th 2014 [5] and this dataset belongs to one on these MOOCs, which is entitled "The Spain of Don Quixote" - Quijote501x[1]. A total of 3530 students enrolled in the course; however, only 1718 students were actively involved with any of the course content of which 164 students obtained a grade of over 60% and thus received a certificate. Therefore around 4.65% of the enrolled students earned a certificate, which is a completion rate similar to the ones reported in the literature. It is a 7-week course where every week there are multimedia resources, discussion forums, practical activities without evaluation, and also a final evaluation activity per week. The first and last week (seventh), students were evaluated with a peer review activity. For weeks 2 to 6, they were evaluated with a multiple choice test of 21–23 questions. Each weekly evaluation contributed a 14% to

[1] https://www.edx.org/course/la-espana-de-el-quijote-uamx-quijote501x-0.

the final grade of the course. For the first three weeks of this course, the evaluation activities deadlines are four weeks after the release date. Then, from the fourth week to the end of the course the evaluation activities deadlines are three weeks after.

3.2 Data Collection and Selected Variables

The main source of data involved the tracking logs of students[2], which contained detailed information regarding all actions performed by the students, a total number of 893.098 events were triggered. We used this file to compute the different variables. The dependent variable is binary and addresses the acquisition of a certificate. We used a total of 11 independent variables to build the model and predict the dependent variable. Two of these variables are related to the progress of students, one regarding the grade achieved in the completed assignments (*problem_progress*) and other regarding the percentage of different video watched from 0 to 100% (*video_progress*). Then, five variables are related to the volume and amount of activity of students, the summation of time invested in problems (*total_problem_time*), the summation of time invested in videos (*total_video_time*), the total time in the course (total_time), the number of sessions (*number_sessions*) and number of events produced by the student (*number_events*). Finally, four variables related to the distribution of the activity with the dispersion of the time invested in each exercise separately (*problem_homogeneity*), dispersion of time in each video separately (*video_homogeneity*), number of days that the student logged in (*number_days*) and dispersion of time invested in each day of the course (*constancy*).

3.3 Method and Tools

With the purpose of analyzing early prediction, we divided the data into seven data batches that corresponded with the data available after each week's deadline. We fed the machine learning algorithms with each one of these batches. Therefore, in a practical sense, we implemented a model with all the data just after first week, a model with all the data just after the second week, and so on. This way we were able to analyze the evolution of the performance of each model as the amount of data available increases in the direction of looking for stability and early detection. We used R software and specifically *caret* package and its functions. We implemented four classification models that are random forests (RF) using *randomForest* package, generalized boosted regression modeling (GBM) using *gbm* package, k-nearest neighbours (kNN) using *knn* package, and a logistic regression using *glm* package. The specific steps that we followed for the training and the evaluation of the models are the following:

[2] http://edx.readthedocs.io/projects/devdata/en/latest/.

1. **Training**: We divided the dataset in training and test with a probability of 0.75 and used *train* function of *caret* package to train the four models. As part of the pre-processing we scaled and centered all the numeric variables. We established that the quality metric that we want to maximize is the ROC, and it was estimated through a 10-fold cross validation repeated and averaged three times.
2. **Model selection**: We used each one of the implemented models of the previous step to predict on the data from the test dataset. We evaluated the results over the weeks using F1-score and AUC and selected the best model.
3. **Evaluation**: We evaluated the selected best model in terms of AUC, F1-score, sensitivity, specificity, Cohen's kappa coefficient and accuracy. We analyzed the importance of variables of the selected model as more data becomes available.

4 Results and Discussion

4.1 Training and Selection of the Model

We partition the data in train (N = 1289, 123 certificate earners) and test (N = 429, 41 certificate earners) dataset. We train the four models using each one of the seven batches following the method described in Subsect. 3.3. Next, we evaluate each one of the models by predicting on the test dataset. Figure 1 represents the quality metrics, i.e. F1-score (on the left) and AUC (on the right), over the weeks for each model.

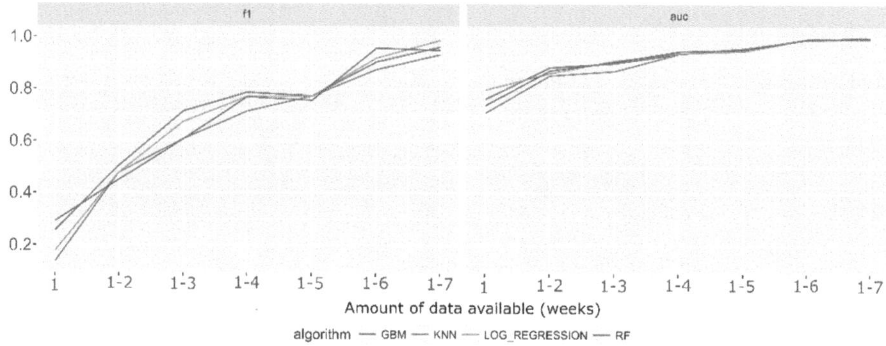

Fig. 1. Evaluation results in the test dataset in terms of F1-score and AUC metrics for the models on each batch of data.

We can see that the performance after the first week in terms of F1-score is a bit higher for the RF model, and afterwards BGM model takes over as the best one. In terms of AUC in the first week log regression is the best, in the second week GBM has the best performance and afterwards the AUC values are very similar. We are looking for a stable model over the weeks, offering always a good performance and specially in the first four weeks, since those are the weeks in which we have chances of sending an early warning to avoid that a student misses the certificate. Considering those premises, in terms of the F1-score and AUC, we consider that the model that provides the best performance for this task is the GBM model, which always performs as the best or second best model over the four first weeks both in terms of F1-score and AUC, offering performance and stability.

4.2 Evaluation Results and Discussion

In this section we analyze the results when predicting on the test data using the selected GBM model. Figure 2 shows the evolution over the weeks for the GBM model in terms of sensitivity, specificity, F1-score, Cohen's kappa coefficient, AUC and accuracy. Additionally, we have added the baseline accuracy of the predictor that always classifies as non-certificate earners (0.904). We can see how the specificity remains high over the weeks, but the sensitivity is very low at the beginning, we are aware of these results but we think this is the correct approach. We want to minimize false positives, since a false positive implies a student who is not going to receive a certificate and still will not be warned by our system due to the classification created by the prediction model. We are less concerned about students who will get a certificate, but receive a warning regarding they are still in risk of not getting a certificate. F1-score increases in a similar trend than the sensitivity does, since F1-score is the geometric mean of sensitivity and specificity. Additionally kappa coefficient also increases over time, the more that the predictor starts behaving differently than the baseline predictor (being able to detect both true negatives and true positives), the more the kappa coefficient increases.

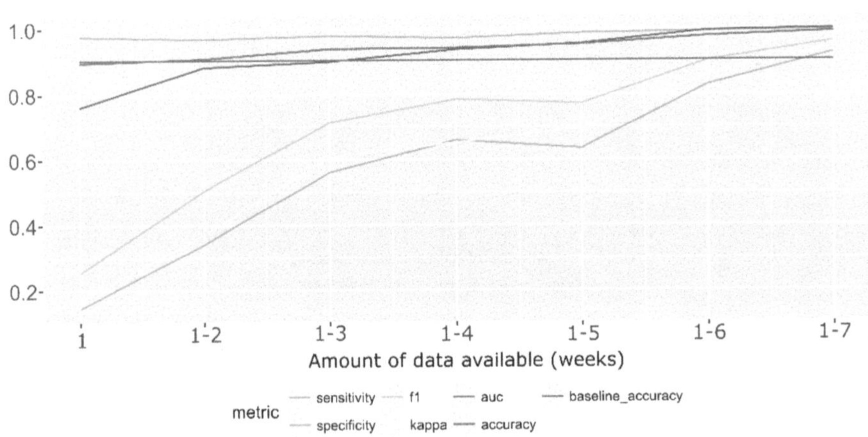

Fig. 2. Evolution of the performance in the test dataset of the selected GBM model over the weeks.

There is a progressive prediction improvement during the first weeks due to the fact that most learners that dropout are likely to do it during the first weeks, therefore activity metrics that show that students are interacting with the platform, are very important during these first weeks. One interesting detail is the effect of the deadlines of week 5, where we can see that in terms of sensitivity, the predictor gets worse and accuracy improves little (this happened also with the rest of the algorithms). Then, after week 6 there is a big improvement in terms of accuracy and sensitivity. These findings suggest that early prediction models should heavily take into account the deadlines of the course, and use them to find the optimal time in which the system should warn students (e.g. just before or after deadlines). These deadlines could even be parametrized into variables and input to the model so that the prediction accuracy improves. By the end of the last week the accuracy is really high (0.991), but the course is finished and the system can no longer send early warnings, that is why we should focus in the first three or four weeks.

We have explored also the influence of the different variables of the GBM model over the weeks. We compute and report the relative variable importance (scaled from 0 to 100) as reported by Friedman [8] of each one of the variables of the model. We plot the variable importance results over the weeks in Fig. 3. The results show an interesting trend where there is a lot of difference in the importance of variables during the first three weeks, where it is distributed among many variables, and at the end of the course, where *problem_progress* is with much difference the most important. We can see that after week 3, the most important variable is *problem_progress*, and *total_problem_time* is the second most important one, the rest of the variables have low relative importance. However we can see that during the first weeks the importance is more distributed among the different variables. The most interesting detail is that at the end of the first week, *number_sessions*, *total_problem_time*, *number_events*, *video_homogeneity*, *total_time* and *video_progress* have more importance towards the prediction than *problem_progress*. Additionally, specially at the end of week two but also at the end of week three, some of these variables still have great importance (specially note

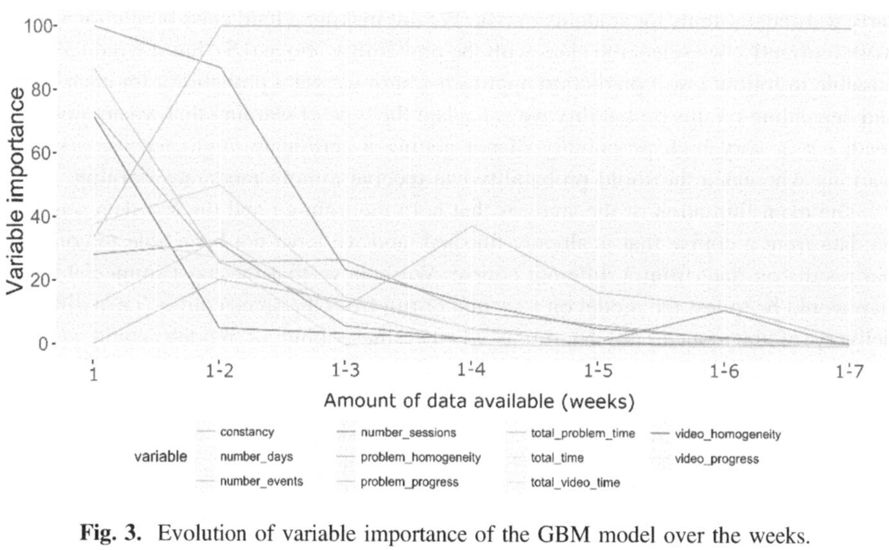

Fig. 3. Evolution of variable importance of the GBM model over the weeks.

number_sessions at the end of week two). These results seem to indicate that in the first weeks of the course some indicators related to the activity of students with the platform are even more useful to early detect students in risk than the indicator related to the progress in problems, specially at the end of the first week. We believe this is a very interesting finding, since we should mostly focused on warning students during the first weeks, since that is the timeframe where we are still able to help and get them back in track to earn their certificate. We were surprised to see that *number_sessions*, being such a straightforward variable, achieved a high importance during the first weeks. By the end of week three, we can see the variable importance of most of the variables have dropped below the 30% of influence and most of the prediction power comes *problem_progress*. Taking into account that the course analyzed is a xMOOC, this extracted result is coherent. These findings suggest that warning models should probably tune the weight of the variables during the different weeks of the course.

5 Conclusions and Future Work

In this study we have approached the implementation of machine learning models with the objective of early predicting which students will fail in the task of accomplishing enough grade to get a certificate, so that interventions (either automatic or by instructors) can be performed before it is too late. Our results suggest that GBM model was the best one in terms of both performance and stability over the first weeks, although the RF and logistic regression models offered also very good performance. Since the performance of the different algorithms might change as more data becomes available, this might raise a question related to whether some algorithms should be used for very early predictions and change to others when the amount of data increases. Following this idea, we found that some of the activity variables had a high importance towards the prediction during the first weeks, whereas after week three the most important indicator was *problem_progress*; this can be of interest implementing an early warning systems for students in risk. We are making a hard class prediction in this work (currently, we select the class with the probability above 0.5), but it would also be possible to follow a soft prediction approach where we get a probability for each class, and depending on this probability we can adapt the type of warning that we are going to send, e.g. a very high probability of not getting a certificate might receive a strong warning whereas a threshold probability can receive a more moderate warning.

The main limitation of the study is that both the training and the test data sets rely on data from a course that is already finished, and we have not been able to compare our results on data from a different course. We believe that the most immediate next step would be to test the model on a second re-run from the same course (i.e. a different delivery of the course) to determine whether these kind of models could at least extrapolate to courses with many similar contents and course structure, e.g. to try to predict using our selected model from this research on the second run of Don Quixote MOOC. A more complex question to ask would be if it is possible to implement a model that can effectively predict on different MOOCs taking into account the different topics, educational resource types and contents.

In the future, more granular analysis would be required to be able to answer such questions, for example, to be able to map the impact of the different learning resources and the structure of the course to the performance of the predictors. This would allow the design of a more general approach that could apply better to different courses. We reported on results after analyzing data after each week of the course, but a more granular data analysis, e.g. each day, could also be tested. Due to the heterogeneity in MOOC learners we would like to add additional variables such as motivation of students or prior education. The final stage of this research could be to perform an A/B experiment in which the treatment group would receive warnings from the system based on a model like this one, and the control group would not; then we would be able to compare if there was improvement in terms of certificate accomplishment rates between the two groups.

Acknowledgments. Work partially funded by the Madrid Regional Government with grant No. S2013/ICE-2715, the Spanish Ministry of Economy and Competitiveness projects RESET (TIN2014-53199-C3-1-R) and Flexor (TIN2014-52129-R) and the European Erasmus+ projects MOOC Maker (561533-EPP-1-2015-1-ES-EPPKA2-CBHE-JP) and SHEILA (562080-EPP-1-2015-BE-EPPKA3-PI-FORWARD). This research work was made possible thanks to Universidad Autónoma de Madrid, which provided us with the dataset, and to Prof. Pedro García, who was the instructor of the selected MOOC.

References

1. Aguiar, E., Lakkaraju, H., Bhanpuri, N., Miller, D., Yuhas, B., Addison, K.L.: Who, when, and why: a machine learning approach to prioritizing students at risk of not graduating high school on time. In: Proceedings of the Fifth International Conference on Learning Analytics and Knowledge, pp. 93–102. ACM (2015)
2. Alexandron, G., Ruipérez-Valiente, J.A., Chen, Z., Muñoz-Merino, P.J., Pritchard, D.E.: Copying@Scale: using harvesting accounts for collecting correct answers in a MOOC. Comput. Educ. **108**, 96–114 (2017)
3. Anozie, N., Junker, B.W.: Predicting end-of-year accountability assessment scores from monthly student records in an online tutoring system. In: Educational Data Mining: Papers from the AAAI Workshop. AAAI Press, Menlo Park (2006)
4. Breslow, L., Pritchard, D.E., DeBoer, J., Stump, G.S., Ho, A.D., Seaton, D.T.: Studying learning in the worldwide classroom: research into edX's First MOOC. Res. Pract. Assess. **8**, 13–25 (2013)
5. Claros, I., Cobos, R., Sandoval, G., Villanueva, M.: Creating MOOCs by UAMx: experiences and expectations. In: The Third European MOOCs Stakeholders Summit (eMOOC 2015), pp. 61–64 (2015)
6. Coleman, C.A., Seaton, D.T., Chuang, I.: Probabilistic use cases: discovering behavioral patterns for predicting certification. In: Proceedings of the Second (2015) ACM Conference on Learning@Scale, pp. 141–148. ACM (2015)
7. Elbadrawy, A., Studham, R.S., Karypis, G.: Collaborative multi-regression models for predicting students' performance in course activities. In: Proceedings of the Fifth International Conference on Learning Analytics and Knowledge, pp. 103–107. ACM (2015)

8. Friedman, J.H.: Greedy function approximation: a gradient boosting machine. Ann. Stat. **29**, 1189–1232 (2001)
9. Guo, S., Wu, W.: Modeling student learning outcomes in MOOCs. In: The 4th International Conference on Teaching, Assessment, and Learning for Engineering (2015)
10. Hill, P.: Emerging student patterns in MOOCs: a (revised) graphical view (2013)
11. Jordan, K.: MOOC completion rates: the data (2013). http://www.katyjordan.com/MOOCproject. Accessed 27 Aug 2014
12. Kelly, K., Arroyo, I., Heffernan, N.: Using ITS generated data to predict standardized test scores. In: Educational Data Mining 2013 (2013)
13. Khalil, H., Ebner, M.: MOOCs completion rates and possible methods to improve retention-a literature review. In: World Conference on Educational Multimedia, Hypermedia and Telecommunications, no. 1, pp. 1305–1313 (2014)
14. Kloft, M., Stiehler, F., Zheng, Z., Pinkwart, N.: Predicting MOOC dropout over weeks using machine learning methods. In: Proceedings of the EMNLP 2014 Workshop on Analysis of Large Scale Social Interaction in MOOCs, pp. 60–65 (2014)
15. Muñoz-Merino, P.J., Molina, M.F., Muñoz-Organero, M., Kloos, C.D.: An adaptive and innovative question-driven competition-based intelligent tutoring system for learning. Expert Syst. Appl. **39**(8), 6932–6948 (2012)
16. Pardo, A., Mirriahi, N., Martinez-Maldonado, R., Jovanovic, J., Dawson, S., Gašević, D.: Generating actionable predictive models of academic performance. In: Proceedings of the Sixth International Conference on Learning Analytics and Knowledge, pp. 474–478. ACM (2016)
17. Ren, Z., Rangwala, H., Johri, A.: Predicting performance on MOOC assessments using multi-regression models. arXiv preprint arXiv:1605.02269 (2016)
18. Ruipérez-Valiente, J.A., Muñoz-Merino, P.J., Delgado Kloos, C.: A predictive model of learning gains for a video and exercise intensive learning environment. In: Conati, C., Heffernan, N., Mitrovic, A., Verdejo, M.F. (eds.) AIED 2015. LNCS, vol. 9112, pp. 760–763. Springer, Cham (2015). doi:10.1007/978-3-319-19773-9_110
19. Sinha, T., Jermann, P., Li, N., Dillenbourg, P.: Your click decides your fate: Inferring information processing and attrition behavior from MOOC video clickstream interactions. arXiv preprint arXiv:1407.7131 (2014)
20. Tabaa, Y., Medouri, A.: LASyM: A learning analytics system for MOOCs. Int. J. Adv. Comput. Sci. Appl. (IJACSA) **4**(5), 113–119 (2013)

Types of Dropout in Adaptive Open Online Courses

Maxim Skryabin(✉)

Stepik, Saint Petersburg, Russia
ms@stepik.org

Abstract. This study is devoted to different types of students' behavior before they drop an adaptive course. The Adaptive Python course at the Stepik educational platform was selected as the case for this study. Student behavior was measured by the following variables: number of attempts for the last lesson, last three lessons solving rate, the logarithm of normed solving time, the percentage of easy and difficult lessons, the number of passed lessons, and total solving time. We applied a standard clustering technique, K-means, to identify student behavior patterns. To determine optimal number of clusters, the silhouette metrics was used. As the result, three types of dropout were identified: "solved lessons", "evaluated lessons as hard", and "evaluated lessons as easy".

Keywords: Adaptive learning · Dropout · Clustering · MOOC

1 Introduction

Massive Open Online Courses (MOOCs) have the potential to enable free online education at scale but a concern is their low completion rate. A meta-analysis conducted by Jordan indicates that the completion rate have an average of 6.5% and ranges from 0.9% to 36.1% (Jordan 2014). Onah et al. suggested a number of reasons for student dropout in MOOCs: no real intention to complete, lack of time, course difficulty and lack of support, lack of digital skills or learning skills, bad experiences, expectations, late start, and peer review (Onah et al. 2014). One of approaches to decrease student dropout is to provide MOOCs personalization and adaptive learning to improve learning experience in MOOCs (Sunar et al. 2015).

Adaptive learning is the mainstream of the contemporary educational science. The key idea is in recommendation of learning activities to students according to their ability and preferences. In the ideal adaptive learning engine, students do not quit it until they do not achieve their learning goals.

2 Related Work

Dropout rates in massive open online courses (MOOCs) are extremely high, and it is a constant theme in the MOOC literature (Rivard 2013; Huin et al. 2016). This topic is also connected with student engagement in MOOCs (see, for example, Sinclair and Kalvala 2016). Some authors identified various clusters of MOOC participants

C. Delgado Kloos et al. (Eds.): EMOOCs 2017, LNCS 10254, pp. 273–279, 2017.
DOI: 10.1007/978-3-319-59044-8_32

according to their activity. Kizilcec et al. (2013) analyzed three computer science MOOCs and identified four clusters of students: 'completing', 'auditing', 'disengaging,' and 'sampling' (Kizilcec et al. 2013). Anderson et al. (2014) clustered students' engagement into five groups: viewers, solvers, all-rounders, collectors, and bystanders (Anderson et al. 2014). Kovanovic et al. (2016) used k-means clustering on 28 MOOCs from the Coursera platform and identified five groups: enrollees, low engagement, videos, videos and quizzes, and social (Kovanovic et al. 2016). Khalil and Ebner (2016) classified four categories of students based on their activity: registrants, active learners, completers, and certified students (Khalil and Ebner 2016).

Unlike traditional massive open online courses where exist lots of literature on completion rates, dropout rates and student engagement, there is not so much literature for adaptive open online courses. Sonwalkar (2013) proposed an adaptive MOOC that offers the learning content according to learning styles (Sonwalkar 2013). Burgos and Corbí (2014) used a rule-based recommendation model to improve students' performance. Yang et al. (2014) proposed a personalized support on MOOCs discussion forums.

However, the field of MOOC personalization and adaptive learning can be benefited with research in the intelligent tutoring systems (ITS) due to its focus on problem-solving behavior. While MOOC research focused on identification of patterns of student behavior through a course, ITS research analyzed student behavior through the process of solving a given problem. Arroyo et al. indentified cognitive, metacognitive and affective factors that influence student behavior (Arroyo et al. 2014). Mills et al. predicted whether student quit instructional texts: they used supervised machine learning algorithms and prediction accuracy for quitting at any point during the text was 76.5% (Mills et al. 2014).

The aim of this study is to identify different patterns of students' behavior before they drop an adaptive course.

3 Context of the Study

As the case for this study, the Adaptive Python course at the Stepik educational platform was selected. Stepik (https://stepik.org/) is an educational engine and MOOC platform focused on IT and STEM courses. In the Fall 2016, the platform contains more than 60 open courses. Every course on Stepik consists of 3–7 weeks (one week = one module) with 100–150 steps, and has 7000 learners on average. The Stepik platform supports different types of problems: close-ended problems (multiple choice quizzes, matching problems, table problems, and sorting problems), open-ended problems (free responses, text problems, number problems, and math problems) and challenges (data challenge, code challenge, and Linux challenge). Both adaptive and non-adaptive courses have launched on the Stepik platform.

In this study, the data from the Adaptive Python course was used. This course contains 347 lessons with code challenge assignments of various difficulties where students need to write the programming code in Python to solve problems. This course uses an adaptive engine developed in Stepik based on the Roskam model (Roskam 1987, 1997). This model uses the response time to measure the student ability.

The adaptive course interface is shown on Fig. 1. Unlike the case of response-time models where students need to provide the correct answer, at Stepik, students can also evaluate the lesson as too easy or too hard.

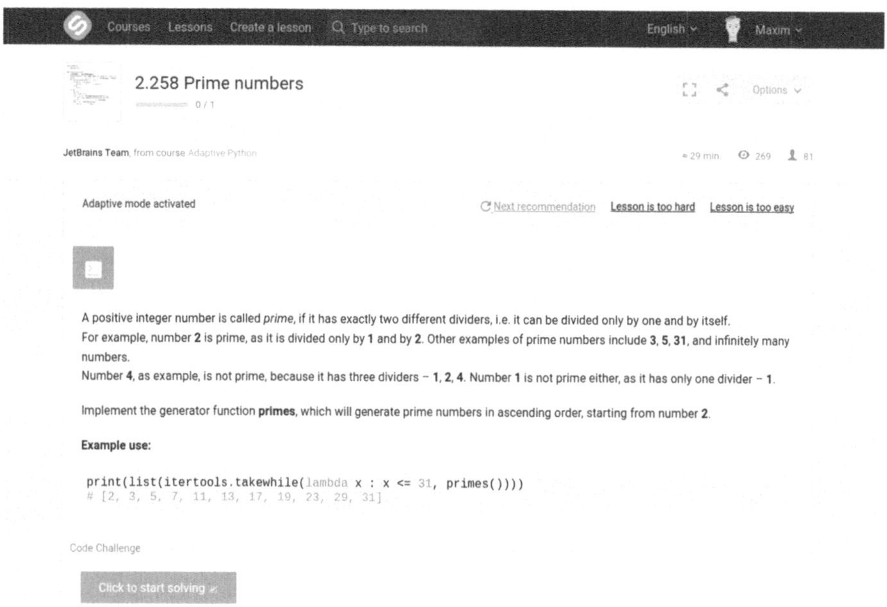

Fig. 1. The adaptive course interface.

Thus, there exist three ways to receive the next recommended lesson: solve the lesson, evaluate the lesson as too easy or as too difficult. When updating the student ability, we compare our prediction with the student performance: solving time, number of attempts, and whether the lesson was evaluated as too easy or too hard. Depending on this, the student ability can increase or decrease.

4 Methods

4.1 Sample

This study uses data from the Adaptive Python course that is launched on the Stepik educational platform. Over the lifetime, this course had over 4500 enrolled students.

We selected the time period from September 1, 2016 to December 15, 2016 that depends on the student activity after the summer break and before winter holidays. We excluded students who studied at the course outside of this period. Anonymous users were also removed.

The final sample contains 685 students and 10994 interactions between students and lessons.

4.2 Measurement

Basic information on student performance inside adaptive course consists of time used for solving lessons, number of attempts, and number of reactions "too easy" or "too hard". Using this information, student behavior before dropping the course was measured by the following variables:

- Number of attempts for the last lesson. If this number is large, the student can be frustrated and it is more likely that he drops the course.
- Last three lessons solving rate. This indicator was calculated as the weighted average whether student solved last three lessons or used evaluation as too easy or too difficult. The latest values have larger weight (backward discounting).
- The logarithm of normed solving time. Normed solving time is defined as student's solving time divided to the average solving time for the lesson. It measures student abilities in comparison with other students. The positive value of its logarithm means that the student needs more time to solve the lesson than in average, i.e., the student ability is lower.
- The percentage of easy lessons. This shows how often students evaluate lessons as easy based on their self-estimation.
- The percentage of difficult lessons. This shows how often students evaluate lessons as difficult based on their self-estimation.
- Number of passed lessons and total solving time. These two variables show student engagement in using the adaptive engine.

4.3 Analysis

A standard clustering technique, K-means, to discover student behavior before dropping the course was applied. First, we cleaned the data and removed outliers with solving time greater than the 97%-percentile. We also normalized all the measurement variables used for clustering analysis to reduce the scale effect. Then, we performed the clustering analysis with the K-means technique.

To determine an optimal number of clusters, the cluster silhouette metrics was used: it is a measure of how similar an individual case to its own cluster compared to other clusters. All the analysis was performed in Python with using the scikit-learn library (Pedregosa et al. 2011).

To identify behavioral patterns before students dropped the courses, we also calculated the frequency of last three reactions. For this purpose, we distinguish the situation whether students solved lesson faster than in average ("fast") or not ("slowly").

5 Results

After cleaning data and removing outliers in solving time, the sample contains 401 students and 4308 interactions between students and lessons. The K-means technique with the silhouette metrics was performed. The optimal number of clusters is equal to 3, the silhouette metrics is equal to 0.478 (see Fig. 2).

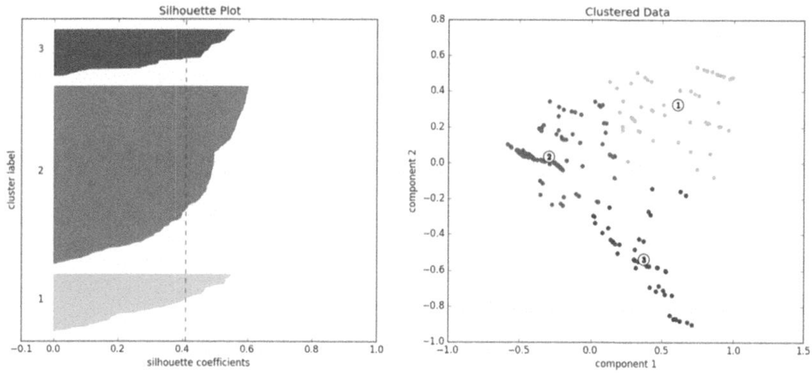

Fig. 2. The silhouette plot and clustered data

The identified clusters define three types of dropout:

1. "Solved lessons" (n = 243; 60.60%) where number of attempts for the last lesson is greater than for other types.
2. "Evaluated lessons as easy" (n = 84; 20.95%) where students prefer to evaluate lessons as easy but not solve them.
3. "Evaluated lessons as hard" (n = 74; 18.45%) where students prefer to evaluate lessons as hard but not solve them.

The descriptive statistics for each cluster are provided in Table 1. Note that there is no significant differences between clusters for total solving time and number of passed lessons (engagement metrics) as well as for the logarithm of normed solving time (proficiency metrics).

The percentage of the last three reactions before students dropped the course was also calculated and ten of the most frequent ones are provided in Table 2. We can note that when the learning content is too difficult for students (because of their self-evaluation as hard or their slow solving), it is more likely that students drop the course.

Table 1. Description of clusters

Variables	Cluster 1	Cluster 2	Cluster 3
Number of attempts for the last lesson	**1.19 (0.11)**	0.62 (0.06)	0.33 (0.07)
Last three lessons solving rate	**0.80 (0.01)**	0.20 (0.02)	0.14 (0.02)
Number of passed lessons	9.20 (0.83)	14.24 (1.74)	12.12 (1.22)
Log(normed solving time)	0.80 (0.07)	0.69 (0.17)	0.59 (0.13)
Percentage of easy lessons	0.04 (0.01)	**0.62 (0.02)**	0.04 (0.01)
Percentage of difficult lessons	0.06 (0.01)	0.03 (0.01)	**0.76 (0.02)**
Total solving time	841.48 (128.55)	595.66 (160.07)	407.10 (166.25)

Bold values show statistically significant difference as compared with the other two clusters ($p < 0.05$). Standard errors are provided in the brackets.

Table 2. The percentage of the last three reactions

Last reactions	Percentage	Last reactions	Percentage
hard, hard, hard	15.65%	easy, easy, easy	3.63%
slowly, slowly, slowly	11.83%	fast, fast, quickly	3.44%
fast, fast, fast	6.87%	slowly, fast, slowly	3.24%
fast, slowly, slowly	5.92%	fast, slowly, fast	3.05%
fast, fast, slowly	4.39%	slowly, fast, fast	2.48%

6 Discussion and Conclusion

Our results indicate that there exist three main patterns of student behavior before they drop the adaptive course. Two of them are related with students' self-evaluation of lessons as hard or easy. This connected with the flow theory where higher challenges than your skills lead to frustration but lower ones lead to boredom (Csikszentmihalyi 1990). Both of them can be reasons for course dropouts.

The pattern "Solved lessons" is related with regular lesson solving. To reduce student dropout, it is necessary to provide students the learning support, for example, in the case where the number of their attempts to solve problems rises. It is important to react on these cases on time as well as predict student dropouts to have an opportunity for pedagogical interventions in advance. The prediction of student dropouts for adaptive courses is one of topics for the further research.

Another topic for the further research is validation of identified clusters with student interview on their learning strategies and motivation. This can provide more insights on student behavior in adaptive courses.

References

Anderson, A., Huttenlocher, D., Kleinberg, J., Leskovec, J.: Engaging with massive online courses. In: Proceedings of the 23rd International Conference on World Wide Web, pp. 687–698. ACM (2014)

Arroyo, I., Woolf, B.P., Burelson, W., Muldner, K., Rai, D., Tai, M.: A multimedia adaptive tutoring system for mathematics that addresses cognition, metacognition and affect. Int. J. Artif. Intell. Educ. **24**(4), 387–426 (2014)

Burgos, D., Corbí, A.: A recommendation model on personalised learning to improve the user's performance and interaction in MOOCs and OERs. In: IITE 2014 International Conference, UNESCO Institute for Information Technologies in Education, Moscow, Russia. 14-15 October 2014 (2014)

Csikszentmihalyi, M.: Flow: The Psychology of Optimal Experience. Harper and Row, New York (1990)

Huin, L., Bergheaud, Y., Caron, P.A., Codina, A., Disson, E.: Measuring completion and dropout in MOOCs: a learner-centered model. In: Proceedings of the European Stakeholder Summit on Experiences and Best Practices in and Around MOOCs (EMOOCs), p. 55 (2016)

Jordan, K.: Initial trends in enrolment and completion of massive open online courses. Int. Rev. Res. Open Distrib. Learn. **15**(1), 133–160 (2014)

Khalil, M., Ebner, M.: What massive open online course (MOOC) stakeholders can learn from learning analytics? In: Spector, M., Lockee, B., Childress, M. (eds.) Learning, Design, and Technology: An International Compendium of Theory, Research, Practice, and Policy, pp. 1–30. Springer International Publishing, Switzerland (2016)

Kizilcec, R.F., Piech, C., Schneider, E.: Deconstructing disengagement: analyzing learner subpopulations in massive open online courses. In: Proceedings of the Third International Conference on Learning Analytics and Knowledge, New York, USA, pp. 170–179. ACM (2013). doi:10.1145/2460296.2460330

Kovanovic, V., Joksimovic, S., Gasevic, D., Owers, J., Scott, A.M., Woodgate, A.: Profiling MOOC course returners: how does student behavior change between two course enrollments? In: Proceedings of the Third ACM Conference on Learning at Scale, pp. 269–272. ACM (2016)

Mills, C., Bosch, N., Graesser, A., D'Mello, S.: To quit or not to quit: predicting future behavioral disengagement from reading patterns. In: Trausan-Matu, S., Boyer, K.E., Crosby, M., Panourgia, K. (eds.) ITS 2014. LNCS, vol. 8474, pp. 19–28. Springer, Cham (2014). doi:10.1007/978-3-319-07221-0_3

Onah, D.F.O., Sinclair, J., Boyatt, R.: Dropout rates of massive open online courses: behavioral patterns. In: Proceedings of the EDULEARN 2014, pp. 5825–5834 (2014)

Pedregosa, et al.: Scikit-learn: machine learning in Python. J. Mach. Learn. Res. **12**, 2825–2830 (2011)

Rivard, R.: Measuring the MOOC dropout rate. Inside Higher Ed., 8 March 2013

Roskam, E.E.: Toward a psychometric theory of intelligence. In: Roskam, E.E., Suck, R. (eds.) Progress in Mathematical Psychology, pp. 151–171. North Holland, Amsterdam (1987)

Roskam, E.E.: Models for speed and time-limit tests. In: van der Linden, W.J., Hambleton, R.K. (eds.) Handbook of Modern Item Response Theory, pp. 187–208. Springer, New York (1997)

Sinclair, J., Kalvala, S.: Student engagement in massive open online courses. Int. J. Learn. Technol. **11**(3), 218–237 (2016)

Sonwalkar, N.: The first adaptive MOOC: a case study on pedagogy framework and scalable cloud architecture—Part I. In: MOOCs Forum, vol. 1, no. P, pp. 22–29 (2013)

Sunar, A.S., Abdullah, N.A., White, S., Davis, H.C.: Personalisation of MOOCs: the state of the art. In: 7th International Conference on Computer Supported Education (CSEDU2015), Portugal, 23–25 May 2015, p. 10 (2015)

Yang, D., Piergallini, M., Howley, I., and Rose, C.: Forum thread recommendation for massive open online courses. In: Proceedings of 7th International Conference on Educational Data Mining (2014)

Exploring the Role of Assessment in Developing Learners' Critical Thinking in Massive Open Online Courses

Catherine Zhao[1(✉)], Sonal Bhalla[1], Lesley Halliday[3], Joanne Travaglia[2], and Julia Kennedy[4]

[1] University of New South Wales, Sydney, Australia
Catherine.zhao@unsw.edu.au
[2] University of Technology Sydney, Sydney, Australia
[3] YourTutor, St Leonards, Sydney, Australia
[4] St Vincent's Hospital, Sydney, Australia

Abstract. Massive Open Online Courses (MOOCs) have provided learners unprecedented opportunities to access university level education. As a form of largely free and self-paced education, MOOCs are less formal than credit-bearing university courses. It is often the case that MOOCs do not count toward a formal university qualification, and that majority learners enter MOOCs for various purposes other than specifically gaining a certificate. As a result, assessment and critical thinking, valued by universities as important learning outcomes are thought to be less relevant to MOOCs learners or designers. In the last couple of years, however, a few universities have started to design credit-bearing MOOCs as part of university programs. The aim is to encourage quality learning and outcomes that satisfy formal university assessment criteria. MOOCs designed to target particular groups of professionals for career advancement are also emerging. Both trends require a rethink of the relevance of assessment and critical thinking in MOOCs. This paper provides a case study of a MOOC targeted at health professionals, which demonstrates how self- and peer-assessment are designed to encourage critical thinking, and includes a discussion on future directions and constraints of this work-in-progress. The paper proposes that critical thinking is relevant for learning in MOOCs and that carefully designed assessment tasks are essential for developing MOOCs' learners' critical thinking.

Keywords: Critical thinking · Self-assessment · Peer-assessment · MOOCs · Learning outcomes

1 Introduction

MOOCs have offered an unprecedented opportunity for people worldwide to access university level education [1, 2]. This situation has sparked significant interest in understanding how to create a learning experience that goes beyond traditional courses. While research largely focuses on learner profiling, learning interventions, and the effectiveness of MOOCs, much less research has been undertaken that explores the role

C. Delgado Kloos et al. (Eds.): EMOOCs 2017, LNCS 10254, pp. 280–289, 2017.
DOI: 10.1007/978-3-319-59044-8_33

of assessment in enhancing learning, and even less in understanding how critical thinking, a core professional skill, could be developed within this context. It is suggested this research gap is due to three main reasons. Firstly, research into MOOCs is considered still to be in its infancy [3] and therefore researchers are still discovering what learners do and under what conditions. Secondly, researchers [4, 5] claim that developing MOOC learners into critical thinkers is virtually impossible, due to the open and self-paced nature of MOOCs [6]. Finally, as MOOCs learners are from diverse backgrounds, demographics, motivations and expectations, a formal qualification is usually not what attracts them to these types of courses [7]. As MOOCs gradually become part of universities' credit bearing programs and more employers start to recognise the value of MOOCs as forms of professional development, learning outcomes become an increasingly important element for educators.

This paper asserts that, as a new format of online university education, MOOCs should aim to fulfil the same primary goal as traditional forms of higher education, that is, to educate graduates as critical thinkers [8].

Accepting that the educational methods utilised in the MOOCs are just as likely to foster critical thinking, as traditional education is one part of this assertion. In addition, the subject areas addressed by MOOCs are often cutting edge social or technological issues (e.g. personalised medicine) and can have strong practical focus (e.g. health leadership that impacts on day-to-day health service quality). Such topics lead themselves to critical thinking, not least of all as they expose learners not only to new content but also to new ways of understanding such content.

The second assertion is that assessment in MOOCs leads to the development of learners' critical thinking, and is based on the notion that assessment is essential in the development of critical thinking in the MOOCs. To this end, both self- and peer-assessment serve an important educational purpose in designing assessments in MOOCs. This is due to the large numbers and limited resources available to undertake such assessments as these forms of assessments have the potential to provide 'logistical, pedagogical, metacognitive, and affective benefits' [9] that can be tapped into the MOOC environment. However, Peer Assessment, to serve as an educational tool, needs to be well thought out, planned and integrated into a course [10].

Research undertaken in the HE context consistently finds four factors that shape critical thinking: abilities to logically reason; abilities to reflect and be open-minded; abilities to be self-aware; and abilities to incorporate moral and ethical considerations [11, 12]. Fife stated the purpose of developing critical thinking is to enable the learner to come up with his [or her] own position towards a problem [13]. Educators, including those who use the MOOC platform, are in a position to design learning tasks to support learners in the development of this skill.

Assessment is the process by which information from tasks is collected and combined in order for both learners and educators to 'make a judgement' about learning progress [14].

Peer assessment is suggested to be useful in 'medical, paramedical, clinical, dental or teaching contexts', which require performance-based assessments [15]. By engaging in peer-assessment tasks, learners are expected to develop abilities to incorporate multiple perspectives into decision-making. This is particularly relevant for health professional leadership development.

Developing skills in self-assessment has the potential for learners to 'wish to continue their learning', 'know how to do so', 'monitor their performance', and 'take full responsibility for their actions and judgments'. Moreover peer assessment along with peer feedback has the potential to 'considerably enhance self assessment' [16].

The nature of assessment has shifted in recent years to the 'improvement of learning' and to the identification of what 'influences learning' [16]. This shift is driven by the rise of online education, where learners have more control of pace and approaches to learning. In the case of MOOCs the increased tension between at scale learning (e.g. thousands enrolled and engaged in a MOOC) and limited teaching (e.g. only a few teaching staff running a MOOC), has meant that learners are expected to self-direct their learning. Additionally, an important aspect is the relationship of all the assessment tasks with each other.

2 A Case Study: Designing Self- and Peer-Assessment in a MOOC for Critical Thinking

2.1 Design Rationale

The Health Leadership (HL) MOOC was designed to support health professionals to develop effective leadership capabilities. The course enabled learners to explore leadership theories, to develop leadership competencies, and to reflect on their application in the health context. Critical thinking is considered an essential element in leadership development [17].

The HL MOOC had a strong focus on assessment as part of the learning process. A set of leadership constructs was developed to enable the development and measurement of critical thinking. The assessment tasks served a dual function; to meet the professional development needs of the participants, and to assist participants in understanding the relationship between assessment and the participants' professional development needs.

The course was organised into six 'stand-alone' modules, with flexible pathways. Each module consisted of content videos, learning activities and assessment tasks focusing on leadership in a specific area that combined current research, practice knowledge, and participants' own experience. Through learning activities, the MOOC encouraged critical reflection and discussion with peers worldwide to explore and expand knowledge and sharing of leadership experiences.

The overall assessment strategy was intended to help learners explore and expand their experiences and their understanding of leadership through self-assessment and weekly journal tasks, and to assist other learners to identify opportunities to further develop their leadership skills through peer-assessment. In particular, an assessment rubric was provided to learners from the beginning to ensure that they were aware of the assessment criteria. Learners were able to complete a self-assessment task to identify and rate their current state of leadership competencies, and to submit a peer-assessment task, which a peer reviewer would be assigned to provide feedback on. The goal of adopting this strategy was to enable learners to develop an action plan that

Table 1. Overall assessment strategies and assessment grades distribution of HL MOOC

Summative assessment tasks	Focus	Learning activities/formative assessment tasks
Quizzes (50 marks)	Encourage learners to deepen understanding of leadership theory and effective practice through examples	Content videos based discussions
		Practice quizzes
Self-assessment (20 marks)	Promote reflection on current leadership capabilities in order to personalise the participants' learning and identify their leadership opportunities	Practitioner videos based discussions
		Journal tasks
Peer assessment (30 marks)	Assist learners to identify opportunities through which they could further examine and explore leadership both in themselves and in others. Help learners address key questions to devise an action plan for future professional development as an individual or in a team	Content and practitioner videos based discussion
		Journal tasks
		Self-assessment recommendations report
		Peer review (2 feedback opportunities)

meets their leadership development needs. The rationale and structure of assessment tasks are explained in Table 1.

2.2 Evaluating the Effectiveness of the Learning Design Decisions

The HL MOOC, offered in 2015 on Coursera, attracted 16,657 enrolments. A total of 4453 (26.73%) participated at least once during the course (so-called 'active learners'). Of these, 653 (14.22%) were 'active learners' who completed the MOOC by passing a number of assessment tasks, with a total of 261 (41.23%) of the 'completed' learners finishing with certification.

As is generally the case with MOOCs, the video materials were 'used' (e.g. viewed and downloaded) most when compared to other learning activities. Usage pattern of video provides information about learners' pace during the course. It is quite evident that despite the fact that all the course modules were released from the beginning, learners tended to follow the course in a linear fashion, indicated by the squares bigger in size diagonally in the heat map (Fig. 1).

In contrast, learners' engagement with assessment tasks presented some diversity in relation to submission patterns (Fig. 2). Despite the recommendation, where learners were asked to submit their self-assessment tasks in week 2, learners appeared to be 'self-paced' in deciding when to engage with this task in order to self-assess their leadership capabilities, with an evenly spread distribution of submission percentages of around 15% across most of the course weeks. The four quizzes were completed in their respective weeks, but quite a few followed their own pace and completed in other weeks.

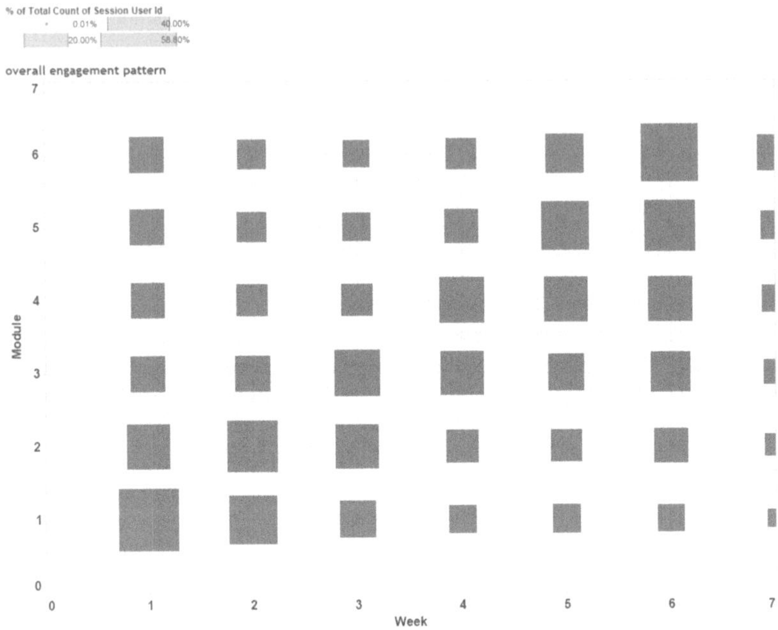

Fig. 1. Overview of learners' engagement with module videos across course weeks

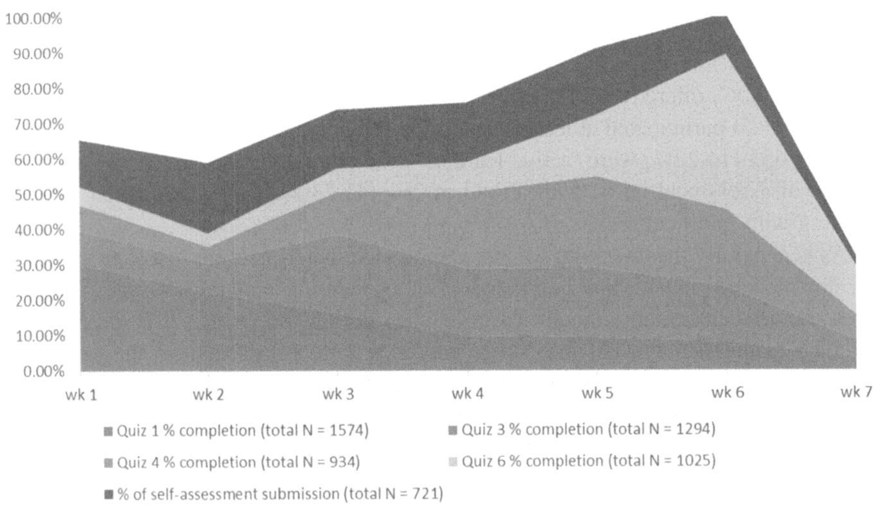

Fig. 2. Overview of learners' submission patterns in quizzes and self-assessment

The different ways in which learners' engaged with the video content and assessment tasks suggest two factors that drive learning behaviours in HL MOOC. The first factor is learners' prior learning experience. HL learners, with the majority in the mid-20s to mid-30s with a Bachelor degree or above, would probably have gone through traditional school and tertiary education, in which classes/courses were designed based on learning a topic on a weekly basis. Thus, when put in a similar setting, their learning behaviour follows a similar learning pattern. The second factor is of learners being introduced to the idea of being autonomous. With most of the learning and assessment tasks made available from the start of the course, learners were given opportunities to make decisions of when to complete these tasks. In other words, the self-paced intention of the design encouraged learners to self-direct their own learning, to a certain extent.

In order to showcase learners' 'growth' in their leadership capabilities, responses to self-and peer-assessment tasks, and the peer-reviews are analysed. 716 learners completed the self-assessment task. 509 learners submitted the peer-assessment task, and 472 of these (93%), completed the self-assessment task as well. In the self-assessment task, learners rated their capacities in four domains consisting of a range of abilities (in Table 2).

Table 2. Overview of 714 participated learners' self-ratings against 4 leadership domains

	Competent to advanced		Developing to competent	
Leadership domains	# of abilities identified	mean ratings (stdv)	# of abilities identified	mean ratings (stdv)
Domain 1	11	2.2(0.7)	4	1.4(1.0)
Domain 2	8	2.2(0.7)	4	1.8(0.7)
Domain 3	8	2.1(0.7)	4	1.8(0.7)
Domain 4	5	2.2(0.7)	7	1.8(1.7)

There was a variance noted in their self-ratings. These abilities were rated against three levels, 'developing' (1 on the scale), 'competent' (2 on the scale), and 'advanced' (3 on the scale). Descriptive analysis (in Table 2) shows the aggregated results of the levels of these abilities, from 'developing to competent' (mean rating < 2) and from 'competent to advanced' (meaning rating > 2). It suggests that learners were able to identify 'gaps' in their abilities across the four domains of leadership.

Peer-assessment submissions were the personal development plans that learners designed to address how they would improve their leadership capabilities. Table 3 presents the frequency distribution of leadership categories in the peer-assessment rubric. Peer-reviewers had the option to select from the categories as feedback, and to provide their own feedback to the assigned submissions. The four most frequently selected categories, which count for more than 50% of the total frequencies, suggest that learners were able to clearly devise an actionable plan to further develop their leadership skills in the future. About 15% of the selected categories suggest poor or incomplete responses to the task. The distribution suggests that learners were able to develop a plan for their development, formulate 'actions' and 'alternative approaches', and 'articulate rationale' and 'evaluate', which resemble the key critical thinking characteristics.

Reviewers were also able to provide customised feedback in addition to using the default categories. 95% of the reviewers (n = 483) chose to provide additional

Table 3. Overview of the frequency distribution of assessment rubric categories

Feedback categories for peer-assessors	# picked	% of overall picked
Leadership competency is clearly identified	1052	16.20%
Identifies at least three actions or steps they will take to improve	848	13.06%
Identifies more than one way and provides additional information on how they will measure and evaluate their improvement	750	11.55%
Provides a detailed rationale about why it is important they develop their skill in this leadership competency	677	10.43%
Provides a rationale about why this is important for their development, but this explanation could be further developed	364	5.61%
Identifies at least one way which outlines how they will measure and evaluate their improvement	301	4.64%
Identifies at least one or two actions or steps they will take to improve	212	3.27%
The answer is minimal, with no rationale provided about why it is important they develop their skill in this area	40	0.62%
There is no answer or does not identify any strategies for evaluating their improvement	30	0.46%
No leadership competency identified	29	0.45%
There is no answer, or does not identify any actions or steps to take to develop their skill	21	0.32%

qualitative feedback. A preliminary text analysis (using the *online version of text analysis tool* Kapiche) reveals some interesting patterns of the ways reviewers formulated feedback for their peers (Fig. 3).

Firstly, many recommendations ($\sim$20% of data coverage) focused on 'think more', which relates to some of the identified leadership competencies e.g. accountability, measurement, and relationship. Secondly, many reviewers demonstrated a forward thinking mindset by encouraging their peers to specifically think about 'goals' and 'achievement' in relation to their abilities. Thirdly, reviewers seemed to have paid good attention to the measurement and the evaluation of competency, and its development and improvement ($\sim$19% of data coverage). Finally, many reviewers appreciated the role of 'communication' in developing effective leadership in the healthcare profession.

In addition to formulating feedback on the assessment tasks, learners were also given an opportunity to feedback on the purpose and role of assessment tasks in the course. The responses indicate a level of thoughtfulness and critical reflection both on the part of the learners and the peer reviewers:

> *"It acknowledges a very practical and pivotal domain for improvement. It addresses the impact on the individual and on the team, which also affects the organization as a whole. There is evidence of self-reflection, and it is oriented in such a way that taking up action on this domain will create a culture of team involvement, strengthened communication and vulnerability."*

> *"The thing I like most about this personal development plan is that it is well written, well-articulated and well laid out. It covers all the questions thoroughly and clearly, identifying the capability to be developed, how it will occur and how the student knows improvement is*

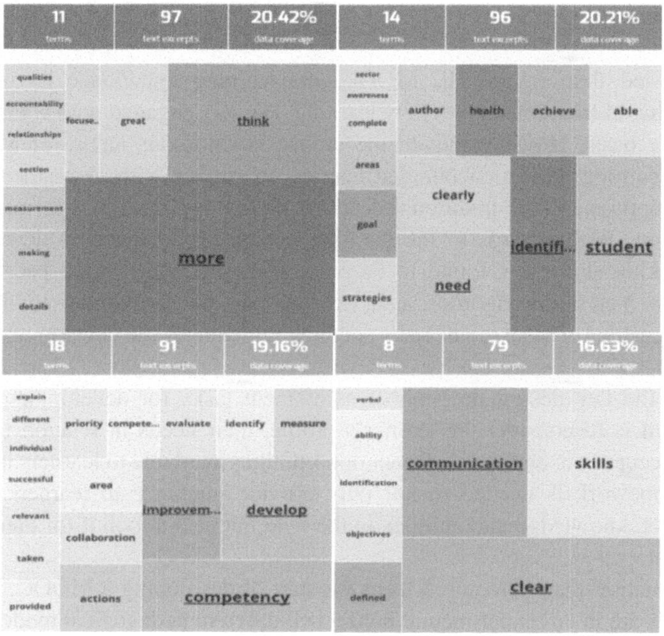

Fig. 3. Descriptive of the top four topic frequencies

occurring. The submission's focus on empathy and compassion is clearly patient focused whilst viewing effective communication with staff and patients as crucial."

A survey tool was used to evaluate the effectiveness of HL MOOC that uses assessment as a strategy for enhancing leadership skills. A post-course survey was available online to learners towards the last week of the course to capture learners' perceptions of their experiences. Of the learners who responded to the survey (n = 106), the majority ($\sim$90%) completed both the self- and peer-assessment tasks. These responses are considered in the evaluation of the course design, despite of a high Margin of Error (7%, at Confidence Interval = 90%), suggesting that this survey data should be used with caution, in relation to its representativeness of the learner cohort that undertook both assessment tasks.

70% of the survey respondents were satisfied with the design features that helped them organise their thoughts, develop their plans, and identify actionable steps to continue working on their future development. Most of these learners (70–90%), acknowledged that their understanding of the area of health leadership was enhanced by completing the relevant assessment tasks and going through course materials. 65% of them stated that they planned to use what they learnt to inform their professional practice, whilst 27% had already used their learnings form the course in their professional area of work.

3 Conclusion

It is suggested that, in the HL MOOC, the learning experience having partially resembled that of traditional university learning, learners engaged with course materials on a weekly basis. However, given the unique autonomous nature of MOOCs, the self-paced learning design encouraged learners to engage with assessment tasks differently as opposed to the traditional deadline driven approach in a formal university course setting. With regards to the learning outcomes, evidence of development of critical thinking skills was found to be present in over 50% of the peer-assessment submissions. Yet, more rigorous analytics need to be carried out to discover the 'inter-relationship' of assessment tasks and how it facilitates the development of critical thinking.

One of the key design decision of assessment tasks for development of critical thinking skill is to consider the learner's profile, their needs in relation to their profession or occupation, and development opportunities available to learners in their field. A solid framework is needed to not only provide guidance to learners on how to acquire skills, knowledge and abilities in the field but also a toolkit for their long-term development.

An evaluation plan is required from the start of developing a MOOC. In the view that MOOCs are in an 'experimental field' [18], different pedagogical models are being tested, and rigorous data is required to justify the effectiveness of these models. To this end, stakeholders should consider upfront evaluation strategies that appropriately address this concern. As a constraint caused by data handling reported in the case study, key data handlers e.g. data science professionals should be involved in the planning process to minimise the risk in this regard.

References

1. Jordan, K.: Initial trends in enrolment and completion of massive open online courses. Int. Rev. Res. Open Distrib. Learn. **15**(1) (2014). http://dx.doi.org/10.19173/irrodl.v15i1.1651
2. Chen, Z., Alcorn, B., Christensen, G., Eriksson, N., Koller, D., Emanuel, E.J.: Who's Benefiting from MOOCs, and Why. Harvard Business Review, 22 September 2015. https://hbr.org/2015/09/whos-benefiting-from-moocs-and-why. Accessed 29 Oct 2015
3. Kumar, S., Mishra, A.K.: MOOCs: a new pedagogy of online digital learning. Int. J. Sci. Innov. Res. Stud. **3**(4), 8–15 (2015)
4. Kop, R.: The challenges to connectivist learning on open online networks: learning experiences during a massive open online course. Int. Rev. Res. Online Distrib. Learn. **12**(3) 20–38 (2011). http://dx.doi.org/10.19173/irrodl.v12i3.882
5. Bates, T.: What's right and what's wrong about Coursera-style MOOCs (Web log post). Online Learning and distance education resources, 5 August 2012. http://www.tonybates.ca/2012/08/05/whats-right-and-whats-wrong-about-coursera-style-moocs/
6. Littlejohn, A., Hood, N., Milligan, C., Mustain, P.: Learning in MOOCs: motivations & self-regulated learning in MOOCs. Internet High. Educ. **29**, 40–48 (2016)
7. Chauhan, A.: Massive open online courses (MOOCS): emerging trends in assessment and accreditation. Digit. Educ. Rev. **25**, 7–17 (2014)

8. Gardiner, L.F.: Redesigning Higher Education: producing dramatic gains in student learning. Report seven. ASHE-ERIC Higher Education Reports 23–229 (1994)
9. Admiraal, W., Huisman, B., Pilli, O.: Assessment in massive open online courses. Electron. J. e-Learn. **13**(4), 207–216 (2015)
10. Suen, H.K.: Peer assessment for massive open online courses (MOOCs). Int. Rev. Res. Open Distrib. Learn. **15**(3) (2014). http://dx.doi.org/10.19173/irrodl.v15i3.1680. Accessed 15 Jan 2017
11. Mason, M.: Critical thinking and learning. Educ. Philos. Theor. **39**(4), 339–349 (2007)
12. Bermingham, M.: Cleaning up 'critical thinking': its four formidable features. Creat. Educ. **6**, 421–427 (2015)
13. Fife, J.D.: Cognitive process in critical thinking. ASHE-High. Educ. Rep. **17**(2), 25–49 (1988). doi:10.1002/aehe.3640170207
14. Athanasou, J., Lamprianou, I.: A teacher's guide to assessment, p. 3. Soc. Sci. Press, Sydney (2002)
15. Falchikov, N.: Improving Assessment Through Student Involvement, pp. 139–141. RoutledgeFalmer, London (2005)
16. Boud, D.: Enhancing Learning through Self Assessment, pp. 14–25. Kogan Page, London (1995)
17. Burbach, M.E., Matkin, G.S., Fritz, S.M.: Teaching critical thinking in an introductory leadership course utilizing active learning strategies: a confirmatory study. Coll. Stud. J. **38** (3), 482 (2004)
18. Vigentini, L., Zhao, C.: Evaluating the 'Student' experience in MOOCs. In: Proceedings of the Third (2016) ACM Conference on Learning @ Scale, pp. 161–164. ACM, April 2016

Author Index

Alario-Hoyos, Carlos 102
Alcarria, Ramón 140
Álvarez-Álvarez, Susana 77
Alvarez-Rodríguez, Jose María 123
Amado-Salvatierra, Hector R. 68
Andujar, Álvaro 263

Babanskaya, Olesya 197
Bachelet, Rémi 134, 150
Bartalesi-Graf, Daniela 3
Baudo, Valeria 113
Benckendorff, Pierre 176
Bernaert, Olivier 29
Bhalla, Sonal 280
Bianchi, Sébastien 29
Bordel, Borja 140
Bossu, Adeline 38
Bote-Lorenzo, Miguel L. 77
Bouchet, François 150
Bouzayane, Sarra 160
Brown, Mark 10, 170
Brunton, James 10
Busquets, Jaime 182

Castañeda, Linda 182
Castaño-Muñoz, Jonatan 233
Chaker, Rawad 134
Cobos, Ruth 263
Corti, Paola 113
Costello, Eamon 10, 170

de Amescua, Antonio 123
De Rosa, Rosanna 20
Deflandre, Jean-Pierre 29
Delgado Kloos, Carlos 263
Deng, Ruiqi 176
Despujol, Ignacio M. 182
Despujol-Zabala, Ignacio 48
Dhorne, Lucie 29
Dimitriadis, Yannis 77
Dogan, Gulustan 188
Duru, Ismail 188
Dyomin, Victor 197

Ebner, Martin 95

Farrell, Orna 10
Ferrari, Chiara 20
Frau-Meigs, Divina 38

Gannaway, Deanne 176
García-Guzman, Javier 123
Gimeno-Sanz, Ana 48
Gosset, Martin 88
Gröblinger, Ortrun 223
Gynther, Karsten 254

Håklev, Stian 58
Halliday, Lesley 280
Hamori, Monika 203
Henderikx, Maartje 210
Hernández, Rocael 68
Hernández Correa, Josefina 102
Hernández-Leo, Davinia 243

Jaramillo-Morillo, Daniel 217

Kalz, Marco 210, 233
Kennedy, Julia 280
Kerr, Ruth 20
Khalil, Mohammad 95
Kopp, Michael 223
Kreijns, Karel 210, 233

Labarthe, Hugues 150
Lynn, Theo 170

Mahon, Conor 10
Manathunga, Kalpani 243
Martín, Diego 140
Martínez-Monés, Alejandra 77
Mozhaeva, Galina 197
Muñoz-Cristóbal, Juan A. 77
Muñoz-Merino, Pedro J. 263

Nair, Binesh 170
Navarro-Laboulais, Cristina 48

Nic Giolla Mhichíl, Mairéad 170
Nortvig, Anne-Mette 254

Ortega-Arranz, Alejandro 77

Pérez-Sanagustín, Mar 102, 217
Pertuze, Julio A. 102
Petzold, Wolfgang 88
Punie, Yves 233

Ramírez González, Gustavo 217
Reischer, Matthias 95
Rodríguez, María Fernanda 102
Ruipérez-Valiente, José A. 263

Saad, Inès 160
Sancassani, Susanna 113
Sánchez-de-Rivera, Diego 140
Sánchez-Segura, Maribel 123
Sanz-Martínez, Luisa 77
Sharples, Mike 243
Skryabin, Maxim 273
Slotta, James D. 58
Solarte Sarasty, Mario 217
Sunar, Ayse Saliha 188

Thirouard, Maria 29
Travaglia, Joanne 280
Turró, Carlos 182

White, Su 188

Yacef, Kalina 150

Zakharova, Ulyana 197
Zhang, Jingjing 170
Zhao, Catherine 280
Zimmermann, Claudia 223

The manufacturer's authorised representative in the EU is Springer Nature Customer Service Centre GmbH, Europaplatz 3, 69115 Heidelberg, Germany. If you have any concerns regarding our products, please contact ProductSafety@springernature.com

Printed and bound by CPI Group (UK) Ltd, Croydon, CR0 4YY
25/09/2026
02222849-0019